D1481057

NAVIES IN MODERN WORLD HISTORY

GLOBALITIES
Series editor: Jeremy Black

GLOBALITIES is a series which reinterprets world history in a
concise yet thoughtful way, looking at major issues over large
time-spans and political spaces; such issues can be political,
ecological, scientific, technological or intellectual. Rather than
adopting a narrow chronological or geographical approach,
books in the series are conceptual in focus yet present an array of
historical data to justify their arguments. They often involve a
multi-disciplinary approach, juxtaposing different subject-areas
such as economics and religion or literature and politics.

In the same series

Why Wars Happen
Jeremy Black

The Nemesis of Power
Harald Kleinschmidt

Monarchies, 1000–2000
W. M. Spellman

*The Global Financial System,
1750–2000*
Larry Allen

*Geopolitics and Globalization in
the Twentieth Century*
Brian W. Blouet

Mining in World History
Martin Lynch

*China to Chinatown: Chinese Food
in the West*
J.A.G. Roberts

Landscape and History since 1500
Ian D. Whyte

A History of Language
Steven Roger Fischer

A History of Writing
Steven Roger Fischer

A History of Reading
Steven Roger Fischer

Cinemas of the World
James Chapman

Navies in Modern World History

LAWRENCE SONDHAUS

REAKTION BOOKS

Published by Reaktion Books Ltd
79 Farringdon Road, London EC1M 3JU, UK

www.reaktionbooks.co.uk

First published 2004

Copyright © Lawrence Sondhaus 2004

Printed and bound by Cromwell Press, Trowbridge, Wiltshire

British Library Cataloguing in Publication Data

Sondhaus, Lawrence, 1958 -
    Navies in modern world history. - (Globalities)
    1.Naval history 2.Navies - History 3.Sea-power - History
    I. Title
    359'.009

    ISBN 1 86189 202 0

Contents

PREFACE AND ACKNOWLEDGEMENTS 7

1 Ruling the Waves: The British Navy, 1815–1902 9
2 The Challenger: The French Navy, 1840s–1890s 49
3 Shaping the Southern Colossus:
   The Brazilian Navy, 1822–31 78
4 Preserving the Union:
   The United States Navy, 1861–5 107
5 By Reason or by Force:
   The Chilean Navy, 1879–92 141
6 A Place in the Sun: The German Navy, 1898–1918 171
7 Empire Builder: The Japanese Navy, 1894–1945 199
8 Red Star Rising: The Soviet Navy, 1956–91 236
9 Upholding the Pax Americana:
   The United States Navy since 1991 265

REFERENCES 288
BIBLIOGRAPHY 318
INDEX 329

Preface and Acknowledgements

Throughout history, navies large and small have played crucial roles in history. In peacetime as well as in war, the timely application of naval force has helped to determine the fate of nations and empires, establishing or altering the balance of power on a regional level or even globally. This collection of case studies demonstrates the variety of ways in which countries have made decisive use of naval power in the years since 1815. In each chapter, an argument is presented that the navy in question, within the given time frame, helped change the course of modern world history.

Five of the chapters, taken together, also provide a linear account of the evolution of naval *matériel*, training and education, and the conduct of naval warfare from the Napoleonic era into the early twenty-first century, through the examples of the British navy during the era of the Pax Britannica (1815–1902), the German navy of Wilhelm II and Alfred von Tirpitz (1898–1918), the Japanese navy as facilitator of empire-building in the western Pacific (1894–1945), the Soviet navy of the Cold War (1956–91), and the United States navy of the Pax Americana (1991–present). The remaining four chapters provide further insight into developments during the nineteenth century. The French navy, as primary challenger to the British during much of the Pax Britannica (1840s–1890s), instigated most of the technological breakthroughs in the transition from the era of the wooden sailing ship to that of the modern steel navy. Two of the three largest countries in the western hemisphere, Brazil (1822–31) and the United States (1861–5), improvised formidable navies to consolidate state power and crush secessionist movements, in each case taking full advantage of the circumstances (human or technological) influencing naval warfare at the time. Finally, the navy of Chile (1879–92) warrants inclusion as an example of how a relatively modest fleet of technologically respectable warships could facilitate the significant expansion of a state, altering the balance of power in an entire continent and commanding respect beyond.

I would like to thank Professor Jeremy Black, editor of the *Globalities* series, for giving me the opportunity to write this volume. I owe a great debt of gratitude to the interlibrary loan staff of Krannert Memorial Library at the University of Indianapolis for processing my scores of requests promptly and efficiently. I would like to thank Jack Green, Robert Hanshew and the rest of the staff of the Curator Branch, Naval Historical Center, Washington, DC, for their help in securing photographs. Professors Paul Halpern and Carlos López Urrutia assisted in my understanding of the French and Chilean navies. The College of Arts and Sciences of the University of Indianapolis provided a grant for summer 2002.

I dedicate this book to my in-laws, Pablo and Emilia Sobarzo, in gratitude for their hospitality during my visits to Chile and, more recently, to their home in the United States.

All photographs are courtesy of the Naval Historical Center (US), Washington, DC (Basic Collection).

ONE

Ruling the Waves:
The British Navy, 1815–1902

The years immediately following the defeat of Napoleon marked the zenith of British naval power, at least in terms of Britain's relative advantage over the world's other significant navies. At the end of the Napoleonic wars, the British navy was roughly twice as large as its nearest rival, the French, which (until the 1840s) posed no serious threat to British interests. As the Industrial Revolution began to affect naval construction, Britain, like any true hegemon, refused to take the lead in developing technologies that promised only to negate its own considerable advantages, yet as the century progressed the country's industrial might would enable the navy to respond decisively to every technological challenge it faced from abroad. Material strength remained the bulwark of British naval supremacy, since the service often lagged behind its rivals in the education and training of personnel; indeed, for the navy the social revolution proceeded at a much slower pace than the industrial. Nevertheless, for eight decades after the defeat of Napoleon the strength of the navy always sufficed to demonstrate to any potential adversary with a coastline the risk of offending British sensibilities. In addition to safeguarding the interests of Britain and its empire, under the Pax Britannica the navy served as the enforcer of moral and legal positions that the British government had taken (and was persuading others to take) on a global level, keeping commercial sea lanes safe against piracy and stopping the seaborne slave trade.

THE FLEET: FROM WOOD AND SAIL TO STEEL AND STEAM

In 1815 Britain had the largest navy the world had yet known, but just how large remains a matter of debate. Figures published in contemporary accounts and those derived from modern research vary widely, depending upon what one counts as a serviceable warship. Throughout the Napoleonic wars the navy typically kept just over 100 ships of the line in commission. In early 1814, during the last months of the conflict, 99 were on active service, supported by 495 frigates, sloops, brigs and other warships. The most generous estimate for 1815 gives figures of 218 ships of the line and over 600 other warships, the latter including 309 frigates and 261 sloops or brigs, counting all ships in reserve ('in ordinary') as well as those under construction or serving in auxiliary roles as receiving ships and training vessels. As soon as Napoleon was exiled to Elba, 19 ships of the line and 93 smaller warships were sold or broken up. The Hundred Days (March–July 1815) featured no further naval action against France, and Napoleon's exile to St Helena prompted further reductions in the fleet. By one account the British navy of 1817 had 98 ships of the line and 263 other warships. Other sources give figures of 146 ships of the line in 1820 and 106 as late as 1830, by which time just 71 were rated 'in good order.'[1]

In the age of sail Britain's large reserve of ships of the line formed the foundation of its peacetime naval supremacy. The navy of 1817 had 14 ships of the line in service and 84 in reserve; in 1830, 14 in commission and another 80 either in reserve or under construction. Such numbers more than sufficed to deter potential adversaries (in 1830 France had, at most, 53 ships of the line), while the large stock of frigates, sloops and smaller warships defended the empire and enforced the values of the Pax Britannica, combating piracy and suppressing the slave trade. Into the late 1830s, the navy typically kept at least three-quarters of its wooden battleships in reserve. With technology changing slowly, soundly built warships had long service lives and, for those in reserve, the Admiralty had to be concerned only with the rotting of the wood; even this problem was remedied, in part, by the practice of providing larger reserve warships with full-length roofs to guard against weather damage. The active British battleships of 1830 included HMS *Revenge*, a veteran of the Battle of Trafalgar (1805), and the reserve list of that year included eleven other ships of the line that had seen action in Nelson's great victory, among them HMS *Victory*, which had been launched in 1765. As the century progressed, however, the introduction of steam propulsion and, later, armour plate drove up the cost of capital ships, while the accelerating pace of technological change decreased their service lives. These factors prompted navies to maintain fewer of the largest units but have a greater share of them in active service at any given time. In the peacetime navy of the twentieth century, for example, it became common practice to keep at least three-quarters of capital ships (initially battleships, later aircraft carriers and nuclear submarines) in commission and no more than one-quarter in reserve.[2]

In Britain the navy allowed the vibrant private sector to take the lead in applying steam technology to ship propulsion. After initially leasing private paddle steamships for service as tugs and towboats, in 1821 the navy purchased its first steamer, the tug *Monkey*. The following year the Admiralty paid just under £10,000 to build the brig-sized tug *Comet*, the first British steamer constructed for naval service. In 1829 the 500-ton *Columbia* became the first armed steamship in the British navy, and the following year the 900-ton *Dee* entered service as the navy's first purpose-built steam warship. The *Comet* and other older steamers subsequently received at least a nominal armament, but they were not taken seriously as warships. In the late 1830s British naval authorities speculated that, in battle, a steamship would be destroyed if it came within 3,000 yards of a ship of the line. Paddle boxes accounted for too much of the broadside, limiting the number of guns a steamer could mount, a disadvantage not made good by the vessel's greater mobility, which came from machinery carried above the waterline, turning large side paddles vulnerable to enemy fire. They were also expensive to build and, afterward, to operate. The British navy's largest paddle steamer, the 3,190-ton *Terrible* (1845), cost £94,650 and achieved its top speed of almost 11 knots only by consuming an excessive amount of coal. Larger than a 74-gun ship of the line, it mounted just 19 guns owing to the size of its paddle boxes.[3]

The advent of screw propulsion transformed naval warfare, first jeopardizing, then enhancing Britain's margin of superiority over its rivals. Following the launching of the sloop *Rattler* (1843) and frigate *Amphion* (1846), in July 1849 the British navy began work on its first screw ship of the line, the *Agamemnon*, in response to the French navy's *Napoléon*, laid down 17 months earlier. Screw steamers could accommodate a traditional broadside armament, and their propellers (unlike side paddles) did not seriously hinder a ship's sailing ability. Screw propellers could be installed in vessels of similar design to conventional sailing warships, from ships of the line to schooners and gunboats; ultimately the numbers of screw-propelled warships converted from sailing warships outnumbered new construction, at least among the largest types. By the time the last screw ships of the line entered service in 1861, Britain had commissioned 58 (including 41 conversions), significantly more than France, which had 37 (including 28 conversions). Seeking a qualitative as well as quantitative advantage, the British ultimately built the largest and most expensive wooden screw warships ever constructed. None surpassed the 6,960-ton, 131-gun three-decker *Victoria* (launched 1859), which cost £150,000.[4]

Concern for coal supply kept most screw ships of the line in European waters, while screw frigates and smaller screw-propelled steamers joined sailing vessels of the same types on overseas duties. Wooden screw battleships led the British and French fleets of the Crimean War (1853–6), but by the end of the decade the first ironclad warships had doomed the lot. In France, the deployment of armoured floating batteries in the Black Sea during 1855 was followed by the decision to build the first armoured frigates. In May 1859 Britain laid down its first armoured frigate, the *Warrior* (illus. 1), in response to the French navy's *Gloire*, begun 14 months earlier. The *Warrior* and *Gloire* were both three-masted warships, armed with 36 guns, plated with 4.5 inches of wrought iron armour, but the British frigate was a 9,140-ton vessel of all-iron construction, while the 5,630-ton *Gloire* was an ironclad wooden ship. The *Warrior* also

1 The British armoured frigate *Warrior* (1861).

had trunk engines capable of 14 knots (one more than its French rival), carried 200 tons more coal in its bunkers, and could set twice as much canvas to the wind. The added speed and range reflected its designer's intention that it be able to function as a traditional frigate, capable of fulfilling missions worldwide, whereas the French built the *Gloire* for line-of-battle service in European waters. By 1862, when the first meeting of armoured warships took place in the American Civil War's Battle of Hampton Roads, Britain and France each had sixteen armoured frigates built or building, but once again the British had achieved a qualitative edge. The smallest of the early British ironclads were similar in size to the largest of the French, and most were of all-iron construction, whereas most of the French vessels were ironclad wooden ships. During the remainder of the 1860s the leading navies of Europe supplemented their initial complements of armoured broadside battery warships with a variety of turret ships (initially patterned after the USS *Monitor*), rams and, finally, central battery or casemate ships. Conceived by chief constructor Edward Reed, the central battery ship was the first design of the ironclad era pioneered by the British, who thus broke from their pre-ironclad tendency to adopt and improve upon the innovations of others. A central casemate in an otherwise unarmoured hull protected the ship's engines as well as a smaller battery of heavier pivoting guns; in many vessels of the type, a recessed freeboard fore and aft of the casemate allowed end-on fire from the end guns. The first larger central battery ship, the 7,550-ton *Bellerophon* (1866), had 6 inches of casemate and waterline wrought-iron armour; the last of the type, a decade later, were plated with wrought iron twice as thick.[5]

The ironclad fleets of the 1870s were a heterogeneous lot, including broadside battery ships, casemate ships, and turret ships of various sizes, many of the last suitable only for coastal defence. In 1870 Britain had 54 armoured warships built or building to France's 51, but still enjoyed a considerable qualitative superiority, with 32 ironclads displacing 6,000 tons or more, to just 12 for France. Even for a country as wealthy as Britain, the financial burdens of construction and maintenance limited the numbers of larger armoured warships. The British navy spent £377,000 to build the *Warrior*, more than double the price of the most expensive wooden screw ship of the line, then another £121,000 to keep it in service between 1861 and 1869. While the *Warrior* was designed for global cruising duties, the lack of adequate overseas maintenance facilities kept it and most other early armoured warships stationed in European waters. Meanwhile, the firepower of unarmoured frigates and smaller warships, built of iron from the 1860s and steel from the 1870s, sufficed to maintain order in the sea lanes and defend or expand the British Empire. France's defeat at the hands of Prussia in 1870–71 further ensured Britain's position of hegemony. With naval construction across the Channel all but stopped, the British navy slowed the pace of its own building programme and also kept far fewer battleships in active service, by 1874 only four in the Mediterranean and four in home waters, the latter backed by ten coastal defence ironclads.[6]

By the early 1880s the *Warrior* and other armoured battleships with inflexible broadside batteries were obsolete. The sinking of the 7,770-ton *Captain*, a fully rigged low-freeboard turret ship lost in a gale off Cape Finisterre in 1870, cast doubts over capital ships of that design as well. The casemate ship dominated the 1870s but the need to plate the central battery with ever-thicker wrought iron armour raised questions about its seaworthiness. The model for future battleships came from Italy, where chief naval engineer Benedetto Brin's revolutionary *Duilio*, an 11,000-ton mastless, high freeboard turret ship (built 1873–80) caused an international sensation. The 11,880-ton *Inflexible* (1874–81), the largest British warship built to date, likewise featured a high freeboard and a heavy primary armament (four 16-inch guns) paired in two turrets amidships. The *Inflexible* was the first battleship fitted with vertical compound engines and electric power for searchlights and interior lighting. The incorporation of such new technologies contributed to the ship's seven-year construction time (unusually long for a British warship) and its unprecedented cost of £812,000, which sparked a *furor* in Parliament. Nevertheless, the *Inflexible* became the general prototype for four other British battleships begun in the late 1870s. These had no masts or yards from the outset (the *Inflexible* lost its original brig rig in a refit in 1885), and were protected with compound (iron-and-steel) armour, introduced in 1877 by the British firms of Brown and Cammell as a lighter-weight alternative to wrought iron.[7]

The development of compound armour helped save the battleship by at least temporarily resolving the dilemma of the need for ever-thicker protection against ever more powerful guns. While Britain kept faith with the battleship throughout the 1880s, laying down another ten in the years 1880–86, most other countries copied the French Jeune Ecole, a strategy based around commerce raiding in which modern steel cruisers and hosts of torpedo boats took centre stage. Responding to the challenge, the British supplemented their battle fleet with nine armoured cruisers, dozens of second- and third-class cruisers, and 159 torpedo boats constructed during the 1880s alone, ensuring that Britain – the country threatened most by the Jeune Ecole – would be superior in all warship types associated with the strategy. Thornycroft's 32-ton *Lightning* (built 1876), capable of 19 knots under forced draught, set the standard for most torpedo boats of the 1880s, while Armstrong's 3,000-ton protected cruiser *Esmeralda* (1881–4), built for export to Chile, served as a general model for the first generation of mastless

2 The British pre-dreadnought *Royal Sovereign* (1891).

steel cruisers. Armstrong also pioneered medium-calibre quick-firing artillery, first installed in the 735-ton torpedo gunboat *Sharpshooter* (1888–9) but soon adopted as the secondary armament for battleships and large cruisers, to ward off torpedo boat attacks. British battleship designers further countered the torpedo threat by making their ships faster than their foreign competition; the *Victoria* and *Sans Pareil* (both laid down 1885) were the first larger warships fitted with triple expansion engines; upon its completion in 1891, the *Sans Pareil* proved capable of 17.5 knots, making it the fastest battleship then afloat.[8]

The revival of the French navy under the Jeune Ecole threat and a Russian naval build-up begun in 1882 prompted the British public and politicians to question whether the navy was strong enough. Criticism initiated in the series 'The Truth about the Navy', published in the *Pall Mall Gazette* during 1884–5, culminated in the winter of 1888–9 in a heated debate over the need to expand and modernize the fleet further. In December 1888 Lord Charles Beresford, a naval officer and member of Parliament, demanded 'a definite standard . . . against the fleets of two powers combined, one of which should be France.' As a measure of British naval strength, the traditional two-power standard had been first proposed by the Napoleonic-era foreign secretary, Lord Castlereagh, shortly after Waterloo, but never formally adopted; qualitative considerations aside, in the sheer size of its battle fleet Britain had not equalled the next two naval powers combined since the days of the wooden ship of the line. When Parliament passed the Naval Defence Act on 7 March 1889, the standard became official, committing Britain to achieve a level of naval supremacy it had not enjoyed since at least the 1850s.[9] The act provided £21.5 million for the construction of eight 14,150-ton battleships of the *Royal Sovereign* class (illus. 2), two second-class battleships, 42 cruisers of various sizes and 18 torpedo gunboats, in order to give Britain a fleet equal to the combined naval strength of France and Russia within five years. In addition to being the largest warships yet built by any navy, the *Royal Sovereign*s set a new standard for battleship construction not fundamentally changed until the all big-gun *Dreadnought* of 1906. The design included four 13.5-inch guns paired in barbettes on the centreline fore and aft, backed by a secondary armament of ten 6-inch quick-firing Armstrong guns, and triple expansion engines capable of 18 knots under forced draught.[10]

Lord George Hamilton, First Lord of the Admiralty at the time, hoped that the sheer size of the British programme would deter other navies from matching it, but in 1889 France resumed battleship construction after a hiatus of six years, while Russia's naval expansion continued unabated. After the resignation of Otto von Bismarck in 1890, Germany cut Russia loose from its system of alliances, giving France (isolated since its defeat in 1871) a natural diplomatic partner. In 1891 a French squadron called on the Russians at Kronstadt, a visit repaid two years later at Toulon; in 1892 and 1894 France and Russia signed a military convention and an overall treaty of alliance. While the military potential of the Franco-Russian combination prompted Germany to develop its fateful Schlieffen Plan, the implications of the new alliance at sea led to another programme of warship construction in Britain, which throughout the era of the Pax

Britannica had never faced a formal alliance of the second and third naval powers. With the last ships of the Naval Defence Act nearing completion, in December 1893 Parliament approved another five-year programme for 1894–8, known as the 'Spencer programme' after John Poyntz Spencer, recently appointed First Lord of the Admiralty. Earl Spencer's plan, which called for seven battleships, 30 cruisers and 122 smaller vessels to be built at a cost of £31 million, was ultimately revised to include nine battleships (the 14,560-ton *Majestic* class) and fewer cruisers. Reflecting the degree of alarm in Britain, all nine *Majestic*s were laid down within fifteen months of the Bill's passage. Their armament included four 12-inch guns in two fore-and-aft centreline turrets, backed by twelve 6-inch quick-firing guns. Improving on the design of the *Royal Sovereign*s, they were fitted with nickel-steel armour and were the first British battleships to carry their heavy guns in modern turrets (a 'turret' now being defined as a fully armoured hood protecting guns in a barbette mounting). By the time the programme was completed, Britain's desire to respond immediately to new construction abroad led to annual appropriations for new battleships, another twenty in the years from 1896 to 1901 alone. These projects enabled Britain to maintain better than a two-power standard in numbers of battleships, while in size, as well as capability, its battleships far outclassed those of other countries. The same was true with cruisers and smaller vessels, the latter including the first destroyers (initially known as 'torpedo boat destroyers'), a new type of warship armed with torpedo tubes and light deck guns, first ordered under the Spencer programme. The programmes authorized by Parliament in 1889 and 1893 foreshadowed the explosion of turn-of-the-century popular navalism that swept most of the world's great powers, with one significant difference. While in other states with representative governments (especially Germany and the United States) the phenomenon went hand-in-hand with growing national ambitions and a self-confident patriotism, in Britain navalism stemmed from a lack of confidence about the country's ability to maintain its nineteenth-century position into the twentieth.[11]

During the era of the Pax Britannica the British navy dominated the world's oceans with a body of personnel whose selection and training were remarkably haphazard, at least through the first half of the nineteenth century. For officers as well as common manpower, the British navy lagged behind its foreign competitors in the institution of regular practices of entry and promotion, as well as in the establishment of educational institutions. The service did not confront these matters earlier because, at least for the remainder of the age of sail, it took for granted the availability of many more qualified officers and seamen than it would ever need, a consequence of the dramatic expansion of the fleet during the Napoleonic wars, and the equally dramatic reduction of its size after 1815, when most officers were put on half-pay (reserve) status and most seamen discharged.

The postwar reductions struck an officer corps that, even in wartime, had been larger than necessary. In 1809, when the fleet reached its wartime peak of 773 ships in commission, just under two-thirds of the 4,444 officers were actually employed aboard ship or ashore; by 1813 the number of officers had risen to 4,873 while their employment rate fell to barely half. In the years 1814–18 the number of seamen fell from 140,000 to 20,000, and the number of warships in commission from 713 to 121, yet the number of officers rose to 5,797, barely 10 per cent of whom were needed for active duty. An overabundance of lieutenants became even worse at the very end of the war when, amid a flurry of promotions at all levels, the Admiralty gave the rank to hundreds of midshipmen and master's mates, so-called 'lieutenancies in lieu of pension', which enabled the recipients to draw a lieutenant's half-pay for the rest of their lives. The institution of half-pay, which had evolved since the 1600s, created a reserve officer corps and provided a pension system but did not function particularly well on either account. Prior to 1815 the half-pay system had also never been tested by a period of prolonged peace, such as that which the navy faced after the Napoleonic wars. The wholesale promotions of 1814–15 had a series of negative consequences, slowing the postwar promotion rate to a crawl and making naval service an unattractive career for potential newcomers to the corps. By 1841 the senior captain was 68 years old, and the senior commander had not been promoted since 1794. Starting in the 1840s the annual number of deaths of Napoleonic-era veterans outstripped the number of new lieutenants commissioned, gradually shrinking the corps; nevertheless, as late as 1850 only around 10 per cent of British naval officers were on active duty, the rest on half-pay.[12]

The British navy of the nineteenth century had no formal retirement age, and officers could remain on half-pay, theoretically available for active duty, until death. Advancing gradually in rank under a strict seniority system, in 1868 the relatively undistinguished Edward Ratsey became the navy's senior admiral aged 90, having spent most of the previous 61 years on half-pay after last commanding a ship in 1807. To avoid such cases the Admiralty attempted to buy out veteran officers with promotion-and-retirement deals, as early as 1807 offering aged British lieutenants half-pay at commander's rank in exchange for forfeiting their right to future active-duty assignments. In 1840 the same offer was made to senior commanders, who became retired captains with no right to return to service. Finally, in 1847–51, 200 elderly captains became rear admirals on half-pay, likewise by forfeiting their right to return to active duty. Out of such measures a formal retirement system gradually evolved.[13] In another decisive step toward the professionalization of the naval officer service, in 1861 the Admiralty introduced the system of 'general commissions', ending the tradition of officers receiving commissions specific to ships or to assignments ashore, between which they would revert to half-pay status. Henceforth, officers with no specific charge were considered at the disposal of the Admiralty. General commissions, retirement programmes, and the deaths of the last survivors from the bloated corps of the Napoleonic wars combined to reduce dramatically the number of officers on the half-pay list eligible to return to active duty. As of 1879 three-quarters of the navy's 170 captains were on active duty, and by the end of the century most officers at all ranks were fully employed, yet at any given time a small minority remained on half-pay, an institution that survived until 1938.[14]

Meanwhile, at least during the 1840s and '50s, the absence of a pension system or retirement age affected the pool of candidates for senior commands at sea. The problem did not emerge earlier because of the number of relatively young British admirals on hand as of 1815, owing to the fact that during the Napoleonic wars it was not uncommon for captains to be promoted to rear admiral while still in their forties. Sir Edward Pellew, later Lord Exmouth, who became a rear admiral in 1804, commanded the navy's bombardment of Algiers in 1816, at 59. Sir Edward Codrington, made rear admiral in 1814, commanded allied forces against the Turco-Egyptian fleet at Navarino in 1827, at 57. In contrast, Sir Robert Stopford, promoted to rear admiral in 1808, was 72 by the time he commanded the allied fleet during the Near Eastern crisis of 1840. In 1845 Admiral Sir David Milne died on active duty, at 82, while serving as commander in chief at Plymouth, and in 1851 Admiral Thomas Cochrane, Lord Dundonald, was 76 when he left his last overseas post as commander of the North American and West Indies station. At the onset of the Crimean War in 1854 Admiral Sir Charles Napier, then 68, received command of the British Baltic fleet, while Admiral Sir James Deans Dundas, 69, became commander of the British Black Sea fleet; their principal competitors for these posts were Cochrane, by then 79, and Admiral Sir John Ommaney, 81, then on active duty as commander in chief at Plymouth. Given the slow pace of postwar promotion within a rigid seniority system, if Lord Nelson had survived he would have finally achieved the navy's highest rank, Admiral of the Fleet, in 1844, at which time he still would have been eligible (at age 87) for an active command.[15] The seniority system notwithstanding, after 1815, as before, the Admiralty retained the right to assign key operational commands to the most competent admiral among those available; in this decision, seniority was just one element considered. Indeed, in this manner Nelson, a vice admiral in 1805, trailing dozens of other officers in seniority, had received command of the fleet that fought at Trafalgar.[16]

In general, however, seniority became more rigid and problematic after 1830, an unintended consequence of a modest reform effort after the more liberal Whigs returned to power in

Parliament in 1830, following years of conservative Tory rule. The new First Lord of the Admiralty, Sir James Graham, closed the last loopholes of extraordinary advancement, which had been exploited by officers with Tory political connections under the long tenure of his predecessor, Lord Melville (1812–30). Indeed, Melville's own son, Richard Saunders Dundas, had benefited from his connections to become a captain in 1824, just nine years after graduating from the Royal Naval College in Portsmouth. Without his father's patronage his career slowed considerably, and he did not become a rear admiral until 29 years later, on the eve of the Crimean War. Nevertheless, his earlier extraordinary promotion put him in the position to become the first British officer commissioned after the Napoleonic wars to reach flag rank; he went on to succeed Napier as commander of the British Baltic fleet in 1855.[17] The career path of David Price was perhaps more typical of the mid-century British senior officer than that of the well-connected Dundas. Price became a captain in 1815, following fourteen years of wartime service, then went on to languish on half-pay from 1831 to 1850 except for brief periods as commander of a ship of the line and superintendent of a dockyard. He continued to creep up the navy list and was made rear admiral in 1850, then became commander of the British Pacific squadron at the outbreak of the Crimean War. Tragically, when faced with the prospect of command under fire for the first time in four decades, Price suffered a nervous breakdown and committed suicide in 1854, on the eve of a disastrous allied assault on the Russian base at Petropavlovsk.[18] Price's demise provides some evidence of the sort of pressure British officers felt throughout much of the era of the Pax Britannica. In the decades after 1815, the ageing of the officer corps and limited opportunities for junior officers created something akin to the 'zero defects' mentality prevalent in the US Navy officer corps of the post-Cold War era, 150 years later. In sharp contrast to the bold 'band of brothers' of Nelson's era, most postwar British officers lived in fear of making a career-ending mistake or failing to measure up to expectations. To make matters worse, in an atmosphere in which active-duty officers dreaded a return to the half-pay list, those sympathetic to innovation or reform rarely risked advocating it.[19]

Years of postwar unemployment or underemployment helped drive many British officers into foreign service, even though (under the Foreign Enlistment Act of 1819) they had to forfeit their half-pay while employed by another country. Cochrane commanded the navies of Chile (1818–22), Brazil (1822–5) and Greece (1825–8), while Napier led the navy of Portugal in the early 1830s. During the same years other British officers commanded the newly established navies of Mexico, Peru and Argentina. In each case, a senior officer accepting these foreign commands took dozens of former subordinates with him on the adventure. Their exploits abroad, in particular the derring-do of Cochrane and his cohort of followers during the Latin American Wars of Independence, provided ample evidence of the survival of the old Nelsonian spirit, a spirit unfortunately stifled by the circumstances of the postwar British navy.[20]

The Royal Naval College at Portsmouth, a preparatory school for boys aged between eleven and seventeen, produced less than 5 per cent of the British officer corps of the Napoleonic wars and barely more than 10 per cent of officers serving in the years 1815–49. The school had been founded in 1733 as the Naval Academy, to provide an alternative to the traditional system of midshipmen being placed by their fathers or guardians directly with ship captains. It enrolled no more than a hundred cadets and, one year, as few as fifteen. Officers commanding warships resented being required to take on the college's graduates as midshipmen, filling spaces they could otherwise assign to boys of their own choice.[21] With 90 per cent of the navy's officers unemployed after 1815, the need for a school to train still more officers understandably came into question. At the same time, concern for the education of midshipmen brought aboard ship via the traditional route led the navy to introduce a system of shipboard schoolmasters starting in the 1820s. Once most larger warships had at least one schoolmaster aboard, the Admiralty, in 1837, closed the Royal Naval College.[22] The decentralized system of training future officers aboard ship remained in place until 1857, when the hulk *Illustrious* became a stationary school for officer candidates, now designated naval cadets. The following year the *Illustrious* gave way to the old ship of the line *Britannia*, which was anchored at Dartmouth from 1863. Under the *Britannia* system, all incoming officer candidates were housed and educated for the first year or two aboard the school ship, before being sent into the fleet for four years of duty at sea. For the first time in history, British officer candidates received a uniform education and, when nineteen, had to pass the same examinations before receiving their commissions as lieutenants.[23]

The practice of training everyone from naval cadets to apprentice seamen aboard stationary school ships lasted until the turn of the century. A shipboard gunnery school dating from the 1830s went ashore in 1891, while naval cadet training went from the *Britannia* to buildings in Dartmouth, an institution known henceforth as the 'Britannia Royal Naval College', to distinguish it from the Royal Naval College at Greenwich, established in 1873 as a graduate school for junior officers entering mid-career, groomed to be the navy's future leaders. The Greenwich school, like the Naval War College in the United States and similar institutions in other countries, provided university-level study in international law, higher mathematics and languages, in addition to courses in naval strategy and tactics. The Royal Naval College at Greenwich was one of six institutions established by the British navy in the 1870s and '80s to provide specialized education or training for officers, the others being torpedo schools in Portsmouth (established 1876) and Devonport (1884), a naval engineering college in Plymouth (1880), a signal school in Portsmouth (1888) and a telegraphy school in Devonport (1889).[24]

Coming in the wake of the earlier standardization of conditions under which Britain's naval officers entered, served in and exited the corps, these schools helped complete the navy's gradual process of professionalization begun in earnest after the Crimean War. The reforms helped transform a service that, before the 1850s, had been largely unresponsive to the social and economic changes that had swept Britain. Geographically, the profile of the officer corps of 1815–49 was remarkably similar to that of the corps of 1793–1815. In each cohort, roughly 70 per cent were from England, almost 15 per cent from Scotland and around 10 per cent from Ireland, with the rest born in

Wales, the colonies or foreign countries. The same ten English counties consistently provided the most officers, with the three southeasternmost counties – Devon, Kent and Hampshire – always leading the way. Socially, the corps of 1815–49 was led by sons of naval officers at 33.3 per cent (1793–1815: 24.1 per cent), followed by sons of the landed gentry at 27.6 per cent (27.4), sons of noblemen at 17.8 per cent (12.0), sons of clergy-men at 7.8 per cent (8.7), sons of army officers at 7.3 per cent (unchanged), and sons of merchants and professional men at 4.6 per cent (12.3). Sons of working-class families – 6.7 per cent of the officers of 1793–1815 – were not represented at all in the 1815–49 cohort, most likely because promotions from the ratings, accounting for roughly 5 per cent of the officers of 1793–1815, all but ceased after the Napoleonic wars. Thus, the groups whose representation declined most precipitously after 1815 (the merchant and professional classes, along with the working class) were the same groups whose importance in British society as a whole was rising. At least for the merchant and professional classes, the decline of representation in the officer corps reflected the lack of opportunity in the postwar navy rather than any prejudice on the navy's part, while the rise in sons of naval officers indicates that at least this group did not lose faith in a naval career when others did. Family connections continued to matter, perhaps more than before. In the officer corps of 1849, an astonishing 59 of the 154 captains who had entered service since 1815 (38.3 per cent) were sons or grand-sons of admirals.[25] Owing to the social profile of the officer corps, most naval officers, as before, came from Anglican religious backgrounds, and their strongest prejudices were anti-Catholic and anti-Irish. Throughout the nineteenth century the Church of England retained its monopoly over naval chaplaincies and shipboard worship services. The navy's Catholics and non-Anglican Protestants (Methodists, Pres-byterians and the like) were limited to attending Sunday services ashore, when ships were in ports where such services were available.[26]

For its common manpower, the British navy of 1815 still relied upon the hire-and-discharge system. Just as officers at sea held commissions specific to a shipboard assignment, seamen signed on when a ship entered commission and were paid off when the ship went into reserve, but unlike idle officers, they had no half-pay between active assignments. The only people kept on the payroll continuously were non-commissioned or warrant officers such as boatswains, gunners and carpenters, whose services were required to maintain ships in reserve as well as those in active service. Nevertheless, amid the reductions of 1814–18 (from a fleet manned by 140,000 seamen to one employing just 20,000), the navy could always count on enough unemployed seamen turning up to man a warship once it was activated. Whereas over half of the British seamen of the Napoleonic era had been forced into naval service by press gangs or sent by localities against their will as 'quota men', after 1815 the navy typically had far more men seeking shipboard positions than were needed and turned away one-half to two-thirds of them. Unemployment drove tens of thousands into the merchant marine or to the navies of other countries, most notably the United States. When Cochrane and other British officers went into the service of the newly independent Latin American countries, they had no trouble recruiting British seamen to follow them.[27] Throughout the nineteenth century, the size of the fleet and its manpower needs rose in times of great international tension, then stabilized at a somewhat higher level afterward. In the wake of the Near Eastern crisis (1839–40) and First Opium War (1839–42), the navy maintained a normal peacetime stand of 40,000 seamen and marines. During the last year of the Crimean War (1855–6), nearly 68,000 were on active service, and afterward the peacetime stand stabilized near 50,000. The European war scare of 1859 and possible hostilities with the United States early in the American Civil War caused an increase to over 70,000 for the years 1860–62, but by the end of the Civil War (1865–6) the numbers stabilized at around 60,000.[28] The number of seamen and marines did not top 100,000 again until the fleet expanded under the Naval Defence Act and the Spencer Programme, and only on the eve of the First World War did it reach 150,000 men, finally surpassing the figure for 1814.

The traditional hire-and-discharge system began to change in 1830, when a gunnery school was established at Portsmouth aboard the old ship of the line *Excellent*. Thereafter, any seaman trained aboard the *Excellent* was guaranteed at least five years of continuous employment, with terms of service renewable at higher pay. Gunnery pay initiated a system of 'proficiency payments', which expanded as the increasing complexity of weaponry and propulsion systems required more seamen to have a greater specialized knowledge. The navy eventually extended higher pay and job security to seamen passing mechanical engineering, signal and torpedo courses. In 1853 Sir James Graham, back in office as First Lord of the Admiralty, implemented a ten-year term of service and minimum age of eighteen for all seamen, and established the first training ship for apprentice seamen. On the new system, a twenty-year reserve liability followed the seaman's active service. In the years after the Crimean War, seamen serving under the new terms (known initially as Continuous Service men) were the first British sailors to be issued official uniforms. Previously, dress had varied by ship and, in some cases, seamen wore no real uniform at all.[29]

These reforms came too late to help the navy through its most serious manning crisis of the nineteenth century, following the outbreak of the Crimean War. The Register of Seamen, established by an Act of Parliament in 1835, theoretically included the names of all British seamen and was to be used to identify men for naval service in time of war. Yet in 1854 of the 250,000 men on the register barely 400 volunteered for duty. Admiral Napier's Baltic fleet had to put to sea with skeleton crews, with Graham advising him to 'pick up some Norwegian sailors' on the way to Russian waters, along with any Swedes who might be willing to sign on. The British navy had resorted to Scandinavian manpower before, in the Napoleonic wars, but in the social and political climate of the 1850s it could not fall back on the devices of impressment or the quota. In any event, as the Industrial Revolution transformed warship design, naval vessels required a crew far more skilled and literate than any press gang could have assembled. Napier's campaign for further reform, pursued after his postwar election to Parliament, in 1858 led to the creation of the Royal Commission on Manning the Navy. The following year, the term of service was extended to twelve years, with an optional renewal of ten years, after which a sailor (by then at least 40 years old) could receive a pension as a so-called 'pensioner reserve' or re-enlist for further five-year terms of active duty. Also in 1859, the Register of Seamen gave way to the Royal Naval Reserve, which by 1862 had 12,000 merchant seamen voluntarily enrolled. A decade later, the reserve included 14,000 merchant seamen and 6,000 'pensioner reserves.'[30]

After 1815 the abandonment of impressment and the quota system brought an end to the high incidences of indiscipline and flogging common aboard British warships during the Napoleonic wars. With all seamen serving willingly and most feeling fortunate to have employment, disciplinary problems declined dramatically. As utilitarianism began to transform Britain's criminal justice system, the philosophy's chief advocate, John Stuart Mill, also numbered among those calling for a reform of the navy's disciplinary practices. At the insistence of Parliament, overall punishment statistics became a matter of public record starting in 1845–6. The decision of the editors of the *United Service Magazine* (eventually known as the *Journal of the Royal United Services Institution*), founded in 1857, to publish flogging statistics for individual warships subsequently helped stigmatize excessive flogging within the officer corps.[31] Whereas the navy's post-1815 'zero defects' mentality initially had worked in favour of draconian discipline, from mid-century onward the opposite was true, as ship captains once most fearful of a career-ending mutiny now most feared being sacked by the Admiralty for being too harsh with their crews.

The British navy experienced no mutinies between 1815 and 1859, but following the mobilization of the fleet during the general European war scare of 1859, officers at least temporarily lost control over fifteen warships, including the Mediterranean flagship *Marlborough* and nine other ships of the line. Lack of leave topped the list of the seamen's complaints, as the navy's recent measures to resolve its manning crisis had not yet had their desired impact, and the captains of the fleet's undermanned ships could not afford to let any men go on leave during an international crisis. Parliament responded with four discipline Acts passed in the years

1860–66, superseding articles of war that had been in effect since 1749. The new codes eliminated many restrictions on shore leave and most corporal punishment, and curtailed the use of solitary confinement and other draconian measures. The last instance of shipboard capital punishment, the traditional hanging from the yardarm, came in 1860. The acts did not abolish flogging but the navy subsequently 'suspended' peacetime flogging in 1871 and wartime flogging in 1879; the last recorded flogging in the British navy occurred in 1880, in violation of the suspension. All punishments were standardized and a 'Table of Summary Punishments' distributed throughout the fleet. Henceforth a Ship's Police enforced discipline at sea rather than detachments of Royal Marines. Once convicted of a crime, prisoners (after 1862) were housed ashore rather than aboard often-squalid prison hulks. On the question of shore leave, key to the mutinies of 1859, it remained a privilege dispensed by the captain until 1890, when it became a seaman's right.[32]

Because unruly behaviour and the ensuing flogging had often stemmed from drunkenness, the reduction of the sailor's rum ration (halved in 1824, and halved again in 1850) did much to improve shipboard discipline. The new limits on alcohol consumption became essential to shipboard safety in the era of the steam warship, since drink and machinery did not mix well. The rum ration survived until 1970 but was considerably less popular after 1850, when the Admiralty began to offer higher pay (eventually as much as 20 per cent more per month) to seamen electing not to take their ration. Such incentives carried considerable weight in light of the fact that rates of pay had remained the same from 1806 to 1844, and again from 1844 to 1859. Just as the onset of the age of steam created friction between sea officers and shipboard engineers, below deck the ordinary seaman shunned the lowly stoker, and resented the fact that stokers were paid at least 50 per cent more than they were, with additional bonuses applied whenever a steam warship was serving in the tropics.[33] All things considered, after 1860 the British navy learned from experience that, for most of its seamen, regardless of their shipboard roles, better pay and treatment produced better and more reliable behaviour.

Lord Palmerston, serving as foreign secretary or prime minister for 24 of the 35 years between 1830 and 1865, shaped the Pax Britannica more than any other British politician or statesman. Famous for his 1847 remark that 'there are no better peace-keepers than well-appointed three-deckers',[34] Palmerston had few scruples about the active use of British naval power to police the world, either in the direct interest of the British Empire and its subjects or to defend causes and principles that Britain had embraced. Under his influence, the British navy would be employed to eliminate the slave trade, suppress piracy, support constitutional governments and, above all else, defend the rights and property of Britain and British subjects abroad. Palmerston's only formal connection with the navy came early in his parliamentary career, when he served for two and a half years as a junior lord at the Admiralty, but in this capacity he set the tone for his future views and policies. His first speech in the House of Commons, in February 1808, defended the navy's infamous 1807 pre-emptive strike against Copenhagen, carried out by Admiral Sir James Gambier in order to keep the fleet of neutral Denmark from falling into French hands, after the Danes had rejected overtures for a British alliance.[35]

Britain employed a combination of diplomacy and naval force to end the maritime trading in slaves. With effect from 1 January 1808, Britain and the United States declared the slave trade illegal. To eliminate illegal slave trading by its own subjects, the British government subsequently confiscated any British vessel caught slaving, fined the owners £100 per slave aboard, and punished the captain and crew with transportation to Australia. These measures sufficed to end illegal British slave trading by 1811. On the diplomatic front, Britain secured pledges from Portugal (in 1810) and Spain (in 1817) to end their slave trade north of the Equator, in the Spanish case in exchange for a cash settlement of £400,000. In 1836 Portugal outlawed the slave trade altogether. Three years later, coinciding with Parliament's passage of Palmerston's Slave Trade Suppression Bill, Britain began hunting Spanish and Portuguese slavers south of the Equator as well as north of it. For the newly independent states of Latin America, Britain offered diplomatic recognition and trade ties in exchange for the suppression of the slave trade. Whereas the republics formed from the former Spanish empire all abolished slavery after declaring their independence, Brazil did not follow suit until 1889, when it became a republic after 67 years as a monarchy. In a treaty signed in 1825 Brazil promised to outlaw the slave trade but subsequently did nothing about it; starting in 1839, when the British navy extended its anti-slavery patrols south of the Equator, scores of Brazilian-flagged slavers were seized every year. By 1852 fewer than 1,000 slaves made it into Brazil, and the trade finally died out altogether in 1855. Meanwhile, in 1840, Britain granted recognition of the Republic of Texas in exchange for its abolition of the slave trade; the treaty became moot in 1845, when the United States annexed Texas. The continuation of slave trading by American vessels (in violation of their own government's ban) and by the French (who did not abolish slavery until 1848) initially posed the greatest obstacles to the British campaign. The Webster-Ashburthon Treaty of 1842, resolving a border dispute between the United States and Canada, committed the us navy to join the British in hunting slavers off the coast of West Africa. Three years later, an Anglo-American-French convention committed the French navy to join as well, but only in pursuit of French slavers. The Americans had no great enthusiasm for the task but at least showed more resolve than the French, who failed to capture a single vessel in the years 1845–8.[36]

Aware that many of its officers and most of its seamen could not have cared less about freeing slaves, the British navy offered lucrative incentives to ensure the enforcement of British policies. An Admiralty court at Freetown, Sierra Leone, awarded prize money (so-called 'head money') based on a headcount of slaves freed. Thus British officers and seamen took a strong interest not just in capturing slavers at sea, but in making sure that as many freed slaves as possible made it back to Africa alive. Initially the British financed the head money payments by auctioning off the seized ships, as it would any other prize of war, but this practice stopped once the navy realized that most of the best slavers it captured ended up back in the trade under new owners. After 1836 captured slave ships were broken up, with the British government absorbing the cost. Better to facilitate operations against the slave trade, in 1840 the British navy separated the West African command from the Cape command and further reinforced both stations. In 1840 they included 34 ships, mostly fast frigates and sloops, up from 11 in 1830. In 1855, at the height of the Crimean War, the navy still had 22 ships assigned to the campaign. The defeat of the Confederate States in the American Civil War made the Spanish Caribbean colonies and Brazil the only places in the western hemisphere still allowing slavery. In 1865, coincidentally the year of Palmerston's death, no prizes were brought before the Admiralty court at Sierra Leone, and the Atlantic slave trade could be considered ended.[37]

After 1865 anti-slavery efforts shifted to the East African coast, where the slave trade centred on the island sultanate of Zanzibar. During the early 1860s the British Cape squadron participated in the first significant attempts to disrupt the trade in the Indian Ocean. In 1864 the Cape station was merged with the East Indies squadron, but as of 1868 the combined force included just seven ships, far from adequate for its far-flung responsibilities. After the sultan of Zanzibar agreed to outlaw the slave trade in 1873, the navy sent the old screw ship of the line *London* to Zanzibar as headquarters ship for a vigorous campaign against East African slavers. By 1884 slaving in the area had all but ceased, but as soon as the *London* was decommissioned and broken up, the trade resumed. Germany, then first establishing its colonial empire, stepped into the breach the following year, proclaiming a protectorate over Zanzibar and establishing a colony on the East African mainland. In 1888–9 British and German squadrons joined forces to end the slave trade as well as arms shipments to anti-German forces in the East African interior. Under the Helgoland-Zanzibar Treaty (1890), Britain traded the North Sea island of Helgoland to Germany for Zanzibar, which remained a part of the empire until 1964. Thus ended the East African maritime slave trade, although isolated cases of slaving continued to be reported. As late as 1922, a British ship in the Red Sea captured an Arab dhow with a cargo of slaves.[38]

Much less idealistic, in a global sense, than the suppression of the maritime slave trade, the peacetime British navy strove to assist British subjects abroad during times of distress. The so-called Don Pacifico affair of 1850 laid to rest any doubts that the government or the fleet did not take these duties seriously. David Pacifico, a Spanish Jew born a British subject at Gibraltar, grew up in Portugal and, as a naturalized Portuguese subject, in 1839 became that country's consul in Athens, at which time he obtained a British passport as further security. He would need it, for Portugal subsequently dismissed him for corruption. He remained in Athens and, in 1847, during the Greek capital's traditional Easter mob action against the local Jewish community, his house was ransacked and burned. Afterward, when Pacifico sued the Greek government for £32,000, Palmerston supported him as a British subject with a legitimate claim against a foreign regime. The intervening revolutions of 1848–9 delayed the British response, but in January 1850 Admiral Sir William Parker anchored at Piraeus with the Mediterranean Fleet, presenting the Greeks with a bill including Pacifico's claims and lesser sums for other British subjects, plus interest calculated from the time of each alleged offence. After the Greeks refused to pay, Parker first seized a Greek warship and then blockaded Piraeus, later widening the blockade to other ports. Foreign-flagged vessels were allowed through the blockade, but all Greek-flagged vessels were seized and interned. When several Greek merchants changed their ships to Russian registry, Parker, with Palmerston's backing, treated as Greek all merchantmen that had been under Greek registry at the onset of the blockade, and seized the Russian-flagged Greek vessels as well. Palmerston persevered under pressure from Queen Victoria, the Tory opposition in Parliament, and other European governments, all of which thought his measures too harsh, and in April 1850 Admiral Napier accepted the Greek capitulation. In 1851 Pacifico finally agreed to a reduced settlement of £6,550. The affair at least temporarily poisoned Britain's relations with both France and Russia, but Palmerston remained unapologetic. In a famous address in the House of Commons, he beat back a vote of no confidence by drawing a direct link between the Pax Britannica and the Pax Romana of antiquity, making the case that, as the world's dominant power, Britain was within its rights to use any means necessary to ensure that a British passport was respected worldwide.[39] But the selective nature of Palmerston's responses to acts of violence against British subjects underscored his powerlessness to respond when the perpetrators were beyond range of the navy's firepower. An example came in 1842, when a Central Asian Muslim ruler beheaded two British army officers sent to Bokhara on a diplomatic mission. Palmerston let the matter drop, since the offending emir and his landlocked state were more than 1,000 miles from the nearest body of water, the Persian Gulf.[40]

During the eighty years of the Pax Britannica (or indeed, during more than a century between the last major naval engagements of the Napoleonic wars and the opening of the First World War) no navy dared challenge the British to a battle at sea. For the remainder of the nineteenth century after 1815, in every battle or campaign involving a British force of squadron strength or larger the opposition came from coastal fortifications or enemy warships anchored in port: Algiers (1816), Navarino (1827), the Near East (1840), the First Opium War (1839–42), the Crimean War (1854–5), the Second Opium War (1856–60) and Alexandria (1882).

With the leading navies of Europe occupied fighting one another from 1792 until 1815, pirates sponsored or sheltered by the North African Muslim states became the scourge of the Mediterranean. Following smaller actions by the US navy, in August 1816 the British navy sent Admiral Edward Pellew, Lord Exmouth, to Algiers with a fleet including five ships of the line, five frigates and seven sloops, reinforced by five frigates and one corvette from the Dutch navy. In what many historians view as the first example of the Pax Britannica in action, Exmouth's ships subjected Algiers and its fleet to a destructive nine-hour bombardment, after which the Bey of Algiers acceded to allied demands to suppress piracy. This 'spectacular reassertion of power in support of European ideals', as Andrew Lambert has called it, cost the allies no ships but over 800 casualties, evidence of the sort of damage strong shore batteries could inflict upon a wooden fleet. After the capitulation of

Algiers, Tunis and Tripoli followed suit, with no bombardment being necessary in either case.[41] In 1819 another British squadron called at the same three ports, to bully their rulers into suppressing the slave trade (from which they had profited handsomely, as the northern termini of caravan routes that crossed the Sahara from the northern outposts of black Africa). In the first instance of Anglo-French co-operation after 1815, the French navy attached a ship of the line and a frigate to the British force.[42] Such coercion compelled the North African states to conform to European standards of behaviour, at least most of the time. When the French annexed Algiers in 1830 the British did not oppose the move, assuming (correctly, as it turned out) that the demise of this one state would cause the conduct of the others to improve still more.[43]

In taking on the slave trade and piracy, Britain showed a willingness to act alone in promoting its ideals but preferred the company of allies. The same was true during the Greek War for Independence, when Britain and France (driven by Romantic-era philhellenism) joined Russia (in its traditional role as protector of Christian subjects of the sultan) to decide the outcome against the Ottoman Empire. In the Treaty of London (7 July 1827) the three countries agreed to send squadrons to Greek waters to bring an end to the war, which the Turks, with the help of their Egyptian allies, were on the verge of winning. Britain's Vice Admiral Sir Edward Codrington served as overall commander of a fleet including three ships of the line and four frigates from Britain, four ships of the line and four frigates from Russia, and three ships of the line and two frigates from France. The Turco-Egyptian fleet, commanded by Ibrahim, son of the pasha of Egypt, Mehemet Ali, included seven ships of the line, fifteen frigates and over forty smaller warships, operating out of Navarino Bay on the Morean coast. When Ibrahim refused to accede to allied demands to evacuate all Egyptian forces from the Greek mainland, on 20 October 1827 Codrington led his fleet into the bay. He had no orders to destroy Ibrahim's warships, but an exchange began as soon as the allies entered the bay. Turco-Egyptian vessels apparently fired upon small boats sent out by the British and French, provoking return fire by the entire allied line. In the two-and-a-half-hour battle Codrington's superiority in ships of the line decided the matter, decimating Ibrahim's fleet by sinking a ship of the line, 12 frigates, 22 corvettes, 19 brigs, and inflicting some 7,000 casualties. Codrington's fleet lost no ships but sustained losses of 177 killed and nearly 500 wounded.[44] History's last major naval battle to include sailing ships alone destroyed the naval power essential to the Ottoman quest to keep Greece in the empire, leading to the establishment of an independent Greek kingdom in 1830.

In the 1820s and '30s Britain used its naval power in support of a liberal revolution in Portugal, where it carried more weight than intimidation by the armies of the conservative Continental powers. Under the more liberal regime of Louis Philippe after 1830, France joined Britain in supporting the liberal cause in Portugal and also in securing the independence of Belgium from the Netherlands.[45] The deployment of British naval forces in Portuguese and Dutch waters kept Palmerston out of a Near Eastern crisis in 1832–3, when the sultan's former ally and nominal vassal, Mehemet Ali of Egypt, marched on Constantinople. The desperate Turks turned for help to the Russians, who intervened to save them but, at the same time, made the Ottoman Empire a virtual Russian protectorate. When the Turco-Egyptian conflict flared up once again in 1839, Britain and France feared Russia would exploit the situation to extend further its influence in the Near East but pursued different solutions to the problem: while Palmerston belatedly committed Britain to the preservation of the Ottoman Empire, the French considered the Turks doomed and placed their faith in a stronger Egypt. The desertion of most of the sultan's navy to Egypt in June 1839 gave Mehemet Ali an overwhelming naval superiority over the Turks and prompted both Britain and France to send squadrons to the Levant. France subsequently backed Mehemet Ali's rejection of a British demand to return the province of Syria to the sultan, causing an open Anglo-French breach and a general European war scare. In November 1839 Louis Philippe increased his fleet in the Levant to thirteen ships of the line and renamed a number of battleships then under construction after French victories in the Napoleonic wars. The following year he reinforced the fleet further, to

3 British ship of the line *Thunderer* (left) and the Austrian frigate *Guerriera* (centre) in the bombardment of Sidon on 26 September 1840.

twenty ships of the line, and sent his own son, navy captain François Ferdinand d'Orléans, Prince de Joinville, to bring the body of Napoleon back from St Helena aboard a French frigate. Riding a wave of nationalism, French premier Adolphe Thiers prepared for war.[46] The aggressive behaviour of France revived the allied coalition of the Napoleonic wars, and in the Treaty of London (15 July 1840), Britain, Russia, Austria and Prussia committed themselves to an armed mediation of the Near Eastern conflict. Admiral Sir Robert Stopford received command of a British fleet that eventually included 26 ships of the line, the most mobilized since 1815, supplemented by small contingents of Austrian and Turkish loyalist warships.[47] The size of Stopford's force sufficed to pressure the French into abandoning the Egyptians. Louis Philippe sacked Thiers, then called home his own fleet, after which Stopford bombarded and seized a series of coastal fortresses, starting in late September with Sidon (illus. 3) and continuing in October and November with Beirut, Tripoli, Haifa, Tyre and Acre. In the last instance, he employed the paddle steamers *Gorgon*, *Vesuvius*, *Stromboli* and *Phoenix* to supplement the firepower of his sailing warships.[48] The allied operations forced Mehemet Ali to return all of his conquests to the sultan; as consolation, he received international recognition as hereditary pasha of Egypt. The Straits Convention of July 1841 sealed Palmerston's victory, as the four allies joined France in agreeing to make the Ottoman Empire a *de facto* collective protectorate of all the great powers, and to close the Dardanelles and Bosphorus to all foreign naval vessels at times when the Ottoman Empire was at peace. Without firing a shot against either France or Russia – then the world's second and third naval powers – Britain had forced the French to abandon the Egyptians and the Russians to relinquish their recently won influence over the Turks.[49]

The British navy fought the First Opium War (1839–42) concurrently with the Near Eastern campaign but under very different circumstances and without allies. Just as Palmerston would later defend Don Pacifico, a known liar and fraud, because he was a British subject whose property had been destroyed, he defended the East India Company, trafficking in opium, because it was a British firm whose property had been destroyed. Regardless of the principles at stake, it could not be denied that the might of the navy – the same power that upheld the Pax Britannica, enforcing British values and preserving the general peace – in this case was brought to bear in support of a morally reprehensible business interest. The East India Company had long been China's principal supplier of opium, over the objections of the Chinese government, which since 1729 had repeatedly tried to ban it. In May 1839 the emperor finally ordered the destruction of £2 million worth of opium (some 20,000 chests) on the docks at Canton, at the time China's only entrepôt for European trade. Three months later the first British warships arrived, the 28-gun frigate *Volage* and the 18-gun sloop *Hyacinth*. In the Battle of Chuenpi (3 November 1839), fought at the mouth of the Pearl River approach to Canton, these two small sailing ships nearly destroyed a fleet of fifteen armed junks.[50] They were reinforced in the summer of 1840 by three ships of the line, eight frigates, eight sloops and brigs, four East India Company paddle steamers, and an Anglo-Indian expeditionary force of 3,600 men aboard 27 transports, all under the command of Rear Admiral George Elliot.[51] Subsequent British operations included a blockade of Canton, the seizure (in July 1840) of

Chusan Island, at the mouth of the Yangtze River, and finally a second attack at Chuenpi (in January 1841), in which the Indian paddle steamer *Nemesis* led the British column and singlehand-edly destroyed eleven armed junks.[52] Elliot lacked the forces necessary to take Canton, however, and in April 1841 Palmerston sacked him for concluding a provisional treaty with the Chinese that the foreign secretary considered too mild. Rear Admiral Sir William Parker replaced him, and in August 1841 attacked the port of Amoy, where the broadsides of two of his ships of the line alone destroyed shore batteries and 26 armed junks. After securing the mouth of the Yangtze River in October 1841, Parker resumed the campaign the following spring with a much stronger force including 25 sailing warships and 14 paddle steamers, supported by 12,000 troops. Following the occupation of Shanghai and other key ports, in July 1842 Parker's flagship *Cornwallis* led eleven frigates and sloops, ten paddle steamers and a train of troop transports up the Yangzte as far as Nanking, which the admiral threatened to destroy unless the Chinese capitulated. The Treaty of Nanking (29 August 1842) gave the British trading rights in Canton, Shanghai and three other ports, an indemnity far surpassing the value of the opium destroyed in 1839, and possession of Hong Kong as a colony. China agreed to lower import duties on British goods but did not formally legal-ize the trade in opium. While they had not joined Britain in the war against China, France and the United States hastened to take advantage of the outcome, in 1844 obtaining similar con-cessions. The First Opium War revealed the degree to which industrialization had enhanced the military and naval superiority of Europe over the non-western world. The broadsides of sailing warships still did most of the damage to enemy warships and coastal forts, but operations crucial to the British victory (most notably the advance inland, on Nanking) would not have been possible without steamships.[53]

The British navy's greatest operation between 1815 and 1914 had its origins in a bid by Napoleon III to challenge Russia's tra-ditional role as protector of Christian shrines in the Near East. When Russia responded by bullying the Ottoman Empire, Britain supported France. After the Russians crushed a Turco-Egyptian squadron at Sinope (30 November 1853), an

4 The *Agamemnon*, a British ship of the line in the bombardment of Sevastopol, Crimea, on 17 October 1854.

Anglo-French fleet entered the Black Sea, to block a Russian naval assault on Constantinople. By the time Britain and France declared war on Russia in March 1854, Admiral James Deans Dundas's British Black Sea force included ten ships of the line, among them the newly completed screw steamer *Agamemnon*.[54] That September, 89 allied warships escorted over 100 transports with 55,000 troops to the Crimean peninsula, for an assault on Sevastopol. The Russian navy chose not to challenge the landings and, afterward, scuttled half of its Black Sea ships of the line to block the entrance to Sevastopol harbour. Russian seamen and naval guns reinforced shore batteries, which on 17 October 1854 warded off an allied fleet that included thirteen ships of the line attempting a close bombardment of Sevastopol (illus. 4). The *Agamemnon* was among four battleships set afire in the six-hour battle, which caused 520 casualties on the allied side.[55] Meanwhile, the Baltic theatre featured no major actions during 1854, as Admiral Napier struggled to operate the under-manned British fleet with little support from the French. During the summer the Admiralty reinforced Napier to a strength of 29 ships of the line (including 13 screw steamers) and pressured him to attack the fortress of Sveaborg (now Suomenlinna), guarding the approach to Helsinki, but he refused, citing the strength of the Russian Baltic Fleet, which included 25 ships of the line (all sailing), commanded by admirals who had no intention of leaving the security of their bases.[56] Over the winter Napier was sacked in favour of Rear Admiral Richard Saunders Dundas, who led an all-steam fleet in the Baltic campaign of 1855, including sixteen mortar vessels and sixteen screw gunboats. These smaller craft took centre stage in the allied bombardment of Sveaborg (9–10 August 1855), which destroyed fortifications ashore along with six Russian ships of the line and seventeen smaller warships in the harbour, inflicting 2,000 casualties. The allies, in contrast, suffered few casualties and lost no ships, thus benefiting from a tactic of leaving behind most of their ships of the line and attacking with vessels that the shore batteries had greater difficulty targeting.[57] One month later, on 7–8 September, the British Black Sea commander for 1855, Rear Admiral Sir Edmund Lyons, joined his French counterpart Vice Admiral A. J. Bruat in ordering a heavy shelling of Sevastopol before a final assault by British and French troops. The Russians scuttled the remnants of the Black Sea Fleet, then abandoned the city.[58] The allies next attacked Kinburn, the last significant Russian fortress on the Black Sea, and which protected the mouths of the Bug and Dnieper rivers. In the force bombarding Kinburn on 17 October 1855, three French armoured floating batteries attracted most of the attention but, as in the Baltic at Sveaborg, screw gunboats and mortar vessels did most of the damage.[59] Anticipating an assault on St Petersburg in 1856, the British ordered 200 screw gunboats and 100 mortar vessels, and built eight armoured floating batteries of their own. Over the winter Russia sued for peace, cancelling these plans.[60] Under the Treaty of Paris (30 March 1856), Russia demilitarized the Black Sea and dismantled coastal fortifications there and in the Baltic. Ironically, given the origins of the war, France soon repaired its ties with Russia, while Anglo-Russian relations remained strained for fifty years.

Shortly after the Crimean War, Britain and France again became rivals, but their partnership held at least in East Asia, where the French joined the British in the *Arrow* War or Second Opium War (1856–60) against China, a conflict touched off by

China's internment of the British-flagged merchantman *Arrow* in October 1856. Palmerston, appointed prime minister in 1855, reacted typically to the seizure of *Arrow*: the small vessel had been constructed in China, was operated by a Chinese crew, had been a pirate boat in the past, and was interned on suspicion of still engaging in piracy, yet to Palmerston it was a simple matter of a foreign government not respecting the British flag. The incident gave Britain an excuse to intervene in China, where the ongoing Taiping rebellion had done much to damage foreign commercial interests. A month after the loss of the *Arrow*, Rear Admiral Sir Michael Seymour bombarded Canton with a British squadron of screw and paddle steamers led by the sailing ship of the line *Calcutta*. Thereafter Seymour dominated the waters off China but lacked the troops to do anything ashore; the outbreak of the Indian mutiny in 1857 made matters worse, because the only British army unit stationed in China (the Hong Kong garrison) had to be withdrawn to reinforce Calcutta. Finally, late in 1857, French reinforcements enabled Seymour to ascend the Pearl River to Canton, which surrendered to the allies in January 1858. Beijing became the next goal, with the allies attempting to force their way inland to the imperial capital via the Peiho River. In May 1858 an Anglo-French force led by screw gunboats (in imitation of the tactic that had first worked at Sveaborg) shelled the forts guarding the mouth of the Peiho at Taku. Once the forts fell, the allies began their ascent of the river and had made it as far as Tientsin when the Chinese sued for peace. But after Britain and France withdrew their forces, China abrogated the Treaty of Tientsin (26 June 1858) and the war resumed. Rear Admiral James Hope, Seymour's successor, attacked the Taku forts again in June 1859, only to have three of his screw gunboats sunk and 400 allied troops killed by Chinese gunners well prepared for the assault. Britain and France then reinforced their expeditionary force to 30,000 men and in August 1860 attacked Taku yet again, this time taking the forts. The allies drove up the Peiho, took Beijing and reinstated the terms of the Treaty of Tientsin, which opened more Chinese ports to foreign trade, allowed foreign merchants and missionaries into the interior of the country, and finally legalized the opium trade.[61] The Second

Opium War left the British position in East Asia stronger than ever but, by leaving the Chinese virtually defenceless against foreign influences, opened the way for the ultimate collapse of Imperial China fifty years later. Late in Palmerston's career, Britain participated in much smaller international naval actions off Mexico (1861–2) and Japan (1863–4), but following his death in 1865 his successors preferred unilateral actions in which Britain would be unencumbered by the need to satisfy temporary allies. Thus began the heyday of Victorian 'splendid isolation.'

During the Second Opium War both Britain and France laid down their first ironclads, but the first significant employment of British naval firepower by an armoured fleet would not come until more than two decades later, at Alexandria in 1882. When Russia went to war with the Ottoman Empire in 1877, for the first time since the Crimean War, Britain did not intervene because the Turks, after the 1860s, had assembled a respectable fleet of foreign-built ironclads while the Russians, since the remilitarization of the Black Sea in 1871, had done little to build up their own naval forces there. But in the first weeks of 1878, with a Russian army bearing down on Constantinople, the British sent a fleet through the Dardanelles to support the Turks. After a brief war scare, the Russians backed down, but afterward resolved to build a formidable Black Sea Fleet, while the British Admiralty wrestled with the problem of how to repeat the show of force in a future confrontation. As the Turks continued to lose their Balkan possessions, Britain became concerned less with defending the Ottoman Empire and more with stopping a revived Russian Black Sea Fleet from breaking out into the Eastern Mediterranean, where it could threaten the Suez Canal, which, after its opening in 1869, became a strategic choke point for Britain's trade and communications with India and the Orient. Egypt remained under nominal Turkish sovereignty, but Britain and France exercised a *de facto* joint protectorate there to safeguard their mutual investment in the Suez Canal. After the war scare of 1878 Britain strengthened its position in the Near East by occupying Cyprus and buying the Suez Canal company shares of the Egyptian viceroy (khedive), Tewfik, a descendant of the late Mehemet Ali. When the Egyptian army officer Ahmed Arabi (Arabi Pasha) led a rebellion against Tewfik in 1882, Britain had reason enough to prop up the khedive, but the prime minister at the time, William Gladstone, at first refused to intervene. Long at odds with the more activist interpretation of the Pax Britannica, Gladstone as a junior MP had been among the leading critics of Palmerston's conduct in the First Opium War and Don Pacifico affair. He continued to hope for the best as Tewfik lost control of Egypt, refusing to act until after the murder of 50 European residents of Alexandria on 11 June 1882. The British navy then joined an international effort to evacuate foreigners from the city, and Gladstone authorized the commander of the British squadron, Admiral Sir Beauchamp Seymour, to prevent Arabi Pasha's forces from strengthening Alexandria's defences. After observing the onset of such work, on 11 July Seymour entered the harbour and bombarded its fortifications. True to Britain's 'splendid isolation', he acted alone (although nine other countries had warships on hand), attacking with a column including the masted turret battleships *Inflexible* and *Monarch*, six casemate ships and six gunboats. At the climax of the ten-hour battle three of the British ironclads closed within 400 yards of the Egyptian stronghold, Fort Meks, but none was seriously damaged, and the squadron suffered just 31 casualties.[62] The navy went on to land 15,000 troops in Egypt, which defeated Arabi Pasha's army at Tel-el-Kebir (13 September), enabling Britain to establish a formal protectorate.

After 1882 Britain's firm grip on the Suez Canal left it in control of all of the world's major sea lanes. The bombardment of Alexandria was the last great exercise of the Pax Britannica, another triumph building upon the earlier gradual destruction of the maritime slave trade, the decisive stand against piracy (at Algiers), support for the freedom of smaller European nations (most notably at Navarino), reduction of the power of autocratic Russia (in the Crimean War), and vigorous defence of the rights of British subjects and merchants (in the Don Pacifico affair and the Opium wars). Far less dramatically, naval vessels had also supported the acquisition of dozens of colonies in Africa, Asia and the Pacific, expanding the British Empire until it covered one-quarter of the earth's surface. By 1890 Britain dominated the world's oceans as no country ever had before. The Naval Defence Act

(1889) and Spencer programme (1893) would soon guarantee the construction of a British fleet stronger than any two competitors, while in the commercial realm, 80 per cent of the world's steam-powered merchantmen flew the British flag.[63] But the Franco-Russian alliance of the early 1890s, linking the second and third naval powers for the first time in the modern era, caused Britain to doubt its ability to maintain its position in the world. In March 1894 Gladstone's successor as prime minister, Lord Rosebery, revealed to the foreign minister of Austria-Hungary that the British navy would not be able to defend Constantinople and the Turkish straits against another Russian assault for fear of having the French attack it from the rear. The formal abandonment of a confident posture in the Mediterranean followed in October 1896, when new British war plans took for granted a successful offensive by the Russian Black Sea Fleet through the straits and into the Aegean Sea, against which the British navy would wage a defensive campaign, seeking to hold Alexandria, Malta and Gibraltar, and block a rendezvous of the Russian and French fleets in the central Mediterranean.[64] The material superiority ensured by the programmes of 1889 and 1893 did nothing to stem the tide of pessimism, and the recent improvements in the education and training of naval personnel likewise were no consolation. Indeed, George Goschen, First Lord of the Admiralty from 1895 to 1900, lived in fear that the British navy, despite all of its advantages, 'might be fatally crippled by a single great disaster.'[65]

The first clear sign of British reticence in an international conflict came in the 1895–6 dispute over the border between British Guiana and Venezuela, in which the United States supported Venezuela. Coinciding with the onset of trouble in South Africa (where Germany provided moral support to the Boers after they rebuffed an unauthorized incursion by British subjects), the Venezuelan dispute caused concerns at the Admiralty that the growing naval power of the United States might undercut the logic of the two-power standard, which, it had been supposed, would guarantee Britain command of the seas worldwide.[66] After the Fashoda Crisis (1898) nearly led to war with France, the escalation of tensions in South Africa led to the Anglo-Boer War (1899–1902), in which Britain further expanded its empire by conquering the Boer states of the Transvaal and South African Republic. During the war, however, the degree of pro-Boer, anti-British public and political opinion in virtually every other country shocked British leaders and made them increasingly self-conscious about Britain's international isolation. During 1899 the Foreign Office and Admiralty took seriously rumours that France and Russia would launch a pre-emptive strike against British strongholds in the Mediterranean, or that Germany would join France and Russia in an anti-British alliance. In response, the Channel Fleet went to Gibraltar, and the Admiralty withdrew warships from other stations to secure the supply line from Britain to South Africa. The navy facilitated the transport of the army to South Africa and blockaded Delagoa Bay to prevent arms from reaching the Boers via Portuguese Mozambique, but otherwise played no direct role in the war, since both of the Boer republics were landlocked.[67]

As First Lord of the Admiralty, Goschen advocated a solution Britain had always avoided: peacetime alliances. As early as February 1896, he remarked that 'we have stood alone in . . . our splendid isolation . . . but if it comes to . . . questions that might strike at our great power, our life, our influence, I do not believe we should find ourselves without allies.'[68] His successor, Lord Selbourne, subsequently persuaded the naval hierarchy that the United States' naval build-up and forthcoming Panama Canal project did not threaten British interests, and (in the wake of the recent Boxer Rebellion in China) that a formal alliance with Japan should be concluded in order to reduce British commitments in the Far East. The Anglo-Japanese alliance of 29 January 1902 required action by one party only if two or more enemy powers attacked the other; more specific naval side agreements, concerning a common signal system and wartime logistics, remained secret.[69] In concluding a strategic alliance with a rising foreign power that did not subscribe to British values, Britain admitted that, on its own resources alone, it could not even safeguard its own interests, much less coerce others to embrace the principles and positions it advocated. The Pax Britannica was dead.

Selbourne, in league with Admiral Sir John Fisher, appointed First Sea Lord in 1904, initiated the process of transforming a

British navy that had been the world's policeman, with substantial overseas stations, to a fleet concentrated much closer to home, prepared to fight a major European war in European waters. Obsolete vessels with little fighting value, sufficient to show the flag in distant waters, went to the scrapyard by the dozen, while a new fleet of warships – in every category, bigger, faster and stronger – gave Britain the force it would need to fight the First World War.[70] The Entente Cordiale of 1904 subsequently resolved outstanding differences between Britain and France, and opened the way for the navies of the two countries to make strategic arrangements further facilitating the concentration of British naval power in home waters. Some historians have pointed out that Britain's turn-of-the-century leaders may have felt they were reacting prudently to changing international circumstances, but in fact, by shifting the focus of the navy from keeping the peace to preparing for war, they may well have helped encourage the very conflagration Britain most needed to avert. In any event, clearly the rather abrupt abandonment of the Pax Britannica and redirection of British naval resources did much to erode Britain's image as a world power and weaken the bonds within its empire.[71]

CONCLUSION

In his first term as First Lord of the Admiralty, a confident Sir James Graham remarked that the British navy must be 'ready at all times and in all places, to sustain our greatness, to assert our rights, and to vindicate our maritime supremacy.' Decades later, in the twilight of the Pax Britannica, an ageing William Gladstone foreshadowed future developments by supporting the much more limited goal of 'a powerful fleet in and near our own waters'.[72] Britain may have applied its naval power inconsistently between 1815 and the turn of the century, but at least until the mid-1890s its navy could still be counted upon to police the world's oceans. Paradoxically, the same force that stopped the slave trade and kept international sea lanes safe against piracy also kept China open to the opium trade. Thus, it played an important part in spreading the western world's most admirable values and concepts of human rights, as well as facilitating one of history's darkest examples of capitalism without a conscience. Ultimately British naval hubris faded only after the second and third naval powers, France and Russia, concluded a formal alliance, on the eve of a series of international crises that underscored Britain's isolation. As the Admiralty adopted a defensive strategy, the Foreign Office began charting a course out of the 'splendid isolation' of the Victorian era, a process that began with the Japanese alliance, continued in the Entente Cordiale, and ultimately led to an understanding with Imperial Russia, Britain's ideological arch-enemy for most of the past 100 years. The British navy remained the world's largest into the 1920s, and was second largest as late as the 1950s, but never again would it rule the waves as it had during the Pax Britannica of the nineteenth century.

TWO

The Challenger:
The French Navy, 1840s–1890s

After 1815 the French navy maintained both its rank as the world's second largest and its long record of repeated failures in challenging the British navy's dominant position. While geography allowed Britain the luxury of a small army, freeing resources to be spent on its fleet, the realities of France's position required a large standing army, dooming its navy to permanent status as the country's second service. The French navy always had its share of leaders who despaired over its fate but, from the early postwar years onward, also a faction that actively sought out new technologies as the means to challenge British maritime supremacy. France played a leading role in the introduction of the screw-propelled battleship, the armoured battleship, the steel cruiser, the torpedo boat, and finally the submarine, in each case pushing Britain to a higher level of achievement in order to maintain its leading position. During the nineteenth century France never approached Britain in industrial capability, yet in most instances the French pioneered the application of new technologies to sea power.

INNOVATION AND FRUSTRATION:
THE TRANSFORMATION IN MATÉRIEL

In the post-Napoleonic twilight of the wooden sailing warship, the French navy maintained roughly half as many ships of the line as the British navy. During his tenure as navy minister (1818–21), Baron Pierre-Barthélemy Portal introduced the peacetime standard of 40 ships of the line and 50 frigates, half of each type to be kept on the stocks, near-ready for launching.

The initial inventory of unfinished ships, all projects begun under Napoleon, were completed as needed, in some cases after decades under construction. Not until 1847 did France launch a three-decker (the 120-gun *Valmy*) laid down after 1815. The navy had more ships of the line than it needed to meet Portal's standard (by the most generous measure, 69 in 1815, 53 in 1830), but not enough frigates (just 38 in 1815), since the Napoleonic wars had decimated the French cruising fleet. A campaign to build more frigates gave France 67 by 1830, as the postwar navy planned to resort to a commerce-raiding strategy should Anglo-French hostilities resume in the short term. Nevertheless, the French frigate force likewise remained around half the size of the British.[1]

International respect for French naval construction waxed and waned throughout the eighteenth century and into the Napoleonic era, but conventional wisdom held that French warships were more solidly built and more durable than their British counterparts. Their reputation fell only in the years after the destruction of the French battle fleet at Trafalgar, when, under pressure from Napoleon to make good the losses, the navy rushed to completion ships built of unseasoned timber, which did not measure up to the traditional high standards of French naval construction. The British copied French hull designs throughout the period and, after 1815, introduced into their own shipbuilding a system of diagonal bracing long used by French naval architects. The British paid perhaps the highest compliment to French shipbuilding by incorporating so many captured French warships into their own fleet. Their navy list of 1815 included thirteen former French frigates; of these, the *Rhin* (completed 1802, captured 1806, hulked in 1838) served longest into the postwar era. The British also used a number of captured French ships of the line well into the postwar era. Still active in 1847, the *Canopus* (ex-*Franklin*), a third-rate battleship slightly larger than the standard 74-gun design, served as a model for Britain's own postwar 84-gun ships of the line.[2]

Foreshadowing their later faith in technology as the key to compensating for the material deficiencies of their fleet, the French moved faster than the British in embracing the paddle steamer. In 1818, two years after a failed British attempt to develop a steamer for a Congo River expedition, the French navy ordered two steamers for colonial service on the Senegal River. One reached its station late in 1819 and the other the following spring, both after making their passage under sail, with their side-paddles stowed. Three more steamers completed for the navy during 1824 included the *Caroline*, deployed to French Guiana under steam. Unlike the Senegal steamers, which had been turned over to the colonial administration, the *Caroline* was added to the French navy list, as were the other two steamers the following year. Most private French steamship builders imported their machinery from Britain. A high tariff on imported British engines, devised by the French government to encourage domestic industry, initially only encouraged expatriate Englishmen to establish machine shops in France, where they dominated early production of steam engines. Concerned about the reliability of these sources in case of war, in 1827–8 the navy established its own facility for building steamships and steam engines at Indret, near Nantes. Nevertheless, the first truly successful French steam warship, the 910-ton *Sphinx*, launched in 1829, was powered by a British engine, albeit one imported to serve as a model for production at the Indret factory.[3] While the British remained sceptical of the fighting value of warships that, owing to their side paddles, could not accommodate a traditional broadside, the French more quickly recognized that the paddle steamer could serve as a platform for a smaller number of heavier guns. Army artillery officer Henri-Joseph Paixhans, whose experiments with shell guns dated from 1809, considered the revolutionary ordnance a perfect fit for steam warships. In his *Nouvelle force maritime* (1822) Paixhans advocated a fleet of smaller steam-powered warships armed with shell guns as the solution to France's inferiority to Britain in sailing battleships.[4] In 1824, after trials targeting the old ship of the line *Pacificateur* showed the potential of the new ordnance, the French navy purchased Paixhans shell guns for the *Caroline* and other paddle steamers.[5] Range posed the greatest problem for Paixhans's guns, since solid shot was heavier than shells and could be fired much farther by the smooth bore guns of the time: an 8-inch shell gun had a range of 800 yards, a comparable conventional 32-pounder 1,300 yards.[6] Nevertheless,

Paixhans persisted in promoting paddle steamers armed with shell guns as substitutes for sailing ships of the line, even though France in the 1820s and '30s lacked the means to implement such a revolution in warship construction. Indeed, Paixhans's early shell guns were as unreliable as the first generation of French-built steam engines. During the 1830s most French navy steamers were built at Indret but private firms were patronized as well; a few British engines were still imported, especially for fast mail packets once the navy assumed responsibility for France's postal steamers. For the most part the navy remained content with replicating the successful *Sphinx*, and only late in the decade decided to build larger steamers, vessels which, in peacetime, would serve government-run transatlantic packet lines.[7]

During the Near Eastern crisis of 1839–40, the French government acknowledged that self-sufficiency in engine construction was a matter of national security. In 1842 King Louis Philippe approved a fleet plan calling for 70 paddle steamers, and while the ensuing volume of orders strained the resources of Indret and private French firms, forcing the navy to turn to the Netherlands for some of its engines, by the mid-1840s the French had developed the capacity to construct even the largest engines on their own.[8] Heartened by the progress, the Prince de Joinville revived the argument that steam propulsion would be the key to overcoming Britain's superiority in sailing warships. A younger son of Louis Philippe, Joinville had entered the navy in 1834 when aged 16, and within nine years rose to the rank of rear admiral with a seat on the Council of Admiralty. In 1844 his controversial pamphlet *De l'état des forces navales de la France* claimed not only that the capital ships of the future would move under steam, but that steamships already were the key to naval power. While the British navy had a greater advantage over the French in steamships (125 to 43) than in ships of the line (88 to 46, as of 1845), Joinville contended that its lead in steamships was actually smaller, because just 77 British naval steamers were armed as warships. He also pointed to the eighteen steamers his own navy then had under construction, and argued that a further emphasis on steam warships would enable the French to 'reign as masters' in the

Mediterranean, and pose a credible invasion threat to Britain itself.[9] In 1841–3 Normand of Le Havre built the French navy's first screw-propelled ship, the *Napoléon* (later renamed *Corse*), a despatch vessel intended for postal service in peacetime. The ship served briefly in 1843 in a squadron commanded by Joinville, who afterward concluded that the future French battle fleet should consist of screw steamers. A revised fleet plan of 1846, funded by 93 million francs budgeted by the French Chamber, included Baron Portal's old standard of 40 ships of the line and 50 frigates (but with more of each in service, 24 and 40, respectively), along with 100 steamers.[10] After building the *Corse* concurrently with the British sloop *Rattler*, in 1845 France launched the screw frigate *Pomone*, converted from a sailing ship, and laid down its first purpose-built screw frigate, the *Isly*, one year before Britain launched its first screw frigate, the *Amphion*. The programme of 1846 still included more paddle steamers than screw steamers, but provided for the first installation of screw propellers in sailing ships of the line, and for the construction of the first purpose-built screw ship of the line, the 5,120-ton *Napoléon*, designed by the rising star among French naval architects, 30-year-old Stanislas Dupuy de Lôme, whom Joinville characterized as 'a young engineer *d'une rare intelligence*'. The navy ordered the new battleship in July 1847 (symbolically, on Bastille Day), but work did not begin until February 1848, unfortunately for Joinville just days before revolution swept his father from power and forced the royal family into exile.[11]

With the Revolution of 1848, political and fiscal instability joined industrial weakness to cause France to lose its early lead in the incipient screw battleship race with Britain. Six different men served as navy minister during 1848 alone, and the president of the new Second Republic, Louis Napoleon Bonaparte, did not adopt the navy's cause until 1851, when the French assembly voted to resume the screw battleship programme. In 1852 the *Napoléon* finally entered service (along with the British *Agamemnon*, begun 17 months later) and the French began to order other new screw ships of the line. Once President Bonaparte established the Second Empire, taking the title Napoleon III, the navy became an important part of his overall programme. Like Admiral Tirpitz in Germany a half century later, Napoleon III considered a powerful battle fleet a diplomatic tool that would be useful against Britain even if France and Britain never actuallly went to war. In the race to outbuild Britain in screw ships of the line, France remained close at first but always suffered from the loss of momentum in the years 1848–51. By the end of 1853, when the two countries prepared to go to war as allies against Russia, the French fleet had nine screw ships of the line (the *Napoléon* and eight others converted from sailing battleships), while the British fleet had ten (including seven conversions). At the end of the Crimean War in 1856, France had 21 (15 conversions) and Britain 23 (18 conversions). The French finally pulled even early in 1858, when each navy had 27 (21 conversions), but by then the British had many more under construction. By 1861, when they commissioned their last screw ships of the line, France had 37 (28 conversions) to Britain's 58 (41 conversions), and the British had another nine building. Not counted in the British totals are nine steamers converted from old sailing 74-gunners and classified as 'block-ships', vessels capable of roughly half the speed of the 12-knot *Napoléon* and *Agamemnon*.[12] Pressure from France drove Britain to build history's largest and most powerful wooden battleships, culminating in the *Victoria*, which had a displacement 35 per cent greater than that of the *Napoléon*, launched just nine years earlier. As in the days of the sailing battleship and the paddle steamer, France found it could not match the industrial and shipbuilding prowess of Britain. While most of its wooden screw steamers were built from French resources, as in the early days of the paddle steamer at least some British engines were imported, including three for battleships built during the Crimean War, when the two countries were allies.[13]

Ironically, by the time the French navy pulled even with the British in screw ships of the line, the French had already stopped building the type in favour of a new capital ship, the armoured frigate. From the onset of the Crimean War Napoleon III had doubted the survivability of wooden battleships. The firepower of the Russian squadron at Sinope (30 November 1853) included 38 Paixhans shell guns, which in their most extensive battle test to date helped destroy a Turkish squadron. Then, in the first

5 The French armoured frigate *Gloire* (1860).

allied naval bombardment of Sevastopol (17 October 1854) Russian artillery ashore battered and drove off a fleet including the best British and French screw ships of the line. In November 1854 the French emperor called for the armouring of ships of the line, but shortly thereafter settled for the construction of armour-plated wooden floating batteries. The first three, the 1,575-ton *Dévastation*, *Lave* and *Tonnante*, could steam at just 4 knots, sufficient only for manoeuvring, and had to be towed from Toulon to their first battle stations off Kinburn (17 October 1855). Their performance in the bombardment of the Russian fort there reinforced Napoleon III's belief that future capital ships must be armoured. Historians still disagree over whether shell guns really were the decisive factor at Sinope or the armoured batteries at Kinburn, but at the time the French emperor was confident they were, and his convictions shaped subsequent developments. After October 1855 the French navy placed no new orders for wooden screw battleships.[14] Even the designer of the first such ship, Dupuy de Lôme, conceded that the type was doomed. Appointed director of construction of the French navy, he drew up plans for the armoured frigate *Gloire* (illus. 5) during 1857. In March 1858 the ship was laid down at Toulon and Napoleon III ordered another five armoured frigates of the same design, prompting Britain to respond with its own ironclad programme.[15]

More so than with wooden screw ships of the line (most of which were converted from sailing vessels of the same type), with its programme of armoured frigates France succeeded in eliminating Britain's position of superiority by redefining the capital ship altogether. Because the introduction of armoured warships made unarmoured wooden battleships obsolete, and few wooden steamers were suitable for conversion to ironclads (France converted none and Britain seven, all from screw battleships still on the stocks at the time), the French navy's past inferiority had no bearing on the new naval race. France completed the 5,630-ton *Gloire* in 1860 and another fifteen armoured frigates by 1867, thirteen of which were near-identical copies of the *Gloire*. Britain responded with its *Warrior* and another fifteen armoured frigates of various designs completed by 1868. In addition to their greater homogeneity, the first French armoured battleships were designed to operate under steam in European waters and thus reflected a clearer sense of purpose than their British counterparts, which featured a greater sailing capability and theoretically could have served on overseas stations as cruisers. The *Gloire* and *Warrior* each took two years, five months to complete. For the sixteen French armoured frigates as a group, construction times averaged just over four years, the same as the average for the first sixteen British armoured frigates. The *Warrior*, however, was more than 60 per cent larger than the *Gloire*, and the largest of the French armoured frigates were the size of the smallest of the British. At the time, French industry could produce enough iron for only one *Gloire*-sized hull per year; as a result, just two of the first sixteen French ironclads were of iron construction. In contrast, all of Britain's initial ironclads were of iron construction (except those built on the cut-down hulls of projected wooden screw battleships). Thus France's industrial capability once again failed to measure up to its naval ambitions, leaving the French with ironclad warships that were smaller and less durable than their British rivals. Whereas the *Gloire* was scrapped in 1879 and one of its sister ships as early as 1871, the *Warrior* survived (ultimately as a museum ship) into the twenty-first century. As the standard armoured battleship quickly grew larger and more complex, the French lagged further behind.

Seven French central battery ships begun in the years 1865–70 averaged 7½ years under construction, while eleven British central battery ships begun between 1863 and 1868 were completed in an average of just over three years.[16] By the time Napoleon III fell from power in 1870, during the disastrous Franco-Prussian War, the French navy had 51 armoured warships built or building (including small rams and monitors suitable only for coastal defence), but only a dozen displaced 6,000 tons or more. Thus in sheer numbers the French ironclad fleet was practically the equal of the British, but it had barely a third as many truly formidable armoured warships. Once again, France lost a naval race it had started, but the pressure it put on Britain drove the international standard of battleship construction to new heights in size, strength and complexity.

The French navy's age-old dream of achieving parity with the British in capital ships – whether they be wooden sailing ships of the line, paddle steamers, wooden screw battleships or armoured battleships – died along with the Second Empire. As early as 1869, future admiral Richild Grivel contended that it was 'a simple question of good sense' for the French navy to adopt a cruiser-based commerce-raiding strategy instead.[17] During the lean early years of the Third Republic, as France gave first priority to rebuilding its shattered army, such thinking gained strength within the officer corps, paving the way for Admiral Théophile Aube to found the Jeune Ecole in the early 1880s. The anti-British 'young school' of French naval thought placed its hopes in modern steel cruisers and torpedo boats rather than battleships, and in commerce raiding rather than fleet-scale actions. Aube spent most of his career on colonial stations before being called home to the Mediterranean in 1883; he served briefly as navy minister in 1886–7, at the peak of the Jeune Ecole's popularity. Impressed during manoeuvres in 1883 by the ability of two 46-ton torpedo boats to ride out a heavy storm, Aube theorized that torpedo boats could be used alongside modern steel cruisers in high-seas commerce raiding and attacks on enemy ports. He supported his arguments by citing the toll taken by Confederate raiders on Union shipping during the American Civil War, and praised 'the spirit of [Raphael] Semmes', captain of the css *Alabama*. Aube used the

6 The French steel cruiser *Milan* (1885).

7 The French protected cruiser *Sfax* (1887).

language of Darwinism to defend such tactics, arguing that 'war is the negation of law . . . Everything is therefore not only permissible but legitimate against the enemy.'[18] Firm in his belief that the development of the self-propelled torpedo had already rendered the British battle fleet worthless, he thought France needed no armoured warships other than coastal defence vessels.[19] Under the influence of the Jeune Ecole, France laid down no new battleships for six years (1883–9). Reflecting the international popularity of Aube's ideas, the battleship programmes of Germany, Italy and Austria-Hungary each experienced a hiatus at least that long, and in 1887 no country laid down a battleship (the only year between the start of construction on the *Gloire* in 1858 and the onset of international naval disarmament in 1922 for which that was the case). While Aube's school developed the overall strategy for the use of modern cruisers and torpedo boats, France's endemic political instability and industrial weakness meant that other countries would lead the way in developing these warship types and the tactics to use them. The French navy's first steel cruiser of any type, the 1,705-ton *Milan* (illus. 6), completed in 1885, and first protected cruiser, the 4,560-ton *Sfax* (illus. 7), completed in 1887, each had a lighter primary armament and less modern appearance than Armstrong's *Esmeralda* and other new cruisers of the mid-1880s. By the time Aube left office France had laid down another thirteen protected cruisers, and had in service four small torpedo cruisers and eight torpedo gunboats. By the end of the decade France had also launched eighteen torpedo boats designed for high-seas service and another 70 coastal torpedo boats, supplementing 58 that predated the Jeune Ecole. Aside from eight small coastal gunboats, the only armoured warship laid down during the hiatus in French battleship construction starts was the 6,680-ton *Dupuy de Lôme*, the navy's first modern armoured cruiser (built 1888–95).[20]

France's Jeune Ecole threat, combined with Russia's concurrent battleship build-up, compelled Britain to outbuild its rivals in cruisers and torpedo craft while also maintaining its lead in battleships. The Naval Defence Act of 1889 confirmed Britain's resolve to remain superior in all warship types. That year France resumed construction of new battleships, and in 1890, in a further sign of the abandonment of the Jeune Ecole, half of the navy's high-seas torpedo boats were reclassified for coastal service, an admission that such vessels could not serve regularly and reliably as ocean-going warships.[21] A host of tactical and technological advances combined to cause navies to turn away from the strategy so soon after adopting it. France itself introduced better boilers, steel shells and smokeless powder, all of which worked in favour of larger warships and against torpedo boats, while other countries pioneered quick-firing medium-range artillery, electric searchlights and torpedo netting further to enable larger warships to ward off torpedo attacks by smaller craft. In the early 1890s the development of light, strong nickel-steel armour, led by Germany's Krupp, put further momentum behind the international revival of battleship construction, a competition in which France would not fare well.[22]

Late in the nineteenth century the French navy commissioned the first truly operational submarines, but the technology developed too late to save the Jeune Ecole in the face of the turn-of-the-century battleship renaissance. Dupuy de Lôme conducted experiments with submarines before his death in 1885. Gustave Zédé continued the effort, and in September 1888 completed the 31-ton *Gymnote*, the world's first genuinely successful submarine. In contrast to its manually driven and steam-driven predecessors, the *Gymnote* drew its power from an electric battery and was the first to feature hydroplanes for depth regulation. In twenty years of service it made roughly 2,000 dives without an accident. After Zédé's death in 1891, his successors laid down another submarine named in his honour. In their *Essai de stratégie navale* (1893), the last major tactical treatise of the Jeune Ecole era, the French naval officers Paul Fontin and Mathieu Vignot noted the success of the *Gymnote* and looked forward to the launching of the much larger *Gustave Zédé* (built 1892–3). This 270-ton vessel, the world's largest submarine for more than a decade after its launch, during manoeuvres in 1898 became the first undersea boat to torpedo and sink a target ship while submerged. The exhibition was arranged by an old Jeune Ecolist, Vice Admiral François Fournier, the leading advocate of submarine warfare within the French naval leadership.[23] France went on to commission a total of 76 submarines in the years 1900–14, many of which were modelled after the highly successful 202-ton *Narval* (illus. 8) of 1900.[24] While the build-up began at a time of Anglo-French tension, it was not as blatantly anti-British as the Jeune Ecole had been; nevertheless, Fournier and its other promoters tended to be anglophobes and former disciples of Admiral Aube, facts that did not go unnoticed in Britain. Until the conclusion of the Entente Cordiale, Admiral Sir John Fisher remained concerned about a return of the Jeune Ecole, primarily because he believed (as did Fournier and

8 The French submarine *Narval* (1900).

diehard Jeune Ecolists) that France's growing submarine force could fill the offensive role Aube had assigned to the torpedo boat. The French had also continued to add torpedo boats long after other navies stopped building the type, and their cruisers – in particular, 23 armoured cruisers laid down between the *Dupuy de Lôme* (1888) and the conclusion of the Entente Cordiale (1904) – were universally recognized as the best larger units in their fleet.[25]

While serving as British Mediterranean commander (1899–1902), Fisher kept a watchful eye on the expanding French submarine force, based at Toulon; later, as First Sea Lord (1904–10) he insisted that Britain have an undersea force second to none. Thus, the same Admiral Fisher who is more famous to history for his *Dreadnought* and battle cruiser designs was also the father of the British submarine service, which by 1914 had commissioned 88 boats, more than any other country.[26] Yet again, the French lost a naval race they had started, but again, not before they had fulfilled their historical role of pressuring the British to push their own naval mastery to new heights. By the time the British achieved Fisher's goal of having the leading submarine force, the French were their allies and both were preparing for war against the Germans. Concern over the rising power of Germany had driven France to conclude the Entente Cordiale with Britain, and after 1904 the

Germans inherited the function of leading naval antagonists for the British.

PERSONNEL, POLITICS, AND POLICY

To some extent the naval officer corps reflected the political instability of nineteenth-century France. The navy, like the country as a whole, had its monarchists, Bonapartists and republicans, with liberal and conservative subgroups under each type. After the Bourbon Restoration, King Louis XVIII initially sought to purge the navy of veteran Napoleonic officers. The ultra-royalist François-Joseph Gratet du Bouchage, last navy minister before the creation of the First Republic, returned to office in 1815 after an absence of 23 years and set about recommissioning hundreds of old monarchists who had not been to sea in a generation. His policies came under fire almost immediately, in a bungled mission to restore French colonial rule in Senegal. In 1816 the royalist officer Captain Hugues de Chaumareys stranded his frigate *Méduse* on the coast of Mauretania, in the process losing almost half the men aboard. The ensuing inquiry confirmed the incompetence of Chaumareys and led to the prompt return to retirement of most of the officers Bouchage had so recently brought back, and the recommissioning of Napoleonic veterans.[27] Thereafter the navy's leadership consisted of men who had shared the common formative experience of baptism of fire against the British during the long war of 1793–1815, and remained cohesive in its anglophobia, if in little else. On matters of policy, within the navy and among French politicians the conservatives typically kept faith with the battle fleet, while the liberals argued for commerce raiding and alternative strategies. When faced with new technologies, conservatives either resisted their adoption or sought to use them to reinvent the capital ship, while liberals more readily embraced applications that challenged or threatened the battle-fleet paradigm. These divisions persisted from the initial adoption of steam propulsion and the shell gun in the 1820s through to the era of the Jeune Ecole and the first submarines late in the century.

During the 1830s and '40s the conservative majority of naval officers remained sceptical about, if not hostile toward, the steam revolution. Indeed, Joinville became so important as an advocate of steam because, as Louis Philippe's son, his own advancement was not contingent upon the approval of conservative admirals, and fellow officers in general were reluctant to criticize him. Indeed, only three officers published rebuttals to his sensational 1844 pamphlet advocating a steam navy. Despite his privileged status and extraordinary promotions, Joinville became genuinely popular within the navy, and most officers appreciated his tireless efforts to advance the cause of their service.[28] Whereas French navy ministers under the Bourbon Restoration of 1815–30 were all civilians, most of those serving Louis Philippe were admirals who had been junior officers in the navy of Napoleon. While the ongoing transformation in naval *matériel* remained the central focus of the navy, between 1830 and 1848 the training and main-tenance of personnel received greater attention than before. At least one historian has alleged that the good leadership of the era resulted in good discipline in the fleet, but Joinville himself painted a less orderly picture, recalling late in life that the senior officers of his youth 'who all had belonged to the old Imperial Navy, clung to that detestable habit . . . of completely neglecting the military side of the ship's drill. The only thing they looked to was navigation.' Thus crews were 'somewhat insubordinate' and 'command[s] were given amidst volleys of oaths, and carried out under a hail of blows dealt by the petty officers.'[29]

Cardinal Richelieu founded the first French naval academy in 1629, but a number of schools opened and closed over the decades that followed. In 1784 academies were established aboard school ships at Brest and Toulon; they did not survive long after the Revolution but were restored by Napoleon in 1810. Branded 'Bonapartist schools' under the Restoration, the academies were replaced in 1816 by a single naval college at Angoulême, which, in turn, closed a decade later. Naval educa-tion stabilized after 1830, when the Naval School (Ecole navale) opened at Brest. The course for cadets began at age 16 (later 17) and lasted five years, emphasizing mathematics and the sciences early in the curriculum and naval subjects only later. Most graduates emerged with a greater appreciation for science and technology than their contemporaries in other navies, reinforcing the growing tendency of the service to seek technological solutions to its perennial strategic problems. The school remained housed aboard school ships until 1914, although gradually more of the course work shifted to buildings ashore, reducing the school ship to a floating dormitory. Just as school ships in Britain serving in a similar capacity later assumed the name *Britannia*, in France (from 1840) three successive school ships were named *Borda*, honouring Jean-Charles de Borda, a renowned mathematician from the pre-revolutionary naval officer corps. Enlightened even by later standards (first-year cadets were segregated from upperclassmen in 1850, to end bullying), the school produced the world's best-educated naval officers. Nevertheless, it had its critics. Old salts considered the curriculum not naval enough, and a perennial complaint concerned the age at which graduates eventually became lieutenants, detractors citing the fact that the British navy's newly minted lieutenants were younger (and presumably more vigorous) than their French counterparts. The navy's annual cohort of new sea officers typically included a small minority educated at the prestigious Ecole polytechnique in Paris, which also provided most of the officers for the service's elite branches, the construction corps and naval artillery corps. Traditionalists among the sea officers resented the fact that, during their years of study, officer candidates from the Ecole polytechnique only spent summers training with the fleet, and thus received their commissions as lieutenants having logged very little time at sea. Yet from the 1830s onward, as an increasing share of the corps of sea officers emerged from the Naval School drilled in the sciences and sympathetic to technological change, more sea officers willingly conceded a greater voice to the graduates of the Ecole polytechnique. Indeed, by the reign of Napoleon III the constructors and artillerists came to dominate the service, led by Dupuy de Lôme and his counterpart in the naval artillery, General Charles-Victor Frébault. Most educational institutions of the French navy opened before their British and other foreign counterparts; one exception was the Naval War College (Ecole de guerre navale), first proposed in 1882 but not opened until 1896.[30]

From the time of their commissioning as lieutenants and throughout the remainder of their careers, French naval officers tended to be older than most of their foreign counterparts of the same rank. Whereas the British navy faced its greatest surplus of officers immediately after 1815, when the large battle fleet of the Napoleonic wars demobilized, the French navy had a similar crisis after 1870, when the Third Republic ended France's last battle-fleet challenge to Britain and slashed naval spending. By 1873, 69 per cent of lieutenants were unemployed or serving in posts on land, as were 80 per cent of commanders and 81 per cent of captains. Promotions all but ceased, and while the Naval School continued to turn out a new class of junior officers annually, the lack of opportunity made the service unattractive to graduates of the Ecole polytechnique. Political circumstances made it impossible for the French to solve their surplus staffing problem as the British had, by buying out veteran officers with promotion-and-retirement deals. Senior admirals dominated the post of navy minister, and at any given time several sat in the Chamber of Deputies and Senate; regardless of their political convictions, virtually all opposed the creation of a comprehensive retirement system. In any event, the navy's reduced budget could not have handled the cost of such a programme. The only piece of legislation to pass came late in the century, in 1896, when lieutenants who had not been promoted within fourteen years were given the option of voluntary retirement. Owing to the system of French naval education, French lieutenants traditionally had been somewhat older than their British counterparts in any event, but by 1894 the gap had widened to a full twenty years: the average French navy lieutenant was 52 years old, the average British navy lieutenant just 32. In many cases, the surplus of officers dictated that vessels that in earlier years would have been given to lieutenants went to commanders instead, and commanders' vessels to captains. When it came to admirals, by the 1880s France faced a problem similar to Britain in the 1830s, with few being fit for command at sea. In 1883, when France's colonial ambitions in Indochina led to a confrontation with the Chinese Empire, just two admirals of the dozens theoretically available were considered vigorous enough to command the squadron dispatched to East Asian waters. The choice fell to 56-year-old Rear Admiral

Amédée Courbet who, ironically, died in the Far East two years later, at the end of the Franco-Chinese War of 1884–5.[31]

While the British navy's policy of promotion-by-seniority became increasingly rigid after the 1830s, in the French navy promotions remained arbitrary and heavily politicized throughout the century. Over the decades, sons of the rising bourgeoisie and declining gentry eventually accounted for most of the Navy School's cadets, and under Napoleon III at least two men of very humble origin rose to the rank of admiral. Family and social connections came to mean less than personal service connections, yet connections continued to matter all the same. Especially after 1870, when so few promotions were available, admirals sitting on promotion boards tended to advance their own protégés, to the detriment of men of equal or greater capability who lacked a well-placed mentor. Officers serving on overseas stations, even those distinguishing themselves in combat, such as Courbet's junior officers of 1884–5, did not fare as well as those whose staff positions at home afforded greater opportunity for networking with the admirals. Sons of admirals and of prominent politicians likewise enjoyed the advantage of a recognizable surname standing out on the long list of officers eligible for advancement. Frustration over the near-impossibility of promotion and the lack of opportunity to serve aboard ship led to a unique 'politicization of naval strategy', as Theodore Ropp has called it, making the Jeune Ecole even more popular among junior officers, since the hosts of torpedo boats required by the strategy would be commanded by lieutenants rather than senior officers.[32]

In rallying behind the Jeune Ecole, the political Left in France considered itself to be striking a blow against what it perceived to be a conservative, pro-clerical, anti-republican naval hierarchy. Amid the modernization of the fleet, Catholicism maintained its hold on the vast majority of French naval officers just as Anglicanism did on the British, giving an aristocratic veneer to a corps that had long ceased to be socially exclusive. Especially on colonial stations (where it eagerly carried the banner of France's *mission civilisatrice*, in the process providing support for Catholic missionaries), the navy embraced formal Catholic ritual as an expression of its French identity. At home, French admirals often embarrassed their political allies with ostentatious displays of Catholicism (such as participating in public religious processions in full uniform), drawing criticism from a political Left that assumed that an officer's personal identification with Catholicism meant he held conservative views on all other matters as well. But the ideological lines were not so cleanly drawn, and key supporters of the Jeune Ecole included senior officers known for their staunch Catholicism. The overall tone of the service notwithstanding, throughout the century the naval officer corps included men from France's small Protestant minority, most notably Admiral Charles Baudin, squadron commander in the Franco-Mexican War of 1838, and Admiral Jean-Bernard Jauréguiberry, commander of the Mediterranean Fleet in the 1870s and later navy minister.[33]

In its various naval challenges to Britain, France always considered its relative shortage of common seamen to be its greatest liability. In Paixhans's early promotion of the steamer armed with shell guns, the Jeune Ecole's torpedo boats, and the first submarines (if not the screw ship of the line and the armoured frigate), the French sought to overcome the British advantage at sea not just with technologically innovative warship types, but with types that required far less manpower than the conventional capital ships of their times. Indeed, Paixhans foreshadowed the 'lean manning' debate of the early twenty-first century by assuming that warships incorporating higher technology would require fewer personnel. With a logic rooted in the pre-industrial era, when France's inferiority at sea was not so much in *matériel* as in personnel (it could build more than enough wooden sailing warships, if it chose to, but could never man a fleet larger than one the British could man), Paixhans argued that smaller, heavily armed steamers were the answer because they would require smaller crews than sailing battleships, and their crews would require less sea-specific knowledge or experience. Thus, for its steam navy France could enlist personnel from 'the total military population' rather than just the coastal population.[34] Under the traditional *Inscription maritime*, which dated from the ministry of Jean-Baptiste Colbert in the late 1600s, seafaring Frenchmen were required to register for potential naval service. In return, they were rewarded with certain economic privileges and pensions after 25 years at sea, counting merchant marine service as well as naval duty. After the French Revolution, the *Inscription maritime* was incorporated into the system of universal military service. In 1835, the same year in which the British finally copied the traditional French *Inscription maritime* by introducing their Register of Seamen, France went a step further by establishing a formal naval conscription, the *Levée permanente*, calling up all seamen automatically at age twenty. The effects were immediate. In 1839, on the eve of the Near Eastern Crisis, the *Inscription maritime* included 45,000 active seamen, of whom 18,000 were serving in the navy, while Britain's Register of Seamen included 190,000 seamen, of whom less than 10,000 had ever seen naval duty.[35] By 1844 some 55,000 French seamen conscripted since 1835 had circulated through the fleet. In the long run, however, the navy's efforts to establish a modern trained reserve were foiled because most of its conscripts came from the fishing population of Brittany, and many of them spoke only Breton. In addition to having the country's lowest literacy rate, Bretons had the least exposure to the Industrial Revolution and to machinery. Volunteers from the interior (from Paixhans's 'total military population') accounted for the rest of the common manpower; these men tended to be better educated and more adaptable but, by the era of the Third Republic, also more easily politicized and harder to discipline.[36]

The educational background of French naval conscripts (20 per cent were illiterate as late as 1910) combined with their lack of familiarity with machinery in civilian life to cause considerable problems for a service that, decade after decade, hoped to use the latest technological breakthroughs to catch up with its British rival. The French navy addressed the shortcomings of its common manpower through training and education, in many cases establishing models followed by other navies in Europe and abroad. Its institutions included an apprentice seamen's school at Brest (founded 1834), artillery training ships (1837), a marine marksmanship school (1856), schools for mechanics (1863), training ships for apprentice seamen, signalmen and topmen (1865), and a floating torpedo school (1869). The reforms in naval training and education concentrated in the reign of Napoleon III followed the decision, in 1856, to recognize specialities among the crews of the fleet.[37]

CHALLENGER AND PARTNER:
FRENCH NAVAL OPERATIONS UNDER THE PAX BRITANNICA

In its first major naval operation after 1815, France demonstrated that it could employ sea power decisively in a cause Britain opposed, provided that the campaign also involved the French army and was supported diplomatically by other European great powers. When liberal revolutions broke out in Spain, Portugal and the Italian states during 1820, the conservative Restoration government aligned itself diplomatically with the absolute monarchies of central and eastern Europe (Austria, Prussia and Russia) rather than with Britain. While Britain sent a naval squadron to Lisbon to safeguard the new constitutionalist regime in Portugal, Austria suppressed the revolutions in Italy, and France volunteered to intervene in Spain. A French army invaded Spain in April 1823 and, within weeks, drove the liberal Cortes from Madrid. When its leaders retreated to Cadiz, forcing King Ferdinand VII to accompany them, Rear Admiral Guy Duperré blockaded the port with three ships of the line and ten frigates. In September 1823, after French troops besieged Cadiz from the land side, liberal resistance collapsed and Ferdinand VII returned to absolute power. Duperré's squadron certainly did not intimidate the British, but by their inaction they acknowledged that, compared to Portugal, the cost of saving the liberal cause in Spain would be prohibitively high.[38]

Coming a year before Paixhans's first experiments with shell guns, and a year before the first paddle steamers were added to the French navy list, the Spanish campaign of 1823 did not involve the application of new technology. The first French naval steamships did not see action until seven years later, in the conquest of Algiers. Duperré, by then a vice admiral, commanded the operation, which involved 103 warships of various sizes and 575 transports ferrying 35,000 troops across the western

Mediterranean during June 1830. His armada included seven steamers but only two, the *Sphinx* and its sister ship *Nageur*, made it to the North African coast under their own power. They participated in the opening bombardment of Algiers, then carried messages to and from Toulon during the ensuing landings and occupation of Algerian coastal territory.[39] Ostensibly undertaken to punish the Algerian regime for its lack of respect for French consular officials and merchants, the conquest failed to serve its intended purpose of distracting public opinion away from the domestic troubles of the regime of King Charles x. Three weeks later the July Revolution of 1830 replaced him with his more liberal cousin, Louis Philippe, a fateful move for the navy since it paved the way for the Prince de Joinville's extraordinary naval career. Britain did not oppose the French conquest of Algiers, for its demise encouraged better behaviour by other North African states, which, like Algiers, had grown rich on piracy and slaving.

Within the Concert of Europe, Louis Philippe initially aligned France with Britain. In the early 1830s French squadrons supported Belgium's secession from the Netherlands and the liberal regime of Portugal in a civil war against conservatives, and showed the western powers' displeasure over Austria's occupation of the Papal States; as with the Navarino campaign in 1827, however, these operations were conducted by sailing warships alone. The French navy's next notable use of steamships came in the Franco-Mexican War of 1838, which erupted after Mexico rejected France's demands for compensation for depredations against French citizens. Better known as the 'Pastry War' (because the aggrieved parties included a baker whose pastry shop had been ransacked by Mexican soldiers), the brief conflict featured an expedition to Veracruz by Rear Admiral Charles Baudin, whose fleet included the *Sphinx*'s sister-ships *Phaeton* and *Météore* as well as four frigates and ten smaller sailing warships, one of them a corvette captained by Joinville. The action included a bombardment of Veracruz and culminated in the seizure of the fortress of San Juan de Ulúa, key to the port's defences. Engine trouble plagued the two steamers throughout the campaign; nevertheless, during the bombardment of 27 November 1838 they managed to tow two of the frigates and two mortar vessels to the positions Baudin desired.[40] Their failure did not dissuade France from using steamers on transatlantic missions. Another two of the *Sphinx*'s many sister-ships, the *Styx* and *Tonnerre*, participated in a blockade of the River Plate in 1840–41, when France joined Britain and the United States in protecting Uruguay from conquest by Argentina.[41]

By the time of the River Plate expedition, Anglo-French relations had deteriorated over the concurrent Near Eastern Crisis. The French naval force in the Levant, commanded by Rear Admiral Julien-Pierre Lalande, rose in strength from three ships of the line in June 1839 to thirteen later in the year and twenty early in 1840, but throughout included just one paddle steamer, functioning as a despatch vessel. Louis Philippe chose Lalande because he was an aggressive commander, ignoring his known republican sympathies and the fact that he was in ill health. The squadron deployed to the Levant in the winter of 1839–40 was the best force of sailing warships ever assembled by France, operated by the best-trained crews, and yet it could not deter Britain from taking a diplomatic course detrimental to the interests of France and its ally, Egypt's Mehemet Ali. After Austria, Prussia and Russia joined Britain in signing the Treaty of London (15 July 1840), Louis Philippe moved decisively to avoid a naval clash with the British, first recalling Lalande, then withdrawing all French warships from the eastern Mediterranean, leaving Admiral Stopford free to conduct his campaign against Egypt's coastal strongholds in the Levant.[42]

Lalande's failure to deter the British from a course detrimental to French interests provided grist for the mill of Joinville's subsequent criticism of the old sailing navy, and arguments for a steam-powered battle fleet. Indeed, the crisis of 1840, and the naval weakness that had compelled France to back down, led to larger naval budgets thereafter, culminating in the programme of 1846.[43] In August 1844, shortly after the publication of Joinville's controversial pamphlet *De l'état des forces navales de la France*, the prince saw his first action as a squadron commander, leading a force including three ships of the line and six large paddle steamers on a punitive bombardment of Tangier and Mogador (now Essaouira) in Morocco. The brief war came after the sultan of Morocco refused to abandon the cause of Abd-el-Kader, an Algerian emir who, since 1832, had enjoyed Moroccan support in his campaign of resistance against French rule in Algeria. The French lost no ships in the shelling, which Joinville called 'much more of a political act than an act of warfare', but suffered a significant casualty afterward, when the paddle steamer *Groenland* ran aground near Larrache and could not be saved. The naval operation, combined with a French army victory over Moroccan forces at Isly, sufficed to force the sultan to brand Abd-el-Kader an outlaw; he surrendered to the French in Algeria in 1847. While steamships played an important part in the operations at Tangier and Mogador, Joinville commanded both bombardments from the ship of the line *Suffren*, and the three ships of the line in his force provided most of the firepower.[44]

The British had warships on hand at both Tangier and Mogador, and protested the bombardments. Indeed, the Moroccan campaign, combined with concurrent Anglo-French tensions over Tahiti, fuelled a mild war scare.[45] In July 1845 Palmerston, then in the Opposition, alarmed the House of Commons by calling the Channel a 'steam bridge' for the French navy, a means for, rather than a barrier to, a French invasion of Britain.[46] The perception in both countries that war might be imminent helped inspire the French chamber to approve the naval programme of 1846. Ironically, when the revolutions of 1848 brought an instability to Europe unprecedented outside of the context of a major Continental war, Anglo-French tensions actually eased considerably. With Joinville in exile and the programme of 1846 a dead letter, the two countries could focus on what they had in common: a general sympathy for liberal revolution, especially in the Italian states. In particular, France and Britain kept a close watch on the situation in the upper Adriatic, where the newly proclaimed Venetian Republic enjoyed the support of Sardinian and Neapolitan squadrons in its quest to fend off a blockade by Austria's modest navy. In September 1848, after Austrian victories on land led to an armistice requiring the Italian squadrons to withdraw, France sent a squadron to the upper Adriatic as a gesture of solidarity with Venice. Its presence deterred the

Austrians from reimposing their blockade of Venice, at least through the winter of 1848–9. Heartened by the French presence, the Sardinian navy violated the armistice and sent its squadron back into the Adriatic, but a second defeat on land, in March 1849, forced the Sardinians to call their navy home yet again. The French squadron remained in the Adriatic until the surrender of Venice in August 1849, but after April did nothing to hinder Austrian operations, owing to a policy shift by the new president of the Second Republic, Louis Napoleon. Concerned for his popularity with conservative Catholic voters, the future emperor reversed France's position on the Italian question and deployed troops to crush Giuseppe Garibaldi's Roman Republic. The force sent to restore the temporal powers of Pope Pius IX included three batteries of artillery backed by 7,500 men, 350 horses and rations for three weeks. The steam navy provided the transport from Toulon to Civitavecchia, and the force commenced its brief, successful campaign just ten days after Louis Napoleon issued his initial orders. The decisive outcome of history's first 'rapid deployment' of troops using steam transport attracted attention worldwide but especially in Britain, where it lent credence to Palmerston's earlier 'steam bridge' rhetoric.[47]

The short-lived Second Republic lacked the means to implement France's plan to achieve superiority over Britain in screw ships of the line, and the first ships built in the competition ended up serving side by side after the two countries went to war as allies against Russia in 1854. While the two navies never formally divided responsibility for the Baltic and Black Sea theatres, the French ultimately sent most of their best warships to the Black Sea and the British, to the Baltic. Yet even in the Black Sea, the French force of screw and paddle steamers, led by the *Napoléon*, was weaker and less impressive than its British counterpart; there, as in the Baltic, the British took the lead in most allied operations. An important exception to this rule came at Kinburn (17 October 1855), where the French deployed the first armour-plated warships in modern world history, the floating batteries *Dévastation*, *Lave* and *Tonnante*. Otherwise, the allied force led by Vice Admiral Bruat and Rear Admiral Lyons included equal numbers of French and British ships of the line, along with a host of shallow-draught paddle steamers, mortar vessels and screw gunboats. As in the British-led attack on Sveaborg in the Baltic two months earlier, the smaller warships inflicted most of the damage at Kinburn and suffered little in return, since they presented smaller targets for the Russian fortress guns. Displacing 1,575 tons apiece and virtually immobile, the three floating batteries were struck a number of times by Russian artillery, but none was damaged. They fired 3,000 rounds into the fortress from a distance of roughly 1,000 yards at a cost of two casualties, both aboard the *Dévastation*, killed when a Russian shot passed through an open gunport. The British reacted calmly to the debut of armour plate (especially when compared to the unbridled enthusiasm on the French side), but in referring to the batteries in his post-battle report to the Admiralty, Lyons expressed hope that the British would build 'as many good ones as the French.'[48]

A dozen years after the end of the Crimean War, France had a new battle fleet centred around the *Gloire* and fifteen other armoured frigates. The British had maintained their predominance by outbuilding the French (in the size of their ironclads if not in sheer numbers), and the other naval powers had joined the ironclad race as well. Yet after pioneering the armoured warship the French navy went three decades before one of its ironclads fired a shot in anger. In the Second Opium War (1856–60) the sailing frigate *Némésis* served as flagship of Admiral Rigault de Genouilly, whose squadron also included three screw corvettes and several smaller steamers.[49] The great distances involved prevented the deployment of armoured floating batteries to East Asia, but when France supported Sardinia-Piedmont against Austria in the War of 1859, the fleet sent into the Adriatic included the *Dévastation*, *Lave* and *Tonnante*. The mere presence of the three batteries, along with six screw ships of the line, sufficed to keep the Austrian navy (which at the time had no warship larger than a frigate) in port for the duration of the brief conflict.[50] Napoleon III's dream of establishing a French satellite empire in Mexico brought a French naval presence to the Mexican coast in 1862. Because the republican forces of Benito Juárez had no warships, the ensuing five-year struggle featured no combat at sea. The

French navy ferried 40,000 troops to Mexico, intercepted seaborne arms shipments intended for Juárez's supporters, and provided military force for the imperial cause in places French troops could not reach by marching overland, most notably the Pacific ports of Mazatlan and Acapulco. During the campaign the French lost just one vessel, the screw gunboat *Amphion*, wrecked off Veracruz in 1866. The French deployed one iron-clad to Mexican waters, even though its presence was hardly justifiable given the lack of opposition. The armoured frigate *Normandie*, sister-ship of the *Gloire*, became the first ironclad to cross the Atlantic when it joined the squadron off Veracruz in 1862–3.[51] By the time of the Franco-Prussian War (1870–71) the French navy had seventeen armoured frigates in service, most of which were deployed to the German coasts when Vice Admiral Louis Bouët-Willaumez's Northern (Channel) Squadron relocated to the Baltic and Vice Admiral Martin Fourichon's Mediterranean Squadron to the North Sea. The ships arrived in August but returned home in September, after Napoleon III's defeat at the Battle of Sedan opened the way for Prussian armies to march on Paris. The vastly outnumbered navy of the North German Confederation included three armoured frigates, which attempted just two sorties, encounter-ing no French warships on either occasion. The navy's greatest contribution during the brief, disastrous war came in the seizing of some 200 German merchantmen during its blockade of the north German ports. Fears of further French naval action all but shut down German overseas commerce for the duration of the war.[52]

After 1870 France recovered its national pride in overseas empire-building, with the navy playing the leading role in the conquest of Southeast Asia, the focal point of French colonial ambition beyond Africa. To secure the future French Indochina, a squadron under Rear Admiral Courbet blockaded Hue in August 1883 and directed an assault on its citadel, forc-ing the capitulation of the emperor of Annam. China subsequently agreed to recognize French control over Indochina, but early in 1884 the accord broke down when China delayed in abandoning its northern Vietnamese strong-hold of Lang Son. Rewarded for the victory at Hue with a promotion to vice admiral, Courbet led a force of five armoured masted cruisers and twenty-six unarmoured warships against the Fukien fleet, the weakest of China's four regional navies. His ironclads included the 5,915-ton barbette ship *Bayard* (built 1876–82) serving as flagship. While the brief Franco-Chinese War (1884–5) occurred in the era of the Jeune Ecole, Courbet had been sent to the Far East too early for his squadron to include the latest torpedo boats. At the decisive Battle of the Min River (23 August 1884) the French improvised torpedo craft from four small steam launches, which participated in the defeat of the Fukien fleet. In a smaller battle at Shei-Poo (14–15 February 1885) the *Bayard* deployed two launches armed with spar torpedoes that sank the 2,630-ton screw frigate *Yu Yuen*, the last remaining larger warship in the Fukien fleet and the largest Chinese warship sunk in the conflict. China's overall loss of five unarmoured screw steamers and two small flatiron river gunboats left Courbet in command of the sea in the war zone, but he lacked the manpower to pressure further the Chinese with landings ashore. Landing parties lost more men to sickness than to Chinese fire, and Courbet himself fell ill after contracting a tropical disease during an aborted invasion of Taiwan. He died aboard the *Bayard* in the nearby Penghu Islands in June 1885, the same month that the war ended with the reinstatement of the terms of 1884. The less than glorious conflict sufficed to secure Indochina for the French, leading to Courbet's posthumous enshrinement as a national hero. In a fitting tribute to the commander of the first French armoured squadron to engage in combat, the navy honoured him by naming its next new battleship (commissioned 1886) the *Courbet*. Eventually, in 1913, France's first dreadnought also received his name.[53]

The French navy's campaign against China was its last in the era in which it could lay claim to being the British navy's primary challenger. By the 1890s, when the Jeune Ecole fell out of fashion and the world's navies again focused on battleship construction, France lacked the industrial capacity, financial resources and political will to maintain its traditional rank as the world's second naval power. Yet even in relative decline, the French navy remained central to British strategic concerns. France's new alliance with Russia forced Britain first to commit to the Two Power Standard, then to conclude that it could no longer afford to remain isolated, and ultimately to align with France in the Entente Cordiale of 1904. Over the next decade France quickly fell from second to fifth in rank among the world's naval powers, passed by the United States and Japan as well as Germany, and never recovered its former maritime glory.

CONCLUSION

Within the French navy, the impetus for change often came from outsiders or peripheral figures, most notably in the cases of Paixhans, an army artillerist, and Joinville, a royal prince. The innovative spirit only gradually became endemic, and even then, it always had its opponents. Yet it became more widespread and remained more influential in France than elsewhere among the great naval powers. Scholars tend to judge military institutions by their record of victories and defeats alone, often obscuring the true significance of their role in or contribution to history. From the 1840s until the end of the 1890s, the challenge posed by the French fleet repeatedly compelled the British to embrace new designs and technologies in order to maintain their position as the leading naval power. In each instance – with the screw-propelled battleship, the armoured battleship, the steel cruiser, the torpedo boat and ultimately the submarine – the British navy benefited considerably from having a credible rival to build against. Because in each round of the competition the British ultimately built more of the ship type in question than the French (or, indeed, anyone else), French naval activity in the nineteenth century may be viewed as a series of exercises in futility. Nevertheless, were it not for the historical role played by the French navy, the application of modern industrial technologies in the naval realm would probably have followed a very different course.

THREE

Shaping the Southern Colossus:
The Brazilian Navy, 1822–31

In Brazil, as in the Spanish American colonies, the Napoleonic wars provided the context for independence. In 1807, with Portugal threatened by French invasion, the ruling Braganza family fled to Rio de Janeiro and did not return to Lisbon until compelled to do so in the wake of the Portuguese revolution of 1820. Dom João (King John VI) left behind as regent his son, Dom Pedro, who astutely assumed leadership of an independence movement that made him emperor of Brazil. In a vast country where all population centres lay along the coast and the interior had no roads, naval force became the key to Dom Pedro's consolidation of power, and remained central to subsequent efforts to keep distant provinces loyal to the imperial government.

After arriving in Rio de Janeiro, the Portuguese royals enhanced their own position and the colony's prosperity by adopting a free trade policy (1808) and granting Brazil the status of a kingdom (1815). While the merchants and landowners of the Spanish colonies rallied behind republican movements, in Brazil prosperity and autonomy kept the same key groups loyal, at least until the Portuguese Cortes revoked both free trade and political autonomy following the return of Dom João to Lisbon in 1821. These measures sparked an independence movement that Dom Pedro quickly embraced, for his own sake and to keep Brazil in the hands of the Braganza dynasty. In January 1822 he refused a direct order to return to Portugal, and on 7 September (still celebrated as Brazil's independence day) he proclaimed the goal 'independence or death!' In October an elected assembly named him 'constitutional emperor' of Brazil, and his coronation followed in December. His quest to make Brazil an independent country enjoyed the support of Britain, whose merchant marine by 1822 handled half of Rio de Janeiro's commerce.[1] In building up his navy, Dom Pedro took full advantage of British goodwill and tapped the vast reservoir of unemployed British officers and seamen, scores of whom entered Brazilian service.

'TO MAINTAIN OUR HONOUR AND DIGNITY': THE CREATION OF THE FLEET

During their wars for independence the Latin American countries organized their navies from ships purchased abroad or defected from their Iberian mother country. Brazil alone had the capability to build its own warships in significant numbers, including vessels as large as ships of the line, in a naval arsenal at Rio de Janeiro that dated from 1763.[2] Frigates and smaller warships could be built in a number of smaller coastal shipyards, one as far north as Belém near the mouth of the Amazon. Other supporting facilities, most of them in Rio de Janeiro, were established in 1808 after the arrival of the Braganzas. But the emergency atmosphere of 1822–3 did not allow the luxury of new construction, and Dom Pedro, like the leaders of the neighbouring republics, assembled his initial fleet from existing warships. Throughout most of 1822, until Portugal declared him a rebel, he took full advantage of his status as crown prince to retain in Brazilian waters as many Portuguese warships as could be officered and manned by naval personnel loyal to him. By the end of 1822 the fleet included the large frigate *Piranga* (ex-*União*), the smaller frigates *Paraguaçu* (ex-*Real Carolina*) and *Thetis*, the corvettes *Maria da Glória* and *Liberal*, four brigs and thirteen schooners, divided roughly evenly between the harbour of Rio de Janeiro and the waters around Uruguay, a predominantly Spanish colony that Portugal had occupied in 1816 and subsequently annexed to Brazil in 1821, amid the ultimate collapse of Spanish rule along the River Plate. The most recent arrivals from Portugal included the *Paraguaçu*, which a squadron visiting Rio de Janeiro had left behind in March 1822 together with 894 men, most of whom entered Brazilian service along with their ship. In September, after Dom Pedro's declaration of independence, the ships of the fleet raised the new green-and-yellow flag of Brazil. Thereafter loyalties wavered aboard many naval vessels, but the Brazilians lost only one larger ship, the *Thetis*, to Portuguese authorities at Montevideo who subsequently could not muster a crew large enough to sail it back to Portugal. It remained anchored at Montevideo throughout the ensuing War for Independence, of no use to either side.[3]

During the southern summer of 1822–3, royalist opposition to Dom Pedro centred on the northeastern city of Salvador in Bahia province, where the Portuguese garrison enjoyed the support of a fleet that grew to include fourteen warships mounting some 400 guns. The Brazilian navy, not counting its schooners, had just eight warships carrying half as many guns. The new government faced a dilemma: without tax revenue from the distant provinces of the north, it lacked the resources to assemble a larger fleet, but it needed a larger fleet in order to secure control over those provinces. In January 1823 Dom Pedro initiated a subscription that soon provided the funds to pay for additional warships. Another four brigs included one purchased from an American privateer, one from a British firm and two from the Brazilian merchant marine. Meanwhile, the naval arsenal in Rio de Janeiro refitted the best of more than a dozen disarmed Portuguese naval vessels anchored in the harbour: the old 64-gun ship of the line *Martim de Freitas* (renamed *Pedro I*), the frigate *Sucesso* (renamed *Niterói*) and a fifth brig. During the same months the navy lost a schooner and three unarmed transports on the River Plate, which went over to the Portuguese at Montevideo. While the defection had little practical significance, it reinforced the government's decision, late in 1822, to hire a foreign commander and foreign officers rather than trust its warships to Portuguese navy veterans of questionable loyalty. The mercenaries were led by Thomas, Lord Cochrane, commander of the Chilean navy from 1818 to 1822, who raised his flag in the *Pedro I* and set out to attack Bahia on 1 April 1823, just ten days after receiving his Brazilian commission.[4]

On 9 November the *Pedro I* returned to Rio de Janeiro in triumph. In just over seven months Cochrane had chased the

Portuguese navy from the New World, secured the northern provinces for Dom Pedro, and made prizes of dozens of merchantmen and transports, in the process losing no warships of his own. The war against Portugal was over, although not officially, since Lisbon had yet to recognize the independence of Brazil. During the seven months of Cochrane's campaign the Brazilian navy continued to grow, albeit modestly. The British merchant brig that had brought Cochrane from Chile was purchased and armed as a warship. The surrender of São Luis in Maranhão province brought with it a Portuguese navy brig, and in capturing the northern Portuguese stronghold of Pará province, the navy inherited a frigate (renamed the *Imperatriz*) nearing completion in the shipyard of Belém. In September the Brazilians captured the Portuguese corvette *Voador* when it entered the harbour of Rio de Janeiro on a peace mission, but under the flag of Portugal rather than a flag of truce; the ship joined the Brazilian navy as the *Itaparica*. Another corvette, the *Maceió*, under construction in the port of that name (in the northeastern province of Alagoas) at the time Brazil declared its independence, joined the fleet upon completion in October 1823.[5] The collapse of Portuguese resistance also freed the frigate *Thetis* from its internment at Montevideo. These additions to the fleet raised its strength to one ship of the line, five frigates, four corvettes and eleven brigs, supplemented by a number of schooners, gunboats and transports.

A further expansion of the fleet during 1824, initiated on rumours from Europe of Portuguese preparations for a counter-attack, enabled Cochrane to deal with a serious uprising in northeastern Brazil, where rebels had proclaimed the 'Republic of the Confederation of the Equator'. Brazilian shipyards began the construction of a 74-gun ship of the line, two frigates and several gunboats, and armed five prizes taken by Cochrane the previous year, including the corvette *Carioca* (ex-*Leal Portuguíz*) and two brigs. During the summer of 1823–4 the navy lost a brig and a schooner seized at Recife in Pernambuco, the centre of the rebellion, but in July 1824 these vessels were recaptured along with another rebel brig. Over the subsequent twelve months the navy added another three brigs – a commissioned prize, a purchased American merchantman and a new vessel launched at Belém – along with the frigate *Dona Paula*, a converted British East Indiaman. No other warships were commissioned before 29 August 1825, when Portugal recognized Brazil's independence, formally ending their war.[6]

By then Cochrane was back in Britain, en route to his next adventure as commander of the Greek navy, and Brazil was preparing to go to war with Argentina over Uruguay, whose predominantly Spanish-speaking population had rebelled against their Brazilian masters. The conflict, known as the Cisplatine War owing to its focus on the River Plate, lasted from December 1825 to October 1828 before ending in a compromise peace that gave Uruguay its independence. Dom Pedro considered a large blue-water navy essential to command international respect, in South American waters and beyond, and used the war to justify further naval expansion. Brazil opened the conflict with a force of one ship of the line, six frigates, five corvettes and fifty-three brigs, schooners and gunboats. During the conflict the navy added the 62-gun frigates *Isabela* and *Príncipe Imperial* (both completed in the United States in 1826) and the smaller frigate *Dona Francisca*, along with three corvettes: the *Duqueza de Goias* (in 1826) and the converted merchantmen *Maria Isabel* and *Bertioga* (in 1827). Brazil also purchased its first pair of steamships, both originally laid down as merchantmen in British shipyards. The 300-ton *Correio Imperial* (ex-*Hibernia*) reached Rio de Janeiro on the eve of the war, and the *Correio Brasileiro* (ex-*Britannia*), of the same design, during 1826. Usually armed with three or four light cannon apiece, they would have little fighting value.[7]

The navy's most formidable warships were its large sailing vessels, but these were of little use on the rivers and inshore coastal waters where the Cisplatine War was fought. The three largest warships Brazil lost were corvettes, one (the *Itaparica*) captured on a river and two (the *Duqueza de Goias* and *Maceió*) abandoned after running aground in shallow water. Under such conditions the brigs, schooners and gunboats of the Brazilian and Argentinian navies saw most of the action, often in bitter fighting, with several of the smallest warships changing hands two or three times during the course of the conflict. As of May 1827, the Argentinian navy (not counting privateers) included two corvettes, four brigs and ten schooners, of which exactly half (one corvette, two brigs and five schooners) had been captured from the Brazilian navy.[8] By 1828 the Brazilian fleet included one ship of the line, nine frigates, five corvettes and sixty-one brigs, schooners and gunboats, with another nine warships (including a ship of the line, two frigates and two corvettes) under construction. That year the naval budget consumed 3,500 contos of réis (£700,000), triple the outlay of 1823, and the fleet quite rightly was held to blame for Brazil's huge budget deficit and spiralling inflation.[9]

The rising cost of the navy in particular and the Cisplatine War in general occasioned fiery speeches in the Brazilian assembly. But Deputy Cuhna Mattos, speaking in 1827, summed up the thoughts of many patriotic Brazilians in concluding that 'to maintain our honour and dignity at sea, we must maintain a large naval force'.[10] Thanks to Dom Pedro's naval build-up, by 1830 Brazil could boast of having the world's eighth largest navy and, in the western hemisphere, the second largest, trailing only that of the United States. In larger warships built-and-building the Brazilian navy's force of two ships of the line and eleven frigates remained clearly inferior to the American navy's ten ships of the line and sixteen frigates but, if measured either in larger warships or in total warships, the Brazilian fleet was stronger than all the other navies of Latin America combined.[11]

The ever more complicated saga of the House of Braganza overshadowed Brazil's effort in the Cisplatine War. Dom João's death in 1826 left the throne in Lisbon vacant. Portugal would not accept Dom Pedro as heir to the throne owing to his role in separating Brazil from the mother country, and the other obvious candidate, his younger brother Dom Miguel, had been exiled after leading a failed rebellion against his father in 1824. The brothers soon hatched a scheme under which Dom Pedro renounced the Portuguese throne in favour of his young daughter, Maria, who would then marry her uncle. Dom Miguel would have the status of prince consort and, for the foreseeable future, rule Portugal as regent for his child-bride, but in 1828 he reneged on the deal and seized the throne for himself, touching off the so-called Miguelist War, a Portuguese civil war in which conservative absolutists favoured Miguel and liberal constitutionalists backed Maria. Dom Pedro's preoccupation with events in Portugal made him increasingly unpopular with patriotic Brazilians, and his abrupt shifts between liberal and absolutist policies only added to the country's instability. Stung by criticism for sacking a popular cabinet, in April 1831 he abdicated unexpectedly and left for Portugal to fight for his daughter's claim to the throne, leaving the Empire of Brazil to his five-year-old son, Dom Pedro II. The regency governing for the young emperor did not share Dom Pedro I's vision of Brazilian sea power. Cost-cutting measures adopted in the months prior to his departure continued after 1831, dramatically reducing the size and strength of the navy.[12]

MANNING THE FLEET:
BRAZILIANS, BRITONS AND 'THE CRUSADE OF LIBERTY'

Owing to the manner in which Dom Pedro first assembled his navy (by invoking his powers as Portuguese crown prince over Portuguese warships in Brazilian waters, before it became clear that there would be an independent Brazil), from its birth the service suffered serious personnel problems. The 160 current and former Portuguese naval officers who were either stationed in or living in Brazil as of 1822 were not pressed to declare their loyalty definitively until the defection to Montevideo of the frigate *Thetis*, in the wake of the formal breach between Brazil and Portugal, underscored the need for vigilance. On 5 December 1822 a commission began passing judgement on the disposition of each officer, and during the subsequent proceedings just 27 elected to return to Portugal. The rest declared their allegiance to Dom Pedro and placed themselves at his disposal. Of these, roughly three dozen were rejected on grounds of advanced age or ill health, leaving the new officer corps with 96 veterans of the Portuguese navy. Despite the fact that the Portuguese naval academy had moved to Rio de Janeiro in 1808 (and remained the only Portuguese naval academy until 1825, when Portugal re-established one in Lisbon following its recognition of Brazil's independence), junior officers were in short supply. Exactly half of the former Portuguese officers (48) held ranks of captain-lieutenant (commander) or above. With increased rank came the increased likelihood that an officer had been born in Portugal rather than in colonial Brazil. All eight admirals were Portuguese-born, and none was considered an attractive candidate to command the fleet. The head of the Brazilian squadron in the River Plate, Vice Admiral Rodrigo José Ferreira Lobo, was unpopular in patriot circles owing to his role in suppressing a revolt against the Portuguese in Pernambuco in 1817. Nevertheless, he was the frontrunner until the desertion of the *Thetis*, which had been his flagship, further tainted his already questionable service record.[13]

The subsequent loss of the schooner *Maria Teresa* and its convoy of transports, taken to Montevideo by a pro-Portuguese officer in January 1823, led to a general questioning of the loyalty of naval personnel and further predisposed Brazilian patriotic circles to accept the decision to hire Cochrane and other foreign officers. By then all of the Spanish American republics had established navies commanded primarily by British and American officers idled after 1815; indeed, the migration had been so extensive that, in the British case, it inspired Parliament to pass the Foreign Enlistment Act of 1819, which among other provisions denied inactive British officers their half-pay while they were employed by another country. The navy of Chile, which Cochrane had served since 1818, provided the most dramatic example of the decisive difference foreign naval talent could make within the context of the Latin American Wars for Independence. Thomas, Lord Cochrane, later 10th Earl of Dundonald, was a highly decorated British veteran of the Napoleonic wars, living in exile in France (after being disgraced in a stock market scandal in 1814) when he accepted command of the Chilean navy. His brilliant campaign against the Spanish navy ranged as far north as the coast of California; the high point came in 1820–21, when his fleet transported the army of General José de San Martín to conquer Peru, the last bastion of Spanish rule in South America. Thereafter he fell out with San Martín, who established himself as dictator of Peru and tried to lure Cochrane and his British officers and seamen into Peruvian service. Cochrane refused, but enough of his officers and men accepted seriously to cripple the Chilean navy. Once Spain had been defeated, Cochrane's relationship with the Chilean government soured over issues of pay and prize money. As early as May 1822 Dom Pedro's chief agent in Britain suggested Cochrane as a potential commander of the Brazilian navy. When offered the position six months later, he accepted: 'The war in the Pacific having been happily terminated by the total destruction of the Spanish naval force, I am . . . free for the crusade of liberty in any other quarter of the globe.'[14]

Dom Pedro accepted Cochrane's stiff demands regarding rank and salary. A vice admiral in Chile, he received the rank of 'first admiral' in Brazil, with compensation at an annual rate of 11,500 milréis (£2,304) when ashore and 17,290 milréis (£3,458) while at sea, sums three times as great as the salary of any other Brazilian admiral, and £500 per year more than what he would have earned as a British admiral commanding a fleet. Cochrane brought four British officers with him from Chile, and another 47 British subjects entered the Brazilian naval officer corps during 1822–3. Six more followed in 1824, one in 1825 and two in 1826, bringing the overall total (including Cochrane) to 61. Most were young, 56 entering at the rank of lieutenant or lower. The British were neither the first nor the only foreign officers hired by Brazil. The prospect of serving under a monarchy made Brazil somewhat less attractive than the Spanish American republics in the eyes of officers from the United States, yet Captain David Jewitt, an American most recently in the service of Argentina, was the first foreigner commissioned by the Brazilian navy, in October 1822. Other early signings included Teodoro de Beaurepaire, formerly of the French navy.[15] Thus the leadership of the fleet Cochrane took into action against the Portuguese had a truly multinational character. The commanders of the nine warships that left Rio de Janeiro in April 1823 included four Brazilians, three Britons, the American Jewitt and the Frenchman Beaurepaire; aboard Cochrane's flagship *Pedro I*, the officers and staff included eight Brazilians, six Britons, two Frenchmen and one German. The Brazilian chaplain aboard the *Pedro I* noted in his diary that the 'care and courtesy' shown by the foreign officers led to their immediate acceptance by their Brazilian peers, resulting in good camaraderie 'in the company of the mess'.[16]

The relative youth of most of the British recruits helped remedy the shortage of junior officers. Cochrane also pressed into service patriotic young Brazilians who flocked to the fleet as volunteer midshipmen. Joaquim Marques Lisboa, the future Admiral Marquis de Tamadaré, entered the navy as a volunteer in March 1823, not yet sixteen, and spent the rest of the year on active duty aboard Captain John Taylor's frigate *Niterói*. In January 1824, after Cochrane drove the Portuguese fleet from Brazilian waters, Dom Pedro ordered Marques Lisboa and other provisional midshipmen and second lieutenants to complete a course of study at the naval academy in Rio de Janeiro, which had just reopened under the name Imperial Naval Academy (Academia Imperial da Marinha). Cochrane and Taylor both disagreed with the imperial decree ordering the young men ashore, reflecting the traditional British preference for practical shipboard training over classroom education. In any event, their studies lasted just six months, cut short in July 1824 when the fleet remobilized on the rumour of an impending Portuguese counter-attack, then stayed on a war footing for the campaign against the Pernambuco rebels.[17]

Cochrane spent the next nine months campaigning against Pernambuco and its allies among the other northern provinces. In consolidating Dom Pedro's rule, the navy continued to place a special trust in its British officers: in midsummer 1824–5 they accounted for 57 of the 170 officers at sea and served as commanders of 13 warships.[18] Cochrane remained an effective commander despite becoming increasingly preoccupied, even obsessed, with prize money. In a development disturbingly reminiscent of his last months in Chile, he argued constantly with the Brazilian government over the sums he felt that he and his men had earned in vanquishing the Portuguese navy during 1823. After leaving the flagship *Pedro I* for the frigate *Piranga*, in May 1825 Cochrane sailed directly from Maranhão to Britain, ostensibly to repair his ship. Having declared his sympathy with 'the struggle for the liberties of Greece' as early as 1822, he was receptive to an overture from the Greek navy and by August 1825 had negotiated the fabulous sum of £57,000 to serve as its commander-in-chief. After he ignored repeated appeals to return to Brazil, in April 1827 the navy formally dismissed him, one month after he finally arrived in Greece to assume his new post.[19] The departure of Cochrane by no means brought an end to the Brazilian fleet's British connection. Only one officer from the *Piranga* stayed behind to accompany Cochrane to Greece – Captain Thomas Sackville Crosbie, who earlier had followed him to Chile and to Brazil. Captain James Shepherd, who likewise had served under Cochrane in both Chile and Brazil, remained in Brazilian service and sailed the frigate back to Rio de Janeiro late in 1825, taking with him fresh British recruits for Dom Pedro's navy. While the British influence remained strong, during 1825 other foreigners entered the officer corps in unprecedented numbers. The navy employed sixteen American, French and Scandinavian officers, including nine who arrived that year. During 1826 a Danish officer served as the first commander of the steamer *Correio Brasileiro*.[20]

Shortly after Cochrane's departure for Britain, a rebellion in Uruguay supported by Argentina brought a Brazilian squadron to the River Plate. Its commander, Vice Admiral Lobo, had not been to sea since leaving the same station in disgrace late in 1822, after losing the frigate *Thetis* to pro-Portuguese mutineers. By the onset of the Cisplatine War with Argentina in December 1825 it had become clear that Cochrane would not return, making Lobo, by default, commander-in-chief of the navy. The 62-year-old admiral was twelve years older than Cochrane and, temperamentally, his polar opposite, extremely cautious even when facing a numerically inferior enemy. After mismanaging the campaign during the summer of 1825–6 he was summoned home to a court martial and never served again. In May 1826 Admiral Rodrigo Pinto Guedes replaced him. The new commander-in-chief was a year older than Lobo and had not been to sea since 1806, a year before he became chief of staff of the Portuguese navy. In that capacity he had followed the royal family to Brazil, where he served as principal naval adviser to Dom João until the king returned to Portugal. Declaring his loyalty to Dom Pedro in 1822, Pinto Guedes served as the highest ranking admiral on Brazil's Supreme Military Council until replacing

Lobo as commander. Upon his arrival in the River Plate he had the good sense to allow his ship captains greater initiative and sacked those he considered too timid, replacing them with officers (mostly British) he could trust to be more aggressive. While he took personal command of the deep-water blockade at the mouth of the River Plate, he delegated to Captain James Norton the inshore blockade of Buenos Aires and to Captain Jacinto Senna Pereira operations on the River Uruguay, which formed Uruguay's western border with Argentina. These two divisions of smaller warships shouldered much of the burden for the rest of the Cisplatine War.[21]

Because smaller vessels dominated the action against Argentina, the conflict provided ample opportunity for junior officers to gain valuable experience commanding schooners or gunboats under fire. Many were young Brazilians who had volunteered for naval service in the War for Independence. The youngest warship commander of the Cisplatine War, Joaquim Marques Lisboa, received his own schooner as a nineteen-year-old second lieutenant, during an ill-fated expedition to Patagonia in 1827.[22] Others were entrusted with considerable responsibilities aboard slightly larger ships. Second Lieutenant Joaquim José Ignacio, the future Admiral Viscount de Inhaúma, at age seventeen served as second-in-command of the brig *Pará* at the Battle of Corales in 1826.[23] Using relatively youthful, aggressive ship commanders further enticed by the prospect of prize money, Pinto Guedes could enforce a strict blockade of the River Plate while only loosely holding the reins. But the navy paid a high price in the number of smaller warships lost or captured by the Argentinians, and the widespread, sometimes reckless seizures of foreign merchantmen ultimately brought pressure from the leading naval powers for a compromise peace.

By 1827 British officers accounted for 58 of the 290 men in the corps, constituting by far the largest foreign contingent. Non-British foreign officers in active service that year included nine Frenchmen, eight Danes and two Americans. Despite comprising just 20 per cent of all officers, the British commanded 14 of the largest 46 warships in the fleet. They dominated Pinto Guedes's deep-water squadron and Norton's division on the River Plate, leaving native Brazilians in control only in Senna Pereira's isolated division on the River Uruguay, where officers were in such short supply that some gunboat commands went to army artillery lieutenants or sergeants. After suffering no fatalities in the War for Independence, four of Brazil's British officers lost their lives in the war against Argentina, killed outright or mortally wounded in the action. Just two deserted to the Argentinians; one, a lieutenant, who took a schooner with him, crossing paths during 1827 with an Argentinian British lieutenant who defected to Brazil. The same high degree of loyalty did not hold true for the British seamen recruited into Brazilian service, at least in the Cisplatine War. Because the Argentinian navy was even more dependent upon British manpower (for two-thirds of its officers and half of its seamen, compared to one-fifth of the officers and one-sixth of the seamen for the Brazilian navy, as of 1827), deserters moved easily between the two navies, selling their services to the highest bidder. Captured British seamen typically accepted the offer to change sides rather than spend months idle (and unpaid) as prisoners of war.[24]

The loyalty of British seamen was not a problem for the Brazilian navy during the War for Independence; indeed, the questionable loyalty of the sailors Dom Pedro's fleet inherited from the Portuguese navy had inspired their recruitment in the first place. While only 17 per cent of the Portuguese naval officers in Brazil opted not to enter Brazilian service in 1822, among common seamen a greater share wished to remain loyal to Portugal, no doubt out of concern for ever being able to return home. Whereas officers were given the opportunity to declare their loyalty to the mother country, Brazil's desperate shortage of seamen led to a decision not to give sailors born in Portugal the same option. As early as the mid-year manoeuvring of 1822 (at which time the warships loyal to Dom Pedro were still flying the Portuguese flag), it became clear that seamen compelled to serve under such circumstances could not be counted upon. As the Portuguese began to consolidate their position at Salvador in Bahia, Dom Pedro sent a squadron under Division Chief Rodrigo de Lamare to reinforce and resupply patriot troops in the north, but when

Portuguese loyalists ashore prevented him from landing in Bahia, the questionable fidelity of his crews made battle out of the question. After he put the troops and supplies ashore at Alagoas, Lamare felt fortunate to make it back to Rio de Janeiro without losing any of his ships to mutinies. The fiasco led to an effort to recruit sailors in Britain as well as officers. Over the months that followed Brazilian agents offering able seamen 13 milréis (£2.60) per month, significantly more than the £1.60 they could earn in the British navy, found no shortage of volunteers. The first 170 British sailors reached Rio de Janeiro in March 1823, coinciding with Cochrane's arrival from Chile. Another 250 departed from Britain in April and May, still in time to participate in the War for Independence.[25] The next great wave of recruits left Britain for Brazil between July and November 1825, as the navy prepared for the Cisplatine War. Of 400 seamen in this cohort, 150 sailed aboard the frigate *Piranga* when it returned to Brazil without Cochrane. By 1827 there were between 1,000 and 1,200 British sailors in Brazilian service. Cochrane had dispersed British seamen throughout the fleet, to bolster the reliability and competence of the Brazilian crews, and did not have to worry about communication problems because virtually every ship in the navy of 1823–5 had at least one British officer aboard. By the time of the Cisplatine War, with British officers accounting for a smaller share of a growing officer corps, most British seamen were segregated aboard ships commanded by British officers, to ease the myriad problems and tensions that would have arisen from requiring British sailors to serve under non-English-speaking officers.[26]

The growing number of British seamen must be considered in light of the overall growth of the navy during the Cisplatine War. The peak of 1,000–1,200 British sailors served in a navy that had just over 7,800 seamen in 1827 and 8,400 in 1828. Portuguese remaining in Brazilian service and all other foreign recruits combined never surpassed the British in number, leaving native Brazilians to account for one-half to two-thirds of the seamen at any given time.[27] The navy had to pursue all avenues of recruitment to complete its crews, because Brazil – notwithstanding its lengthy coastline and dependence upon the sea –

had relatively few civilian mariners. Most fishermen were mulattos who never ventured out of sight of the coast, and many seamen employed in the coastal trade were slaves. Initial efforts to recruit white Brazilian seamen were less than successful because there were few of them to begin with, and because the navy made up for the high wages paid to attract foreign seamen by offering far less to its own. During the summer of 1822–3 able seamen recruited at home were paid just 8 milréis (£1.60) per month, far less than the 13 milréis (£2.60) offered to British recruits. Ordinary seamen fared even worse, at 6.50 milréis (£1.30). As early as March 1823 the navy ministry recognized that, even with British recruits on the way, decisive measures had to be taken to boost recruitment at home. The navy raised the monthly wages offered to able and ordinary seamen to 10 milréis (£2) and 8 milréis (£1.60), respectively. Dom Pedro also agreed to allow slaves to serve aboard warships, and granted convicts pardons in exchange for enlistment.[28] When all other measures failed, Brazil resorted to impressment to man its fleet. During the Cisplatine War, this practice included forcing into service prisoners from prizes taken on the blockade at the mouth of the River Plate.[29]

The dramatic downsizing of the Brazilian navy following the end of hostilities with Argentina and the subsequent abdication of Dom Pedro I brought an end to the dependence upon foreign officers and seamen, most of whom returned home or moved on to other adventures. The foreign recruits had been a mixed lot, yet most served competently and many with distinction. The British in particular had a lasting impact on the culture of the Brazilian navy, which adopted many British naval traditions in substance as well as in form.[30] On the road to independence the vast country had not held together easily, and its unity would remain in question throughout the long regency of the child-emperor Dom Pedro II. During those years of vulnerability, when units of the country's army frequently rallied behind regional or republican uprisings, the imperial government could count upon the professionalism of a fleet whose officers and seamen would do their duty in the cause of national unity.

The first naval confrontation of Brazil's War for Independence stemmed from Dom Pedro's initial rejection, in January 1822, of a direct order to return to Lisbon. Two months later the ship of the line *Dom João VI* led a Portuguese squadron into Rio de Janeiro harbour, but Dom Pedro managed to persuade them to depart without him, securing the added bonus of the frigate *Real Carolina* (eventually renamed *Paraguaçu*), which the squadron's commander agreed to leave behind. Rodrigo de Lamare's ill-fated voyage to Bahia (July–September 1822), although still sailing under the Portuguese flag, was the first naval mission with a Brazilian purpose, sent by Dom Pedro to reinforce and resupply patriot troops in the northeast. When the *Dom João VI* led another squadron to Brazil late in the year it came on a mission of war, escorting transports and bound not for rebellious Rio de Janeiro but the Portuguese loyalist stronghold of Salvador in Bahia.[31]

The first months following the Brazilian declaration of independence were relatively quiet at sea, since the summer of 1822–3 passed without a major confrontation. Activity in the patriot camp reached a fever pitch in late March, as soon as Cochrane arrived from Chile and other officers and seamen from Britain. Barely a week later, the fleet departed from Rio de Janeiro on its first sortie under the Brazilian flag, a force of two frigates, two corvettes and two brigs led by Cochrane in the ship of the line *Pedro I*. On 4 May 1823, 30 miles (48 kilometres) off Salvador, he met a Portuguese force consisting of the *Dom João VI*, two frigates, four corvettes and four armed merchantmen. Attacking the Portuguese line from its starboard (eastern) flank in a line-ahead formation, he hoped to break it between the seventh and eighth ships, isolating the rearguard and destroying it before the *Dom João VI* and the rest of the enemy line could turn to join the engagement. Ultimately only the *Pedro I* succeeded in breaking the line and, when it was crossing the bow of the armed merchantman *Princeza Real*, it managed only a half-hearted broadside instead of the devastating raking fire Cochrane expected. As the admiral learned before breaking off the battle shortly thereafter, the inexperience of hastily drilled gun crews combined with the open disobedience of some pro-Portuguese seamen to foil his plan. The heat of battle exposed the strongest pro-Portuguese sentiments aboard the corvette *Liberal* (ex-*Gaivota*) and the two brigs, whose officers barely retained control of their ships. Afterward Cochrane complained that 'one half of the squadron is necessary to watch over the other half'. He redistributed his personnel, consolidating the British seamen aboard his flagship and the corvette *Maria da Glória*, which continued to show the flag off Salvador until help arrived from Rio de Janeiro. On 12 June he took the *Pedro I* and *Maria da Glória* on a daring night-time raid into Salvador harbour, following tactics he had used successfully in November 1820 with Chilean warships against the Spanish squadron at Callao, Peru. This time the wind failed him and he inflicted no damage on the enemy; nevertheless, his boldness unnerved the Portuguese. By July Cochrane had added to his squadron another frigate and three brigs, the reinforcements coming via Rio de Janeiro with dozens of British officers and hundreds of seamen who, distributed throughout the fleet, assured the reliability and operational competence of all ships.[32]

In early July 1823 the Portuguese decided to abandon Salvador and head for home, but Cochrane chose to pursue them in their retreat, hoping to inflict enough damage to their squadron to preclude a future counter-attack. The captains of the Portuguese warships refused to turn and fight, remaining focused on their mission of escorting their vulnerable convoy of merchantmen and troop transports. Cochrane took full advantage of their plight, giving chase with the *Pedro I*, two frigates and two smaller warships, seizing sixteen prizes and 2,000 prisoners. After the rest of the squadron turned back to Brazil, John Taylor's frigate *Niterói* continued the pursuit to the coast of Portugal, taking seventeen more prizes by November 1823. In the meantime, Cochrane deployed the rest of his ships to support local patriots against Portuguese loyalists in the northern provinces of Brazil. He personally commanded a show of force at São Luis, which secured the allegiance of Maranhão province, and sent a detachment to Belém, at the mouth of the Amazon, to secure Pará province while he set sail for Rio de Janeiro with the rest of the fleet. By the time of his arrival in early November, ships under his direction had claimed 73 prizes worth £250,000.[33]

Aside from the fighting off Salvador on 4 May 1823, the only conventional battle between Brazilian and Portuguese warships occurred on the River Plate off Montevideo, where the Portuguese had formed a squadron from the defected schooner *Maria Teresa* and its convoy of three transports, armed as two corvettes and a brig. For months they made no effort to challenge a Brazilian blockade of the port, which grew to include the corvette *Liberal*, three brigs and three schooners, under the command of Captain Pedro Nunes. By the time they finally attempted to break out, on 21 October 1823, Montevideo was the last Portuguese outpost on territory claimed by Brazil. The action on that day was heated but inconclusive, with neither side losing a ship. Nunes forced the Portuguese squadron to return to Montevideo, which surrendered a month later, ending the War for Independence.[34]

After playing a leading role in securing the independence of Brazil, the navy almost immediately faced the task of preserving Dom Pedro's empire against a separatist, republican revolt. During the winter of 1823–4 five northeastern provinces formed the Republic of the Confederation of the Equator. Cochrane's fleet deployed against them in August 1824, and the following month the rebel capital of Recife, Pernambuco, fell to a joint operation by the imperial army and the navy, the latter including the flagship *Pedro I*, two frigates, two corvettes, a brig and a schooner. The fleet remained engaged until May 1825, helping the army subdue the remaining rebels, when the admiral abruptly left for Britain following the surrender of the last of the northern provinces.[35]

With the Brazilian navy in a state of confusion over Cochrane's departure, Argentina first lent its support to a rebellion in Uruguay, then announced its intention to annex the province, prompting Brazil to declare war in December 1825. Across the River Plate, Admiral Lobo faced an adversary who would have posed a challenge even for Cochrane: the 50-year-old Irish adventurer William George Brown, commander of the Argentinian navy during its war against Spain (1814–18), recalled to service from the merchant marine in January 1826. Unlike most British officers in Latin American service, Brown had served in the British navy only briefly, as a common sailor, before passing into merchant service and making his way to South America. Against Spain, he had distinguished himself at small-unit riverine warfare, blockade running and commerce raiding, expertise that would serve him well in the Cisplatine War. At the start of the conflict the Argentinian navy consisted of two laid-up brigs; under Brown's direction, and with considerable help from other foreign officers and seamen, within months it would give the Brazilians all they could handle. From Montevideo due south to Cabo San Antonio, the mouth of the River Plate is 120 miles (193 kilometres) wide; at Buenos Aires, 140 miles upstream from Montevideo, the river is still 35 miles (56 kilometres) wide. At the time, before modern dredging deepened the channel, ships drawing more than 20 feet were at risk of running aground if they ventured farther upriver than Montevideo, and the approaches to Buenos Aires were so shallow that no ship drawing more than 15 feet could get within five miles of the city. These geographic realities neutralized Brazil's considerable advantage in larger warships, because its ship of the line, frigates and most of its corvettes could not get within firing range of Brown's ships at Buenos Aires unless he chose to come out.[36]

The first naval engagement of the war, the Battle of Corales (9 February 1826), took place in the River Plate 20 miles downstream from Buenos Aires. Brown sortied with an Argentinian squadron consisting of his flagship, the corvette *25 de Mayo* (the former merchantman *Comercio de Lima*), manned entirely by British and Americans, followed by three brigs, a schooner and nine gunboats. Lobo's squadron included the corvettes *Liberal*, *Itaparica* and *Maceió*, six brigs, two schooners and three gunboats. The two forces duelled for three and a half hours before Brown, abandoned earlier by the rest of his squadron, finally broke off the action and returned to port. Lobo did not give chase for fear of running his larger warships aground. Neither side lost a ship, and casualties on both sides were light. After Corales, Lobo made the fateful decision to scatter his brigs, schooners and gunboats to defend various strategic points along the Uruguayan shore of the River Plate, while pulling back his corvettes well out into the estuary, some 100 miles (160 kilometres) from Buenos Aires. In the Battle of Colonia (26 February–14 March 1826), Brown took advantage of Lobo's redistribution of forces to attack one of the Brazilian strongholds on the Uruguayan shore. Repeated assaults by Argentinian warships, eventually accompanied by land attacks from Uruguayan patriot forces, ended only when Lobo finally sent reinforcements. The battle cost Argentina a brig, three gunboats and over 300 casualties, many more than the Brazilians suffered. Even though Brown failed to win the battles of Corales and Colonia, in each case his bravado contrasted sharply with Lobo's caution. Within days of the relief of Colonia, Lobo was sacked. In the interregnum before Pinto Guedes took command in May 1826, Brown continued his aggressive posture. Twice during April he took his flagship *25 de Mayo* on daring raids into the harbour of Montevideo, the second time surprising and almost capturing the Brazilian frigate *Imperatriz*.[37]

The arrival of Pinto Guedes signalled not only a tightening of the Brazilian blockade, but a more assertive stance on the River Plate as well. Captain James Norton's inshore division won the battles of Los Pozos (11 June 1826) and Lara-Quilmes (30 July 1826), in the former recapturing a schooner lost earlier, in the latter turning back a sortie spearheaded by Brown's *25 de Mayo* and the corvette *Congresso Nacional*. Battered by broadsides from Norton's 38-gun *Niterói*, the only Brazilian frigate light enough to operate on the River Plate, the Argentinian flagship limped back to its anchorage, capsized and sank.[38] Considering Norton's division too strong to challenge, Brown turned his attention to Captain Jacinto Senna Pereira's division on the River Uruguay. Senna Pereira had more experience on the river than any other Brazilian officer: before the War for Independence he had commanded a flotilla there during the Portuguese conquest of Uruguay (1816–21). At the Battle of Jaguary (29 December 1826), in which both forces had a brig and sixteen schooners or gunboats, Senna Pereira turned back an attack by Brown, then pursued him 60 miles (96 kilometres) downriver as he retreated toward Buenos Aires. There, in the Battle of Juncal (8–9 February 1827), Brown turned the tables, capturing a wounded Senna Pereira along with the brig that served as his flagship. After the engagement the defeated Brazilians scattered up the Uruguay, to be hunted down piecemeal by the Argentinians in the days that followed. Brown returned to Buenos Aires in triumph, with a train of thirteen prizes.[39]

The elimination of the Brazilian division on the River Uruguay raised Argentinian morale but did nothing to change the situation in the River Plate, where Buenos Aires's access to the open sea remained blocked. The Brazilian blockade threatened a lucrative trade dominated by the world's three largest merchant fleets, and deprived the government of Argentina (then a loose confederation of provinces) of customs revenue critical to its survival. During 1825 a total of 387 foreign merchantmen had docked at Buenos Aires, bringing in £2 million worth of goods. Roughly £1 million came in British vessels, £360,000 in American and £260,000 in French, and Argentina collected £429,300 in customs revenue on the imports. With the blockade in place for the last eleven months of 1826, just 20 foreign merchantmen got through, of which only two made it from June onward, after Pinto Guedes succeeded Lobo and tightened the noose. Argentinian customs revenue for 1826 plummeted to £81,900. The situation grew bleaker the following year. During the first three months of 1827, just £18,750 worth of British goods entered Buenos Aires, and no exports left for Britain; in comparison, in the last six peacetime months (July–December 1825), British imports had totalled £455,000 and exports to Britain £325,000. Among the leading commercial powers Britain alone recognized the Brazilian blockade, since its establishment was consistent with the British concept of blockade employed most recently in the Napoleonic wars. But because Britain's own merchants suffered the greatest losses, it took the lead in trying to mediate an end to the war, suggesting as early as mid-1826 a compromise that would leave Uruguay independent. Meanwhile, by late 1826 the United States and France both indicated that they would not respect the Brazilian blockade, and would fight to defend the right of their merchants to trade with Buenos Aires. At the same time, with the Portuguese succession in doubt following the death of Dom João in 1826, Dom Pedro needed the support of Britain and France to implement his plan to place his daughter Maria on the throne in Lisbon. In

November 1826 he ordered Pinto Guedes to abandon the strict British concept of the law of blockade, according to which ships entering the Plate estuary were seized on fairly loose pretexts, in favour of the more lenient American concept, which required each passing ship to be stopped individually and informed of the blockade. This allowed a ship to be seized only if it resisted on the spot or subsequently refused to honour the blockade. As a result of this loosening of the rules, 42 foreign merchantmen made it into Buenos Aires during 1827, more than double the total for the previous year.[40] Fortunately for the United States, it would not have to observe such strict rules in its own blockade of the Confederate States in 1861–5, owing to the intervening adoption of international laws of blockade at the Congress of Paris (1856).

Unable to break the Brazilian blockade, Argentina resorted to a campaign of commerce raiding, using some regular naval vessels but mostly privateers. The first fourteen Argentinian privateers put to sea during 1826, and a total of 57 had sortied by the time the war ended in 1828. Collectively they claimed 405 prizes, most of them (248) taken by the 27 privateers active during 1827. The privateer fleet was multinational, and even more diverse than the regular Argentinian navy. One cannot assume that all corsair crews shared the same nationality as their captains, but of the latter roughly 20 per cent were American and 10 per cent British, while Italians and Frenchmen (practically unrepresented in the regular navy) accounted for 20 per cent and 15 per cent, respectively. They ranged as far as the North Atlantic in search of their prey, but had their best luck in attacking Brazil's extensive coastal commerce and targeting its slave trade, which had continued despite Dom Pedro's 1825 promise to the British to outlaw it, in exchange for recognition of Brazil's independence. As a special incentive for its privateers to go after Brazilian slavers, the government in Buenos Aires offered £40 'head money' for every slave brought alive to Argentina (where the adult males among those freed were required to serve in the army for four years, as the price of their redemption). In 1826 Argentina purchased three warships from Chile for use as commerce raiders, the frigate *Buenos Aires* (ex-*O'Higgins*) and the corvettes *Montevideo* (ex-*Independencia*) and

Chacabuco, but only the latter survived to enter Argentinian service, as the *Montevideo* proved to be unfit for the voyage around Cape Horn and returned to Chile, while the *Buenos Aires* was lost at sea with all hands. Brown met the *Chacabuco* at Cape Corrientes in Patagonia in October 1826, then took it on a raid of the Brazilian coast with the schooner *Sarandí*. By the time of their return in December, they had taken thirteen prizes, in the most successful raid of the war by units of the regular navy. In 1827 Argentina declared a blockade of the entire coast of Brazil, which it could not enforce, but under this pretext Argentinian-flagged privateers started preying upon not just Brazilian ships, but ships of all flags found off the coast of Brazil. The British deployed more warships to stop the practice, and even France and the United States, otherwise pro-Argentinian, took measures to protect their own merchantmen from the scourge. Thus the objections of the great powers by the end of 1827 stopped the belligerents from making full use of their most effective weapons of war – Brazil had to loosen its blockade of the River Plate, and Argentina had to rein in its privateers. During 1828 thirteen new commerce raiders put to sea, but the numbers of prizes taken fell dramatically. Only a dozen Argentinian privateers survived the war; another 27 were captured, and 18 shipwrecked.[41]

To avoid the Brazilian blockade at the mouth of the River Plate, most Argentinian privateers operated out of the smaller rivers and small coastal ports of Patagonia. In February 1827 Pinto Guedes sent one of his most distinguished British officers, Captain James Shepherd, to destroy the privateer base at Carmen de Patagones on the Rio Negro. His squadron included the corvettes *Duqueza de Goiás* and *Itaparica*, the brig-schooner *Escudeira* and the schooner *Constança*, the last under the command of nineteen-year-old Marques Lisboa, then a second lieutenant. The expedition encountered problems from its first action, on 28 February, when the flagship *Duqueza de Goiás* ran aground under the guns of Argentinian batteries while forcing the mouth of the Rio Negro. The corvette was lost along with 38 of its crew, but Shepherd pressed on to Carmen, 16 miles (25 kilometres) upriver, where he was killed on 7 March in a botched attack on the privateer base. Captain-

Lieutenant William Eyre of the *Itaparica* inherited command of the landing party, which surrendered after Argentinian privateers blocked their escape by seizing the three surviving Brazilian warships, left behind in the Rio Negro manned by skeleton crews. Adding to the magnitude of the disaster, Argentina promptly hired 184 of the British seamen taken prisoner at Carmen and commissioned the three captured warships as commerce raiders; they went on to take nineteen prizes. Six months later Eyre, Marques Lisboa and 91 other prisoners from the expedition seized an Argentinian brig and escaped to Montevideo. Of Shepherd's 654 men, they were the only ones to return to Brazil.[42]

The debacle at Carmen de Patagones, coming a month after the defeat and capture of Senna Pereira at Juncal, focused the attention of the Brazilian court and assembly on the conduct of the naval war. Pinto Guedes weathered the storm of criticism, and the navy soon saved face when Norton's division on the River Plate won another decisive victory over Brown's squadron. At the Battle of Santiago Bank (8–9 April 1827), Norton deployed the frigate *Dona Paula* and sixteen smaller warships to stop a sortie out of Buenos Aires by the corvette *Congresso Nacional*, the schooner *Sarandí* and two brigs. The operation ended in disaster for the Argentinians when their two brigs ran aground and could not be refloated. Norton closed with his smaller warships but also had the *Dona Paula* towed within range of the two stricken vessels, which were destroyed with great loss of life. Brown was fortunate to escape with his remaining pair of warships. After the battle the action subsided from May to August 1827, while the British attempted to mediate a peace settlement. When Argentina rejected the proposed terms as too favourable to Brazil, the fighting resumed.[43] Shortly thereafter, Pinto Guedes sent the corvette *Maceió* and two brigs on a second expedition to Patagonia, which fared no better than the first. Eyre, promoted to captain after his recent escape from captivity in Argentina, commanded the mission; his officers included Marques Lisboa and other veterans of the disaster at Carmen de Patagones. On 20 September Eyre's flagship *Maceió* and one of the escorting brigs ran aground en route to attack a privateer base in the Bay of San Luis, 65 miles (105 kilometres) north of

Carmen. The two ships were then destroyed in a storm that drowned 50 men. Marques Lisboa was among those rescued by the crew of the surviving brig, while Eyre made it ashore to be captured again by the Argentinians, along with 82 of his men.[44]

Thus it was the pressure from Britain, France and the United States, rather than the naval operations of Brazil, that reduced the damage done by Argentinian privateers. Nevertheless, some of the most spectacularly successful commerce raiders sortied during the last year of the war, after the great naval powers went on record opposing the tactic. In sheer audacity none surpassed the year-long voyage of the brig *General Brandsen*, under the American George DeKay, which between June 1827 and June 1828 captured, destroyed or looted 26 of the ships it stopped. Its prizes included the Brazilian navy brig *Cacique*, captured off Pernambuco on 9 September 1827 and subsequently pressed into service as its partner, claiming two prizes of its own. DeKay took the two ships as far north as New York, where they were refitted and their crews replenished midway through the northern winter of 1827–8. On his homeward voyage DeKay ultimately pressed his luck too far. While the *Cacique* put in safely at Carmen de Patagones, the *General Brandsen* ran aground in the River Plate on 17 June 1828 while attempting to run the blockade into Buenos Aires. Norton closed on the stranded Argentinian brig with the corvette *Bertioga*, a brig and a schooner, and lost an arm in the ensuing battle. DeKay and his crew abandoned the *General Brandsen* and watched its ultimate destruction from the shore. Brown could do nothing to save the ship, his own force having been reduced to one brig and a handful of schooners and gunboats, charged with defending Buenos Aires. As privateers assumed a greater importance in the Argentinian war effort at sea, the foreign officers and seamen that the regular navy had depended upon were drawn away by the more attractive and lucrative privateering arm, and local men Brown conscripted or impressed in Buenos Aires were more trouble than they were worth, in at least three cases in 1827–8 mutinying and deserting en masse.[45]

With the war winding down, on 5 July 1828 a French squadron under Rear Admiral Albin-Reine Roussin entered the harbour at Rio de Janeiro to support the French ambassador's protests over issues arising from the blockade of the River Plate. Within two weeks the force had grown to include the ship of the line *Jean Bart*, three frigates, two corvettes and three brigs, more than enough to intimidate the Brazilian warships on hand: the ship of the line *Pedro I*, frigate *Príncipe Imperial*, corvette *Carioca*, two brigs and a gunboat. Dom Pedro's government bowed to the show of force, and on 21 August the French declared their satisfaction that the dispute had been resolved. During the weeks that the French were anchored at Rio de Janeiro, events in Portugal further distracted the emperor and made the conclusion of peace imperative. His daughter Maria had left for Portugal aboard the frigate *Imperatriz*, escorted by the frigate *Dona Francisca*, for her wedding to her uncle, Dom Miguel, and subsequent coronation, only to have Dom Miguel seize the throne while she was en route, touching off the Miguelist War. More eager than ever to enlist British and French support for his daughter's cause, Dom Pedro agreed to the compromise peace Britain had proposed two years earlier, which created an independent Uruguay as a buffer between Brazil and Argentina.[46]

Before the treaty was signed, one last battle enabled the Brazilian navy to end the war on a high note and the Argentinian navy to go out in a blaze of glory. In June 1828 a public subscription had paid for the purchase and arming of three foreign merchantmen in Buenos Aires: the corvette *Gobernador Dorrego* (ex-French *Mandarin*), the brig *General Rondeau* (ex-American *Allison*) and the schooner *Argentina* (ex-French *Hydre*). Under the command of Frenchman Jean Soulin, the three warships evaded the blockade, then set sail on a raid up the coast of Brazil. They took just three prizes before being intercepted by Captain George Broom's corvette *Bertioga*, Marques Lisboa's schooner *Rio da Prata* and a brig in the Battle of Chico Bank (23 August 1828), off the coast of Rio Grande do Sul. Soulin sacrificed his flagship, the *Gobernador Dorrego*, to facilitate the escape of the other two ships. The *Argentina*, badly damaged, put in at Carmen de Patagones, but the *General Rondeau* ended up taking another eight prizes (all after the conclusion of peace) in a raid that lasted into 1829 and ranged from the Caribbean to the coast of West Africa.[47]

Five days after the engagement at Chico Bank, representatives of Brazil and Argentina signed the treaty ending the Cisplatine War. In late September 1828 the Brazilian navy ended its blockade of the River Plate, and the following month the two governments formally ratified the peace. Dom Pedro's advisers immediately began to ponder how the Brazilian navy could be deployed in support of Maria's candidacy for the Portuguese throne, but for the moment her prospects appeared too bleak to justify the effort. In October 1829 the *Imperatriz* brought her back to Rio de Janeiro, where she remained until departing for Portugal with her father in April 1831, when he relinquished the throne of Brazil to Dom Pedro II.[48]

CONCLUSION

Because the regency ruling in the name of Dom Pedro II did not subscribe to his father's vision of Brazilian naval power, the new government had few reservations about reducing the fleet to a peacetime footing a fraction the size of the force that ended the Cisplatine War. The navy contracted from 76 warships and just over 8,400 personnel in 1828 to 17 warships and 1,500 personnel in 1833. At least part of the reduction in manpower came at the expense of the foreign contingent. Even before Dom Pedro I's abdication, a law of 15 November 1830 discharged all foreign naval officers, excepting only those who were veterans of the War for Independence. By 1835 there were just 22 British officers remaining in a Brazilian naval officer corps of 270. For those who remained, Brazilians as well as foreigners, the overall downsizing of the fleet slowed promotions to a crawl, as reflected in the service records of three future admirals who had served as teenagers in the War for Independence and otherwise enjoyed relatively rapid advancement throughout their long careers. Joaquim Marques Lisboa, the future Marquis de Tamandaré, spent nine years (1827–36) as a first lieutenant; Joaquim José Ignacio, later Viscount de Inhaúma, spent eight years (1829–37) as a first lieutenant; and Francisco Manoel Barroso da Silva, the future Admiral Baron do Amazonas, spent seven years (1829–36) as a first lieutenant, then another thirteen years (1836–49) at the next grade of captain-lieutenant.[49] But even at its worst, the pace of advancement in the Brazilian navy remained much faster than in the British, French or American navies of the same era.

After reducing the navy so dramatically in warships and manpower, the regency government did not hesitate to call upon it to aid in the suppression of the frequent rebellions that plagued the empire during the childhood and adolescence of Dom Pedro II. The authorities had little choice, since every uprising involved at least some mutinous army troops (while only one involved naval personnel), and in the era before railroad construction, loyal troops could best be moved to distant provinces by sea. In April 1831, September 1831 and April 1832, warships helped put down rebellions in Pernambuco. In July 1831 naval artillery assisted in suppressing an army mutiny in Rio de Janeiro (but three months later the same artillery unit attempted its own rebellion, the only time that naval personnel tried such a thing). The navy helped suppress another attempted coup in the imperial capital in April 1832. Warships were deployed against the revolt of the Farrapos in Rio Grande do Sul (1835–45), when a republic was proclaimed in Bahia (1837), against the revolt of the Cabanos in Pará (1835–40), and against an uprising in neighbouring Maranhão (1839–41). The leader of the Cabanos, Nogueira Angelim, recognized the importance of naval power and, by marketing himself as a friend of Britain, tried to get Division Chief John Taylor and the rest of the blockading squadron's British officers and seamen to desert to his side. They did not, and naval power proved decisive in suppressing the uprising. Rebellions became much less common after the end of the regency in 1840 and the formal coronation of Dom Pedro II the following year, but in 1849 the navy again was called upon to facilitate the suppression of a revolt in Pernambuco.[50]

Under the regency and during the subsequent reign of Dom Pedro II, Brazil subscribed to classic continental balance-of-power goals. As a legacy of the Cisplatine War, Brazil consistently asserted its strategic interest in keeping both Uruguay and Paraguay independent as buffer states against Argentina, preventing the latter from recreating a single state the size of the old Spanish viceroyalty of Rio de la Plata, in the form of a modern republic.[51] While warships, especially on the rivers, might play a role in maintaining these goals, fundamentally they required military power rather than naval power. The French exercise in 'gunboat diplomacy' at Rio de Janeiro in 1828 also had a lasting impact on Brazil's view of its own sea power. By the end of the Cisplatine War the Brazilian government recognized that it had many more warships than it needed to defeat any naval rival on the South American continent, yet its fleet was far too small to challenge a great naval power, and thus it had prudently made peace when a squadron of one of those powers appeared. From their birth, the countries of Latin America recognized the importance of naval power; in the era of the First World War, Brazil would join Argentina and Chile in purchasing dreadnought battleships, and in the last decades of the twentieth century both Brazil and Argentina would operate aircraft carriers. But from the late 1820s onward none would maintain a fleet larger than it needed to defend its interests within Latin America.

The navy was crucial to the establishment of Brazil's independence and to the preservation of its unity afterward. In light of the fragmentation of the former Spanish America (ultimately into sixteen independent countries on the mainland alone), it was not a foregone conclusion that the former Portuguese America would remain united as a single state, which ranks today as the world's fifth largest both in size and in population. If not for the efforts of the Brazilian navy, it is likely that several Portuguese-speaking states would have emerged, leaving modern Latin America with a very different map and a different history in the long term.

FOUR

Preserving the Union:
The United States Navy, 1861–5

In November 1860 the anti-slavery candidate Abraham Lincoln won the United States presidential election. By the following spring, eleven of the southern slaveholding states had seceded from the Union and formed the Confederate States of America, and two more had rival Union and Confederate state governments. Rebel forces in South Carolina, the first state to secede, on 12 April 1861 fired the first shots of the American Civil War against Fort Sumter, the island fortress guarding the mouth of Charleston harbour. To accomplish the missions of blockading the long southern coastline, securing control of the Mississippi and other southern rivers, and hunting down Confederate raiders and blockade runners on the high seas, Lincoln's government required a fleet roughly seven times the size of the United States navy of 1861. The success of the expansion effort owed much to the organizational skills of navy secretary Gideon Welles, a Connecticut politician and newspaper editor who had gained valuable experience as head of the navy's Bureau of Provisions and Clothing during the Mexican-American War (1846–8).[1] The growth in *matériel* and personnel proceeded in a makeshift and at times haphazard fashion, and some critics have alleged that the navy could have done more for the war effort once it was fully mobilized.[2] Nevertheless, just as the Brazilian navy had facilitated the establishment of a united Brazil, the United States navy played a central, though largely unrecognized, role in the preservation of the Union during the American Civil War.

At the beginning of 1861 the US navy had 90 warships (including 40 steamers), of which 42 (26 steamers) were in commission, 27 (9 steamers) in reserve and 21 (5 steamers) 'in an unserviceable condition.'[3] The core of the fleet included six screw frigates and fourteen screw sloops commissioned within the past five years; another four screw sloops were on the stocks and nearly completed. Northern proprietors owned over 90 per cent of the American merchant marine, the world's second largest after the British, and their vessels included dozens of steamships that the navy could convert to warships; by the end of 1861 the navy had purchased 79 of these, along with 58 sailing ships. As it identified merchantmen suitable for conversion, the Navy Department recalled all ships from the Mediterranean and East Indian stations, and left just one sailing ship on the Brazil station and one on the African station. As early as July 1861 the active fleet had doubled in size to include 82 ships mounting 1,100 guns.[4] When the southern states seceded no warships fell intact into Confederate hands, but in their evacuation of the Norfolk Navy Yard in April 1861 Union forces burned four ships of the line, four frigates, two sloops and a brig, all of them sailing vessels except for the screw frigate *Merrimack*.[5]

The US navy instituted the blockade with its screw sloops and armed merchant steamers, eventually reinforced by 35 screw gunboats and 47 so-called 'double-ended' paddle steamers laid down between 1861 and 1864.[6] The Union began building armoured warships only in response to the rebel government's attempts to acquire ironclads. In May 1861 the Confederacy allocated $2 million for the purchase of ironclads in Europe, as a first step toward the creation of a fleet of ironclad blockade-breakers and unarmoured blockade runners and raiders. Over the summer, Confederates at New Orleans converted the screw tugboat *Enoch Train* into the 385-ton armoured gunboat CSS *Manassas*, an ironclad ram with a 'turtle-back' casemate protecting its lone gun. By the end of the year the Confederates had begun another six ironclads: two at New Orleans, two at Memphis, one at Savannah and one at Norfolk, the last on the hull of the former *Merrimack*, whose

9 The armoured frigate USS *New Ironsides* (1862).

machinery had survived intact when the ship burned to the waterline in the destruction of the navy yard there. During the winter of 1861–2 the deficiencies of the southern industrial base slowed work on the five ironclads being built from the keel up, while work on the *Merrimack* forged ahead. It was completed in February 1862, two months before any of the others was launched, and renamed CSS *Virginia*.[7] Meanwhile, in July 1861 the Union navy ordered seven ironclads for river service, the so-called city class gunboats, and in September three ironclads for coastal or high seas duty: the 4,510-ton frigate *New Ironsides* (illus. 9), 950-ton sloop *Galena* and 990-ton *Monitor*. While the frigate and sloop were conventional broadside battery warships, the *Monitor*, designed by John Ericsson and built by the Continental Iron Works of New York, was little more than an armour-plated raft, mastless, with a pair of 11-inch smoothbore Dahlgren guns in a revolving turret protected by eight inches of wrought iron. Fearful that the Confederate ironclads would be operational before its own were completed, the Lincoln government spared no expense in rushing the initial projects to completion. The seven river ironclads were completed in January 1862, and the *Monitor*, after less than four months on the stocks, in February 1862.[8]

10 USS *Monitor* and CSS *Virginia* at the Battle of Hampton Roads, 9 March 1862.

The mastless *Virginia* carried ten heavy guns: six 9-inch smoothbore Dahlgrens from the old *Merrimack*'s armament, and four muzzle-loading rifles (two 7-inch and two 6.4-inch) designed by Confederate artillerist John Brooke, a former US navy officer. All guns were housed in a casemate amidships, a wooden structure 2 feet thick with angled sides plated with 4 inches of armour. When fully loaded the *Virginia* displaced 3,500 tons and rode so low in the water that the deck fore and aft of the casemate was awash. The *Virginia* could fire six of its guns in either broadside, since the heaviest two rifles were installed as pivot guns fore and aft on the centreline, capable of firing end-on or to either side through portals in the casemate, while the other eight guns were mounted four to each broadside. In contrast, the *Monitor* could only fire its two guns one at a time, at a rate of one shot every seven or eight minutes. Both vessels were very slow – the *Monitor* steamed at just 6 knots, the *Virginia* 7.5 – but the *Virginia*'s draught of 22 feet (6.7 metres), more than double that of the *Monitor*, limited its scope of operations in coastal waters.[9] The *Monitor* and *Virginia* fought to a draw on 9 March 1862, in the second day of the Battle of Hampton Roads (illus. 10), leaving each side pleased with the performance of its own ship. Assistant secretary of the navy Gustavus Fox, witness to the battle from nearby Fortress Monroe, became a strong 'monitor' enthusiast, as did the US navy's chief engineer, Alban Crocker Stimers. Aside from a small number of river gunboats on each side, all subsequent Confederate ironclads were smaller versions of the *Virginia*, and all Union ironclads were monitors.[10]

Late in 1862 the *Monitor* was reassigned from Hampton Roads to the blockade of Charleston. On the night of 30–31 December it sank in a storm off Cape Hatteras. The disaster highlighted the glaring deficiency of the monitor design – when at sea, its low freeboard left the deck awash and the ship in constant danger of sinking – but the sinking did nothing to dampen the enthusiasm of Fox and Stimers for their monitor programme. Because the navy, as of 1862, could not build iron warships, much less armoured ones, in its own shipyards, the programme initially depended entirely on private industry. In addition to designing the first Union ironclad to show its worth in battle, Ericsson also had wealthy business partners who were well connected politically. He wanted his consortium (which built twelve of the first fourteen monitors) to have exclusive rights to construct the type, but Welles recognized that a single group of builders could never produce the number of monitors the navy would ultimately want. Furthermore, for political reasons the navy had to spread the lucrative ironclad contracts among builders in several states, including those along the Ohio River. Delays there were longer than in eastern yards, and the first monitor completed in the west, the *Catawba* at Cincinnati, was not launched until April 1864. The need to build large numbers of monitors very quickly in a variety of locations in the midst of a technological revolution led to countless design changes and delays while the vessels were under construction. Unfortunately for the firms building the ironclads, the construction of the *Monitor* raised unrealistic expectations about the speed with which subsequent vessels could be built. The monitors of the *Passaic* class, larger (at 1,875 tons) and technologically more complex than the original *Monitor*, were expected to be completed in four or five months, contracted to take no longer than six, but took an average of nine. The *Passaic* itself (launched in November 1862) came in at eight months, the slowest project among its sister ships at thirteen.[11]

Including the original *Monitor*, 42 single-turret monitors begun during the war were completed by 1866. The first double-turret monitor was laid down in March 1863, and nine were in service by the end of 1865. The former screw frigate *Roanoke*, a sister-ship of the *Merrimack*, emerged from a radical reconstruction (April 1862–June 1863) as the war's only triple-turret monitor, a giant vessel of 4,395 tons armed with six heavy guns, including two 15-inch Dahlgrens. The *Roanoke* had a much higher freeboard than any other monitor but rolled so badly on the high seas that its guns could not be trained on a target. Its only two sea voyages were from New York to Hampton Roads in the summer of 1863 and back to New York in April 1865 to be decommissioned. Aside from the *Roanoke*, the only Civil War monitors specifically intended for high seas duty were Ericsson's 4,440-ton *Dictator*, armed with two 15-inch Dahlgrens in a single turret, and the slightly larger *Puritan*, designed to carry two 20-inch Dahlgrens. The *Dictator* was commissioned in November 1864 but kept out of action by engine problems, while the *Puritan* was never finished. Nevertheless, the prospect of a large seagoing monitor caused alarm in Britain, where the principal promoter of the turret ship, Captain Cowper Coles, wrote a letter to *The Times* of London arguing that a multiple-turret ship with 15-inch guns would be superior to the *Warrior* and other European broadside battery ironclads.[12] Of the 52 monitors of all types completed for the US navy between 1862 and 1866, all but the *Dictator* and the double-turret *Onondaga* (illus. 11) had wooden hulls, and most would not remain structurally sound for long after the war's end. Overall, the shortcomings of the monitors reflected the circumstances under which they were built. Welles and Fox gave Chief Engineer Stimers broad discretion to get the job done, but his premium on speed of construction over quality led to wasteful cost overruns on ships that more often than not had serious mechanical problems after entering service. The Navy Department tolerated his approach in a crisis atmosphere but not after that crisis had passed. In June 1864, with most major southern rivers and ports in Union hands and no new monitors being laid down, Stimers was sacked.[13]

11 The monitor USS *Onondaga* (1864).

The decision to replicate the *Monitor* to the exclusion of other ironclad types may have reflected poor process, but Ericsson's design had the advantage of being the first completed and of fighting well enough in its baptism of fire to justify its construction. Of the other two seagoing Union ironclads laid down in October 1861, the sloop *Galena* took six months to finish and, a month after its commissioning in April 1862, was riddled by enemy shot in a duel with Confederate batteries along the lower James River. The *Galena* was such a failure that the Navy Department ordered the removal of its 2-inch armour plate, after which it served as a conventional wooden screw sloop.[14] The armoured frigate *New Ironsides*, at 4,510 tons more than four times the size of the *Monitor* or the *Galena*, nevertheless was built in just ten months. Aside from its speed, at 6.5 knots just half that of its European peers, it would have been a match for the armoured frigates of other navies, mounting fourteen 11-inch Dahlgrens and two 150-pounders behind 4.5 inches of armour. Upon completion it reinforced the Union blockade of Charleston, where it saw most of its wartime duty.[15] Aside from the *New Ironsides*, the *Galena* and the monitors, the 840-ton *Keokuk* was the only ironclad to see coastal action in the Civil War fleet of the US navy. From a distance it appeared to be a small double-turret monitor, but it had stationary gunhouses (each with one pivoting 11-inch Dahlgren) instead of revolving turrets. The *Keokuk* had an iron hull but a novel (and weak) type of armour consisting of alternating layers of iron and oak. Commissioned in February 1863, like the *Galena* it was holed repeatedly by enemy fire in its first action, at Charleston two months after its commissioning.[16]

From the start naval officers commanded the Union's river gunboats, but they served under the US army until July 1862, when their flotillas were transferred from the jurisdiction of the War Department to the Navy Department. The seven 'city class' gunboats, completed in January 1862, were joined that month by the double-hulled *Benton*, a river boat conversion which, like the purpose-built ironclads, had 2.5 inches of casemate armour, a centreline paddle wheel, and engines capable of 5.5 knots. The *Benton* carried 16 guns, the 'city class' 13. All were designed by James Eads of St Louis, a famous engineer and bridge-builder. Between 1862 and 1864 the navy commissioned another eight armoured river gunboats, all with side paddles. Of all the converted river boats only the *Benton* had armour thick enough to be considered a legitimate ironclad. More lightly protected 'tinclads', such as the 1,000-ton stern-wheeler *Essex*, fitted with 0.75-inch side armour, and a great number of 'timberclads', with thick wooden planking, offered their crews protection against rifle fire from the river banks but could not stop artillery of any calibre. The navy's monitors included five single-turret and four double-turret vessels built with extraordinarily shallow draught specifically for river duty. Two of the single-turret monitors had stern paddle wheels rather than screw propellers.[17] Concerns that Confederate raiders would victimize California's poorly defended ports led to the assignment of one monitor, the *Camanche*, to the Pacific coast. Built in Jersey City in 1862–3, it was disassembled and shipped around Cape Horn to San Francisco, then reassembled and commissioned in the spring of 1865. For many years it was the only US armoured warship permanently stationed on the Pacific.[18]

Of the five new Confederate ironclads laid down in 1861, one (at Savannah) was completed as a floating battery and the other four (at New Orleans and Memphis) were destroyed as a result of Union actions on the Mississippi during 1862. Only one of the four functioned as a warship under its own power, the

Memphis-built css *Arkansas*, which fought for just three weeks in July–August before being sunk. Its loss left the Confederates temporarily with no armoured warships, but from 1862 to 1865 river shipyards from Shreveport in northwest Louisiana to Tarboro in eastern North Carolina kept busy building various versions of the *Virginia* prototype. By 1865 a total of 22 Confederate ironclads had served at one time or another, and at least 30 more were under construction at war's end. The only one not of wood construction was the css *Atlanta*, converted at Savannah from the 800-ton iron-hulled *Fingal*, a blockade runner built in Britain.[19] Confederate attempts to acquire ironclads in Britain or elsewhere in Europe met with failure, thanks in part to the vigilance of the us ambassador to Britain, Charles F. Adams, and other diplomatic and consular personnel, who warned their host countries that selling warships to the Confederacy would be considered a hostile act against the United States.[20] The decisive Union victories at Gettysburg and Vicksburg in July 1863 made it unlikely that any European country would extend diplomatic recognition to the Confederacy, much less intervene on the Confederate side in the war. Three months later the British government confiscated two 2,570-ton double-turret rams being built by Laird for the Confederate navy; they entered British service as the *Scorpion* and *Wivern*.[21] Arman of Bordeaux built two 1,400-ton rams for the Confederacy, but sold one to Prussia, which commissioned it as *Prinz Adalbert*. The other entered service as css *Stonewall* but was still crossing the Atlantic when the war ended, and in May 1865 surrendered to Spanish authorities at Havana.[22] All other ironclads laid down for the Confederacy in Britain and France were either sold to European navies or never finished. At one point Confederate agents considered ordering armoured warships in Austria, from the Cantiere Navale Adriatico of Trieste, but nothing came of the plan.[23]

The Confederacy had better luck acquiring fast wooden steamers for service as commerce raiders or blockade runners. The latter were a heterogeneous lot of screw or paddle steamers, sharing only the common features of powerful engines and a draught shallow enough to operate in the coastal waters of the southern states. They rarely crossed the Atlantic, more typically carrying their cargoes (usually cotton) from Confederate ports to Havana in Spanish Cuba or Nassau in the British Bahamas, the nearest European-controlled ports. While most blockade runners were private business ventures, reaping their greatest profits from luxury items imported for the southern elite, some were commissioned by the Confederate government to bring in military supplies or machinery.[24] Most commerce raiders were screw sloops. The css *Florida* (by Miller of Liverpool, completed March 1862) and css *Alabama* (by Laird, completed July 1862) were the first ships built for this purpose for the Confederacy in European shipyards. Both left British waters unarmed, loaded their guns from tenders in the Atlantic, then operated with British crews commanded by Confederate officers.[25] British and French shipyards laid down another six commerce raiders for the Confederacy but in the end delivered none of them. Ultimately Confederate agents found it both cheaper and easier to buy existing fast merchantmen in Britain or France and have them converted to commerce raiders. Their search for bargains took them as far as Austria, a country then financially strapped by its ironclad competition with Italy. In February 1863 the Austrian navy offered a Confederate agent 26 screw and paddle steamers for the price of a single armoured frigate, but the ships were either too slow or drew too much water to function as raiders, and none was purchased.[26] The best judges of a ship's potential as a commerce raider were the captains of the raiders themselves, who sometimes converted prizes on the spot into 'satellite' cruisers manned by prize crews under junior officers. The most successful converted raider, the css *Shenandoah* (ex-*Sea King*), was also the first composite (wood-and-iron) hulled cruising warship. Starting in the 1850s the trend toward ever-longer wooden steamships had resulted in serious hogging or sagging problems in some designs, prompting British shipbuilders in the early 1860s to begin constructing them with iron frames. At first all composite ships were either merchantmen or transports built to carry British troops to India. The *Sea King*, completed in 1863, remained unarmed until being purchased by the Confederates in 1864.[27]

At the peak of its wartime strength, the US navy had in commission 649 warships of 510,396 tons, armed with 4,600 guns. The fleet included 49 ironclads, 113 unarmoured screw steamers, 52 paddle steamers, 323 other steamers used for auxiliary purposes and 112 sailing ships. The numbers would have been even greater if the Navy Department had not stopped ordering new warships in 1864. After the collapse of the Confederacy in April 1865 dozens of warships under construction were never finished. The United States maintained a formidable fleet at least until Napoleon III's decision, in February 1866, to withdraw French troops from Mexico, where they had supported the regime of Emperor Maximilian. Thereafter, a sweeping demobilization reduced the active force to a fraction of its wartime size.[28]

DIVIDED LOYALTIES: OFFICERS AND SEAMEN

Following the creation of the US navy in 1798, its officers, like most of their British counterparts, began their careers by being placed as midshipmen by their fathers or guardians directly with ship captains, often at very young ages. David Glasgow Farragut, victor of New Orleans and Mobile Bay during the Civil War, secured a midshipman's warrant in 1810, at the age of nine, thanks to his father's friendship with Captain David Porter. Farragut entered service the following year, in time to see action in the War of 1812 aboard Porter's frigate *Essex*. Thereafter, he had a typical experience in the peacetime navy. After passing his lieutenant's exam in 1819, he waited three years for his next assignment to sea, and then it was only as a 'passed midshipman', because no lieutenancies were available. His commission finally came in 1824, by which time he had already been in service thirteen years. The navy only gradually standardized the process through which young men became officers. In 1836 the minimum age of entering midshipmen was fixed at 14. Nine years later, navy secretary George Bancroft established the Naval Academy at Annapolis, which initially admitted students aged 13–15 for a six-year course of study and training (three at Annapolis and three at sea), after which they were eligible to sit for the lieutenant's exam. While assigned to the academy, students were designated 'acting midshipmen' until 1862, then midshipmen. In 1846 the navy formalized a system distributing the appointment of midshipmen geographically, using a formula based upon each state's number of seats in the House of Representatives.[29]

By the end of the War of 1812 the navy had established a system under which officers almost always were promoted by seniority alone. This practice continued through the Civil War years. In 1866 one US senator noted that 'since the time of Stephen Decatur' only six naval officers had received merit promotions.[30] Farragut languished as a lieutenant for seventeen years before being promoted to commander in 1841. He served another fourteen years – including in the brief war with Mexico (1846–8), the only formal hostilities between 1815 and 1861 – before becoming a captain, then the highest rank in the service. Farragut's promotion to captain, aged 54, would have come even later if not for a series of forced retirements authorized by Congress in 1855. Officers of his generation went unemployed for years at a time, but the problem never approached the magnitude of that facing the British navy after the Napoleonic wars. For example, in 1840 just over 60 per cent of US navy officers (lieutenants and above) were on active duty, while as late as 1850 the figure for the British was around 10 per cent.[31]

Like the British navy of the same era, the US navy before the Civil War had no retirement age. Inactive officers remained in the corps, on half-pay, eligible for command until they resigned or died, blocking the advancement of younger men. On the eve of the forced retirements of 1855, the youngest captain was 56. That year, Congress created a board of fifteen officers charged with composing 'a list of officers who should be compelled to retire', but the board never devised objective criteria for its decisions. In an officer corps traditionally riven by divisive cliques, bitter personal rivalries and petty, backbiting behaviour, the recommendation that 201 of the navy's nearly 700 officers should leave the service did not go unchallenged. It made matters worse that the board's most prominent figure, Captain Matthew Calbraith Perry, recently returned from his mission to force Japan open to trade with the United States, disassociated himself from the process and later argued for the reinstatement of many men he had earlier voted to sack. Ultimately the retired officers were given a chance to appeal, and of the 118 who did so, 64 were returned to service. Thus the reform effort resulted in the forced retirement of just 137 officers and, by failing to establish a retirement policy, did nothing to solve the problem of the ageing officer corps. Six years later, in 1861, the oldest commanders were 58 to 60, while the oldest lieutenants were 48 to 50 and veterans of 34 years of naval service. The wartime need to clear the ranks of captains and commanders for younger men physically fit to serve aboard ship led Congress, in December 1861, to pass a law requiring all naval officers to retire at age 62 or after 45 years of service, whichever came first. Only the president could waive these limits, in individual cases and with the approval of the Senate. The first such waiver was granted to Farragut, who was 63, with 53 years of service, when he led the Union fleet into Mobile Bay in 1864, and died six years later as the navy's highest ranking officer.[32]

Because the navy bore the responsibility of representing the United States overseas, its officers before the Civil War typically had a higher sense of national loyalty than state loyalty, while in the army the opposite was the case. Before 1861 Navy Department leaders rarely showed concern for sectional divisions within the naval officer corps, and those who did found it impossible to act on their fears. For example, in 1843 the Senate did not confirm President John Tyler's designated secretary of the navy, David Henshaw, after naval officers, including Farragut, protested against his stated intention to send northerners south and southerners north when assigning important naval posts on land, such as the commands of navy yards.[33] Some undeniable strains began to show after 1855, when the appeals process following the forced retirements became highly politicized, with the congressional allies of some aggrieved officers alleging sectional prejudice. Captain Franklin Buchanan, a slaveowner from Maryland who had served as first superintendent of the Naval Academy, then as Perry's flag captain on the mission to Japan, subsequently criticized the United States' refusal to join Britain and France in the Second Opium War (1856–60) as pusillanimous 'Yankeeism'. But such sentiments did not preclude his appointment to an important, potentially sensitive post on the eve of the war. In 1859 Buchanan became commander of the Washington Navy Yard, and his lifelong friend, Captain Samuel F. Du Pont, from the slaveholding state of Delaware, commander of the Philadelphia Navy Yard.[34]

In the spring of 1861 almost all southern army officers remained loyal to their states and resigned their commissions when their states seceded. In contrast, just over half of all southern naval officers remained loyal to the Union, but the precise figures vary depending upon which ranks are included and, indeed, how one defines a 'southerner'. Maryland and Delaware, slaveholding states considered 'southern' before the war, never seceded from the Union and, as a result, are treated differently by some sources. Official statistics are misleading because the Navy Department considered an officer to be from the state where he had resided when he first received his midshipman's warrant. Thus Buchanan, the Maryland slaveowner, was officially a Pennsylvanian because his family was living in Philadelphia when he entered the navy at age fifteen. By one account, the 571 captains, commanders and lieutenants of 1861 included 253 southerners (44.3 per cent). Of this group, 126 (49.8 per cent) resigned their commissions.[35] Including masters and passed midshipmen (ranks later redesignated as lieutenant junior grade and ensign) along with midshipmen and warrant officers (NCOs), the overall number rises to 1,563, including 677 southerners (43.3 per cent). Of this group, 321 (47.4 per cent) resigned.[36]

While some southerners left the service even before their states seceded, others took months to make their decision. Ironically the most prominent naval officer of the first state to secede refused to resign his commission: South Carolina's 71-year-old Captain William Shubrick, a squadron commander in the war with Mexico and, as recently as 1858–9, commander of a squadron in South American waters, decided to remain loyal to the Union.[37] Farragut, born in Tennessee but 'officially' from Louisiana (since his family resided in New Orleans when he entered the navy), likewise never considered resigning. Between assignments Farragut had made his home in Norfolk, where he met and married his late first wife and his second wife, both Virginians. His family and most of his friends out-side the navy were southerners. Nevertheless, on 18 April 1861, the day after Virginia seceded, he left Norfolk for New York, which became his new home. His application for an active command came with one condition: 'I cannot fight against Norfolk'. Fortunately for the us navy, no one asked him to.[38] The most interesting resignation cases were four Marylanders. Lieutenant Raphael Semmes, future captain of the raider css *Alabama*, embraced the rebel cause eagerly, going south in February 1861, at a time when the Confederacy included just seven states. In contrast, one of the oldest officers in the corps, Captain Isaac Mayo, agonized for weeks before submitting his resignation. Secretary Welles gave all resigna-tion letters a curt acknowledgement, simply informing the writer that his name had been removed from the roll of com-missioned officers, but of all the recipients of those notes, Mayo alone committed suicide. For Lieutenant John Taylor Wood, Naval Academy instructor and future commander of the raider css *Tallahassee*, and for Franklin Buchanan, com-mander of the Washington Navy Yard, the key moment came a week after the shelling of Fort Sumter, when a regiment of Massachusetts infantry en route to reinforce Washington clashed with a pro-secessionist mob in Baltimore, shooting down several civilians. Convinced that Maryland would secede, they resigned their commissions. Buchanan soon regretted doing so and in May applied for reinstatement, only to be rebuffed by Welles. Both Wood and Buchanan waited until September 1861 to go south.[39] The Confederate government offered us navy officers commissions at the same grade they held before resigning, but because none brought their warships with them, those accepting the offer remained idle while ves-sels were acquired for them to command. Frustrated at the long wait, some joined the Confederate army instead. An of-ficer of Buchanan's stature did not have to wait for work. As soon as he arrived in Richmond, the rebel capital, he assumed the highest administrative position in the Confederate navy and went on to become its most distinguished officer. Those resigning usually paid a high price in lost friendships. Delaware's Du Pont, who remained loyal to the Union, never answered a letter in which Buchanan explained his actions, and never spoke to his old friend again.[40]

Because the Naval Academy dated only from 1845, relatively few of the naval officers of the Civil War had been educated at Annapolis. In the postwar peacetime navy the academy would produce almost all the new officers, but the pre-war corps of 1861 included barely 100 of its graduates. Aside from a small number of the youngest lieutenants, all were masters or passed midshipmen. In the wake of the bloodshed in Baltimore (19 April 1861), the Navy Department decided to move the Naval Academy from Annapolis to Newport, Rhode Island, for the remainder of the academic year; it would not return to Annapolis until the autumn of 1865. With the arrival of the summer of 1861 the second and third classes received emergency commissions, joining the graduating senior class as new lieutenants. But the infusion of youthful, inexperienced junior officers failed to compensate for the loss of nearly a quarter of the corps as a result of the resignations of southerners, much less cover the growing needs of a fleet that ultimately would expand sevenfold. The navy resorted to commissioning 7,500 volunteer officers between 1861 and 1865, most of them from the merchant marine, most of whom did not serve for the entire war. Regular officers continued to hold the most prominent posts, but by the time the navy reached its peak strength in 1865 they accounted for just one-seventh of a corps of 6,700. Long-suffering older lieutenants benefited the most from the rapid expansion, receiving dizzying promotions.[41] David Dixon Porter rose the most dramatically. Son of the hero of the War of 1812, Porter was 48 when the war began and still a lieutenant after 32 years of service; a mere eighteen months later, he was an acting rear admiral and commander of the navy's Mississippi River squadron. At the end of the war almost all volunteer officers were discharged with three months' pay. In the peacetime establishment of 857 officers approved by Congress in July 1866, just 150 places (17.5 per cent) were reserved for wartime volunteers who wished to remain in the service. Even this relatively small number (half of whom were commissioned as ensigns) created controversy in the postwar officer corps, as promotions again slowed and academy graduates considered the former volunteers to be blocking their way.[42]

The shortage of trained officers paled in comparison to the shortage of common manpower. The United States, like Britain, never conscripted sailors, traditionally relying upon volunteers. Over the years since the US navy's last major conflict, the War of 1812, Congress had done much to make the service attractive, offering better pay than foreign navies and abolishing flogging in 1850, thirty years before the British navy's last recorded use of the lash. As in the British fleet, the age of steam brought additional compensation for men with mechanical skills and for stokers; in the United States, as in Britain, such bonuses initially were a source of discontent for ordinary seamen whose pay scale remained unchanged for years at a time, in the American case from 1820 to 1854. The raises of 1854 were followed the next year by the introduction of the honourable discharge and re-enlistment bonuses for men in that category. Nevertheless, the navy still offered a life of lower pay and longer cruises than the American merchant marine. The peacetime fleet remained chronically undermanned, and in March 1861 there were only 207 sailors aboard receiving ships or elsewhere in ports awaiting assignment. All other personnel were assigned and thus not immediately available for newly commissioned or recommissioned warships.[43]

The wartime navy offered the same three-year enlistments as the Union army but had difficulty competing with the generous bounties offered by the northern states for army volunteers. To make matters worse, under the quota system for the number of troops each state had to raise for the war effort, states received no credit for men sent into the navy. These factors combined to leave the blockading fleet and high seas warships perpetually short of seamen, since thousands of men who had been to sea as merchant mariners, fishermen or whalers ended up in the army. On the rivers of the western theatre, where typically the only regular navy man aboard a vessel was its commander, the crews were a hodgepodge of Great Lakes sailors, rivermen, coastal and merchant seamen, and soldiers pressed into service to fill vacancies. In 1863, with the three-year enlistments of 1861 due to expire in another year, the army averted the looming manpower shortage by introducing conscription. The navy, in contrast, remained an all-volunteer force throughout the war.

Its recruiters exploited the situation after 1863 by openly advertising naval service as a way to avoid the draft, and further sweetened the deal by offering enlistment bounties. It also helped the cause that, in 1864 and 1865, states finally received credit toward the quota for their sailors.[44] When the navy still fell short of keeping its warships manned once its own three-year enlistments began to expire, in 1864 Congress agreed to lift an 1813 ban on the enlistment of foreigners. Their numbers aboard some ships rose dramatically, for example, to 35 per cent of the crew of Farragut's flagship *Hartford* by September of that year. Reflecting the desperation of the situation, in 1864–5 the navy even enlisted Confederate prisoners of war. Hundreds of ex-Confederate soldiers were more than willing to swear oaths to the Union and join the fleet in order to escape another chilly winter in northern prison camps. They proved to be remarkably reliable as sailors, but out of concern for security, the navy limited their numbers to 16 per cent of the crew aboard larger ships, and to 6 per cent aboard ships crewed by less than 100 men.[45] Overall, the complement of seamen, fixed at 7,600 in the pre-war peacetime navy, rose to 13,000 by July 1861, 34,000 by July 1863 and 51,500 by April 1865. The state of New York alone accounted for 30 per cent of all wartime naval enlistments, followed by Massachusetts with 17 per cent. While the Union army, a million men strong at the end of the war, suffered 110,000 battle deaths and 335,000 total deaths during the war, the navy lost 1,800 men in battle and 4,800 from all causes. The likelihood of dying in service was roughly three times greater for the Union soldier than for the Union sailor.[46]

African Americans provided another valuable source of manpower. Blacks were not allowed into the us army until 1862 but had always served aboard us navy ships, although after 1839 their number had been limited to 5 per cent of enlisted men. After the start of the Civil War their share increased dramatically, to 15 per cent by the spring of 1862 and 23 per cent by the autumn of 1863. Of the estimated 90,000 men who served in the us navy at one time or another during the years 1861–5, roughly 18,000 were black. Of these, some 1,500 were foreign born, mostly from the Caribbean; approximately half of the rest were 'contrabands', slaves freed in southern states during the war (mostly from along the Mississippi or the coastal areas of the Carolinas), and the remainder were from states that did not secede (including 2,300 from the former slaveholding state of Maryland). African Americans served aboard virtually every naval vessel but were more numerous aboard storeships and colliers than seagoing warships. Black sailors were most likely to be found in combat roles on the western rivers; as of the spring of 1864 they accounted for 34 per cent of the manpower in Porter's Mississippi squadron. The war had a long-term impact on the US navy's racial composition. At the end of 1865, with much of the force already demobilized, blacks accounted for 15 per cent of the manpower remaining; they continued to make a significant contribution through to the end of the First World War, when the navy stopped recruiting African Americans.[47]

Like the Union army, the navy of 1861–5 faced a rapid expansion and the rapid training and assimilation of a volunteer force. Much more so than the army, it had to accomplish this feat in the midst of a technological revolution, and won the war with a force spearheaded by warship types that did not even exist when the fighting began, employing tactics improvised along the way. With the fate of the country in the balance, a naval officer corps notorious for its infighting proved to be more loyal, more cohesive and produced more competent leaders than its army counterpart. In contrast to the army's leading generals, most of whom were loath to part with the lessons they had learned at West Point, most of the navy's leading admirals embraced change and became more effective commanders as a result. The admirals rose to the occasion despite their age, on average almost a dozen years older than the generals. Indeed, aside from the elderly Winfield Scott, all of the most prominent Union generals of the Civil War were younger in 1861 than David Dixon Porter, the youngest of the most prominent wartime admirals.[48]

COASTAL, RIVERINE AND HIGH SEAS OPERATIONS

From the start of the Civil War the Lincoln administration recognized the importance of establishing a naval blockade of the southern coast, to prevent the Confederacy from exporting cotton and other cash crops or importing weapons and machinery from Europe. The coastline to be covered measured 3,549 miles (5,711 kilometres); including 'bays and inlets', 6,789 miles (10,925 kilometres); including the coastline of all coastal islands, 11,953 miles (19,236 kilometres). The operation marked an early test of the international law of blockade recently laid down in the Declaration of Paris (1856) following the Crimean War. During the first weeks of the war the navy maintained a legal and effective blockade only at Hampton Roads, where Union forces still held Fortress Monroe. Between June and December 1861 more than 150 ships entered Charleston; during the three summer months of 1861, 42 entered Wilmington, North Carolina. Yet as early as July 1861, when the British navy sent two warships to cruise the Confederate coast (one to the Atlantic ports and one to the Gulf ports) to observe the effectiveness of the blockade, both reported a legal blockade in effect. As more ships were added and a greater vigilance imposed, the navy decentralized the coastal command. Initially the entire operation came under the direction of Captain Garrett Pendergrast, pre-war commander of the Home squadron. The first subdivision (May–June 1861) created an Atlantic squadron under Captain Silas H. Stringham and a Gulf squadron under Captain William Mervine. The second subdivision (September 1861) created a South Atlantic squadron under Captain Du Pont and a North Atlantic squadron under Captain Louis M. Goldsborough, who soon gave way to Captain Samuel P. Lee; meanwhile, Captain William McKean replaced Mervine in the Gulf. The final subdivision (February 1862) created a Western Gulf squadron under Captain Farragut, leaving McKean responsible for the Eastern Gulf.[49] Along with a separate inland command for the Mississippi River and its tributaries, the four coastal commands provided the navy with its organizational structure until the end of the war.

From the start the blockading navy pursued a strategy of 'converting the blockade of principal points into an occupation'.[50] Fort Hatteras, a stronghold on the Outer Banks of North Carolina, was the first point on the Confederate mainland to fall, succumbing on 27–8 August 1861 to a bombardment by

Stringham's Atlantic squadron, including the screw frigates *Minnesota* and *Wabash*, the large paddle steamer *Susquehanna* and three gunboats. More than 900 marines and soldiers carried by leased transports were landed to secure the fort, taking 615 prisoners in 'the first Union victory of the war'.[51] After taking command of the new South Atlantic squadron, Du Pont led a similar operation against Port Royal, South Carolina, only with the army providing many more troops. On 7 November 1861 he subdued shore batteries using the guns of the *Wabash*, the *Susquehanna*, the sailing sloop *Vandalia*, and sixteen gunboats and armed merchant steamers. A makeshift rebel flotilla of five small armed merchantmen, none mounting more than two guns, offered little resistance. The following day some 30 transports landed 12,000 troops to occupy Hilton Head and Port Royal islands. Two months later, on 5–7 February 1862, the army contributed the same number of men to an attack on Roanoke Island, North Carolina, to follow up on the earlier capture of Fort Hatteras. Captain Goldsborough led the assault on the crucial island, commanding the passage between Albemarle Sound and Pamlico Sound, relatively shallow safe havens for blockade runners separated from the Atlantic by the Outer Banks. A makeshift force of 19 shallow draught screw and paddle steamers (river boats, ferries and tugs, armed with 48 heavy guns) carried out the operation, while 46 small transports ferried the 12,000 troops. In a battle against a Confederate flotilla of two paddle and six screw steamers, Goldsborough's force suffered no losses while the rebels had to scuttle one badly damaged vessel. Union forces secured Roanoke Island and went on to seize the small ports along the mainland shore of the two sounds. These operations closed all North Carolina ports except Wilmington, which had access to the sea via the Cape Fear River, flowing directly into the Atlantic. Meanwhile, in April 1862, Union troops based at Port Royal attacked and captured Fort Pulaski on the Savannah River, all but closing Savannah, Georgia, to blockade runners. Perhaps of greater significance, the navy's conquests caused the collapse of the coastal plantation culture of the South Atlantic states, as thousands of slaves fled to freedom at the Union enclaves on the water, and retreating Confederates destroyed homes and crops to deny their use to the enemy.[52]

After the capture of Roanoke Island, Goldsborough resumed command in Hampton Roads, where the css *Virginia* (ex-*Merrimack*) neared completion in the Norfolk Navy Yard. The us navy had already seen what an armoured warship could do against an unarmoured blockading force months earlier (12 October 1861) on the Mississippi, downriver from New Orleans, where the tiny css *Manassas*, the world's first self-propelled ironclad to engage in combat, rammed the screw sloop uss *Richmond*. The attack did not sink the *Richmond* but forced it to abandon its station. The *Virginia*, ten times the size of the *Manassas*, sortied into Hampton Roads on 8 March 1862, under the command of Franklin Buchanan, to attack blockaders led by the screw frigates *Minnesota* and *Roanoke* (half-sisters of the original *Merrimack*) and three sailing ships: the sloop *Cumberland* and the frigates *St Lawrence* and *Congress*. The *Virginia* first rammed and sank the *Cumberland*, then used gunfire to destroy the *Congress*. The *Minnesota*, *Roanoke* and *St Lawrence* all ran aground while trying to join the battle, providing stationary targets for the Confederate ironclad to attack in turn. Buchanan was wounded shortly after the *Virginia* began to exchange shots with the *Minnesota*, and his incapacitation, along with a falling tide and approaching darkness, brought an end to the day's action. The *Virginia* returned the next day, under temporary commander Lieutenant Catesby Jones, to finish its work. As Jones approached the *Minnesota* he found it protected by the *Monitor*, which had arrived from New York the previous evening. Lieutenant John Worden led the *Monitor* out to intercept the *Virginia*, initiating history's first engagement between armoured warships. Throughout the four-hour duel the survivors of the previous day's debacle were content to watch the *Monitor* do its work; the *Minnesota*, still hard aground, caught fire after being hit by shells from the *Virginia*, but otherwise the Union wooden ships remained safely out of the fray. The two ironclads failed to damage each other seriously, even though they exchanged shots at a range of less than 100 yards. The *Monitor*'s smaller size and shallower draught made it far more mobile than the *Virginia*, but its revolving turret proved so unmanageable that for much of the engagement Worden kept it stationary, and aimed its guns by moving the entire ship.

Late in the battle the *Virginia* fired a shell that struck the pilot-house on the *Monitor*'s foredeck, seriously wounding and blinding Worden. The *Monitor* then withdrew, and with the tide falling, the *Virginia* likewise withdrew. Worden, the only casualty aboard either ironclad, survived his wounds and even recovered his eyesight. In the following weeks Commodore Josiah Tatnall took the *Virginia* out on two more sorties. On 11 April Tatnall steamed well out into Hampton Roads, but Goldsborough declined battle, keeping the *Monitor* and his wooden warships safely under the guns of Fortress Monroe. On 8 May 1862, while the *Monitor* and other Union warships bombarded Norfolk's defences in preparation for an assault on the city, the *Virginia* came out again but Tatnall chose not to engage the superior force facing him. Norfolk fell on 10 May and, since the *Virginia* drew too much water to retreat up the James River toward Richmond, Tatnall ran the ship aground and set it on fire. Unfortunately for the Union, General George B. McClellan, whose Peninsular campaign had advanced to the outskirts of Richmond, did not appreciate what the navy could do for his army, and the two services failed to cooperate to exploit the situation. The *Monitor* did not see battle again before it sank off Cape Hatteras at the end of the year.[53]

While the navy tightened the noose on Norfolk, New Orleans became the next target, because Farragut was instructed to take the city before its two ironclads, css *Louisiana* and css *Mississippi*, were completed. Without them, the guns of Fort Jackson and Fort St Philip, flanking the Mississippi 90 miles (145 kilometres) below the city, posed the greatest challenge to an attack by the Western Gulf squadron, since Confederate naval forces under Commander John K. Mitchell included just the one-gun ironclad *Manassas* and nineteen small wooden steamers carrying a total of twenty guns. Porter accompanied Farragut with a separate force consisting of six gunboats, the sailing sloop *Portsmouth* and twenty mortar schooners, which started shelling Fort Jackson and Fort St Philip on 18 April 1862, six days before the battle. On 19 April Mitchell added another warship, the sixteen-gun *Louisiana*, which had to be towed downriver to the forts because it could not yet move under its own power. Porter's flotilla lost one of its schooners but continued to bombard the two forts through the pre-dawn hours of 24 April, when Farragut ran the gauntlet between them. The Union column included the screw sloops *Hartford*, *Pensacola*, *Brooklyn* and *Richmond*, supported by the paddle steamer uss *Mississippi* and twelve smaller steamers. Farragut's largest warship, the screw frigate *Colorado*, drew too much water to ascend the river and had to be left behind in the Gulf. The *Manassas* attacked Farragut's column as it approached the forts, ramming the uss *Mississippi* and the *Brooklyn* but failing to sink either of them. The column passed successfully, at a cost of 163 casualties and one gunboat sunk, in the process sinking sixteen of the Confederate gunboats. After the *Manassas* was scuttled by its own crew, Mitchell had just the *Louisiana* and three gunboats remaining. Later on 24 April, as Farragut's ships approached New Orleans, local Confederates set on fire the unfinished css *Mississippi* along with dozens of river boats and the city's warehouses and docks. Farragut took the surrender of New Orleans and held the city until Union troops arrived to take over on 1 May. Meanwhile, Porter took the surrender of the bypassed forts downriver, but during the negotiations Mitchell blew up the *Louisiana* and burned his other surviving vessels. Farragut subsequently detached ships upstream, which took the surrender of Baton Rouge and Natchez. After the operation the Western Gulf squadron established its base at Pensacola, Florida, which the Confederates abandoned on 10 May; the city had been useless to them, since Fort Pickens, guarding its harbour, had remained in federal hands since the start of the war.[54]

New Orleans had four times the population of any other Confederate city, and the cotton trade had made it one of the world's busiest ports before 1861.[55] Its surrender devastated the Confederacy, leaving Galveston, Texas, and Mobile, Alabama, as the leading Gulf ports still in rebel hands. Inexplicably, even after the loss of New Orleans the Confederates left Galveston only lightly defended, and late in 1862 Farragut took it easily with a detachment under Captain W. B. Renshaw including one gunboat, one former revenue cutter and two former ferry boats, landing just 260 troops. On 1 January 1863 the Confederates counter-attacked, using two 'cottonclad' steamers (river boats padded with bales of cotton as protection against rifle fire) manned by sharpshooters. Renshaw had failed to blow up the railroad causeway linking Galveston to the Texas mainland and, with the Union vessels in disarray, rebel troops rushed across to reoccupy the city. Renshaw's flagship, the former ferry boat *Westfield*, ran aground early in the battle and was blown up to avoid capture; unfortunately, Renshaw and several of his crew did not abandon ship fast enough once the charges were set, and were killed in the explosion. Another Union warship, the cutter *Harriet Lane*, surrendered as the battle ended. Farragut, outraged at the debacle, sent the screw sloop *Brooklyn* at the head of a mixture of regular warships and armed merchantmen to reimpose the blockade; lacking the necessary troops, he did not attempt to retake Galveston, which remained in Confederate hands until the end of the war. The blockade was back in effect by 8 January, but the navy was in for further humiliation off the Texas coast. During the intervening week Raphael Semmes had put in at Galveston with the css *Alabama*; the raider departed as the *Brooklyn*'s group approached but continued to cruise in the area. On the night of 11 January it showed itself off Galveston and succeeded in drawing off a lone pursuer, the armed merchantman *Hatteras*. The *Alabama* carried eight guns, all heavier than the *Hatteras*'s makeshift battery of four, and easily outgunned it in their engagement, which resulted in the *Hatteras* becoming the only us navy warship sunk by a Confederate raider in the entire war. On 21 January 1863 the navy lost two more armed merchantmen, the sailing ships *Morning Light* and *Velocity*, captured by another pair of 'cottonclad' steamers at the mouth of the Sabine Pass. The attack occurred in a dead calm, which immobilized the Union warships and made them easy prey. Their capture led the navy to avoid using sailing vessels on blockade duty in places where the rebels had steamers of any type.[56]

After Farragut became the navy's first rear admiral as a reward for his victory at New Orleans, Du Pont received the same rank in belated recognition of his earlier Port Royal victory. With it came the expectation that he would use the South Atlantic squadron, reinforced by ironclads, to capture Charleston. Du Pont loved the armoured frigate *New Ironsides* but had no confidence in monitors and doubted he could take

Charleston unless the army provided him with a large body of troops for a combined operation. His views put him at odds with the Navy Department, especially assistant secretary Fox, the leading proponent of monitors and of the view that the navy should take Charleston alone rather than share the glory with the army. In any event, the War Department was obsessed with taking Richmond and would never agree to give Du Pont the number of troops he wanted. Pressured to act, on the afternoon of 7 April 1863 he steamed into Charleston harbour with the flagship *New Ironsides*, the ill-designed *Keokuk* and seven *Passaic* class monitors, leaving his unarmoured ships behind. Floating mines and other obstacles cast adrift in the harbour dispersed his column, after which the ships fell into the crossfire of Fort Sumter and the formidable shore batteries. The *Keokuk*, leading the column, was holed repeatedly and barely survived to sink the next day. Four of the monitors were damaged, but the rest came through unscathed along with the *New Ironsides*, which Du Pont had kept toward the rear of his column. His ten ironclads managed just 139 shots in the 90-minute battle, compared to 2,229 for the forts and shore batteries. The Confederate navy had a small squadron in the harbour – including the ironclads *Palmetto State* and *Chicora*, which had damaged two of Du Pont's wooden gunboats in a sortie against the blockade on 31 January – but its ships did not attempt to join the battle. For all the ammunition expended, Union casualties numbered just 23 (one killed), Confederate casualties 14.[57] A month before his failure at Charleston, Du Pont had detached the monitor *Montauk* (commanded by Worden of *Monitor* fame) to destroy the raider css *Nashville* at anchor in Georgia's Ogeechee River; two months after the battle, he sent the monitor *Weehawken* into Warsaw Sound where it captured the ironclad css *Atlanta* after a brief duel.[58] Otherwise, he did nothing more with the considerable resources allocated to him, and hurt himself politically by blaming the monitors for his failure at Charleston. He even filed charges against Chief Engineer Stimers, who was exonerated by a court of inquiry during the summer. The affair split the navy into pro- and anti-Du Pont factions, mirroring its anti- and pro-monitor factions. Ultimately the controversy made it impossible for Du Pont to keep his post. During the course of the war Lincoln sacked countless generals for failing to achieve victory in battle; Du Pont would be the only admiral to lose his post for the same reason.[59]

In July 1863 Rear Admiral John Dahlgren, the famed artillerist, replaced Du Pont as commander of the South Atlantic squadron. He had lobbied for the post, and would hold it for the rest of the war. As soon as he arrived off Charleston, he initiated a series of aggressive actions using the ironclads and amphibious landings with troops grudgingly provided by the army, many of them from newly raised Colored regiments. Between 6 July and 8 September Dahlgren systematically forced the Confederates to abandon most of the city's outer forts and batteries; then, during the remainder of the year, Union gunners used these positions to pummel Fort Sumter into a useless wreck. But the inner batteries of Charleston remained intact, and even Fox gave up the notion of the navy taking the city by storm, finally conceding that the cost would be prohibitive. Charleston remained in rebel hands until February 1865, when it fell to General William Tecumseh Sherman's army. After the summer of 1863 the blockade of the city again became routine, the relative calm interrupted only by Confederate experiments with new blockade-breaking technologies. In October 1863 the Confederate semi-submersible *David* detonated a spar torpedo against the hull of the *New Ironsides*. The first torpedo boat attack in history caused minimal damage to its victim, which remained on station for another eight months before steaming to Philadelphia for repairs. In February 1864 the Confederate submarine *H. L. Hunley*, powered by a hand-cranked propeller, detonated a spar torpedo against the hull of the wooden screw sloop *Housatonic*. The *Housatonic* became the first ship ever sunk by a spar torpedo, but the *Hunley* also sank as a consequence of the attack, drowning its entire crew.[60]

With Charleston sealed to blockade runners, Mobile became the lifeline for supplies to support the army attempting to defend Atlanta when Sherman began his March to the Sea. The Confederate government entrusted its defence to Franklin Buchanan, by then a rear admiral. The warships at his disposal included a newly completed ironclad, css *Tennessee*, built at

Selma on the Alabama River. The Union sent Farragut to attack the port, with the best ships of the Western Gulf squadron. At dawn on 5 August 1864 he led a force into Mobile Bay including the large screw sloops *Hartford*, *Brooklyn*, *Richmond*, *Monongahela* and *Lackawanna*, six smaller screw sloops and gunboats, and three paddle steamers. Most important of all, he had just received four monitors, the single-turret *Tecumseh* and *Manhattan* from the Atlantic, and the double-turret *Winnebago* and *Chickasaw* from the Mississippi. The *Tecumseh* headed the column but struck a mine and sank as the battle opened. Thereafter the *Tennessee* led three rebel gunboats against the Union line, and the battle soon became a mêlée. The *Hartford*, *Monongahela* and *Lackawanna*, the latter two fitted with iron bow plates, each rammed the *Tennessee* but damaged themselves as much as their target. At the end of the desperate four-hour struggle, the *Chickasaw* closed on the *Tennessee* and shelled it until Buchanan surrendered. Farragut had lost no warships after the *Tecumseh* but most of his wooden vessels suffered damage, and his 342 casualties included 172 killed, 120 of whom went down with the *Tecumseh*. Buchanan was among 32 casualties aboard the *Tennessee*; wounded through one leg in 1862 at Hampton Roads, he was wounded in the other at Mobile Bay, and spent most of the rest of the war convalescing as a Union prisoner. The victorious Farragut, meanwhile, became his country's first vice admiral early the following year. Union forces occupied the outer forts of Mobile Bay later in August 1864, closing the port to blockade runners. The city of Mobile remained in Confederate hands until the last days of the war, and the bay remained a treacherous hornet's nest of mines. On 27–28 March 1865, during the final assault on the city, the monitors *Milwaukee* and *Osage* struck mines and sank. After the end of the war mines in the bay claimed a Union gunboat and four smaller unarmed vessels.[61]

Right up to the last months of the war, the emergence of a single Confederate ironclad from a secure river shipyard could cause considerable havoc for the Union blockade. The css *Albemarle*, completed in April 1864 on the Roanoke River in North Carolina, provided one such example. Modelled after the general *Virginia* prototype, the *Albemarle* drew just 6 feet of water, half as much as most monitors, and put Albemarle Sound into play for the first time in over two years. After showing its mettle shortly after its completion by sinking a Union gunboat, the *Albemarle* spent most of its brief career anchored in the Roanoke, where its mere presence affected US naval operations in the entire region. Finally, in October 1864 daredevil Lieutenant William Cushing used a steam launch armed with a spar torpedo to sink the *Albemarle*. As with the submarine *Hunley*'s sinking of the *Housatonic* eight months earlier, the attacker sank along with its victim after delivering the blow, but in this instance Cushing and most of his party survived.[62] The elimination of the *Albemarle* left the new commander of the North Atlantic squadron, Rear Admiral Porter, free to concentrate on the capture of Wilmington, the last open Confederate port. On 24–5 December 1864 the *New Ironsides* joined the screw frigates *Minnesota*, *Colorado* and *Wabash* in leading a bombardment of Fort Fisher at the mouth of the Cape Fear River, guarding the approach to Wilmington. Afterward Porter considered the fort sufficiently weakened, and was disappointed that his army counterpart in the operation, General Benjamin Butler, chose not to use the 3,000 troops on hand to attempt to take it. Porter resumed the bombardment on 13 January 1865, this time with the *New Ironsides* and four monitors anchored in a line 1,200 yards from the fort, and a more co-operative partner, General Alfred Terry, standing by with 8,000 troops. The five ironclads kept up the shelling for three days, resupplied with ammunition under cover of darkness. On the third day, 15 January, the rest of the fleet joined the bombardment, and Porter added nearly 2,000 sailors and marines to the troops ashore. The lightly armed naval party threw itself against one wall of Fort Fisher, suffering 393 casualties but drawing enough rebel fire to enable Terry's soldiers to take the fort from the other side. Smaller forts upriver fell after Fort Fisher, and in February 1865 Wilmington surrendered.[63]

Porter ended the war as the victor of Wilmington, but only after spending most of the conflict on the Mississippi, commanding the river squadron from October 1862 to October 1864 as it slowly took control of the Mississippi and other western rivers of the Confederacy, isolating Texas, Arkansas and

Louisiana from the other rebel states for the second half of the war. Earlier, Porter's predecessor, Captain Andrew Hull Foote, used the 'city class' armoured gunboats and the converted iron-clad *Benton* to support General Ulysses S. Grant's army at Fort Henry on the Tennessee River (6 February 1862) and Fort Donelson on the Cumberland River (13–16 February 1862). While Fort Henry surrendered to Foote before Grant's troops arrived, Fort Donelson drove off his squadron and surrendered only after being besieged by Grant. At Fort Donelson the flag-ship *St Louis* took 59 hits, one of which gave Foote the wound that forced him to leave his post three months later. In the meantime, he directed his ironclads in the reduction of Island No. 10 on the Mississippi (16 March–7 April), and sent timber-clads up the Tennessee River to support Grant at the Battle of Shiloh (6–7 April). Promoted to rear admiral in July 1862 along with Farragut and Du Pont, he saw no further action before dying the following year. Commander Charles H. Davis, the interim squadron chief, lost the ironclads *Cincinnati* and *Mound City* (both later repaired) in a skirmish with an unarmoured Confederate squadron on the Mississippi at Fort Pillow (10 May), but later routed the same enemy squadron in forcing the surrender of Memphis (6 June).[64] The retreating rebels destroyed one of the two ironclads under construction there but saved the css *Arkansas*, which entered service in July. The *Arkansas* remained active only until August, when it was scuttled after engaging the Union tinclad *Essex* during a Confederate attempt to recapture Baton Rouge. After taking over from Davis, Porter did not have to contend with another Confederate ironclad, while ultimately eight side-wheel ironclads joined the *Benton* and the surviving 'city class' gunboats in his own force. During Grant's Vicksburg campaign, the navy lost the river ironclad *Cairo* to a mine in the Yazoo River and the paddle steamer uss *Mississippi* (sent up from the Gulf by Farragut) to Confederate batteries at Port Hudson. The fall of Vicksburg on 4 July 1863 and Port Hudson five days later left Union forces in control of the entire length of the Mississippi, cutting the Confederacy in half.[65] The navy did not fare as well in Porter's Red River campaign (March–May 1864), which had as its goal the capture of Shreveport, in northwest Louisiana, for use as a

12 The Union screw sloop USS *Kearsage* and the Confederate raider CSS *Alabama* duel off Cherbourg, 19 June 1864.

base of operations for an invasion of Texas. Porter took his flotilla 300 miles (480 kilometres) up the winding river but had to turn back, 100 miles from his objective, when the Union army retreated. The shallow river posed a greater obstacle than resistance from the Confederates. Falling late spring water levels threatened to strand the gunboats on the retreat, and some of his ironclads made it out only after their armour was removed to lighten their draught.[66] Union control of the Mississippi and other western rivers caused the region's plantation culture to break down, just as it had earlier around Union enclaves on the South Atlantic coast. The waterways became magnets for runaway slaves, and the navy's river steamers towed thousands to freedom aboard commandeered boats and barges.[67]

In the war on the high seas, the CSS *Alabama* was the most successful Confederate raider, in two years sinking or capturing 69 ships, including the armed merchantman *Hatteras*. In a slightly longer career the CSS *Florida* sank or captured 37 ships, and three 'satellite' cruisers it armed took 21 more. On 19 June 1864 the screw sloop *Kearsarge*, commanded by Captain John Winslow, a Union loyalist from North Carolina, sank the *Alabama*, commanded by Semmes, of Maryland, in a 90-minute battle off Cherbourg (illus. 12). On 31 October 1864 Captain Napoleon Collins's screw sloop *Wachusett* ended the career of the *Florida* by capturing it in a surprise attack in the neutral harbour of Bahia,

Brazil; instead of rewarding him for his ingenuity, the navy subsequently dismissed Collins from the service for violating
international law.[68] The next most successful Confederate raiders
managed to conclude their careers without being captured or
destroyed. On its only cruise, setting out from and returning to
Wilmington in August 1864, John Taylor Wood's iron-hulled css
Tallahassee captured 33 ships in just ten days. Under the name css
Olustee, the same raider destroyed another six ships on a second
cruise later that year, before being converted to a blockade
runner. The css *Shenandoah* likewise completed just one cruise,
but it was the longest by any Confederate warship, an eastward
circumnavigation of the globe from October 1864 to November
1865, starting and ending in Britain. Its 38 victims included 25
New England whalers, sunk in the north Pacific between April
and June 1865, after the collapse of the Confederacy but before
its commander, James Waddell, received word that the war had
ended.[69] The Confederate navy's raiders captured or sank 259
sailing ships but only two steamers. Their greatest impact came in
the flight of American shipowners to foreign flags, with 715 ships
being transferred to the British merchant marine alone. In comparison, the us navy inflicted far greater losses on Confederate
blockade runners, capturing or sinking 295 steamers and 1,189
sailing ships.[70] The Confederacy's use of commerce raiders built
in Britain and manned by British crews further strained an Anglo-
American relationship damaged earlier in the war when the screw
sloop uss *San Jacinto* stopped the British steamer *Trent* on the
high seas (8 November 1861) and removed two Confederate
agents headed for Britain. The British demanded the release of
the agents no later than 30 December 1861, and the us government heightened tensions by not complying until 27 December.
During the brief 'Trent affair' the British reinforced their garrison
in Canada from 7,000 troops to 17,500, and sent roughly one-
quarter of their fleet (almost 50 warships manned by 15,000
seamen, including six screw ships of the line) to their North
American and West Indies station. Anglo-American relations
remained tense until 1871, when Britain agreed to pay the United
States a sum to be determined by arbitration (ultimately $15.5
million) for damages inflicted by British-built Confederate
raiders.[71]

On land, the American Civil War remained very much in doubt until the summer of 1863 and was still undecided until the summer of 1864. At sea, in contrast, the Union from the start systematically tightened the noose on the rebel states. Its blockade of the southern coast grew increasingly stronger, and the Confederacy was gradually starved of the materials it needed to continue the war. Not everything the Union navy attempted actually worked – it could not force its way into Charleston harbour, or take and hold Galveston, or ascend the Red River to Shreveport – but in general, it did what it needed to do, in a deliberate but timely fashion, to win the war and preserve the Union. Just as the toll taken by the US navy against Confederate blockade runners far surpassed the damage done by Confederate raiders against the US merchant marine, the US navy brought about the destruction of the Confederate navy while losing very few warships of its own. Aside from the ill-designed *Keokuk*, sunk by coastal artillery, the only Union ironclads destroyed by Confederate action (four monitors and three armoured river gunboats) all fell victim to mines. The only others sunk (the original *Monitor* and the monitor *Weehawken*) were claimed by storms. The Union also lost very few of its next-most valuable warships, wooden screw steamers. After abandoning the screw frigate *Merrimack* in the Norfolk Navy Yard in April 1861, the US navy lost only the screw sloop *Housatonic*, sunk by the submarine *Hunley*. Confederate warships sank no Union ironclads, and (aside from the *Hunley*) none managed to sink an unarmoured steamer larger than a gunboat. Of the 22 operational Confederate ironclads, the US navy only sank one – the CSS *Albemarle* – but captured another four and, in league with advancing US army troops, forced the Confederates to destroy the rest.[72]

Like Brazil and the other Latin American naval powers, in the nineteenth century the United States rarely maintained more than the minimum naval force it needed to defend its interests. During the American Civil War, the US navy assembled a fleet impressive in sheer numbers of warships and in firepower, but tailored for the specific tasks of blockading the southern coast and hunting down rebel blockade runners and commerce raiders. Thus, it had relatively little value as a fighting force against other leading navies; indeed, almost all of the ironclads were shallow-draught monitors incapable of action on the high seas. As soon as the Confederacy was defeated, the navy, like the army, quickly demobilized to a peacetime footing somewhat larger than the pre-war level but still much smaller than the wartime force. Two ironclads were sold to France and two to Peru; most of the rest were laid up and, aside from a few mobilized for coastal defence during the Spanish-American War (1898), none served long into the postwar era.[73] Ericsson claimed that the laid-up Civil War monitors, if properly maintained, would last fifty years. Indeed, the last were not scrapped until after 1900, but the dizzying technological revolution of the first decade of the armoured warship did not suddenly stop after 1865, and most of them were obsolete within a few years of the end of the war.[74]

Two decades passed before the United States, in the 1880s, began to construct a modern navy, mostly in response to developments elsewhere in the western hemisphere. In the meantime, the us navy very rapidly returned to being a force of modest size, incapable of offensive action against even the weakest of the great powers of Europe. As the force shrank, the industrial base that had built the fleet of monitors likewise evaporated; none of the Ohio River shipyards survived, and many of the northeast shipyards failed as well.[75] The us navy's achievement of 1861–5 may have been ephemeral and, given a greater degree of interservice co-operation (still a problem in the United States in the twenty-first century), the Civil War might have been won sooner. But if the navy had not assembled a force capable of blockading the southern states, seizing control of their rivers and containing the rebel government's efforts on the high seas, the Union most likely would not have been preserved. Through the imposition of the blockade and worldwide vigilance against all who would help the Confederate cause, the us navy made it too risky for the leading European powers to extend to the Confederacy the diplomatic recognition and military aid critical to its survival.

FIVE

By Reason or by Force:
The Chilean Navy, 1879–92

In the 1870s Peru supported Bolivia in a dispute with Chile over nitrate deposits discovered in the coastal Atacama Desert, where Chilean companies did most of the mining in an area in which international borders had remained ill-defined. Reflecting its national motto 'by reason or by force', when Chile failed to secure its interests by peaceful means it fought for them, and emerged victorious in the War of the Pacific (1879–84). While the contested nitrate-rich provinces remained central to the campaigns in this 'saltpetre war', the naval action ranged along the entire 4,500-mile (7,240-kilometre) Pacific coast of South America, justifying the formal designation of the conflict. Chile's triumph brought a significant expansion of its territory, elevating it to the first rank of regional powers with Brazil and Argentina, and forever altering the balance of power within South America. The rise of the Chilean navy also had broader implications for the western hemisphere. By the end of the War of the Pacific it had three armoured warships more formidable than any vessel in the US navy, a development that, combined with the acquisition of modern battleships by Brazil and Argentina, helped inspire the United States to lay down its first modern steel warships in 1883.

THE REVIVAL OF THE CHILEAN FLEET

As Bernardo O'Higgins surveyed the field of battle at Chacabuco in 1817, where he had joined forces with José de San Martín to secure the independence of Chile in a decisive victory over the Spanish army, he declared that 'this triumph and a hundred more will be insignificant if we do not control the sea.'[1] As founding president of the Chilean republic, O'Higgins subsequently hired Lord Cochrane to serve as vice admiral and commander of the Chilean navy. Under Cochrane's direction (1818–22) the navy played a central role in the Latin American Wars for Independence, chasing the Spanish fleet from the Pacific coast of South America and ferrying San Martín's patriot army from Chile to Peru, facilitating the conquest of the last stronghold of Spanish colonial rule on the continent. On the eve of Cochrane's departure for Brazil in 1822, Chile had a fleet including one ship of the line, three frigates, three corvettes and three brigs. But the resignation of O'Higgins in 1823 ushered in lean years for the Chilean navy, just as the abdication of Dom Pedro I would for the navy of Brazil. His successors did not share his vision of Chilean sea power, and by 1826, with the Spanish threat eliminated, the navy retained just one brig in active service. Thereafter Chile followed what became the Latin American custom of never maintaining more warships than were absolutely necessary to defend its interests within the region. The Chilean navy remobilized for a war against a hostile confederation of Peru and Bolivia (1836–9), ultimately growing to include a frigate, three corvettes and six smaller vessels, which enabled it to command the sea and transport an army from Chile to Peru, forcing the dissolution of the confederation. But afterward the navy once again practically disbanded, maintaining only two schooners in active service. During the subsequent years of peace the navy remained small; its first screw steamers, the corvette *Esmeralda* (completed 1855) and gunboat *Maipú* (1857), both built in Britain, were the only active warships when Chile joined Peru in a war against Spain (1864–6). The Spanish took advantage of the American Civil War to demand that Peru repay debts dating from the colonial era, and overawed the combined Peruvian-Chilean squadron with a force ultimately including the armoured frigate *Numancia* (the first ironclad to circumnavigate the globe), five unarmoured frigates and two gunboats. Ironically the Spanish suffered the war's only loss of a warship, the screw schooner *Covadonga*, captured in 1865 by the Chilean navy, which subse-

13 The Chilean screw corvette *Abtao* (1865).

quently commissioned it as a replacement for the discarded *Maipú*. Spain gave up the fight (as France did in Mexico) only under pressure from the United States following the defeat of the Confederacy, and only after having its squadron bombard Callao, Peru, and Valparaíso, Chile, before departing.[2]

The material foundations of the Chilean and Peruvian fleets of the War of the Pacific were laid during the war against Spain, when the allies took decisive steps to remedy their naval weakness. British shipyards built the 3,500-ton armoured frigate *Independencia* and the 2,030-ton ironclad turret ship *Huáscar* for Peru, and laid down the screw corvettes *O'Higgins* and *Chacabuco* for Chile. Each of the allies also bought screw corvettes originally laid down as raiders for the Confederate States: Peru, two in France, and Chile, two in Britain. The *Independencia* and *Huáscar* reached the Pacific in 1866, shortly after the Spanish squadron departed. Of the four would-be Confederate raiders, the two purchased by Peru arrived in time to see action in the war, as did the Chilean *Abtao* (illus. 13), while the fourth ship, the *Pampero*, was captured at Madeira by the Spanish navy shortly after leaving Britain for Chile. To save money, the Chilean government suspended construction on the *O'Higgins* and *Chacabuco* once the war ended. But as soon as the Spanish threat subsided, relations between Chile and Peru began to deteriorate. Chilean miners discovered saltpetre near the Bolivian port of Antofagasta, raising the stakes in an old dispute over the exact location of the borders between the desert provinces of Chile, Bolivia and Peru. In 1868 Peru further augmented its fleet with the single-turret monitors *Atahualpa* (ex-*Catawba*) and *Manco Capac* (ex-*Oneota*), purchased from the United States, but protested when Chile finally completed the purchase of the *O'Higgins* and *Chacabuco*, delivered the same year. Thereafter, diplomacy did little but raise false hopes for a peaceful solution. In 1872 Chile and Bolivia agreed to a border at the 24th parallel (24°s latitude), just south of Antofagasta, and under an 1874 treaty Bolivia agreed not to raise taxes on Chilean companies mining between the 23rd parallel and 24th parallel for a period of 25 years. Meanwhile, in 1873 Bolivia concluded a secret anti-Chilean alliance with Peru, and in 1874 the Peruvian government dealt a blow to Chilean miners in its own desert provinces of Tacna and Tarapacá by nationalizing all nitrate deposits there. Amid the confusion, in 1872 the Chilean congress authorized the construction in British shipyards of the composite-hulled screw corvette *Magallanes* and the 3,370-ton casemate ships *Cochrane* and *Valparaíso* (later renamed *Blanco Encalada*), designed by Edward Reed. The *Cochrane* and *Magallanes* reached Chile by the end of 1874, the *Blanco Encalada* early in 1876. The arrival of the new warships inspired Peru to conclude a friendship treaty with Chile later in 1876. This development, together with the 1874 Chilean-Bolivian treaty and economic problems stemming from the worldwide depression of 1873, led the Chilean government to the premature conclusion that the new ironclads were not needed. During the Russo-Turkish War (1877–8) the *Cochrane* and *Blanco Encalada* were offered for sale to both Russia and Turkey, as well as to Britain, which wanted to block their sale to Russia. At the same time, Chile made overtures to Argentina to resolve their age-old Andean border dispute. Bolivia and Peru interpreted these initiatives as signs of weakness and became bolder in their own policies toward Chile.[3]

In February 1878 Bolivia placed a new export tax on saltpetre, violating the Chilean-Bolivian treaty of 1874 and threatening the profitability of the Compañía de Salitres y Ferrocarril de Antofagasta, a Chilean railway and nitrate mining firm with investment capital equalling £1 million. After the company refused to pay the tax, in January 1879 the Bolivian government confiscated its assets, which were to be sold at auction on 14 February. That morning, the casemate ships *Blanco Encalada* and *Cochrane* and the screw corvette *O'Higgins* anchored in the bay of Antofagasta and landed 800 troops, more than enough to secure the city of 8,500 residents, three-quarters of whom were of Chilean nationality.[4] Bolivia protested at the occupation and appealed to Peru for help. The War of the Pacific had begun, but the Chilean navy was not in fighting trim. Lack of money for operations and maintenance left even the five latest acquisitions in poor condition by early 1879. The two ironclads needed to have their hulls cleaned and their boilers and engines serviced, while the corvettes *Magallanes*, *Chacabuco* and *O'Higgins*, the next-newest warships, all needed new boilers.[5] The older screw corvettes *Esmeralda* and *Abtao* and the screw schooner *Covadonga* were in worse shape, capable of only 3–5 knots under steam. Fortunately for Chile, the Peruvian navy was in little better condition. Like the Chilean casemate ships, the Peruvian ironclads *Huáscar* and *Independencia* had boiler and engine problems, which reduced their speed to 11–13 knots. Neglect and inactivity had taken its toll on the *Manco Capac* and *Atahualpa*, which were capable of just 4 knots and, as mastless monitors, useful only for harbour defence. The screw corvette *Unión* (one of the ex-Confederate raiders) and screw gunboat *Pilcomayo* (built in Britain in the mid-1870s) were Peru's most formidable unarmoured warships.[6]

Inland fighting between Chile and Peru continued until July 1883, and between Chile and Bolivia until April 1884, but the naval campaign of the War of the Pacific ended in January 1881, when the Peruvian naval base at Callao fell along with the capital city of Lima. In the 23 months of action at sea, the Chilean navy captured the *Huáscar* and forced the sinking or scuttling of the remaining three Peruvian ironclads. The unarmoured *Pilcomayo* was also captured. The Peruvian navy sank Chile's oldest screw steamers, the *Esmeralda* and *Covadonga*, along with an armed transport. In the course of the fighting both navies introduced flotillas of torpedo boats (in Chile's case, twelve boats built in Britain in 1880–81), and each lost one of the small craft in action. During the war Peru attempted to purchase armoured warships in Europe, but its options were limited. Aside from Austria-Hungary, which had three casemate ships roughly the same size as Chile's *Blanco Encalada* and *Cochrane*, the options all were either too small, too large or too old (the last including the first armoured frigate, France's *Gloire*, decommissioned in 1879). Captain Luis Lynch of the Chilean navy headed a special wartime mission based in Paris that, in league with Chilean diplomats, successfully tracked and foiled Peruvian attempts to buy ironclads. Aside from a few torpedo boats, no naval vessels purchased abroad by Peru made it to the Pacific in time to see action in the war. Peru ultimately bought the 1,700-ton unarmoured cruiser *Lima*, a merchantman converted in Britain in 1881, which became the flagship of its small postwar navy. For the next quarter-century it remained Peru's largest warship.[7]

The Chilean navy of the early 1880s may have been insignificant by European standards, but the destruction of the Peruvian fleet and the addition of the *Huáscar* to the *Blanco Encalada* and *Cochrane* at least temporarily made Chile the most formidable naval power in the western hemisphere. Indeed, Chile's naval strength enabled it to disregard the pro-Peruvian sentiments of the United States throughout the War of the Pacific and to reject an 1882 American mediation effort pushing for a peace without annexations. In March 1884 one Ohio congressman noted that the US navy had 'not one ship . . . that could stand fifteen minutes against any one of the three great Chilean war vessels.' According to Rear Admiral John Worden, who as a lieutenant had commanded the *Monitor* at Hampton Roads in 1862, by the end of the War of the Pacific 'the Chilean navy could have stood three miles beyond the range of the best guns we have . . . at the Golden Gate, and dropped 500 pound shells into the heart of San Francisco'. Throughout the decade comparative references to the naval power of Chile dominated a debate in the United States over the need for a stronger fleet, inspiring appropriations

14 The Chilean protected cruiser *Esmeralda* (1884).

for the construction of modern steel warships starting in 1883.[8] With the US navy still years away from restoring its own credibility as a fighting force, Chile engaged in a bit of 'gunboat diplomacy' of its own. In 1885, when relations between the United States and Colombia reached a boiling point over issues related to the province of Panama, where a French company had begun work on a canal, the Chilean government sent the navy's newest warship, the protected cruiser *Esmeralda* (illus. 14), to the Panamanian coast as a sign of solidarity with the Colombians.[9] After having owned islands as far as 400 miles (640 kilometres) offshore since independence, in September 1888 Chile sent the armed transport *Angamos* (Captain Policarpo Toro) to assert a claim to Easter Island, 2,350 miles (3,800 kilometres) west of the Chilean coast. Ambitious Chileans even dreamed of inheriting the Philippines from Spain. Thus, the postwar Chilean navy appeared destined for a greater significance not just in the South American balance of power, but within the second rank of the world's naval powers.

During the war Chile ordered two cruisers from Armstrong's Elswick shipyard, to be named after the lost corvette *Esmeralda* and its heroic captain, Arturo Prat. Both vessels had steel hulls, no side armour, impressive speed (16.5 knots) and a heavy primary armament (two 10-inch guns), a combination that captured the imagination of cruiser advocates in the subsequent era of the Jeune Ecole. While the 1,350-ton *Arturo Prat* had a nominal rigging and no armour at all, the 3,000-ton *Esmeralda* had two military masts, an armoured deck and some armour protecting its guns, making it the prototype for the protected cruiser of the late nineteenth century and the early twentieth. The *Arturo Prat* (laid down 1879, launched 1880) was not ready for delivery until June 1883, the same month that the 3,000-ton *Esmeralda* (laid down 1881) was launched. With the naval campaign of the War of the Pacific long over, the Chilean government decided to sell the *Arturo Prat* to Japan (where it became the *Tsukushi*) and await delivery of the more formidable *Esmeralda*. Within months of the *Esmeralda's* arrival in 1884, the *Blanco Encalada* went to Britain for a complete overhaul, followed by the *Cochrane*, which returned to service early in 1887. Both received new boilers and a new armament of 8-inch Armstrong breech loading rifles. The *Huáscar*, rearmed with the same new Armstrong ordnance in 1880, received a steam winch for its turret in 1885.[10]

As Chile enhanced its naval strength, Brazil, which already had the largest navy in Latin America, continued to lead the region in armoured warship acquisitions with the 5,610-ton *Riachuelo* (launched 1883) and 4,920-ton *Aquidaba* (1885), both built in Britain, but the fall of the monarchy in 1889 brought smaller budgets and harder times for the Brazilian navy. By then Argentina had emerged as Chile's strongest naval rival. After purchasing its first ironclads, two small coastal defence monitors (1874), the Argentinian navy subsequently acquired the 4,200-ton casemate ship *Almirante Brown* (1880), two small coastal battleships, two protected cruisers, eight small gunboats and twenty-two torpedo boats. The Argentinian build-up coincided with tensions over the Chilean-Argentinian border in the Andes, which had been resolved in principle in 1878 and by treaty in 1881, only to re-emerge in the actual demarcation of the boundary.[11] Chile did not shrink from the competition. Indeed, the first president elected after the War of the Pacific, José Manuel Balmaceda (term 1886–91), made sure the Chilean army and navy received their share of the mineral wealth they had conquered. By 1890 the annual budget was 3.4 times larger

15 The Chilean battleship *Capitán Prat* (1893).

than it had been in 1875, and export duties (mostly on nitrates) accounted for almost three-quarters of the national income. Given the surplus of revenue in Chile and the progress of re-armament in Argentina, Balmaceda saw no reason to allow the armed forces to return to their normal state of peacetime neglect. He retained a German military adviser to modernize the army, ordered the latest Krupp artillery for shore batteries at the naval bases of Valparaíso and Talcahuano (near Concepción), and in 1887 persuaded the Chilean congress to appropriate the equivalent of £400,000 over a three-year period for the purchase of new warships abroad. Naval spending rose from 4.5 per cent of the national budget in 1887 to 11.2 per cent in 1889, and Balmaceda sent a special naval mission to Paris to co-ordinate the spending spree. Projects funded included three launched in France in 1890: the 6,900-ton battleship *Capitán Prat* (illus. 15) and the 2,050-ton protected cruisers *Presidente Errázuriz* (illus. 16) and *Presidente Pinto*, along with two copies of the British navy's revolutionary torpedo gunboat *Sharpshooter*, the 710-ton *Almirante Lynch* (1889) and *Almirante Condell* (1889), built in Britain.[12] While these ships were still under construction the navy, or at least most of it, supported the leaders of the Chilean congress in a rebellion against

16 The Chilean protected cruiser *Presidente Errázuriz* (1892).

Balmaceda, on the grounds that he had violated the constitution by expanding the powers of the executive at the expense of the legislature. The Civil War of 1891 divided the personnel of the fleet as well as its ships. The split was particularly traumatic for career officers who had enjoyed unprecedented professional advancement and public acclaim as a result of the navy's performance in the War of the Pacific.

'CONQUER OR DIE': PERSONNEL AND THEIR TRAINING

Balmaceda's decree of April 1890, assigning names to the new warships, also authorized the motto 'Vencer o Morir' (Conquer or Die) to be displayed aboard all Chilean naval vessels. Eventually it became the official motto of the service, ironically bestowed by a president the navy had helped overthrow.[13] The Civil War of 1891 and subsequent installation of a naval officer, Jorge Montt, as president of the republic broke two trends that had made Chile relatively unique among the countries of Latin America: the government changed by force of arms for the only time in a period of 94 years (1830 to 1924), and a serving officer rather than a civilian occupied the presidency. Chile also had a strong tradition of civilian control over the army and navy, reflected in the leadership triumvirate of the minister of war and navy, commandant general of the navy and squadron commander. While the commander, of course, was always a high ranking naval officer and usually the senior officer in the service, the minister was usually a civilian (though sometimes a soldier) and the commandant general often was either a civilian or a soldier. From 1818 to 1885, civilians served as commandant general for a total of 28 years, army officers for 23 years (though not after 1860) and naval officers for just 17. Among the naval officers in the post, the longest-serving were Cochrane's second-in-command from the War for Independence, Manuel Blanco Encalada, who held it from 1818 to 1821 and again from 1847 to 1852, and Robert Simpson, who rose from being one of Cochrane's British midshipmen to hold it three times between 1843 and 1853. The commandant general supervised the naval administration and handled logistical matters but had no control over the commander of the active squadron. The same was not true of the minister for war and navy. On at least two crucial occasions, strong civilian ministers were involved directly in planning and directing naval operations: Diego Portales at the onset of the war of 1836–9, and Rafael Sotomayor during the first half of the War of the Pacific. Sent north to the war zone by the president to keep an eye on the generals and admirals, Sotomayor supervised every detail of the navy's war effort in 1879–80, assigning and replacing squadron commanders and even warship captains, and meddling in the plotting of strategy. Postwar changes gave the navy a greater degree of political independence and operational freedom from civilian micro-management. In 1887 Balmaceda divided the ministry into separate war and navy ministries, and from 1886 onward naval officers at the rank of rear admiral filled the post of commandant general. In 1897 the latter gave way to the new post of director general, which former president Jorge Montt, armed with the rank of vice admiral, occupied until his retirement in 1913, functioning as a true naval commander-in-chief.[14]

Over the six decades between the War for Independence and the War of the Pacific, the Chilean navy struggled to train and maintain a cadre of competent officers and seamen. The age of sail afforded Chile the luxury of applying a 'militia' concept to its fleet, keeping very few warships and personnel in service until a crisis justified a temporary expansion, then reducing the numbers again as soon as peace returned. Given the overall tendency of Latin American countries to maintain minimal naval forces in peacetime, such an approach was feasible, but when it survived into the age of steam and armour plate it placed unrealistic expectations on the small career cadre responsible for leading the service in wartime. The navy's uneven performance in the war against Spain (1864–6) and at the onset of the War of the Pacific in 1879 demonstrated that the traditional policy could have dire consequences. Fortunately for Chile, the Naval School produced a generation of gifted officers who came of age just in time to assume leadership roles during and after the war. Their professionalism, leadership ability and, in some cases, heroism made the difference between victory and defeat.

The first Chilean naval academy dated from 1818, when O'Higgins established the Academy of Young Midshipmen (Academia de Jóvenes Guardias Marinas) at Valparaíso. It operated intermittently over the years that followed, during which time the most promising young officers and officer candidates were placed with foreign navies. These included Patricio Lynch and José Galvarino Riveros, both admirals during the War of the Pacific. Lynch, a teenaged midshipman in the war of 1836–9, served in the British navy from 1840 to 1847 and saw action in China during the First Opium War, while Riveros embarked in 1849 for an extended cruise with the French navy. This system did not work particularly well, since officers who had 'seen the world' aboard the larger warships of a leading navy had great difficulty adjusting to the circumstances of naval service in Chile after their return. In 1847 the Chilean naval academy closed altogether, and for the next eleven years most aspiring naval officers were educated alongside army cadets at the Military School (Escuela Militar) in Santiago, their studies on land supplemented from 1848 by cruises aboard the training ship *Chile*. During the same years some young men were simply taken on as midshipmen by Chilean warship commanders, as in the traditional British or American practice. These included

Luis Lynch, who as a teenager served aboard two schooners commanded by his older brother Patricio, following his return to Chile from British service.[15]

In August 1858 a new Naval School (Escuela Naval) opened in Valparaíso, offering a three-year curriculum. The first instructors were two hired French officers, Jean Feillet and Anatole Desmadryl. Students were designated cadets while at the school, and received the rank of midshipman upon graduation. The initial cohort entering in 1858, 26 young men known in Chilean history as 'the class of the heroes', included five of the most prominent figures of the War of the Pacific: Arturo Prat, Juan José Latorre, Carlos Condell, Luis Uribe and Jorge Montt. While the school typically admitted boys aged ten to twelve, older boys and young men were accepted, leading to a considerable range of ages among cadets. In the entering class of 1858 Prat (at ten) was the youngest and Condell (at fifteen) among the oldest. Another future hero of the War of the Pacific, Ernesto Riquelme, entered in 1874 when aged 22, after earning a bachelor's degree at the Instituto Nacional in Santiago. Such differences in age at time of entry meant that, by the time of the War of the Pacific, officers with a variety of ages and levels of experience could be found at virtually every rank. Prat became a second lieutenant at seventeen, after his baptism of fire in the war against Spain, and rose three more ranks to become a *Capitán de Fragata* (equivalent of Commander in the British or American navies) at age 29, while Riquelme was still a midshipman when he died at age 27.[16]

Initially the Naval School curriculum involved classroom instruction ashore and shipboard experience aboard the paddle steamer *Independencia* and the navy's two screw steamers, *Esmeralda* and *Maipú*. When the latter ship was discarded after the war with Spain, the *Esmeralda* became the primary training vessel. In 1870 the school closed and its cadets were sent to the Military School in Santiago, which henceforth was to serve as a common academy for the Chilean armed forces. The experiment lasted just one year, and the Naval School reopened in February 1871 with all classroom instruction as well as practical training held aboard ship in Valparaíso harbour. The 900-ton screw steamer *Valdivia* (ex-*Henriette*), which had been purchased and armed in Britain during the war against Spain, functioned briefly as the school ship before the role passed in April 1871 to the *Esmeralda*. The old corvette continued to serve the cadets until 1876, when the Chilean government, facing a budget crisis stemming from the depression of 1873, closed both the Naval School and the Military School. At that point the navy mustered all of its cadets straight into the fleet as midshipmen.[17]

At the onset of the War of the Pacific the government decided to reopen the Military School, with effect from March 1879, but the Naval School did not reopen until shortly after the naval campaign against Peru ended in January 1881. During the war a few future naval officers began their studies at the Military School, then transferred to the Naval School in 1881, but most applied directly to the navy for placement with the fleet and, if accepted, were designated 'aspirants' until their promotion to midshipmen. Amid the fervour of wartime patriotism, a number of teenaged schoolboys and university dropouts embarked upon naval careers in this manner. After reopening in 1881 the Naval School continued its three-year curriculum, with the academic year typically commencing in March, around the start of the southern autumn, and ending in December, around the start of summer. In the postwar years most entering cadets were fourteen or fifteen years old, but well into the twentieth century the school continued to enrol boys as young as thirteen. The Civil War of 1891 disrupted instruction but only for that year, and in 1893 the school moved into new permanent quarters in Valparaíso (in the buildings that, since 1967, have housed the Naval and Maritime Museum of Chile). By the early 1890s the introduction of longer training cruises for cadets usually extended the training period into a fourth or fifth year.[18]

Chile was the first country in Latin America to introduce a universal military service obligation, but not until 1900. Even thereafter, the navy remained virtually an all-volunteer force, as it had been since the founding of the republic in 1818.[19] For the first half-century of its existence the navy recruited its common manpower under the traditional British-style hire-and-discharge system, which allowed the greatest flexibility for a service maintaining few active warships in peacetime. Chile's

Apprentice Seamen's School (forerunner of the later Escuela de Grumetes) opened in 1869 at Valparaíso aboard the screw steamer *Valdivia*. The three-year training course initially accepted boys aged ten to fourteen; in 1873 the navy shortened the course to two years and raised the age limits for admission from fourteen to eighteen. When the cost-cutting measures of 1876 temporarily closed the Naval School, the Apprentice Seamen's School survived in reduced form, its enrolment (which had exceeded 60 boys in the early 1870s) limited to 50. At the outbreak of the War of the Pacific the navy closed the school and dispersed the boys among the ships of the fleet. During the war years apprentice seamen applied directly to the navy for placement aboard warships, just as boys of a higher social status and educational background applied for placement as officer aspirants. While the education of officer candidates returned to normal with the reopening of the Naval School in 1881, the Apprentice Seamen's School did not reopen until 1887. That year the navy acquired the sailing bark *Almirante Simpson* for use as a school ship at Talcahuano, and two years later bought the sailing frigate *Domingo Santa Maria* as a school ship at Valparaíso. Throughout the nineteenth century, as wooden sailing warships gave way to iron and steel warships powered by steam, even the leading navies continued to use wooden sailing vessels as training ships for cadets and apprentice seamen; ironically the Chilean navy, which had not used a sailing ship for training purposes since the founding of the Naval School in 1858, acquired the *Almirante Simpson* and *Domingo Santa Maria* at a time when most other navies were phasing theirs out. In the twentieth century the navy continued to use sailing ships to train seamen, sporadically until the acquisition of the four-masted bark *Esmeralda* (built 1946–54), which was still taking cadets and apprentice seamen on annual training cruises early in the twenty-first century. After reopening in the late 1880s the Apprentice Seamen's School operated separate schools at Talcahuano (designated 'No. 1') and Valparaíso ('No. 2'), but in 1907 the navy consolidated the training effort at Talcahuano, which became its permanent site.[20]

In the wake of the War of the Pacific, the Chilean navy established a number of specialized schools for the education and training of its officers and seamen, their creation reflecting the prevailing international trend of greater professionalization at a time when naval service was becoming increasingly complex. The Mechanics' School (Escuela de Mecánicos), founded in 1889, the Pilots' School (Escuela de Pilotines), established in 1890, and the Artillery and Torpedo School (Escuela de Artillería y Torpedos), founded in 1892, each served a special need for Chile's growing navy. The Pilots' School doubled as a merchant marine academy, educating officers for civilian maritime service while also serving as a training institute for the navy's own navigators. The Artillery and Torpedo School, created in the heyday of the Jeune Ecole, reflected a strong French influence. In the late 1880s the navy hired French engineers to serve on its faculty, but the Civil War of 1891 delayed its formal founding until the following year. The navy also operated an Office of Hydrography and Navigation, established in 1874, which among other functions oversaw the navy's efforts to map the fragmented coastline and rivers of the south of Chile.[21]

In the years before the War of the Pacific the Chilean navy maintained a peacetime force so small that it could be staffed by around 650 officers and seamen.[22] By the end of the naval war against Peru in 1881, it took roughly 2,000 officers and seamen to man the active warships of the fleet. Owing to the size and number of new warships acquired over the ensuing decade, by the early 1890s the peacetime stand of active manpower afloat would be just as large. At least one historian has emphasized that 'Chile had to hire foreigners to man its fleet' in 1879,[23] but there is little evidence of a wholesale reliance upon non-Chilean manpower to staff the rapidly expanding force of that year. Rosters of crews from May 1879 show relatively few non-Spanish surnames: just five of the 198 men aboard the *Esmeralda* (including First Engineer Edward Hyatt, an American from Cincinnati, Ohio) and four of 116 aboard the *Covadonga*.[24] Of course one cannot assume an English surname to mean that the officer or seaman was a foreign hireling or recent immigrant from Britain or the United States. Of the large numbers of foreigners who fought in the South American navies in the Wars for Independence, some settled permanently in their adopted countries and became the forefathers of naval families, sending generations of officers and seamen into the service. At the highest level, two of Robert Simpson's sons also became admirals, and Juan Williams Rebolledo (squadron commander in 1879 and commandant general of the navy on the eve of the Civil War of 1891) was the son of John Williams, also known as Juan Guillermos, a British officer in Chilean service during the War for Independence. Throughout the nineteenth century, and the twentieth as well, the presence within the officer corps of at least a minority of men with British heritage reinforced the Chilean navy's adoption of the British navy as its role model. Indeed, the surnames and maternal surnames (*apellidos maternos*) of Chilean admirals on active service in 2003 indicate that at least one-third (8 of 27) had some British heritage.[25]

FROM THE WAR OF THE PACIFIC TO THE CIVIL WAR OF 1891

After opening the War of the Pacific by using the casemate ships *Cochrane* and *Blanco Encalada* and the screw corvette *O'Higgins* to help secure Antofagasta, squadron commander Rear Admiral Williams Rebolledo landed troops north of the 23rd parallel at the smaller ports of Cobija and Tocopilla, and on 23 March 1879 took Calama, Bolivia's last outpost on the Pacific Ocean. By early April, after Peru committed its army and navy to the defence of Bolivia, Williams moved up the coast to blockade Iquique, main port of the Peruvian province of Tarapacá. The two navies spent the first month of the war convoying troops, the Chileans from Valparaíso north to Antofagasta, the Peruvians from Callao to Arica, main port of the province of Tacna and their southernmost unblockaded port. Meanwhile, Chilean warships continued to blockade Iquique in between. After escorting troops to Arica, the Peruvian ironclads *Independencia* and *Huáscar* continued south to challenge the Chilean blockade of Iquique, then the landings at Antofagasta, en route passing (without encountering) most of the Chilean squadron, which Williams took north to disrupt the Peruvian convoys between Callao and Arica. Off Callao Williams learned that Peru had already transported its army to Arica and had sent the *Independencia* and *Huáscar* down the coast to Iquique, where he had left his oldest operational warships, the screw corvette *Esmeralda* and screw gunboat *Covadonga*, to maintain the blockade. Williams took his squadron back down the coast at full steam but was still en route on 21 May, when the two Peruvian ironclads fell upon the *Esmeralda* and *Covadonga* at Iquique.[26]

On the morning of 21 May 1879 the *Esmeralda* (Captain Arturo Prat) held its station at Iquique and engaged the *Huáscar* (Rear Admiral Miguel Grau) for three hours and forty minutes, taking a beating in order to enable the *Covadonga* (Captain Carlos Condell) to escape to the south, with the *Independencia* (Captain Guillermo Moore) giving chase. For much of the morning Prat positioned the *Esmeralda* between the *Huáscar* and the waterfront of the Peruvian city, forcing the ironclad's gunners to be extraordinarily careful in order to avoid killing their own countrymen with missed shots. Prat's strategy worked, at least until Peruvian forces ashore began peppering his ship with artillery and rifle fire. When the crossfire began to take its toll among his men, Prat made the fateful decision to leave his position, even though he had no hope of successfully breaking out of the harbour. Grau promptly closed with the *Huáscar* and rammed the *Esmeralda* three times, sinking it just after noon. In arguably the greatest act of bravado in a naval battle since John Paul Jones captured HMS *Serapis* from the stricken *Bonhomme Richard* a century earlier, Prat responded by ordering his crew to board the *Huáscar* from the deck of his sinking ship. He was killed on the deck of the Peruvian ironclad alongside a seaman who scrambled aboard with him; when Grau rammed the *Esmeralda* again, Lieutenant Ignacio Serrano and a second wave of a dozen borders met the same fate. Prat's second-in-command, Captain Luis Uribe, subsequently refused to strike his flag, and the *Esmeralda* sank with its colours still flying. Midshipman Enrique Riquelme continued to work one of the old corvette's guns until the very last, and was among those who perished with the ship. While the *Huáscar* lost just one of its crew in the battle, 148 of the *Esmeralda*'s 198 officers and seamen were killed; Uribe was among those pulled from the water, taken prisoner aboard the *Huáscar*, then turned over to the Peruvian garrison of Iquique. During the same hours an equally compelling drama unfolded down the coast from

Iquique, as the *Covadonga* steamed toward Antofagasta with the *Independencia* in hot pursuit. In the early afternoon off Punta Gruesa, the shallow-draught steamer passed safely over uncharted rocks, which trapped the much heavier Peruvian frigate. With the *Independencia* hard aground, Condell doubled back and placed the *Covadonga* across its bow, out of reach of its broadsides, and raked it repeatedly. The Peruvians returned fire with their deck rifle, but once its ammunition was exhausted Moore struck his flag. While the *Esmeralda*, an unarmoured ship whose captain refused to surrender, lost three-quarters of its crew that day, the *Independencia*, an ironclad that did haul down its colours, suffered just 5 killed and 18 wounded out of a crew of 300. The *Covadonga* lost 4 killed and 3 wounded out of 116. Shortly thereafter the *Huáscar* arrived to chase off the *Covadonga*, salvage the *Independencia*'s heavy guns and rescue the survivors. The battles of 21 May reduced by half the armoured strength of Peru's navy, while the valiant fight of the *Esmeralda* made Prat a national hero.[27]

Having secured a clear advantage at sea, Chile set about transporting more troops to the north for an eventual march on Lima. The war and navy minister, Sotomayor, appointed Rear Admiral Patricio Lynch to co-ordinate the effort, which the Peruvian navy sought to disrupt by using the *Huáscar* as a raider. Sometimes cruising alone, sometimes with the screw corvette *Unión*, the *Huáscar* could strike with impunity as long as neither of the two Chilean ironclads was in the vicinity. Admiral Grau developed an uncanny ability to evade them but had an early brush with disaster on the night of 9–10 July in the harbour at Iquique, where he had hoped to sink the Chilean navy's coaling barque *Matías Cousiño*. He found only the screw corvette *Magallanes* (Captain Juan José Latorre) maintaining the blockade there but, unfortunately for Grau, Latorre sought to emulate the earlier heroism of his old classmate Prat and duelled with the *Huáscar* for 45 minutes, closing to within 300 metres, even though his own ship had the speed to flee. The *Matías Cousiño* escaped, and Latorre's bold action detained the *Huáscar* long enough for the casemate ship *Cochrane* (Captain Galvarino Riveros) to reach the scene, turning the tables and forcing Grau to flee. In the weeks that followed the *Huáscar* enjoyed its greatest success, destroying a number of small cargo vessels and, on 23 July, capturing the Chilean transport *Rimac* off Antofagasta. This setback prompted Sotomayor to sack Williams, elevate Riveros to rear admiral and squadron commander, give Latorre the vacated command of the *Cochrane*, and get personally involved in formulating a plan to trap the *Huáscar*. In the process they all but ignored the *Unión*, which in August ranged as far south as Punta Arenas on the Strait of Magellan in a futile attempt to interdict merchantmen carrying arms shipments to Chile from Europe. The Chilean navy waited until after the threat of the *Huáscar* was removed before it launched a similar mission against merchantmen carrying weapons to Peru from the United States; eventually, over the summer of 1879–80, the *Amazonas* and later the corvette *O'Higgins* ranged as far north as the coast of Panama but had no luck in their efforts.[28]

For the purposes of hunting down the *Huáscar* the Chilean squadron was split into two divisions, one consisting of Riveros's flagship *Blanco Encalada*, the screw schooner *Covadonga* and the coaling barque *Matías Cousiño*, the other of Latorre's *Cochrane*, the screw corvette *O'Higgins* (Captain Jorge Montt) and the armed transport *Loa*. Meanwhile Grau remained bold in his use of the *Huáscar*, on 28 August bombarding Antofagasta in broad daylight and engaging the Chilean warships there – the screw corvettes *Abtao* and *Magallanes* – before Riveros arrived with the *Blanco Encalada* to chase him off. On the morning of 8 October Latorre's division finally spotted the *Huáscar* steaming with the *Unión* off Punta Angamos, north of Antofagasta. Grau immediately sent away the unarmoured *Unión*, prompting Latorre to send the *O'Higgins* and *Loa* to chase it, leaving the two ironclads to duel alone. The ensuing battle featured the first use of armour-piercing Palliser shells, which the 9-inch Armstrong guns of the *Cochrane* fired with deadly accuracy as the range fell to 2,000 metres and less. Riveros arrived with the *Blanco Encalada* some 45 minutes after the fighting began, but Latorre's ship continued to dominate the action. By the time the *Huáscar* surrendered another 45 minutes later, the Chileans had recorded perhaps the best gunnery performance in the history of modern naval warfare, impressing British observers with an amazing 27 hits on 76 rounds fired. Of the 205 men aboard the *Huáscar* 61 were killed, including Grau. The guns in the turret of the *Huáscar* (which had to be cranked by hand until the installation of its steam winch in 1885) managed just three hits against the two Chilean ironclads, killing none and wounding seven aboard the *Cochrane*, and causing no damage to either ship. Unlike the *Independencia*, the *Huáscar* was not damaged beyond repair, and a boarding party led by Lieutenant Juan Simpson foiled the crew's efforts to scuttle the ship. Recommissioned within weeks, it saw its first action under Chilean colours in February 1880.[29]

Taking full advantage of Chile's command of the sea, Rear Admiral Lynch orchestrated the transport of 9,500 troops from Antofagasta northward to Pisagua, where they were put ashore unopposed early in November 1879 after Latorre's division, consisting of the *Cochrane* and three unarmoured warships, shelled the landing site. Meanwhile, Riveros took the *Blanco Encalada* and the rest of the squadron farther north to blockade the harbour of Arica, where he captured the screw gunboat *Pilcomayo* on 18 November. After escorting the convoy to Pisagua, Latorre added his division to the blockade at Iquique, where the Peruvian garrison surrendered on 23 November, finally freeing Uribe and other survivors of the *Esmeralda* who had been held prisoner there since May. Over the same weeks, the Chilean army marched inland from Pisagua, and on 27 November defeated a joint Peruvian-Bolivian army at Tarapacá, securing for Chile the southernmost Peruvian province of the same name. Thereafter, the action centred around Arica, principal seaport of Tacna, the neighbouring province to the north. On 27 February 1880 the old Peruvian monitor *Manco Capac*, anchored there as harbour watch, exchanged fire with the *Huáscar* when the latter arrived to shell the port. Riveros and Latorre soon arrived with the rest of the squadron, which joined in the bombardment. Army units put ashore in early March subsequently laid siege to Arica from the land side. The Peruvian garrison held out for three months, but on 6 June, sensing the end was near, the naval detachment blew up the *Manco Capac* to keep it out of Chilean hands. The following day Chilean troops stormed the city and forced its surrender.[30]

In April 1880, after the initial bombardment of Arica, Riveros left Latorre's division behind to blockade the port while he took the *Blanco Encalada*, the *Huáscar* and the rest of the squadron north to blockade Callao, in preparation for the final Chilean assault on Lima. Following the capitulation of Arica, Latorre brought the *Cochrane* and its unarmoured escorts to join him. Against this overwhelming force the Peruvians deployed a flotilla of torpedo boats, some improvised, others purchased in Britain over the past several months. Copying tactics used by the Russian Black Sea fleet against the Ottoman navy in the recent Russo-Turkish War (1877–8), they managed to sink the armed transport *Loa* in July and the screw gunboat *Covadonga* in September. Thereafter, fears of losing a larger or more significant warship prevented Riveros from maintaining a tighter blockade. Chile soon deployed its own torpedo boats, and the rival torpedo flotillas subsequently dominated the action in and around Callao harbour, with each losing one boat.[31]

Because Rear Admiral Lynch's performance as co-ordinator of troop transports in 1879 had given him such valuable expertise in the logistical side of amphibious operations, the war and navy minister, Sotomayor, appointed him to command the army's expeditionary force for the final strike against Lima. His forces embarked from Arica and in November 1880 landed up the coast at Pisco. From there, Lynch began his march on Lima, staying near the coast so that Riveros's squadron could provide covering fire as he advanced. The navy's heavy guns supported the army in its decisive victory at Chorrillos (13 January 1881), which forced the Peruvians to abandon their capital. Three days later the Peruvian navy scuttled its last ironclad, the immobile Callao harbour watch *Atahualpa*, then surrendered. Over the following months the Chilean navy took the surrender of the smaller Peruvian ports north of Callao; the capitulation of Paita to the *Huáscar* in June 1881 left the entire coast of Peru in Chilean hands. The end of the campaign at sea did not bring an end to the war, since neither Peru nor Bolivia would agree to terms. After occupying Lima, Lynch co-ordinated the fight against Peruvian resistance in the interior for another two and a half years. In October 1883, three months after the fighting ended, Peru formally ceded to Chile the provinces of Tacna and

Tarapacá with the ports of Arica and Iquique. At the same time, Bolivia refused to acknowledge the Chilean conquest of its Pacific coastal province and port of Antofagasta. An invasion from Peru by Lynch's army led to a truce in April 1884, finally ending the fighting, but Bolivia was never occupied by Chilean troops and waited until 1904 to sign a formal peace treaty.[32]

Even before the end of the War of the Pacific, Arturo Prat had been enshrined not just as the greatest hero of the navy or of the war, but as the nation's greatest hero of all time, a status he retained into the twenty-first century. By association, his pre-war and wartime friends and comrades shared at least a bit of his glory, while senior officers who had not appreciated him in life benefited less from his death. The only exception was Lynch, a senior naval officer who had commanded troops rather than ships during the War of the Pacific and, afterward, received the greatest short-term rewards. Promoted to vice admiral in 1883, he served as ambassador to Spain from 1884 until returning to Chile shortly before his death in 1886. Rear Admiral Williams Rebolledo, who had disliked Prat, left him at Iquique to die commanding the worst ship in the navy, and botched the hunt for the *Huáscar* afterwards, did not fare as well. He never held another command at sea, but recovered enough to be named director of the Naval School for the 1889 term, then command-ant general of the navy the following year. His successor as squadron commander, Riveros, hardly distinguished himself by joining the war and navy minister, Sotomayor (or at least Sotomayor's supporters, after his death in May 1880), in claim-ing credit for planning the capture of the *Huáscar*. Nevertheless, his earlier role as director of the Naval School between 1859 and 1863 allowed him to claim a special bond with 'the class of the heroes'. Under a special law he retained the prerogatives of squadron commander after giving up the post in August 1881. Riveros remained a powerful figure within the navy, serving on the board that determined promotions, but died in 1892 with-out having received the honour of promotion to vice admiral (the navy's highest rank until 1948). Latorre ultimately, and quite correctly, received credit for capturing the *Huáscar* and securing command of the sea for Chile, and emerged as the navy's greatest living hero. Promoted to rear admiral, in 1884 he was sent to Britain to supervise the refitting of the *Blanco Encalada* and *Cochrane*, then, after a brief return to Chile as commandant general of the navy, in 1887 was sent back to Europe to supervise the construction of the new warships authorized under Balmaceda. Among the leaders of 'the class of the heroes', Condell received the least recognition, despite his role in luring the *Independencia* onto the rocks at Punta Gruesa on 21 May 1879, clearly the war's early turning point. Sent to Europe from 1881to 1884 to supervise the construction of the cruisers *Arturo Prat* and *Esmeralda*, he returned to be promoted to rear admiral and was squadron commander when he fell ill and died in 1887, at the age of 44.[33]

Luis Uribe, Prat's boyhood friend, Naval School classmate and second-in-command aboard the *Esmeralda*, emerged after the war as the navy's greatest critic of Chile's pre-1879 naval weakness and strongest advocate of a postwar reform of the service. In his book *Los Combates navales en la Guerra del Pacífico, 1879–1881* (1886) he alleged that the overall poor state of the navy had prolonged the war against Peru. The successes of 1879 had been achieved because 'fortunately' the Peruvian navy was 'more disorganized' than the Chilean, and decisive victory ultimately came because of 'the poor state of discipline and organization' of the Peruvian navy rather than Chilean brilliance. Uribe made a series of suggestions to improve the navy's command structure and readiness, almost all of which were implemented within the next dozen years. Some initial changes came on his watch as commandant general of the navy (1887–9). In 1888 he had the honour of leading the division that escorted Prat's remains from Iquique to be reinterred in a monumental tomb in Valparaíso, taking part in ceremonies that secured his own share of the glory of his fallen comrade.[34]

Captain Jorge Montt, one of the less prominent members of 'the class of the heroes', ended up playing the greatest role in his country's history. After the War of the Pacific he captained the *Blanco Encalada* on its postwar voyage to Britain for renovation but held no position of importance before being appointed maritime governor of Valparaíso in 1890. Serving in that capacity, and still awaiting promotion to rear admiral, he allied himself with the leaders of the Chilean congress against President

Balmaceda when a constitutional crisis paralysed the government later that year. For a complex set of reasons rooted in the peculiarities of Chile's constitution and political culture, the congress voted to depose the president with effect from 1 January 1891.[35] While the army rallied behind Balmaceda, keeping him in office, thanks to Montt's efforts every warship in the fleet larger than a torpedo boat supported the congress. Designated 'chief of the Naval Division' by the congress, Montt raised his flag aboard the *Blanco Encalada* and ferried congressional leaders north to Iquique, where he headed a junta that used the nitrate wealth of the Atacama Desert to fund the creation of a congressional army. The navy enabled the junta to ferry thousands of its supporters to the north for military training, which became easier once Balmaceda's chief German military adviser defected to the congressional cause. Just as the hopes of the junta hinged on its ability to create an army, Balmaceda's quest to stay in power required the creation of a navy. Armed merchantmen were not the answer; just two were requisitioned and manned, one of which promptly deserted to Iquique. Attentions turned to the battleship, cruisers and torpedo gunboats under construction in Europe, ships formidable enough to turn the tide in the president's favour.[36]

Latorre, whom Balmaceda had sent to Europe in 1887 to supervise the new warship projects, decided to remain loyal to the president and in March 1891 rebuffed a telegram from the junta urging him to support the congressional cause. The junta then declared his commission revoked and sent agents to Europe to foil his efforts to send the new ships to Balmaceda; while work slowed on the *Capitán Prat* and the two cruisers under construction in France, the torpedo gunboats *Almirante Condell* and *Almirante Lynch* – already en route from Britain – made it safely to Chile later in March. Meanwhile, the two admirals who outranked Latorre did nothing to stop Montt. Williams, commandant general of the navy at the outbreak of the Civil War of 1891, sent Balmaceda a letter reassuring the president of his 'complete personal support' but at the same time resigned his post, noting the 'impossibility' of continuing to serve under the circumstances. While one of his sons died fighting for the president, Williams remained on the sidelines as the Civil War ran its course. Riveros, who would die the following year, likewise was not a factor. Aside from Latorre all other officers of note supported the junta, with the exception of Uribe, who reacted to the breach between the navy and the president by requesting retirement – at the age of 44. Owing to their ambivalence, Williams and Uribe shared Latorre's fate in having the junta declare their commissions revoked.[37]

The navy had no difficulty operating without these admirals and the small number of junior officers who remained loyal to Balmaceda. Yet, despite the overwhelming superiority of the congressional forces in numbers of warships, the presidential forces registered their greatest success of the war at sea. On 23 April the *Almirante Lynch* led a raid on the port of Caldera, where it sank the *Blanco Encalada*, the first armoured warship to fall victim to a self-propelled torpedo. It was also the most expensive Chilean warship ever to be sunk, and the 182 lives lost were the most ever in a single Chilean warship, far surpassing the 148 killed when the *Esmeralda* was sunk in 1879. The loss of a recently renovated battleship that had many good years left in it (its sister ship *Cochrane* served until 1908, and as a hulk until 1933) hurt the navy in the long run but did not delay the junta's battle plan against the president. Because Balmaceda did not command the sea and had no way of knowing where the navy would land the congressional army once it was ready to fight, he had to disperse his 33,000-man army to garrison coastal cities from Coquimbo to Concepción. On 20 August 1891 Montt's fleet put the junta's army of 9,300 ashore unopposed at Quintero, near Valparaíso; the following day, in the Battle of Concón (fought close enough to the shore for the cruiser *Esmeralda* and the old corvette *O'Higgins* to provide fire support), the troops overwhelmed regular army units. Most of the prisoners taken at Concón promptly defected to the congressional cause, and Balmaceda's forces began to crumble. At the Battle of Placilla (28 August), the junta's army crushed what was left of the presidential army, enabling the leaders of the congress to return to Santiago in triumph. Balmaceda sought refuge in the Argentinian embassy, where he committed suicide on 19 September, one day after his presidential term would have ended. Later that year an election confirmed Montt as president of the republic, but during his five-year term (1891–6) he reigned rather than ruled, keeping faith with the congressional leaders whose cause he had embraced.[38]

The navy got off to a bad start in the quest to heal its divisions. Of Balmaceda's three significant warships, the *Almirante Condell* and armed merchantman *Imperial* steamed to Callao, Peru, at the end of the war but were returned to Chile several weeks later. The *Almirante Lynch* remained in Valparaíso, where its crew had to seek refuge aboard American and German warships when some of the junta's troops, fresh from the victory at Placilla, sought revenge against them for their earlier sinking of the *Blanco Encalada*.[39] Among the senior officers whose commissions had been revoked, Uribe was the first to be restored to his former rank and served as director of the Naval School from 1892 to 1895. Latorre remained in exile until returning to Chile under an amnesty after being elected to a senate seat from Valparaíso in 1894, by a party consisting of former supporters of Balmaceda. In 1897 Montt's successor as president, Federico Errázuriz, restored Latorre's rank of rear admiral and the following year appointed him to the cabinet as foreign minister. In that capacity he laid the groundwork for the Chilean-Argentinian 'Pact of May' 1902, which resolved the Andean border dispute. Latorre had to wait until 1908 for his long-deserved promotion to vice admiral; that year, the ageing Williams, in private life since 1891, likewise became a vice admiral. As a reward for defeating Balmaceda, then respecting the primacy of the congress in Chilean politics, Montt advanced to the head of the navy's rank list, serving as director general of the navy with the rank of vice admiral from 1897 until his retirement in 1913. On 8 October 1911, at a ceremony commemorating the thirty-second anniversary of the Battle of Angamos, Montt finally made amends with his old classmate Latorre, who died the following year.[40]

As president, Montt suffered the consequences of the junta's 1891 efforts to delay the delivery of the battleship *Capitán Prat* and the cruisers *Presidente Errázuriz* and *Presidente Pinto* from France. After supporting Peru in the War of the Pacific, in the Civil War of 1891 the United States openly backed Balmaceda, sending some of its new protected cruisers to Chilean waters and, in one incident, seizing a cargo ship carrying arms from San Diego to the junta in Iquique. After Balmaceda's defeat, American cruisers transported some of his followers to Peru and the US embassy in Santiago gave others sanctuary. Chilean-American tensions boiled over in October 1891, when two sailors from the cruiser USS *Baltimore* were murdered in a brawl with Chilean sailors and civilians while on shore leave in Valparaíso. President Benjamin Harrison, facing a difficult re-election campaign in 1892 (which he would lose), took an extraordinarily hard line against Chile, demanding a formal apology and damages of $75,000, an exorbitant sum at a time when the customary compensation in such cases was $5,000 per life lost. Even with the navy in a weakened state (following the loss of the *Blanco Encalada*, with the new warships not yet arriving from France) Montt feared an American naval war or invasion attempt less than the likelihood that Peru, Bolivia and Argentina would intervene in a Chilean-American war and, supplied and bankrolled by the United States, resolve by force their various territorial claims against Chile. In January 1892 Montt apologized, defusing the war scare; the crisis ended six months later, when Chile transferred the $75,000 to the United States.[41]

CONCLUSION

After the War of the Pacific, the mineral wealth of the Atacama enabled Chile to join the much larger Brazil and Argentina in the first rank of Latin American powers. But the Civil War of 1891, the Chilean-American war scare of 1891–2 and the impending emergence of the United States as a modern world naval power tempered Chile's ambitions. Indeed, facing war with the United States in 1892, Chile responded in much the same way that Brazil had when facing war with France in 1828. In the future, the country would remain faithful to the Latin American tradition of maintaining naval forces only great enough to defend its interests against peers within the region.

For the next decade Chile focused on its new rivalry with Argentina. The cruisers *Presidente Errázuriz* and *Presidente Pinto* reached Chile in February 1892 and September 1892; the *Capitán Prat* arrived in May 1893.[42] By 1898 Armstrong had launched two armoured cruisers and another three protected cruisers for Chile, and by 1901 other British shipyards had delivered a torpedo gunboat, six more torpedo boats and six destroyers. Argentina responded with four armoured cruisers built in Italy, and another two protected cruisers, a torpedo gunboat and four destroyers built in Britain. In 1901, on the eve of the resolution of their border dispute, Argentina ordered two more armoured cruisers in Italy, while Chile ordered the 11,800-ton pre-dreadnought battleships *Constitución* and *Libertad* in Britain, but the 'Pact of May' 1902 required the two navies to sell these warships. On the eve of the Russo-Japanese War of 1904–5, Japan bought the two unfinished Argentinian cruisers, while Britain purchased the two Chilean battleships (which became HMS *Swiftsure* and *Triumph*) to keep them out of Russian hands.[43] Brazil's acquisition of dreadnought battleships prior to the First World War led Argentina and Chile to order dreadnoughts of their own, and after the Second World War both Brazil and Argentina bought surplus British aircraft carriers, but through all of the changes in naval warfare in the twentieth century the leading Latin American powers continued to measure their naval strength against each other rather than by more general external criteria.

The bitter legacy of the War of the Pacific remained evident throughout the twentieth century. After waiting until 1904 to accept its defeat formally, landlocked Bolivia repeatedly pressed Chile to return at least part of its lost coastal province. As of 2003 the two countries had not had diplomatic relations since 1962 (aside from a brief rapprochement in the years 1975–8), and Bolivia continued to commemorate the anniversary of Chile's occupation of the last of its coastal ports, Calama (23 March 1879), as its annual 'Day of the Sea' (*Día del Mar*). The day typically featured presidential addresses reiterating Bolivia's post-1945 protests to the United Nations and the Organization of American States over Chile's conquest of Antofagasta province. The territorial issue became more than symbolic at the dawn of the twenty-first century, when natural gas deposits worth billions of dollars were discovered in southern Bolivia, which could only be exploited for export if a pipeline were built to the Pacific coast. While economic considerations called for a shorter pipeline across northern Chile, within Bolivia a more expensive plan for a pipeline across southern Peru was more popular politically. In 2002 Bolivia insisted that any pipeline deal with Chile would have to include the creation of a coastal 'extraterritorial enclave' under Bolivian control, a concession Chile had no intention of making.[44] Peru, which recovered part of Tacna province (although not the port of Arica) in a 1929 border adjustment, still considered Chile its principal maritime rival when it finally rebuilt its navy in the last decades of the twentieth century. Meanwhile, the turret ship *Huáscar*, converted to a Chilean national memorial after leaving service in 1898, became the world's only contested museum ship. As late as August 1999 President Alberto Fujimori demanded its return to Peru.[45]

SIX

A Place in the Sun:
The German Navy, 1898–1918

The first years of the twentieth century witnessed the emergence of Germany as a naval power of the first rank, thanks to Admiral Alfred von Tirpitz's promotion of the fleet as the cornerstone of a new *Weltpolitik* that would make Germany a world power. In this quest he had the enthusiastic support of Emperor Wilhelm II and his foreign secretary (later chancellor) Bernhard von Bülow. Alluding to the boast 'the sun never sets on the British Empire', late in 1897 Bülow introduced Tirpitz's first fleet expansion bill to the Reichstag with the observation 'we now demand our place in the sun'.[1] Tirpitz secured the Reichstag's approval for the First (1898) and Second (1900) Navy laws, establishing a programme that soon created the world's second largest battle fleet and, in the process, brought a dramatic change to Anglo-German relations. Throughout his long tenure as chancellor, ending in 1890, Otto von Bismarck had never viewed British naval power as a threat to German interests. As recently as 1889 he had praised the British fleet as 'the greatest factor for peace in Europe'.[2] As long as Germany was content to dominate the European mainland, leaving Britain the oceans and the colonies, the two countries had no reason to clash. But the Tirpitz plan, coinciding with German advances on Britain's leading position in trade and industry, compelled Britain to join France and Russia in the Triple Entente, solidifying the rival armed camps of pre-1914 Europe and making the ultimate conflict far more likely.

Between the unification of Germany and the passage of the First Navy Law, the Imperial German navy grew considerably but to no coherent grand design. At its birth in 1871, it inherited three armoured frigates (two built in Britain and one in France) from its predecessors, the Royal Prussian navy (to 1867) and the navy of the North German Confederation (1867–71). Eleven armoured warships added over the next seventeen years included four casemate ships, four barbette 'sortie corvettes' and three masted turret ships. As early as 1883 Germany, at least briefly, could claim the honour of having the third largest armoured fleet behind Britain and France, but the country only slowly developed a self-sufficient naval-industrial complex. Two of the casemate ships were built in Britain and almost all of the rest had British armour plate or other components imported from Britain; the casemate ship *Oldenburg* (built 1883–6) was the first battleship in the fleet constructed entirely of German steel. During the 1870s and '80s a 'Prussian school' of naval thought slowly evolved, rooted in the Continental military thought of Karl von Clausewitz. The 'Prussian school' promoted an offensive mentality, ironically for a navy materially incapable of assuming such a posture. The accession of a pro-navy emperor, Wilhelm II, brought an increase in battleship construction starting in 1888, and in the early 1890s Krupp (already world-renowned for its artillery) became the world leader in armour production, yet throughout the first decade of the new reign naval expansion followed no particular plan. Eight 3,500-ton coastal battleships of the *Siegfried* class (built 1888–96; see illus. 17) had little fighting value, and the four 10,000-ton *Brandenburg* class battleships (built 1890–94), Germany's largest to date, were dwarfed by their British contemporaries of the *Royal Sovereign* class. Three battleships of the 11,100-ton *Kaiser Friedrich III* class (laid down 1895–8) and the 10,700-ton armoured cruiser *Fürst Bismarck* (1895) each had a primary armament of four 9.4-inch guns and likewise were inferior to the largest warships of the leading navies.[3]

In 1890 an American naval officer, Alfred Thayer Mahan, published *The Influence of Sea Power upon History, 1660–1763*,

17 A German *Siegfried* class coastal battleship, photographed in the early 1890s.

the first of a series of books providing battle fleet proponents with historical arguments to support their cause. Mahan drew his examples from the early modern competition for empire between Britain and France, but his works were especially influential in his own country and in Germany, where his followers included Wilhelm II and Alfred Tirpitz, neither of whom had been enthusiastic advocates of the battleship. During the era of the Jeune Ecole the opportunistic Tirpitz had embraced torpedo warfare and rose to become head of the navy's torpedo service, before reading Mahan and turning to the battleship in 1891. Wilhelm II, meanwhile, had advocated the cruiser as the warship type best suited to support his dream of a global German colonial and commercial presence, and only slowly came round to the battleship even after his first reading of Mahan. As early as 1893, when Tirpitz was still a captain, serving as chief of staff in the High Command in Berlin, his critique of the navy's annual manoeuvres encouraged officers to remedy their deficient education in 'tactics and strategy' through the 'study of naval history', especially 'the works of Captain Mahan'.[4] Because Mahan shared many strategic assumptions with Clausewitz, the earlier work of the navy's own 'Prussian school' accelerated the reception of his ideas in Germany. Reading the military and naval history of the preceding century, both Mahan and the 'Prussian school' had seized upon the

Napoleonic-Nelsonian faith in the offensive and quest for the decisive battle as the transformational concepts in modern warfare. But since the 'Prussian school' reflected the Continental focus of Clausewitz, Tirpitz needed the underpinning of Mahan to formulate a global vision in which the German navy would have a central role. The evolution of this vision was reflected in his *Dienstschrift* IX of June 1894 and subsequent 'risk theory', first disclosed publicly in December 1899. The First (1898) and Second (1900) navy laws set Germany on a course of naval expansion grounded in Tirpitz's argument that a battle fleet just two-thirds the size of the British would have sufficient strategic value to justify the considerable expense of its construction. Throughout his campaign to expand the fleet, Tirpitz freely acknowledged his debt to Mahan. The 1895 German translation of Mahan's first book was its first non-English edition; after Tirpitz became state secretary of the Imperial Navy Office, he had thousands of copies distributed to support his arguments for the First Navy Law.[5]

Shortly after his appointment in June 1897, Tirpitz warned Wilhelm II that Britain was Germany's 'most dangerous enemy . . . against which we most urgently require a certain measure of naval force as a political power factor'.[6] The emperor likewise viewed Britain as the obvious obstacle to Germany's further rise to world power, and eagerly endorsed Tirpitz's plan for a further expansion of the fleet even though it would bring an end to the generally friendly relations the two countries had enjoyed since German unification. In a speech to the Reichstag in December 1897, Tirpitz used ominous Darwinian language in characterizing the expansion of the fleet as a 'question of survival' for Germany.[7] The First Navy Law, passed by the Reichstag in April 1898, sanctioned a fleet of 19 high seas battleships and 8 coastal battleships, 12 large cruisers, 30 small cruisers and 12 divisions of torpedo boats, to be completed by 1905. The battleships included 12 already built or building: the four 7,600-ton *Sachsen* 'sortie corvettes' (commissioned 1878–83), the 5,200-ton casemate ship *Oldenburg* (1886), the four 10,000-ton *Brandenburgs* (1893–4) and the first three battleships of the 11,100-ton *Kaiser Friedrich* III class (under construction). The coastal battleships were the eight 3,500-ton *Siegfrieds* (1890–96) already in service. The twelve large cruisers included ten already built or building: the old battleships *König Wilhelm*, *Kaiser* and *Deutschland* (recently rebuilt as armoured cruisers), the protected cruiser *Kaiserin Augusta* (1892), the five vessels of the 5,700-ton *Hertha* class (under construction) and the 10,700-ton armoured cruiser *Fürst Bismarck* (under construction). The 30 small cruisers included 23 already built or building: nineteen older units (1883–96) and four 2,650-ton *Gazelle*-class warships (under construction). Before passing the First Navy Law the Reichstag focused on the number of new warships needed to meet its goals – seven battleships, two large and seven small cruisers – which would expand the fleet by 30 per cent in just seven years. Largely lost in the debate was the provision for the future automatic replacement of warships: battleships after 25 years, large cruisers after 20 years and smaller cruisers after 15 years. Under the First Navy Law, work began on the last two battleships of the 11,100-ton *Kaiser Friedrich III* class (1898), five battleships of the 11,800-ton *Wittelsbach* class (1899–1900), the 8,900-ton armoured cruiser *Prinz Heinrich* (1898) and the 9,100-ton armoured cruiser *Prinz Adalbert* (1900). Most of the new small cruisers were units of the *Gazelle* class.[8]

The international situation subsequently favoured Tirpitz's quest for a much greater commitment to naval expansion. Amid anti-British sentiments stemming from the Anglo-Boer War in South Africa (1899–1902) and outrage over the Boxer Rebellion in China (1900), where the German ambassador and German missionaries had been among the first foreigners killed, the Reichstag in June 1900 passed the Second Navy Law. Much more than the First Navy Law, the new legislation (raising the authorized strength of the fleet to 38 battleships, 14 large and 38 small cruisers) reflected Tirpitz's conviction that a battle fleet in home waters would give Germany leverage in all international conflicts, including those far from home. The newly authorized units included eleven battleships (the small *Siegfried*s were now counted as full-sized battleships, for replacement purposes) but only two large and eight small cruisers. The new larger units included the five 13,200-ton battleships of the *Braunschweig* class (laid down 1901–2), five battleships of the 13,200-ton *Deutschland* class (1903–5; illus. 18) and

18 A German battleship of the *Deutschland* class (1906).

the 11,600-ton armoured cruisers *Gneisenau* (1904) and
Scharnhorst (1905; illus. 19); meanwhile, in 1901–3 work began
on three armoured cruisers to replace the three renovated old
battleships that Tirpitz had counted as large cruisers under the
First Navy Law. The new battleships remained smaller and
less heavily armed than their British counterparts, but the
*Braunschweig*s and *Deutschland*s carried a primary armament of
11.1-inch guns, an improvement over the 9.4-inch guns of the
Kaiser Friedrich III and *Wittelsbach* classes. The Second Navy
Law solidified Tirpitz's reputation as Imperial Germany's most
successful politician in the post-Bismarck era. The emperor
showered him with honours, including elevation to the nobility
in 1900.[9]

The automatic replacement provision of Tirpitz's navy laws,
guaranteeing that a future more left-wing legislature could not
undo his master plan, took on greater significance as the years
passed and the anti-military Social Democratic Party (SPD)
became by far the largest party in the Reichstag, growing from
14 per cent of the seats in 1898 to 28 per cent in 1912. By 1906
37 of the authorized 38 battleships and all fourteen large cruisers
were either in commission or under construction, and that year
Tirpitz secured Reichstag approval for a supplementary law

19 The German armoured cruiser *Scharnhorst* (1907).

further increasing the number of large cruisers to 20. With the next large cruiser not due for its twenty-year replacement until 1912 (the *Kaiserin Augusta*, commissioned in 1892), the six new large cruisers filled the gap of 1906–12 and guaranteed that one of the type would be laid down every year indefinitely. At the same time, at least one new battleship (and in some years two or three) would be laid down every year as well, without further approval from the Reichstag. Since it was taken for granted that all replacement ships would have to measure up to the standards of the time in which they were ordered, Tirpitz had *carte blanche* to replace smaller old warships with larger new ones. Eventually the oldest battleships in the fleet of 1898, the four 7,600-ton *Sachsen*s, would be replaced by four 18,900-ton battleships of the *Nassau* class, while the smallest, the eight 3,500-ton *Siegfried*s, would be replaced by units of the 22,800-ton *Helgoland* class and 24,700-ton *Kaiser* class.[10]

During its first years the German naval build-up caused little alarm in Britain. Admiral Sir John Fisher (First Sea Lord 1904–10 and 1914–15) spent his first year in office still convinced that Britain's traditional rivals, France and Russia, were its most likely future enemies, and the world's sea lanes the likely battleground. Battle cruisers were the key to his vision of a

British fleet with truly global reach. These battleship-sized cruisers, armed with battleship guns but with some of their armour plating sacrificed for the sake of speed, would be able to outgun any warship they could not outrun, and vice versa. Laying down his first capital ships in 1905–6, Fisher placated battleship proponents with the *Dreadnought*, a ship of 18,110 tons with ten 12-inch guns, armour as thick as 11 inches and a speed of 21 knots, while ordering three battle cruisers of the *Invincible* class, ships of 17,370 tons with eight 12-inch guns, no more than six inches of armour and a speed of 25 knots. The *Dreadnought*, built in an unprecedented fourteen months (October 1905–December 1906) was intended as a test platform for the unprecedented hull size, all big-gun armament and turbine engines that would also be featured in the three *Invincibles*. Yet while the *Dreadnought* was under construction, changes in the international arena determined that battleships of its type, and not battle cruisers, would be the core of the future British fleet. The Anglo-French Entente Cordiale (1904) had survived the Moroccan crisis of 1905, while the Russo-Japanese War (1904–5) had practically destroyed the Russian navy. Germany, with its fleet further strengthened by the supplementary law of 1906, now appeared to be Britain's most likely future adversary, and battleships of the *Dreadnought* design, better suited for a warfare in the confined space of the North Sea, appeared more useful than battle cruisers, whose potential global range was no longer as relevant. Because the size, speed and firepower of the *Dreadnought* rendered all other battleships obsolete, it became the new model capital ship not just for the British fleet, but for the rest of the world's navies as well.[11]

The onset of the 'dreadnought revolution' raised the stakes of the Tirpitz plan by forcing Germany to build much larger (and much more expensive) battleships than had been anticipated. The admiral remained undeterred, however, and raised costs still more by insisting that future units in the 'large cruiser' category be built as battle cruisers, even though no other European navy copied the design from the British. The type had no particular relevance to the German strategic situation, yet it appealed to Tirpitz because it would allow him to build another twenty battleship-sized vessels under legislation already approved by the Reichstag. These, plus the 38 battle-ships already approved, would give him a fleet of 58 capital ships (dreadnoughts and battle cruisers), against which Britain would have to build at least 90 in order to maintain better than a 3:2 margin of superiority. Thus Tirpitz embraced the changes in capital ship design, even though in the short term they caused his fleet to fall further behind the British. The Germans laid down their last pre-dreadnought battleship, the final unit of the 13,200-ton *Deutschland* class, in August 1905, just two months before the British began work on the *Dreadnought*. They laid down their first dreadnought, the *Nassau*, in June 1907, by which time the British had the *Dreadnought* itself in service and another four dreadnoughts under construction, along with the three battle cruisers of the *Invincible* class. The *Nassau* displaced 18,900 tons, 43 per cent more than the *Deutschland* (compared to the *Dreadnought*'s 18,110 tons, just 13 per cent more than the last British pre-dreadnoughts) and its construction placed unprecedented demands on the German naval-industrial complex. As long as it took Germany to gear up for the production of warships as large as the *Dreadnought*, it would have taken longer still to produce its equal in firepower and speed. Rather than delay the *Nassau* and its three sister ships any longer, Tirpitz had them fitted with a primary armament of the same 11.1-inch guns as previous classes of German battleships, and with triple-expansion engines capable of just 19.5 knots. In 1908 the Reichstag passed another supplementary law, allowing Tirpitz to accelerate bat-tleship construction. By March 1909 he had laid down the four units of the 22,800-ton *Helgoland* class, still slower than their British counterparts (owing to their triple expansion engines) but equal in armament, with 12-inch guns. Meanwhile, in the 'large cruiser' category, Tirpitz followed the 15,800-ton armoured cruiser *Blücher* (laid down 1907) with the 19,400-ton *Von der Tann* (1908; illus. 20) and 23,000-ton *Moltke* (1909), Germany's first battle cruisers and first capital ships with tur-bine engines. These projects combined allowed Germany almost to pull even with Britain in the naval arms race, since Parliament had funded just two new capital ships (one dread-nought and one battle cruiser) in its budget for 1908–9. By

20 The German battle cruiser *Von der Tann* (1911).

March 1909 Germany had ten dreadnoughts and battle cruisers built or building to Britain's twelve, and was on a pace to achieve near-parity in capital ships.

Thereafter the British moved decisively to stay ahead in the competition. In late March 1909 Parliament approved the naval estimates for 1909–10, including three dreadnoughts and one battle cruiser to be laid down by December 1909, with another three dreadnoughts and one battle cruiser to follow early in 1910 if Germany refused to end the arms race. At the same time, the Admiralty dropped its traditional two-power standard in favour of a 60 per cent capital ship advantage over the German fleet, close to the 3:2 ratio of British superiority Tirpitz had been willing to concede, but still not enough to bring the Germans to the negotiating table. By May 1910 Britain had laid down all eight capital ships of its 1909–10 programme. Further widening the British lead, Australia and New Zealand paid for two battle cruisers, begun in Britain in June 1910. They were the last of an astonishing ten capital ships laid down in Britain within a span of twelve months, demonstrating a resolve to make whatever financial sacrifices were necessary to stay ahead. During the same months Germany began just three: the first two dreadnoughts of the 24,700-ton *Kaiser* class and the 23,000-ton battle cruiser *Goeben*.

Thus, a year after achieving a tantalizing near-parity with the British in capital ships built or building, Tirpitz faced a 22:13 deficit. He had assumed all along that German naval construction could push Britain to a breaking point, beyond which it would be unwilling or unable to maintain its superiority. Proven wrong, he became more amenable to negotiations, and in 1911 offered to accept a 3:2 (15:10) British advantage in capital ships, close to Britain's goal of a 60 per cent (16:10) advantage, as long as the British included in their total the battle cruisers *Australia* and *New Zealand*, along with any future ships funded by the overseas dominions. At the same time, attempting to use the fleet as the political lever Tirpitz had always claimed it would be, Chancellor Theobald von Bethmann Hollweg insisted that an Anglo-German naval treaty be part of a broader agreement including Britain's explicit recognition of the territorial status quo in Europe, including Germany's possession of Alsace-Lorraine. The British found these conditions unacceptable, and the race continued. In 1910–11, and again in 1911–12, the Germans laid down four capital ships (three dreadnoughts and one battle cruiser) and the British, five (four dreadnoughts and one battle cruiser), narrowing the capital ship gap slightly, to 32:21. Meanwhile, displacement tonnage and gun calibres increased while further improvements in turbine design kept speeds at 21 knots for dreadnoughts and 26–27 for battle cruisers. Falling short in the quantitative race, the Germans sought a qualitative edge, but here too they had difficulty keeping up. The new German capital ships of 1911–12 were the first three dreadnoughts of the 25,800-ton *König* class and the 26,600-ton battle cruiser *Derfflinger*, all armed with 12-inch guns. Britain responded with the four dreadnoughts of the 25,000-ton *Iron Duke* class and the 28,430-ton battle cruiser *Tiger*, all armed with 13.5-inch guns.

In February 1912 Britain sent its war minister, Lord Richard Haldane, to Berlin in a final attempt to reach a settlement, but Bethmann Hollweg's insistence that any Anglo-German naval treaty must include broader political conditions doomed the negotiations before any discussion of numbers took place. The recently appointed First Lord of the Admiralty, Winston Churchill, subsequently poisoned relations still more by calling the German navy a 'luxury' fleet. Tirpitz rejected Churchill's idea of a one-year 'naval holiday' and in March persuaded the Reichstag to pass another supplementary navy law adding three more battleships to the authorized strength of the German fleet. It would be his last political victory, because the following year the Reichstag funded a significant expansion of the long-neglected German army. By 1913–14 the navy's share of the German defence outlay fell to just under 25 per cent, down dramatically from an all-time high of over 35 per cent in 1911–12. The navy budget still included one new battle cruiser per year (the 26,700-ton *Lützow* in 1912–13 and the future *Hindenburg* in 1913–14) but just one new *König* class dreadnought in 1912–13 and the first two 28,500-ton *Bayern* class dreadnoughts in 1913–14. Over the same two years Britain doubled the German effort, laying down ten dreadnoughts of the *Queen Elizabeth* and *Royal Sovereign* classes, giant battleships displacing 27,500–28,000 tons, armed with eight 15-inch guns.[12] Battle cruiser construction resumed after Fisher returned to office as First Sea Lord in October 1914, with five laid down during the first six months of 1915. Meanwhile, in Germany, another two *Bayern* class dreadnoughts and a battle cruiser were included in the estimates for 1914–15, all of which were under construction by early 1915.

By the outbreak of the First World War, Britain had laid down 42 capital ships (33 dreadnoughts and 9 battle cruisers) since the onset of the dreadnought revolution, of which 29 (21 dreadnoughts and 8 battle cruisers) were in commission. Germany had 27 (20 dreadnoughts and 7 battle cruisers) built or building, including 18 (14 dreadnoughts and 4 battle cruisers) in commission. In active capital ships and counting those still under construction, the Germans fell just short of Tirpitz's goal of a 3:2 British: German ratio. But by the end of the summer of 1914 further developments tipped the balance even more in Britain's favour. The British seized three foreign dreadnoughts (two Turkish, one Chilean) nearing completion in British shipyards, while the German battle cruiser *Goeben*, trapped in the Mediterranean at the outbreak of hostilities, saved itself by steaming for Constantinople and raising the Turkish flag. These changes left Britain with a commanding 45:26 lead in capital ships built or building, and ensured its ability to blockade Germany successfully for the duration of the war. Just as he had abandoned the Jeune Ecole and the torpedo boat in favour of the battleship in the early 1890s, after the start of the war Tirpitz abandoned the battleship in favour of the submarine. Though as administrative head of the navy he had no direct responsibility for operational decisions, from November 1914 until his resignation in March 1916 he became an increasingly vocal advocate of submarine warfare as the key to a German victory at sea. Germany had just 36 undersea boats when the war began, compared to 88 for Britain, but would employ a total of 335 by the end of the war, compared to 269 for Britain. The Tirpitz plan finally became a dead letter in January 1917, when Germany abandoned the two dreadnoughts and five battle cruisers it then had under construction in order to reallocate shipyard personnel and resources from the capital ship programme to submarine construction. The move came on the eve of the fateful decision to launch a new campaign of unrestricted submarine warfare, a decision that drew the United States into the First World War, ultimately ensuring Germany's defeat.

NAVAL PERSONNEL AND 'THE SPIRIT OF THE ARMY'

In Imperial Germany the navy was a relatively new armed service without longstanding traditions. Consequently, its officer corps followed the lead of the army in its organization, values and attitudes, and continued to do so throughout the reign of Wilhelm II to 1918, even after it became a national elite in its own right.[13] While it is true that the largely bourgeois sea officers of the Wilhelmine era eagerly emulated the aristocratic standards and values of the army officer corps, the influence ran deeper than mere imitation within the social context of the time. Three Prussian generals – Prince Adalbert (to 1871), Albrecht von Stosch (1872–83) and Leo von Caprivi (1883–8) – played a central role in the creation and administration of the navy before the accession of Wilhelm II, and it was from them that naval officers derived their mentality toward the state and society, as well as toward the men serving under their command.[14]

The Imperial German navy's Prussian predecessor was founded in 1815, but thirty years later it had no active warships and just one officer, an ageing Swede nearing retirement. On the eve of the revolutions of 1848–9 and the concurrent German-Danish War, a Dutch commander and three Prussian lieutenants were hired. In the spring of 1849, after helping to draft a stillborn plan for the short-lived German navy of the Frankfurt Parliament, Prince Adalbert of Prussia, a general in the army artillery, became supreme commander of the Prussian navy. As the service expanded over the next decade, practical experience meant more than bloodlines when commissions were awarded. Adalbert transferred army officers to serve in the naval artillery, marines and administrative posts, while former merchant mariners and a small number of foreigners accounted for most of the sea officers until the Naval School (established at Danzig in 1853, then moved to Stettin and Berlin before settling at Kiel in 1866) could produce enough graduates to meet the navy's needs. At the start of the wars of German unification (1864–71), the senior officers on the *Rangliste* below Adalbert included eight captains whose first duty had been in the merchant marine. Writing in 1862, the prince lamented that his officer corps included 'a collection of diverse elements', with too few sons of noblemen or army officers and too many sons of merchants or merchant mariners. Even though 'almost without exception' the former merchant mariners and foreigners had proven to be good officers, he wanted the naval officer corps of the future to be a 'union of professional and social comrades' (Vereinigung von Berufs- und Standesgenossen), recruited from 'elements imbued with the spirit of the army'.[15]

After Adalbert's retirement in 1871, General Albrecht von Stosch took command of the navy as head of the new Imperial German Admiralty. He inherited a terrible morale problem, since the navy's negligible role in the wars of German unification, culminating in its relative inactivity during the Franco-Prussian War (1870–71), had left deep scars especially on the psyche of junior officers. Indeed, the formative experience of spending most of the French war at anchor in Wilhelmshaven aboard the armoured frigate *König Wilhelm* helped Tirpitz develop his later convictions about the need for a strong battle fleet.[16] Others of his generation did not stay with the navy long enough to see it emerge from the gloom. In 1871–2 twelve men at the ranks of *Unterleutnant* and cadet (including nine with noble titles) transferred to the army, more than would normally do so in a decade. Sharing Adalbert's vision, Stosch took decisive steps to enhance the image and exclusivity of the naval officer corps. He organized the officers of the Baltic and North Sea stations along the lines of the officers of army regiments, down to their mess and courts of honour, and encouraged social rituals mirroring those of the typical regiment. He also purged officers from less prestigious social backgrounds, regardless of their merit. Of the twenty most senior officers (admirals and captains) on the *Rangliste* of 1872, ten were retired by 1878; all had served in the merchant marine before entering the navy, and none had noble titles, hereditary or acquired. Those driven out included Captain Johannes Weickhmann, recipient of an Iron Cross for his service as commander of the raider *Augusta* in 1870–71, deemed unacceptable because he had humble origins and was 'somewhat rough in form'. Stosch also retired lower-ranking captains and lieutenants who had entered the navy from the merchant marine as auxiliary officers during the wars of German unification, and removed all such officers from the rolls of the reserve *Seewehr*, ensuring that even in a future wartime emergency the navy would not have to use officers tainted by prior experience in the merchant marine.[17]

Stosch redoubled efforts to recruit noblemen, but in the wake of the war of 1870–71 he could do little to make the navy appear as attractive as the army, and the service attracted even fewer noblemen than it had before. In the five classes (or 'crews', as they were known) entering before the Franco-Prussian War, from 1866 through to 1870, 28 per cent of the cadets held noble titles; for the eleven classes of the Stosch era, 1872 to 1882, the figure fell to 17 per cent. The 'crew' of 34 cadets entering in 1881 included an all-time low of just one nobleman.[18] In 1883, 103 of 417 sea officers (24.7 per cent) held noble titles. Five years later, the figure stood at 107 of 514 (20.8 per cent), and in 1897, on the eve of the Tirpitz plan, 148 of 746 (19.8 per cent). The concepts of social exclusivity copied from the army remained the ideal after 1888, when Caprivi left office and Wilhelm II finally put admirals in charge of the navy. Such goals became increasingly unrealistic, however, once the growth of the fleet required a further expansion of the officer corps. The German nobility, though augmented by hundreds of new additions after 1871, could not possibly keep up with the rate of growth, and the ennoblement of a number of common naval officers did little to raise the overall percentage of nobles in the corps. Tirpitz, the son of a civil servant, did not place great value on bloodlines until after 1900, when Wilhelm II elevated him to the nobility. Before Tirpitz, only four common naval officers had been ennobled, but between 1900 and 1918 the emperor elevated another 28.[19]

After the Naval School settled at Kiel, it adopted a curriculum focusing on subjects directly related to naval service, and allowing for more time at sea. Thereafter, future officers received their general education at a Gymnasium or Realschule, and entered the school somewhat later than their contemporaries at other naval academies. The four-and-a-half-year routine began with a six-month preparatory course at the school, followed by one year aboard training ships and two aboard ships in the fleet, then a final year back at the school. In 1872 the entry age limit of seventeen was raised to nineteen for applicants holding the *Abitur*, signifying the completion of the exams that qualified a student for university admission. In 1894, 40 per cent of entering cadets held the *Abitur*; by 1914, the number stood at 90 per cent. Eventually, as both the age and academic background of entering cadets rose, the navy reduced its course of education and training to three and a half years, dispensing with the six-month preparatory period and one of the years that cadets spent in the fleet, but adding six months in special training courses. The shortened curriculum included a first year aboard training ships, a second year in general classes at the school, six months in special training courses, and finally a year serving in the fleet. The higher academic expectations further enhanced the exclusivity of the officer corps by requiring the entering cadet to have spent his teenaged years in school, all but closing the corps to young men from the merchant marine or the ranks of the navy's common sailors (the last of the latter to achieve an officer's commission did so in 1881). As a counterpart to the army's War Academy (Kriegsakademie), in 1872 Stosch established the Naval Academy (Marineakademie) at Kiel, with a two-year curriculum intended to provide further education for distinguished junior officers destined for higher command positions. Alumni included Tirpitz (1874–6) and, years later, Erich Raeder (1903–5), who went on to command the navy from 1928 to 1943. Army officers had to pass through the War Academy to gain appointments to the general staff, but navy officers routinely rose to prestigious posts without attending the Naval Academy; thus, it never became as important as its army counterpart. While the Naval Academy remained in Kiel through the First World War, in 1910 the Naval School moved to Mürwik, near Flensburg.[20]

Throughout its history, the officer corps of the Imperial German navy remained roughly two-thirds Prussian. The ratio holds true for virtually every sample population, from the eve of German unification to the eve of the First World War, even as the corps expanded. For example, Prussians accounted for 27 of 40 men in the 'crew' of 1869, and 130 of 197 in the 'crew' of 1907. Most of the non-Prussians were from the northern coastal states, with the notable exception of the Hanseatic cities of Hamburg, Bremen and Lübeck, where the navy's prejudice against sons of merchants and merchant mariners depressed recruiting. In the years before the First World War barely one-eighth of entering naval cadets came from southern Germany; in 1907 Bavaria provided just eight of the 197. Because Prussia (outside the Rhineland in the west and the Polish lands in the east) had few Catholics and the other northern states almost no Catholics at all, the corps of sea officers was overwhelmingly Protestant. The navy, like the army, commissioned no Jews, and virtually all of the small number of baptized Jews in the officer corps were from very wealthy families.[21]

To serve the needs of Tirpitz's expanded fleet, the corps of sea officers grew to include 2,388 men by 1914, roughly triple the size of the corps of 1897. During the same years the com mon manpower of the navy (including petty officers) experienced a similar pattern of growth, from 25,000 men in 1897 to 73,500 in 1914. Enlisted men typically entered at age 20, after being conscripted, but the navy accepted volunteers as young as 17. Under the North German Confederation's Federal Military Law of 1867, adopted by Imperial Germany in 1871, the navy automatically received all conscripts who had served at least one year in the merchant marine or aboard fishing vessels, as well as those with other other skills relevant to the needs of the service. The latter included locomotive machinists and stokers, who entered the navy from all over Germany. Otherwise, most naval conscripts came from the coastal provinces of Prussia, the Hanseatic cities or Mecklenburg. The standard three-year term of service was followed by a nine-year reserve obligation. The German navy included the unique category of 'deck officers' (*Deckoffiziere*), with status below sea officers but above other petty officers, who aboard ship assumed many of the roles that junior officers or senior petty officers filled in other navies. They grew in number as the navy became more modern technologically and new jobs were created that did not fall into the traditional realm of the officer or the petty officer; in the German navy, a disproportionate number of these functions fell by default to deck officers. By 1914 there were just over 3,000 of them, compared to 16,000 petty officers and just under 54,500 ratings. Deck officers lobbied for officer status right up to 1918, but they continued to be categorized with the common manpower, as high-ranking petty officers. In a service that still had a separate corps of engineer officers long after most other navies had integrated their engineers and sea officers, it would have been unthinkable for men with the educational level, social background and shipboard function of deck officers to receive equal status with sea officers.[22]

THE PRISONER AND THE JAILER: WARTIME OPERATIONS

Because the anti-British assumptions of the Tirpitz plan required the consolidation of German naval power in the High Sea Fleet, based on the North Sea at Wilhelmshaven, the Imperial German navy never had the same degree of global presence as the British and French navies, or the American and Soviet fleets of later years. Aside from small cruisers used as station ships off the coasts of the African and Pacific colonies Germany had claimed in the

1880s, the only warships routinely assigned overseas (and the largest permanent presence beyond European waters) cruised off East Asia. The squadron there, based at the German colonial enclave of Tsingtao (Qingdao), China, from 1898, had been commanded by Tirpitz in 1896–7, between his promotion to rear admiral and his appointment to head the Imperial Navy Office. When war broke out in the summer of 1914, it was led by Admiral Count Maximilian von Spee.

Spee's warships included the armoured cruisers *Scharnhorst* and *Gneisenau*, two light cruisers, four gunboats and one destroyer. When Japan entered the war on the side of the Entente (23 August 1914), Germany gave up hope of holding its Pacific possessions, and Spee took his armoured cruisers eastward across the Pacific. The light cruiser *Emden* was detached to the East Indies and Indian Ocean as a raider, while the rest of the squadron remained behind at Tsingtao, where the ships were scuttled prior to the base's surrender to the Japanese (7 November 1914). By then, the *Scharnhorst* and *Gneisenau* had rendezvoused off the coast of Chile with three light cruisers that had been operating in the waters of the Americas; on 1 November, off Coronel, the five vessels engaged and defeated a smaller British squadron, sinking two armoured cruisers. The victory came one day after Britain's Admiral Fisher returned as First Sea Lord. He recognized immediately that the pursuit of Spee's squadron was precisely the sort of mission for which his battle cruisers had been designed, and sent Admiral Sir Doveton Sturdee with two of them, *Invincible* and *Inflexible*, to the South Atlantic to intercept Spee as he rounded Cape Horn and made for home. The battle cruisers arrived at the Falkland Islands just before Spee raided the base at Port Stanley, not expecting to find superior enemy forces there. In the Battle of the Falklands (8 December 1914) Sturdee's battle cruisers, reinforced by three armoured cruisers and four smaller cruisers, sank the *Scharnhorst*, the *Gneisenau* and all but one of the German light cruisers. Losses included Spee and 2,100 of his men. By the summer of 1915 allied (mostly British) warships had hunted down all German light cruisers attempting to function as raiders; meanwhile, of sixteen armed merchantmen sent out to prey upon allied commerce, all but three were sunk, scuttled, wrecked or interned in neutral ports.[23]

As the naval conflict unfolded and the North Sea became the main theatre of surface operations, the Germans pursued a strategy of using Rear Admiral Franz Hipper's battle cruiser squadron as bait to draw a portion of the British Grand Fleet into battle with the rest of the High Sea Fleet, reasoning that if the entire German battle fleet could be brought to bear to destroy a part of the British fleet, Germany's numerical inferiority in capital ships could be erased at a single stroke. The first such sortie to result in contact with the British went terribly wrong for the Germans. In the Battle of Dogger Bank (24 January 1915), Hipper's squadron of three battle cruisers and the armoured cruiser *Blücher* lured out five British battle cruisers under Vice Admiral Sir David Beatty, which pursued them back towards Wilhelmshaven. In the four-hour engagement, the Germans lost the *Blücher* and nearly 800 dead, while one German and two British battle cruisers sustained significant damage. Wilhelm II responded to the defeat by relieving Admiral Friedrich von Ingenohl, commander of the High Sea Fleet and Hipper's superior, for keeping the main body of German dreadnoughts too far from the battle cruisers to come to their aid or to trap the British battle cruiser squadron. The emperor kept Ingenohl's successor, Admiral Hugo von Pohl, on such a short leash that the High Sea Fleet practically rusted at anchor until early 1916, when Pohl gave way to Vice Admiral Reinhard Scheer.[24]

After assuming command, Scheer persuaded the emperor to allow the High Sea Fleet to resume a regimen of sorties, with Hipper's battle cruisers again used to lure out the British. Unlike Ingenohl on the day of Dogger Bank, however, Scheer intended to keep the German dreadnoughts close enough to come to Hipper's aid and destroy the British forces that came out to chase him. Sorties in February, March and April of 1916 resulted in no contact with British capital ships, but Scheer's fourth sortie, on 31 May, resulted in the Battle of Jutland, the largest naval engagement of the war. In the pre-dawn hours of the 31st, five battle cruisers under Hipper's command steamed northward from Wilhelmshaven, parallel with the coast of Danish Jutland, headed in the direction of the Skaggerak, with Scheer's sixteen dreadnoughts, six pre-dreadnoughts and a host of smaller warships following some 50 miles (80 kilometres) behind. As in the Battle of Dogger Bank, Beatty's battle cruisers came out to intercept Hipper, followed by the rest of the Grand Fleet under Admiral Sir John Jellicoe, coincidentally also roughly 50 miles behind. Owing to a recent exchange of ships between Beatty and Jellicoe, Beatty had six battle cruisers and four dreadnoughts, and Jellicoe twenty-four dreadnoughts and three battle cruisers. Hipper encountered Beatty just before 16:00 that afternoon, and immediately turned south, drawing the pursuing British squadron toward Scheer's superior force. During the hour-long chase German gunfire sank two British battle cruisers, but Beatty kept up the pursuit until sighting Scheer's dreadnoughts. Around 17:00 he reversed course and steamed northward, with Hipper and Scheer giving chase, drawing the entire High Sea Fleet back toward Jellicoe's advancing force. As the two fleets came into contact at 18:15, Beatty's ships joined Jellicoe's line in a west–east crossing of the German 'T', pounding Hipper's battle cruisers at the head of Scheer's column, approaching from the south. During this phase the British lost a third battle cruiser, while Hipper had to abandon the badly damaged battle cruiser *Lützow*, which sank early the next morning. Scheer broke off the action after less than an hour, then doubled back toward Jellicoe's line for another brief exchange before finally turning away and heading for home around 19:30. Jellicoe then made the fateful decision not to pursue the retreating Germans, which he reconsidered at 20:00, only after giving them a safe lead in the ensuing chase. The battle continued sporadically throughout the night of 31 May–1 June. By dawn the next day the High Sea Fleet was back in Wilhelmshaven, minus the *Lützow* and ten other warships: the pre-dreadnought *Pommern*, four light cruisers and five destroyers. The British suffered much more, losing three battle cruisers, three armoured cruisers, one destroyer flotilla leader and seven destroyers. The German dead numbered 2,551, the British 6,097.[25] The outcome disheartened a British navy that had expected another Trafalgar, but amid the gloom a London journalist best summed up the strategic situation post-Jutland: the prisoner had assaulted its jailer but was now safely back in its cell.[26]

Even though the British navy remained in command of the North Sea, the Germans hailed the Battle of Skaggerak (their name for the Battle of Jutland) as a great victory. Scheer received a promotion to full admiral and Germany's highest military medal, the Iron Cross *Pour le Mérite*. Yet the man who led Germany's most formidable surface fleet in its greatest battle ever conceded shortly afterward that Britain could be defeated at sea only through a redoubled effort at unrestricted submarine warfare, which the navy had tried for seven months in 1915. He also integrated u-boats into subsequent surface fleet operations. When Scheer took the High Sea Fleet out again on sorties in August and October 1916, and a portion of it out on a third sortie in November, each time it was accompanied by submarines that attempted to lay traps for British capital ships lured out of their bases. The strategy failed because Scheer encountered no British capital ships, but his u-boats managed to sink two light cruisers on the August sortie. Meanwhile, the British Grand Fleet, likewise resorting to the use of submarines against enemy capital ships, had much greater success. British submarines torpedoed one German dreadnought during Scheer's August sortie and two during the November sortie, all of which managed to limp home to Wilhelmshaven. By late 1916 Scheer agreed with Wilhelm II that such operations were not worth the risk. The High Sea Fleet attempted just one more fleet sortie into the North Sea, in April 1918, with the same result: no British capital ships encountered, and one German dreadnought torpedoed (but not sunk) by a British submarine. Otherwise, the capital ships of the High Sea Fleet spent the last two years of the war (November 1916–November 1918) rusting at anchor in Wilhelmshaven, with the monotony broken only in October 1917, when Scheer sent Vice Admiral Erhard Schmidt with roughly half of the battle fleet (ten dreadnoughts and a battle cruiser) through the Kiel Canal and into the Baltic to secure the Gulf of Riga from the Russian navy. An earlier (August 1915) operation with the same goal had failed, but by the time of the second effort a German army offensive had forced the Russian army to abandon the city of Riga, depriving the defending warships of their port facilities and making the German navy's task much easier.

In the Battle of Moon Sound (17 October 1917) Schmidt's capital ships, supported by a host of smaller warships, overwhelmed a Russian squadron consisting of two pre-dreadnoughts, two armoured cruisers and lighter vessels; the Russians withdrew after losing one of their old battleships, and Schmidt's fleet successfully landed 25,000 troops to secure crucial islands in the gulf. German losses in the brief campaign included a dozen smaller craft sunk and one dreadnought temporarily disabled after striking a mine.[27]

Three weeks after Moon Sound, the Bolshevik Revolution brought V. I. Lenin to power in Russia. The Germans had provided Lenin with transportation home from his exile in Switzerland, gambling that he would cause enough trouble to knock Russia out of the war, enabling Germany to concentrate its forces on the Western Front and achieve overall victory. This scheme ultimately failed, as did the other great German gamble of 1917, the resumption of unrestricted submarine warfare. The German navy had just 37 submarines in commission when its initial, modest campaign of unrestricted submarine warfare began in February 1915. Over the next seven months it rarely had more than six U-boats on patrol in the waters around the British Isles at any given time, yet 787,120 tons of allied shipping were sunk at a total cost of fifteen U-boats lost. The largest single allied vessel sunk, the 30,400-ton Cunard liner *Lusitania*, by *U-20* off the coast of Ireland on 7 May 1915, went down with 1,200 of its passengers, including 128 Americans. Over the objections of Tirpitz, then in his last months at the Imperial Navy Office, Wilhelm II agreed with the rest of his generals and admirals that the results of the campaign were not worth the risk of alienating the United States and other neutral countries. But by the winter of 1916–17 the allied blockade was causing food shortages in Germany and its ally Austria-Hungary, raising the question of how long they could sustain their war effort even though their armies were entrenched on allied soil on all fronts. A campaign of restricted submarine warfare (during which U-boats attacked most of their targets while surfaced, after a warning, using their deck gun rather than torpedoes) sank 1,535,860 tons of allied shipping over the five months from September 1916 to January 1917. Such results, achieved at a cost of ten U-boats lost, reflected the potential of the submarine strategy now that Germany had many more U-boats in service than in 1915. When unrestricted submarine warfare resumed in February 1917, Germany had 105 U-boats in its fleet and around three dozen deployed around the British Isles, and the abandonment of seven capital ship projects (two dreadnoughts and five battle cruisers) ensured that German shipyards would be able to build more than enough submarines to replace future losses. In the first three months alone the Germans sank a staggering 1,945,240 tons of allied shipping while losing just nine U-boats; by the end of the year, 5,820,675 tons had been sunk. The United States responded by declaring war on Germany (6 April 1917) and, even though its army would not deploy in force on the Western Front until the summer of 1918, it had an immediate impact in the war at sea. The US navy (then the world's third largest, behind the British and German) threw its assets into the balance, and under American pressure the British agreed to an allied convoy system that brought a dramatic reduction in the average monthly tonnage lost, from 651,655 tons per month (February–June) to 427,065 tons per month (July–December).[28]

In February 1918, one year into the campaign, the Germans were still sinking allied shipping at a rate greater than the tonnage could be replaced, despite an impressive effort at new construction and the incorporation into the US merchant marine of dozens of German ships interned in American ports earlier in the war. Yet an ever more effective convoy system further reduced the average monthly tonnage claimed by U-boats, to 306,965 tons per month (January–August 1918). Thereafter, the overall collapse of the German war effort brought an abrupt drop in submarine sorties; U-boats sank just 171,970 tons in September, 116,240 in October and 10,230 in the first eleven days of November. The total of 2,754,155 tons sunk by U-boats in 1918 included 166,910 tons claimed by six long-range submarines sent to the eastern coast of the United States, one of which laid a mine off Long Island that sank the armoured cruiser *San Diego* (19 July 1918), the only larger US warship lost in the First World War. The German High Command had assumed that, even if the United States responded to the resumption of unrestricted submarine warfare by entering the war, u-boats would prevent significant numbers of American troops from being shipped to Europe. But German submarines sank just three transatlantic troop transports (one of which limped into Brest before going under), in the process killing a mere 68 American soldiers, while another 2,079,880 made it safely to Europe. The warships convoying the transports came through unscathed, with one exception: the French armoured cruiser *Dupetit-Thouars*, torpedoed by *U-62* on 7 August 1918.[29]

In the autumn of 1918 the navy collapsed along with the rest of Imperial Germany, after it became clear that the army could no longer hold the Western Front. The monarchy's last chancellor, Prince Max of Baden, belatedly tried to appease the United States by formally declaring an end to unrestricted submarine warfare on 21 October. Scheer, since August 1918 Chief of the Supreme Navy Command, agreed to the recall of the u-boats but did not want the German surface fleet to end the war at anchor. In collaboration with Hipper (his successor as head of the High Sea Fleet) he devised a plan to send Germany's remaining eighteen dreadnoughts and five battle cruisers on a suicidal raid to the mouth of the Thames, to draw out the British fleet for a final battle. The High Sea Fleet was scheduled to sortie on 29 October, but when given the order to raise steam, the crews of nine dreadnoughts and four battle cruisers mutinied, forcing the admirals to abandon their mad scheme. Hipper subsequently dispersed the mutinous ships to various north German ports, inadvertently facilitating the participation of radicalized sailors in the revolution that swept those cities in early November. Ultimately the officer corps relinquished control of the mutinous ships without a fight, suffering casualties of just four wounded and none killed in the transition.[30] Over half of the ships were still in the hands of their crews ten days after the Armistice, on 21 November, when the High Sea Fleet (or at least its newest and best ships: eleven dreadnoughts, all five battle cruisers, eight light cruisers and fifty destroyers) steamed for Britain, not for the mouth of the Thames but for the Grand Fleet base at Scapa Flow in the remote Orkney Islands, where the warships were interned pending the outcome of the Paris Peace Conference. Under the command of Vice Admiral

Ludwig von Reuter, the skeleton crews of the ships remained isolated as the victorious allies deliberated the fate of Germany. Reuter did not even know that the Armistice had been extended past its original limit of 21 June 1919, to allow the peace conference to finish work on the treaty. The British fleet happened to be out of the harbour on an exercise that afternoon, giving Reuter the opportunity to scuttle his warships. As the German fleet carried out the order, confused British guards fired on sailors abandoning the sinking vessels, inflicting 30 casualties. The 1,860 survivors were hailed as heroes when the British repatriated them to Germany in January 1920.[31]

CONCLUSION

In light of all the money and effort spent on building the dreadnoughts and battle cruisers of the High Sea Fleet, it is worth noting that of the 26 actually completed, just one – the battle cruiser *Lützow*, at Jutland – was lost as a result of battle damage. Sixteen were scuttled at Scapa Flow, and another nine (most of them older units of the *Nassau* and *Helgoland* classes) were scrapped under the terms of the Treaty of Versailles. Of the fifty completed for the British navy by the time of the Armistice, five were lost, of which just three (the ill-fated battle cruisers at Jutland) succumbed to the gunfire of the High Sea Fleet. Such figures reflect the sobering reality that the most valued and most expensive naval units of the First World War spent most of their time at anchor, while smaller surface warships and submarines did much of the fighting. Ultimately 53 per cent of all U-boats (178 of 335) in commission in 1914–18 were lost, 134 of them to allied anti-submarine operations, and 4,474 German submariners were killed. U-boats sank a total of 11.9 million tons of allied shipping during the war, but their efforts ultimately failed to starve Britain into submission or stop the flow of troops from the United States and the British dominions to the battlefields of Europe.[32]

The postwar Treaty of Versailles prohibited the navy of the Weimar Republic from having submarines. In reducing the German armoured fleet to the size of its inter-war Swedish counterpart, the treaty also required the scrapping of older dreadnoughts not scuttled at Scapa Flow, leaving the surviving pre-dreadnoughts of the 13,200-ton *Braunschweig* and *Deutschland* classes as the largest German warships. Ironically, one of these old battleships, the *Schleswig-Holstein*, fired the first shots of the Second World War on 1 September 1939, after entering the harbour of Danzig ostensibly as a friendly visitor. Adolf Hitler considered the Tirpitz plan to have been a grave mistake and did not allow the construction of a surface force even approaching the size of the High Sea Fleet; nevertheless, after denouncing the Treaty of Versailles he sanctioned the construction of large battleships (most notably the *Bismarck* and *Tirpitz*) and armoured cruisers, as well as submarines. In the Second World War the German navy once again attempted significant surface operations early in the conflict before focusing its effort on submarine warfare; over twice as many u-boats were built, all of them much larger and more capable than their counterparts of 1914–18, yet the German submarine campaign of 1939–45 was relatively less successful than the earlier effort. In a war that lasted 30 per cent longer, just 22 per cent more Allied shipping was sunk (14.6 million tons), at a cost of four times as many u-boats (at least 754 lost) and six times more submariners killed (27,491, with 5,000 taken prisoner). The mortality rate for German submariners, far higher than for surface fleet sailors during the First World War, rose to an astounding 70 per cent for those serving in the Second World War, during which 429 u-boats were lost with no survivors.[33]

The German challenge to Britain's naval position before 1914 clearly changed the course of world history. Without the tension of the pre-war Anglo-German naval race, it strains the imagination to believe that Britain would have formed an alliance with its former rivals, France and Russia, against Germany. To be sure, the rising industrial and commercial might of Imperial Germany posed a threat to Britain's global position, and Britain traditionally had not countenanced having a single military power dominate continental Europe. Yet the direct, unambiguous threat posed to Britain's security by the Tirpitz plan as it unfolded, year by year, was crucial in conditioning the British public and political leaders to view war with

Germany first as possible, then likely, then unavoidable. After playing such a central role in the outbreak of the First World War, the German navy also bore the responsibility of embittering the conflict between 1914 and 1918 through its pioneering use of submarine warfare, and thus contributed much to the atmosphere in which the fateful, flawed peace of 1919 was concluded.

SEVEN

Empire Builder:
The Japanese Navy, 1894–1945

In 1868, fifteen years after Commodore Matthew C. Perry's warships forced Japan to open to trade with the outside world, the Meiji Restoration established a government determined to protect the country's sovereignty by selectively embracing modernization and westernization. The Imperial Japanese navy played a central role in this process and, as Japan grew stronger and more confident, the navy developed an offensive capability crucial to the expansion of the empire. During the 1880s the navy assembled a force of modern steel cruisers, most of them foreign-built, which it used to defeat the Chinese navy in the Sino-Japanese War of 1894–5 and secure Japan's first colonial acquisitions, Taiwan and the Pescadores. Over the next decade Japan purchased an entire new fleet of foreign-built pre-dreadnought battleships and armoured cruisers, which destroyed much of the Russian navy in the Russo-Japanese War of 1904–5, securing Port Arthur and the former Russian sphere of influence in Manchuria, along with a free hand in Korea, which soon became a Japanese possession.

With the demise of the Russian Pacific fleet, the Japanese navy focused on the United States navy as its most likely future rival. By 1914 Japan's industry had improved to a point where the navy could end its dependence upon foreign (mostly British) shipyards and build even the latest models of dreadnoughts and battle cruisers from domestic resources. During the First World War the Japanese navy, allied with the British, seized most of Germany's Chinese and Pacific holdings. The postwar demise of the Imperial German navy left Japan with the world's third largest fleet, a status confirmed in the 5:5:3 capital ship ratio of Britain, the United States and Japan in the Washington Naval

Treaty of 1922. After the regime of naval arms limitations collapsed in the mid-1930s, the Japanese navy expanded beyond the size of the British to become the world's second largest and 80 per cent the size of the US navy. In the early stages of the Second World War, Japan's conquest of Southeast Asia, the East Indies and the Philippines, and the serious threat it posed to allied territories as distant as Alaska, Hawaii, Australia and India, bore witness to the historical significance of its formidable fleet.

NAVAL MATÉRIEL: FROM DEPENDENCY TO SELF-SUFFICIENCY

In its first two decades the Imperial Japanese Navy grew only modestly and acquired almost all of its warships abroad. Its first ironclads were the 1,400-ton[1] ram *Adzuma*, the former CSS *Stonewall*, purchased from the United States. By the end of the 1870s the fleet included three armoured corvettes and a casemate ship, all built in British shipyards, supplemented by a number of wooden steamers either purchased abroad or built in Japan under foreign supervision. Thereafter the Japanese embraced the Jeune Ecole wholeheartedly, and (aside from one small armoured cruiser) commissioned no new armoured warships between 1878 and 1897. In the years between 1885 and 1894 the navy added its first steel-hulled warships, nine protected cruisers and five unarmoured cruisers, building two of each type in Japanese shipyards, under foreign direction, and purchasing the rest abroad. At the Battle of the Yalu (17 September 1894), the principal engagement of the Sino-Japanese War, Admiral Yuko Ito's order of battle included seven protected cruisers – ranging in size from the 4,220-ton *Matsushima* (illus. 21) to the 3,100-ton *Akitsushima* – along with the 2,400-ton armoured cruiser *Chiyoda*, the casemate ship *Fuso* and an old armoured corvette. The Chinese force included two 7,220-ton German-built battleships, three small armoured cruisers and five protected cruisers. While the Japanese won the battle without losing a ship, in the process they learned valuable lessons in *matériel*. One Chinese battleship took 200 hits in the engagement, the other 150, yet neither sank; the Japanese,

21 The Japanese protected cruiser *Matsushima* (1891).

meanwhile, were fortunate not to lose several of their protected cruisers, which were badly damaged, or the two ageing iron-clads in their column, which had no place in a modern naval battle.[2] With China defeated and Russia emerging as its new primary rival, Japan abandoned the Jeune Ecole and built a new fleet centred around battleships and armoured cruisers.

Between 1897 and 1904 the Japanese navy commissioned six pre-dreadnought battleships, eight armoured cruisers, another eight protected cruisers and twenty-three destroyers. Seven submarines laid down in 1904 were not commissioned until after the Russo-Japanese War. The battleships, ranging in size from the 12,320-ton *Yashima* (1897) to the 15,140-ton *Mikasa* (1902), were improved versions of the British navy's *Royal Sovereign* and *Majestic* classes. The armoured cruisers ranged in size from the 7,630-ton *Kasuga* (1904) to the 9,700-ton *Asama* (1899), and included four built in Britain, two in Italy, one in Germany and one in France. The eight protected cruisers commissioned between 1896 and 1904, ranging from the 2,660-ton *Suma* to the 4,900-ton *Kasagi*, included five built in Japanese shipyards, two in the United States and one in Britain. The first sixteen destroyers were built in British shipyards, the last seven in Japan; the first five submarines were built in the United States, the last two in Japan.[3] At this stage, Japan was as helpless

22 The Japanese battleship *Hatsuse* (1901).

as the leading Latin American powers when it came to constructing a large armoured warship; indeed, its dependence on
foreign shipyards for anything larger than a protected cruiser
weakened its claim to first-rate naval power. The problem
would be resolved only after further improvements in the
Japanese steel industry, which became more productive thanks
to the aid of Vickers and other British producers. While
Japanese foundries produced a small quantity of armour plate as
early as 1901, until 1914 European firms (almost exclusively in
Britain, Japan's ally from 1902) continued to provide most of the
armour and even most of the steel for warship construction on
domestic slips. Heavy artillery and the rangefinders to aim guns
had to be imported from Britain, but by 1904 the Japanese were
able to manufacture their own medium-calibre and light-
calibre artillery, gun mountings, shells, torpedoes, mines, shipboard machinery, boilers and radio telegraph sets.[4]

In its decisive victory at the Battle of Tsushima (27–8 May
1905) the Japanese navy lost no warship larger than a torpedo
boat, but it paid a price for its overall victory in the Russo-
Japanese War. Russian mines claimed two of its new British
battleships, the *Yashima* and the *Hatsuse* (illus. 22), three protected cruisers, and one small armoured cruiser that had been
captured from China in the 1894–5 war.[5] Having recommis-

sioned several captured Chinese warships a decade earlier, after 1905 the Japanese fleet incorporated warships the Russians either surrendered at Tsushima or scuttled later at Port Arthur: eight battleships, one armoured cruiser and three protected cruisers. These renovation projects enabled the navy to expand rapidly in the short term, but most were not worth their cost. Japan returned two of the battleships and the armoured cruiser to Russia in 1916, when the two countries were allies in the First World War.[6]

The Russo-Japanese War yielded no clear lessons for future naval warfare, but the world's navies soon focused on the unprecedented distances at which the two fleets opened fire and scored hits on enemy warships. At Tsushima, Russian shells struck the Japanese flagship *Mikasa* from 7,000 metres (4.3 miles). Some historians have drawn a direct connection between Tsushima and the emergence of the British *Dreadnought* and battle cruiser designs, but the battle played no role in the initial conceptualization of the all big-gun battleship. In 1903 *Jane's Fighting Ships* published Vittorio Cuniberti's article titled 'An Ideal Battleship for the British Navy', in which the chief engineer of the Italian navy (whose idea had been rejected as impractical in his own country) proposed the all big-gun design. The man behind the construction of the revolutionary *Dreadnought*, Admiral Sir John Fisher, likewise developed the idea long before Tsushima. Nevertheless, the Japanese were the first to place orders for all big-gun battleships, contracting for two late in 1904, several months before Tsushima and a year before the British laid down their *Dreadnought*. The 19,370-ton vessels, designed for twelve 12-inch guns, were to be built in Japan, an ambitious undertaking for a country whose largest domestically built warship completed to date was a 4,160-ton protected cruiser. The Kure Navy Yard laid down the *Satsuma* in May 1905, five months before work began on the *Dreadnought*, but the vessel and its eventual sister ship (the *Aki*, laid down at Yokosuka in 1906) were completed without their intended armament owing to the prohibitive cost of importing the necessary heavy artillery from Britain. Ultimately they received a mixed armament of 12-inch and 10-inch guns, and held the honour of being the largest pre-dreadnoughts built by any navy. The two projects were a learning experience for the Japanese, who still depended heavily upon foreign construction materials (roughly 60 per cent for the *Satsuma*) and took an inordinately long time to build the ships: 58 months for the *Satsuma* and 60 for the *Aki*. Aside from the altered armament, other changes made while the ships were under construction were all for the better, including the installation of Brown-Curtis turbine engines imported from the United States.[7]

Upon their completion, the *Satsuma* (1910) and *Aki* (1911) gave the battle fleet a nucleus of eight pre-dreadnoughts, including the four survivors of the Russo-Japanese War plus two 16,400-ton units of the *Kashima* class, improved versions of the *King Edward VII* design ordered on the eve of the war and built in Britain (1904–6). Other recent projects included the four domestically built units of the 13,750-ton *Tsukuba* class (1905–8) and 14,640-ton *Ibuki* class (1905–11), which the Japanese laid down as armoured cruisers but, upon completion, rated as battle cruisers, despite the fact that they were smaller, less heavily armed (with just four 12-inch guns apiece) and slower (at less than 22 knots, with triple-expansion engines) than genuine battle cruisers. In Japan the gap between construction starts of the last pre-dreadnought and first dreadnought lasted from March 1906 to January 1909, longer than the hiatus for Britain, Germany and the United States, but far shorter than the delays in the programmes of France, Russia, Italy and Austria-Hungary. For the two dreadnoughts of the 21,440-ton *Settsu* class (built 1909–12), construction took 35 and 42 months. The navy managed to reduce building times even though the ships were larger and more of the materials (roughly 80 per cent) came from domestic sources. While their twelve 12-inch guns were imported from Britain, their Brown-Curtis turbine engines were manufactured under licence by Kawasaki. They also featured Krupp armour manufactured under licence in Japan (which had produced its first Krupp armour plate for the armoured cruisers of the *Tsukuba* class, laid down four years earlier). The *Settsu*s were followed by Japan's first true battle cruisers, three units of the 27,500-ton *Kongo* class, begun over the winter of 1911–12 in domestic shipyards on the model of the prototype *Kongo*, laid down in January 1911 in Britain, by Vickers. At the outbreak of the First World War the British navy seized all warships under construction in British shipyards for foreign navies, but the *Kongo* (completed August 1913) escaped this fate. The last Japanese capital ship built abroad, the *Kongo* featured eight 14-inch guns and a speed of 27.5 knots, and upon delivery was arguably the most formidable battle cruiser in any navy. Construction times for its sister ships (completed 1914–15) averaged just under 36 months. The three Japanese-built *Kongo*s were constructed by the Yokosuka Navy Yard, Mitsubishi's Nagasaki shipyard and Kawasaki's Kobe shipyard; the latter two were the first capital ships completed by private Japanese firms, reflecting the country's growing industrial capacity. For its next eight dreadnought projects, the navy divided its orders between these firms and its own shipyards at Kobe and Yokosuka, with each of the four building two units. The 30,600-ton *Fuso* (built 1912–15) and its sister ship *Yamashiro* (1913–17) were followed by the 31,260-ton *Ise* (1915–17) and its sister ship *Hyuga* (1915–18), the 33,800-ton *Nagato* (1917–20) and its sister ship *Mutsu* (1918–21), the 39,330-ton *Kaga* and its sister ship *Tosa* (both laid down 1920). Thereafter each of the four shipyards laid down one battle cruiser of the 41,220-ton *Amagi* class (1920–21). The *Fuso*s and *Ise*s carried twelve 14-inch guns, the *Nagato*s eight 16-inch guns, and the *Kaga*s and *Amagi*s ten 16-inch guns. Impressive construction times (the *Ise*, for example, was completed in just 31 months) provided further evidence of the recent dramatic improvements in Japanese industry.[8]

After the defeat of Russia, Japan considered the United States its most likely future enemy at sea, and measured the progress of its own naval build-up against the growth of the US navy. Assigned to the Naval Staff College between 1907 and 1909, the theorist Tetsutaro Sato promoted the concept that Japan must have a fleet 70 per cent as strong as the American fleet if it were to have any chance of victory in a future war. The '70 per cent standard' became an article of faith for the Japanese navy, and remained so for another three decades.[9] In 1910 the navy also set the goal of an 'eight-eight' fleet of eight battleships and eight battle cruisers. If one counts the four large pre-dreadnought battleships commissioned after the Russo-Japanese War and the four large armoured cruisers re-rated as battle cruisers, Japan had achieved its goal in capital ships built or building when the First World War began. But the core of the Japanese battle fleet fell far short of 70 per cent of the strength of the us navy, which had fourteen dreadnoughts built or building by 1914. The six dreadnoughts and four battle cruisers begun after 1915 took Japan just beyond its 'eight-eight' goal in dreadnoughts and true battle cruisers built or building by 1921, but by then the us navy had almost twice as many capital ships (twenty-nine dreadnoughts and six battle cruisers) either in service or under construction.[10] Unarmoured warships laid down between 1905 and 1922 included 23 light cruisers, 121 destroyers and 56 submarines, over twice as many light cruisers as the us navy but far fewer destroyers and submarines.[11]

The elimination of the Russian threat in East Asia and subsequent Anglo-Russian rapprochement under the Triple Entente made the Anglo-Japanese alliance of 1902 less important to the British, and in the post-1905 naval rivalry between Japan and the United States Britain's sympathies clearly lay with the Americans. When the alliance was renewed in 1911, the British insisted upon an amendment clarifying that neither party would ever be obligated to fight the United States. Thereafter, traditionally anglophile Japanese naval leaders valued the British connection far less.[12] Nevertheless, in August 1914 Japan honoured its alliance with Britain and took advantage of the opportunity to seize some of Germany's Asian and Pacific colonies: China's Shantung Peninsula with Tsingtao and Kiaochow Bay, the Marshall Islands and the Caroline Islands. Operational wartime losses included one destroyer and one protected cruiser sunk, and two protected cruisers wrecked. Accidents did the greatest damage, as magazine explosions claimed two capital ships, the battle cruiser (re-rated armoured cruiser) *Tsukuba* in January 1917 and the dreadnought *Kawachi* in July 1918, at a cost of over 1,000 lives.[13]

After the end of the First World War a number of factors worked in favour of the limitation of naval armaments. Britain was deeply in debt to the United States and had no hope of maintaining its traditional superiority in the face of an American naval build-up accelerated during the war. The United States remained apprehensive about the Anglo-Japanese alliance, due to lapse at the end of 1921, and would have viewed its renewal as a hostile act. In Japan, navy minister Admiral Tomosaburo Kato, architect of the recent build-up of the fleet, concluded that his country had no hope of winning a naval arms race and would fall even further behind the United States in naval power. General sentiment favoured arms reduction for economic as well as idealistic reasons, in the latter case rooted in the widespread belief that the pre-war arms races, especially the Anglo-German capital ship competition, had helped cause the First World War. When one of the leading Republican isolationists in the US Senate, William E. Borah of Idaho, sponsored a successful resolution calling for the world's three leading naval powers to conclude a naval arms reduction treaty, the British welcomed the news. The Senate resolution led to the Washington Naval Conference, which began on 12 November 1921.[14]

As the conference opened, US Secretary of State Charles Evans Hughes shocked the delegates with a proposal that all capital ships then under construction should be scrapped and none laid down during a 'naval holiday' of ten years. He called for the United States, Britain and Japan to agree to a tonnage ratio of 5:5:3 in all warship types. Reflecting its '70 per cent standard' *vis-à-vis* the United States, Japan wanted a ratio of 10:10:7. The US navy's Admiral Robert E. Coontz, chief of naval operations, wanted a 3:2 superiority over Japan or 3:3:2, the same ratio favoured by Britain.[15] The treaty, signed on 6 February 1922, included the 5:5:3 ratio, giving Japan a slightly lower figure than it wanted (10:10:6 rather than 10:10:7) in exchange for prohibiting the United States from building or upgrading any Pacific fortifications west of a line stretching from Alaska's Aleutian Islands to Hawaii to Panama. The ratios applied to battleships, battle cruisers and aircraft carriers, but not to other cruiser types, destroyers or submarines. The actual tonnage ratios for capital ships (battleships and battle cruisers) were 525,000 for the United States and Britain and 315,000 for Japan; for aircraft carriers, the limits were 135,000 for the United States and Britain and 81,000 for Japan. The signatories were allowed to enhance the side armour of their existing capital ships, up to a maximum of 3,000 tons per ship. New

23 The Japanese carrier *Kaga* (1928), photographed in 1936, after reconstruction.

battleships and battle cruisers were limited to 35,000 tons and 16-inch guns, with none to be laid down until 1931. Carriers were limited to 27,000 tons, but each of the three navies could have two of 33,000, with no restrictions on when new units could be built. As with existing capital ships, an additional 3,000 tons of armour could be added to existing hulls designated for conversion to carriers. Qualitative restrictions on cruisers (other than battle cruisers) were meant to ensure that vessels equivalent to capital ships would not be built within that otherwise unregulated type. 'Treaty cruisers', as they came to be known, were limited to 10,000 tons and 8-inch guns, but navies could construct as many of them as they wanted.[16]

Unlike the British and Americans, who ultimately let their navies slip below the strength permitted under the treaty, as long as the naval arms regime of 1922 remained in effect the Japanese were aggressive in doing whatever the rules allowed, and sometimes more. The tonnage limit on capital ships allowed Japan to keep its ten newest completed units: the six battleships of the *Fuso*, *Ise* and *Nagato* classes, and the four *Kongo* class battle cruisers. By 1931 all four *Kongo*s had received enhanced armour and other improvements, and were re-rated as battleships.[17] Japan spent its aircraft carrier allotment by converting the *Amagi* class battle cruiser *Akagi* (commissioned

1927) and the battleship *Kaga* (1928; illus. 23) to serve as the two large carriers allowed under the treaty, supplemented by the much smaller *Hosho* (built 1919–22) and *Ryujo* (1929–33). The two capital ship conversions added 6,000 tons to the Japanese carrier quota, with the resulting 87,000 tons spent (at least officially) as 33,000–34,000 for each of the large carriers and around 10,000 for each of the smaller units. The *Akagi* and *Kaga* each carried 60 aircraft, the *Ryujo* a remarkable 48, the *Hosho* 26.[18] In the semi-regulated cruiser category, by 1930 the United States enjoyed less than a 5:4 advantage in treaty cruiser strength over Japan. Four light cruisers laid down in 1922 were followed by twelve heavy cruisers (begun 1922–8), the latter armed with the 8-inch guns allowed under the Washington treaty. While the initial units were well below the 10,000-ton limit, the last eight heavy cruisers (the *Myoko* and *Takao* classes) weighed in at between 12,000 and 13,000 tons, raising the question of whether Japan's naval architects and shipyards lacked the ability to produce ships to the precise specifications (not an easy task; British and American designers sometimes overshot the mark by a few hundred tons), or the Japanese were deliberately cheating. The Japanese heavy cruisers were superior to their counterparts in firepower as well as in size. While the *Myoko*s and *Takao*s each carried ten 8-inch guns, just two US navy heavy cruisers were as formidably armed. Most American units of the type carried nine 8-inch guns, the British six or eight.[19]

The American-to-Japanese ratio narrowed to less than 5:3 not just in cruisers but in other unregulated warship types as well. In warships other than capital ships, by 1930 the Japanese fleet had a strength equalling 74 per cent of the US navy. In the unregulated categories, the navy laid down another 26 destroyers and 14 submarines by 1929, years in which the US navy laid down no new destroyers and just five submarines. The new Japanese destroyers of the late 1920s displaced over 2,000 tons (almost twice as much as the newest American destroyers) and had an armament including six 5-inch guns, making them more powerful than many light cruisers. In building their submarines – mostly larger units, capable of long-range operations – the Japanese purchased German U-boat plans and gained access to German submarine technology thanks to Kawasaki's partnership with the Dutch firm of IvS (Ingenieurskantoor voor Scheepsbouw), which employed German engineers and former German submariners unable to practise their craft in the Weimar Republic under the Versailles Treaty. Along with the material build-up in destroyers and submarines, the Japanese became leaders in developing innovative new tactics for both types, paying special attention to night operations for torpedo flotillas. These efforts exemplified the Japanese quest for qualitative advantages to overcome its quantitative disadvantages *vis-à-vis* the us navy in most categories of warships.[20]

By placing a premium on quality and by building up to (or somewhat beyond) their limits in the regulated types, the navy ensured that Japan would be able to dominate the western Pacific. Nevertheless, the compromise of the '70 per cent standard' and the goal of an 'eight-eight' fleet of battleships and battle cruisers outraged a vocal faction within the naval officer corps, which condemned the Washington Naval Treaty and considered war with the United States inevitable. The prospect of further restrictions on the growth of the fleet only deepened the divisions within the Japanese navy, which was relieved when the Geneva Naval Conference (1927) failed owing to an Anglo-American disagreement over extending the limits to cover cruisers. But as the Great Depression spread from the United States worldwide, economic considerations added momentum to earlier proposals to expand the regime of arms limitations, and to extend the 'naval holiday' past its expiration date in 1931. On 21 January 1930 the London Naval Conference convened to take up these matters. The Japanese delegation remained in disarray throughout the three months of meetings, the civilian diplomats open to concessions, the naval officers opposed. The London Naval Treaty, signed on 22 April 1930, preserved the 5:5:3 ratio for American, British and Japanese battleships and aircraft carriers, but at a slightly lower level for battleships (requiring Japan to decommission the *Kongo* class unit *Hiei*). Limits were extended to cruisers, destroyers and submarines as well. Japan henceforth was limited to 60 per cent of the American cruiser tonnage total (5:3) and could build no more heavy cruisers with 8-inch guns. Its destroyer limit was 70 per cent of the American tonnage total, but this translated into just

105,500 tons, for a navy that already had 132,495 tons in destroyers. Japan received the right to parity with the United States only in submarines, and at a level (52,700 tons) that required it to decommission one-third of its existing undersea force (of 77,842 tons). The 'naval holiday' for battleship construction was extended to the end of 1936, at which time the additional limits would also come due for renewal.[21]

While the London treaty further divided the naval officer corps, and drove a wedge between Japan's leading diplomats and most of its naval leaders, throughout the early 1930s the fleet did not lose ground *vis-à-vis* the Americans or the British, who (as before) did not take full advantage of their tonnage allotments. Indeed, Japan still had arguably the world's most modern navy, having built more than double the tonnage of the United States since 1922. But as Japan's behaviour in the international arena grew more aggressive, those within the naval establishment who wanted to quit the regime of arms limitations gained the upper hand. The Japanese invasion of Manchuria in 1931 led to further hostilities with China and condemnation by the League of Nations. In March 1933 Japan announced its intention to quit the League, and in December 1934 the government announced that it would not agree to an extension of naval arms limits past the end of 1936. Japan sent a delegation to the Second London Naval Conference (December 1935–January 1936), convened to head off a new arms race, but from the start its envoys took positions that made a general agreement impossible. The Japanese would agree to quantitative limits only if they received parity with the British and Americans in all warship types; in response to an appeal for new qualitative limits, they called for the elimination of all battleships and aircraft carriers, a proposal they knew no one would accept. The Japanese walked out of the conference, leaving the other naval powers to conclude a treaty necessarily full of loopholes, which allowed the signatories to exceed its limits in response to the building projects of others, including those outside the agreement, namely the Japanese. Thus, when Japan not unexpectedly failed to abide by the limits of a treaty it did not sign, it invalidated the agreement for everyone else. When the earlier treaties expired on 31 December 1936, the inter-war regime of naval arms limits ended.[22]

By the time the restrictions lapsed, Japan had already begun preparing in earnest for the anticipated future war with the United States. During 1936 navy leaders approved plans for the 68,000-ton battleships *Yamato* (built 1937–41; illus. 24) and *Musashi* (1938–42). The largest battleships ever built by any navy, they carried nine 18.1-inch guns mounted in three triple-gun turrets. At the same time, work began on renovating the decommissioned battleship *Hiei*, which would return to service in 1940. The remaining three units of the *Kongo* class received a second renovation during the 1930s, and the six units of the *Fuso*, *Ise* and *Nagato* classes were rebuilt as well. The most dramatic expansion of the fleet came in its carrier arm, where the *Akagi* and *Kaga* emerged from renovation with displacements of over 40,000 tons and the capacity to carry 91 aircraft apiece. While the small *Hosho* was left relatively untouched (and would be relegated to training purposes during the Second World War), the *Ryujo* was rebuilt to displace over 12,500 tons. In anticipation of the end of naval arms limits, the navy had laid down the *Soryu* (built 1934–7) and *Hiryu* (1936–9), each displacing close to 20,000 tons. They were followed by the *Shokaku* (1937–41) and its sister ship *Zuikaku* (1938–41), at just under 30,000. Conversion projects begun by 1941 yielded another eight carriers by 1942. The *Zuiho*, *Shoho* and *Ryuho*, former submarine tenders, emerged with displacements at or just below 15,000 tons, while the *Junyo*, *Hiyo*, *Taiyo*, *Unyo* and *Chuyo*, former passenger liners, ranged from 20,000 to 27,000 tons. The twelve battleships and sixteen carriers built or building as of 1941 would form the core of the Japanese fleet in its war against the United States, but in the years 1937–41 the navy expanded its strength in the smaller classes of warships as well. In cruisers, Japan built four with 6-inch guns (completed 1935–7), permitted under the London Naval Treaty, before resuming construction of heavy cruisers armed with 8-inch guns (another two, completed 1938–9). Japan recommissioned two captured Chinese light cruisers (5.5-inch guns) in 1937, and completed three new light cruisers with the same calibre of armament in 1940–41. Between 1930 and 1941 the Japanese navy added another 61 destroyers and 48 submarines.[23]

24 The Japanese battleship *Yamato* (1941).

In order to sustain the build-up, the navy had to rely increasingly on private shipyards, which ended up constructing 59 per cent of all Japanese naval tonnage for the years 1926 to 1945. The sheer number of ships being built between 1937 and 1941 was impressive enough, but in ships completed during those years the US navy still outpaced the Japanese in every type but aircraft carriers, where the United States commissioned just four. In a further ominous sign, Japan's build-up reflected practically the maximum that its economy and industry could support, while the concurrent American effort was a relatively insignificant sideshow to an economy still on a peacetime footing. In 1937, the first year since 1921 with no international limits on naval construction, both the United States and Japan spent just over $1 billion on defence, but while the US total represented just 1.5 per cent of a national income of $68 billion, the Japanese figure was 28 per cent of a national income of only $4 billion.[24]

Between 1942 and 1945 the Japanese navy fell only further behind, overwhelmed by the wartime production of the United States. During those years Japan completed 1 battleship (the *Musashi*), 10 carriers, 5 cruisers, 61 destroyers and 121 submarines, while the US navy added 8 battleships, 112 carriers (including 82 escort carriers), 48 cruisers, 354 destroyers and

203 submarines. The ten carriers included four purpose-built vessels: the *Taiho* (built 1941–4) and the sister ships *Unryu*, *Amagi* and *Katsuragi* (1942–4), the former displacing over 30,000 tons, the latter trio around 20,000. The *Shinano*, a converted sister of the giant battleships *Yamato* and *Musashi*, emerged in 1944 as the war's largest carrier at nearly 70,000 tons. Other conversions included the *Chiyoda* (1943) and *Chitose* (1944), both former seaplane carriers; the *Kaiyo* (1943) and *Shinyo* (1943), both former passenger liners, and the *Ibuki* (80 per cent complete at war's end), originally laid down as a heavy cruiser. The *Shinyo* displaced around 20,000 tons, the others closer to 15,000. The five wartime cruiser projects were all light cruisers with 6-inch guns: the four units of the *Agano* class (completed 1942–4) and the *Oyodo* (1943).[25] Special attack weapons, limited in the pre-war and early war years to midget submarines, took on a greater significance in 1944–5, when most of the conventional units of the fleet were either sunk or idled for lack of fuel. To defend Japan against the anticipated American invasion, in August 1945 the navy had on hand around 400 midget submarines, 120 manned torpedoes and 2,000 explosive motor boats, the latter two types being suicidal for those operating them.[26]

Less than seventy-five years after Japan began its process of modernization and industrialization, it had the world's second largest navy, one of the most formidable fleets ever assembled by any maritime power. Its construction was arguably the most remarkable technological achievement of any non-Western country up to that time. The aggressive expansionist policies it served led to its own destruction along with that of Imperial Japan, but the battered ruins of the Japanese military and naval industrial complex formed the foundation for the eventual post-war revival that made Japan a modern economic powerhouse. By the late twentieth century firms such as Mitsubishi and Kawasaki were known worldwide for their production of automobiles, motorcycles and other consumer goods, rather than for battleships, aircraft carriers and other weapons of war.

In the first decades after the Meiji Restoration, prominent samurai families from the domain of Satsuma dominated the officer corps of the Japanese navy. They owed their position to loyalty rather than competence, since Satsuma had risen up in the name of the emperor against the last Tokugawa shogun in 1868. Whether they hailed from Satsuma or some other part of the country, most of the officers in the navy's early years came to the service with no prior experience at sea, but this factor, along with the overall lack of maritime tradition among the Japanese elite, made the corps more receptive to new strategies, tactics and technologies.[27]

In 1869 the Imperial Naval Academy opened in Tsukiji, a suburb of Tokyo; in 1888 it moved to Etajima on Japan's Inland Sea, not far from Hiroshima. The course of study, initially four years, included the mixture of naval and general education subjects typical to other naval academies along with a rigorous physical fitness component and the inculcation of traditional martial values. By the time of the Russo-Japanese War, the Imperial Naval Academy had a three-year curriculum and produced around 200 graduates per year, who were commissioned as ensigns. As early as 1871 entering cadets had to pass competitive examinations, and by the 1890s the officer corps had diversified to include men from all over Japan, commoners as well as the descendants of samurai. By the 1920s the Japanese naval leadership finally reflected this diversity as well; over the same years the early Satsuma dominance gradually declined, starting in the lower ranks of the corps and slowly spreading upward to the admirals.[28]

British naval advisers first came to Japan in the last years of the shogunate, and exchanges continued until the end of the Anglo-Japanese alliance after the First World War. One mission in particular, which brought three dozen British officers to Japan between 1873 and 1879, had a lasting significance, shaping the curriculum of the Imperial Naval Academy as well as importing British attitudes of professionalism and British traditions, the latter influencing even the design of the navy's uniforms. British influence declined temporarily during the navy's flirtation with the French Jeune Ecole, but the Naval Staff College, a war college established at Tsukiji in 1888, reinforced the connection by embracing British concepts of strategy and tactics. The navy translated into Japanese the lectures, articles and books of the world's leading naval thinkers and writers, initially just the British and French, in 1896 joined by Alfred Thayer Mahan, the American battle fleet proponent. Mahan's *The Influence of Sea Power upon History, 1660–1783* became required reading at both the Imperial Naval Academy and the Naval Staff College. After 1893 graduates of the Naval Staff College served on a separate Navy General Staff. Graduation from the Naval Staff College became a key to the eventual achievement of admiral's rank, but without becoming an absolute requirement. Indeed, graduation at or near the top of one's class at the Imperial Naval Academy did just as much to accelerate future promotions. Officers could also enhance their prospects by studying abroad. Naval officers were among the scores of young Japanese sent overseas after 1868 to further their education for the good of the country. Many of them went to naval schools in Britain and elsewhere, but some attended civilian universities. Admiral Ito's second-in-command in the Sino-Japanese War of 1894–5, Rear Admiral Kozo Tsuboi, spent two years in New York at Columbia University in the early 1870s. Future admiral Heihachiro Togo, fleet commander in the Russo-Japanese War, studied naval science in Britain from 1871 to 1878, while future admiral Isoroku Yamamoto, fleet commander in the Second World War, studied at Harvard University from 1919 to 1921, before returning home to teach at the Naval Staff College.[29]

Until the policy became impossible to sustain, the navy deliberately sought to operate the smallest, best-trained force possible, rather than sacrifice its quality of training and level of competence simply for the sake of expansion. Gombei Yamamoto (no relation to Isoroku Yamamoto) has been hailed as 'the architect of modern Japanese naval power'. An early (1874) graduate of the Imperial Naval Academy, he became a leading reformer after being posted to the navy ministry in 1891. He went on to serve as navy minister (1898–1906) and eventually prime minister (1913–14 and 1923–4). Born in

Satsuma, he nevertheless dealt a fatal blow to that domain's grip on the naval leadership in 1893, when he forced the retirement of 10 per cent of the navy's officers, most of them senior officers from Satsuma. His relentless reforming spirit and emphasis on professionalism ended the problematic regional cliques within the corps.[30]

As would be the case in the management of the typical large Japanese corporation decades later, in the navy of the early twentieth century a loyal, relatively competent officer could count on a lifetime career in the service following his graduation from the Imperial Naval Academy; indeed, for years the navy practically guaranteed that all academy alumni would rise at least to the rank of captain.[31] Entrance examinations became increasingly competitive as the years passed, but once young men secured admission to the academy they became members of a cohort within which a general harmony reigned, at least until professional differences of opinion created new divisions within the corps. The Washington Naval Conference (1921–2) and the subsequent regime of naval arms limits split the officer corps into two mutually hostile groups: a moderate, realist 'treaty faction' and a belligerent, hard-line 'fleet faction'. The realists, led by navy minister Admiral Tomosaburo Kato, believed Japan's limited industrial strength would doom the country's chances in a naval race or future naval war against the United States. From the start he accepted Secretary Hughes's 5:5:3 proposal as the best possible deal for Japan, even though it sacrificed the navy's hallowed '70 per cent standard' *vis-à-vis* the American fleet and his own goal of an 'eight-eight' force of battleships and battle cruisers. The leader of the hard-liners, Naval Staff College president Vice Admiral Kanji Kato, acknowledged Japan's industrial weakness but argued that this factor made it all the more important for the navy to be free to build the strongest possible force in peacetime, to compensate for the inability of the country's industrial base to augment the strength of the fleet in a hurry once war appeared imminent. The hard-liners were realistic at least in that they knew Japan's hopes in a future war against one or both of the leading naval powers would hinge on a decisive early victory, which a fleet entering hostilities in a state of numerical inferiority could not possibly achieve. During the Washington negotiations Kanji Kato considered anything less than parity with the United States and Britain a dishonourable bargain. Tomosaburo Kato prevailed only because he had seniority over Kanji Kato, and covered himself by gaining approval for the 5:5:3 ratio from all key political and naval figures in Tokyo. Nevertheless, the acrimonious episode featured such un-Japanese behaviour as the junior Kato going over the head of the senior Kato by wiring Tokyo from Washington to express his dissent. At the moment the Japanese delegation agreed to the 5:5:3 ratio, a defiant Kanji Kato declared that 'as far as I am concerned, war with America starts now'.[32]

Fair deal for Japan or not, the Washington Naval Treaty saddled the Japanese navy with commitments that the vast majority of its officer corps did not accept. The small 'treaty faction' survived, and for another decade continued to dominate the navy ministry, but the cause of avoiding war with the United States soon lost its strongest advocate when Tomosaburo Kato, who served briefly as prime minister as well as navy minister following his return from Washington, died of cancer in 1923. His most prominent ally, future admiral Kichisaburo Nomura, ironically went on to serve the agenda of the hard-liners, first as commander of the force at Shanghai that involved the navy in Japan's aggression against China (1932), then as ambassador in Washington on the eve of Pearl Harbor, maintaining the fiction that Japan was interested in a peaceful resolution of its differences with the United States. Meanwhile, Kanji Kato continued to lead the much larger 'fleet faction', which dominated the Navy General Staff and command positions in the fleet. From the prominent posts of vice-chief of the staff (1922–6), then fleet commander (1926–8), then chief of the staff (1928–30), he promoted the notion that war with the United States was inevitable. His faction gained strength, especially among junior and mid-career officers, in part because the limits of the treaty also limited career opportunities within the service and delayed anticipated promotions. As chief of the Naval General Staff at the time of the London Naval Conference, Kanji Kato was in a position to stack the Japanese delegation with hard-liners. Ultimately Japan accepted the treaty only because Emperor

Hirohito favoured it. The delegation to London included Isoroku Yamamoto, recently promoted to rear admiral, who impressed the conference with his fluent English and moderate demeanour, but the enigmatic Yamamoto did little to represent the 'treaty faction' among the Japanese negotiators. Indeed, his good relations with Kanji Kato saved his career in the stormy years that followed.[33]

The London treaty only exacerbated the factionalism within the naval officer corps. The emperor rewarded Kanji Kato's intransigence by promoting him to the largely ceremonial Supreme War Council, where he remained until his retirement in 1935, aged 65. He died four years later, thus witnessing the end of the hated treaty limits but not the disaster that struck Japan after 1941. During the 1930s those urging fidelity to the treaties (or indeed, advocating any sort of peaceful course at all) became potential targets for assassination by ultranationalist groups. The links between these groups and hard-liners within the army and navy remain unclear, but by intimidating the realists and other moderates they paved the way for a dictatorship in which the dominant 'fleet faction' would place the navy at the disposal of army leaders determined to expand the empire in the Pacific as well as on the Asian mainland. The 'treaty faction' within the officer corps practically died out after Kanji Kato succeeded in placing one of his own protégés, Admiral Mineo Osumi, in the post of navy minister (1932–6), giving the hard-liners control over the ministry, the strongest bastion of the realists. During his tenure Osumi forced a number of pro-treaty admirals into early retirement.[34] The purge was by no means complete, since the outspoken Admiral Soemu Toyoda held a prominent post in the ministry as late as 1937 and then returned to sea, ultimately to become the last wartime commander of the fleet in 1944. Toyoda opposed the leaders of the 'fleet faction' and hated their ideological allies in the army, 'whom he often dismissed as "horseshit" or "animals"', according to one Japanese source.[35] Such dissenting cases aside, by the 1930s the naval officer corps as a whole bore the marks of the same ultranationalist extremism that dominated the army and led Japan down the path to conflict with the United States. The defeat of the realists reflected the overall flight from reason, and in the ensuing intensified focus on strategic and tactical matters most navy leaders lost sight of the broader picture of Japan's interests and the navy's role in defending them.[36]

The officer corps included 7,849 men in 1928 and 8,184 as late as 1932, but grew rapidly thereafter to reach 9,749 in 1936, the last year of naval arms limits. In the years immediately preceding the Second World War the dramatic expansion in *matériel* coincided with a tremendous growth in the number of officers, to 11,029 in 1937, 23,883 in 1941, and finally 34,769 in 1942. The navy failed to plan adequately for the tremendous growth in the size of the fleet after 1936, and it proved to be easier to build the warships than it was to train competent officers to command them and sailors to man them. The rapid expansion of the corps from 1937 to 1941, and continuing during the Second World War, required a relaxation of standards for the sake of numbers. Even then, the navy could not recruit and train enough officers to meet the needs of the fleet: in 1941 nearly 5 per cent of the posts in the corps went unfilled, a total of 1,151 vacancies. Wartime attrition left the navy especially short of mid-level officers such as lieutenant commanders and commanders. In some cases lieutenants filled their roles, and to alleviate the resulting dearth of lieutenants, the navy shortened the course at the Imperial Naval Academy, commissioned some warrant officers, and called up more reserve officers. The wartime fleet suffered terribly from the fact that Japan, alone among the leading naval powers, did not have a comprehensive naval reserve system. The reserve officer corps traditionally was kept very small, and included only graduates of Japanese merchant marine academies.[37]

The Imperial Japanese armed forces drafted their common manpower under the Universal Conscription Act of 1873, but the army controlled the draft and typically sent the fleet the worst of the annual cohorts. At least in its earliest years the navy preferred recruiting volunteers with experience in the country's substantial fishing fleet. Even after the growth in size and number of warships necessitated the employment of conscripts, volunteers continued to make up a significant share of the manpower, accounting for roughly one-third of it between the late 1920s and the onset of war with the United States. In sheer numbers this translated into around 25,000 volunteers in 1928 but 95,000 in 1941. Common manpower numbered 72,746 in 1928 and 75,638 as late as 1932, but grew rapidly thereafter to reach 97,718 in 1936, the last year of naval arms limits. In the years immediately preceding the Second World War the dramatic expansion in *matériel* required a rapid growth in personnel, to 122,984 in 1937, 287,476 in 1941, and finally 394,599 in 1942. As with the officer corps, with its common manpower the navy until the 1930s emphasized quality over quantity and attempted to function with the smallest, best-trained force possible. The navy's increased dependence on conscription before and during the Second World War only exacerbated its rivalry with the army, since the latter had a manpower crisis of its own. The army continued to send the fleet the worst of the draftees, and further weakened the navy by conscripting thousands of its civilian workers into the army. Remarkably, through all of the manning problems, the loyalty and discipline of the common Japanese sailor remained a constant upon which officers could depend. It had no equal in other navies.[38]

In leading the navy to disaster, Kanji Kato and the hard-liners of the 'fleet faction' had helped lead the country to disaster as well. Their quest to defeat the US navy, hopeless in any event, suffered from the fundamental contradiction between their own belligerence and the institutional culture of the navy, which emphasized professionalism and quality of training over sheer size and numbers. After the First World War, amid the hubris of the country's emergence as a great power on the world stage, this philosophy changed, but the navy's personnel policies did not. The campaigns against China (1894–5), Russia (1904–5) and Germany (1914) were all relatively brief, reinforcing the short-war mentality of the Naval General Staff and shaping its subsequent approach to war with the United States. In pursuing a course that risked embroiling the navy in a longer war against the American fleet while not preparing a force capable of fighting such a war, Japanese navy leaders committed their fatal error.[39]

Three of the four major wars of the Imperial Japanese navy, against China (1894–5), Russia (1904–5) and the United States (1941–5), began with Japanese forces launching some sort of pre-emptive strike before the formal declaration of war, an approach reflected in the old samurai adage 'win first and fight later'.[40] The baptism of fire of the modern Japanese navy came in the Battle of P'ung Island (25 July 1894), off Inchon, where four protected cruisers under Rear Admiral Tsuboi ambushed and routed a weaker Chinese force convoying troops to Korea, then the focal point of Sino-Japanese rivalry. The decisive Battle of the Yalu (17 September 1894) began when Admiral Ito's Combined Fleet, including seven protected cruisers and three smaller or older armoured vessels, encountered a more formidable Chinese force that had just landed troops near the mouth of the Yalu River. In the six-hour battle the Chinese had lost an armoured cruiser and four protected cruisers, while the Japanese lost no ships at all. The victory gave the Japanese command of the Yellow Sea, enabling them to seize the Liaotung Peninsula with Port Arthur, then the Shantung Peninsula with Weihaiwei, forcing China to surrender in February 1895. In the peace settlement Japan acquired Taiwan and the Pescadores, but pressure from the European powers (especially Russia) forced the return of the Liaotung and Shantung peninsulas to China.[41]

Three years after Japan's victory, Russia leased the Liaotung Peninsula from China and began developing Port Arthur as a naval base, linked by rail across Manchuria to the Trans-Siberian Railway. The Russo-Japanese tensions over Korea and Manchuria led to a rupture of diplomatic relations on 6 February 1904; two days later, without first declaring war, the Japanese sent ten destroyers on a surprise attack against the Russian Pacific squadron at Port Arthur, where they torpedoed two battleships and a cruiser (all of which were repaired). In the first high-seas actions of the war, Admiral Togo's Combined Fleet turned back an attempt by the Russian Pacific squadron to break out of Port Arthur and run for Vladivostok. No ships were sunk at the Battle of the Yellow Sea (10 August 1904), but the unprecedented range at which the battle was fought – both sides were fully engaged between 8,000 and 9,000 metres (5–5.6 miles) – attracted international attention. Days later four Japanese armoured cruisers defeated the Vladivostok cruiser squadron at the Battle of the Sea of Japan (14 August 1904); the Russian squadron lost one armoured cruiser and afterward remained in port for the rest of the war. Over the months that followed, most of the Russian warships bottled up at Port Arthur (five battleships and two cruisers) were sunk by the siege guns of the Japanese forces surrounding the city or scuttled to avoid capture before the base surrendered on 2 January 1905.[42] Meanwhile, in October 1904 the Russians sent Admiral Zinovy Rozhestvensky with the 'Second Pacific Squadron' (actually most of their Baltic Fleet) around Africa to the Far East to relieve Port Arthur. After learning en route that Port Arthur had fallen, Rozhestvensky made for Vladivostok instead, on a course that would take him through the Strait of Tsushima, between Japan and the southern tip of Korea. Passing through the strait on 27 May 1905, the Russian fleet, led by eleven battleships and three armoured cruisers, encountered Togo's Combined Fleet led by four battleships and eight armoured cruisers. The Japanese were outnumbered but their oldest armoured warship had been commissioned in 1897, and three of their four battleships were larger than any ship in the Russian fleet. The encounter began at 13:40, when Togo crossed the Russian 'T' from east to west, then reversed course to recross the 'T' from west to east. At 14:08 the Russians hit Togo's flagship, the 15,140-ton *Mikasa*, from a distance of 7,000 metres. The Japanese began returning fire at 6,400 metres, and their superior gunnery soon took its toll, sinking four Russian battleships between 15:00 and 19:30, and two later, along with an armoured cruiser. The Russians scuttled another battleship and two armoured cruisers before surrendering the rest of their fleet on the morning of 28 May. Of the 38 warships of all sizes in the Russian fleet, only one (an armed yacht) made it through to Vladivostok. The Battle of Tsushima cost the Japanese navy just three torpedo boats and 110 men killed; Russian casualties included 4,830 men killed and 5,917 captured, the latter including Rozhestvensky. Peace talks opened in the wake of the Japanese victory, and in September 1905 the Treaty of Portsmouth gave Japan the southern half of Sakhalin Island, a free hand in Korea (annexed in 1910), and the Russian lease to the Liaotung Peninsula and Port Arthur.[43]

Tsushima reinforced the navy's conviction that modern naval wars would be short and resolved in decisive Mahanian engagements between battle fleets. This legacy lived on in the lecture halls of the Imperial Naval Academy and the war gaming of the Navy Staff College, and in the men who commanded the navy of the Second World War, many of whom (like Isoroku Yamamoto, an ensign when wounded at Tsushima aboard one of Togo's armoured cruisers) experienced their baptism of fire in 1904–5.[44] The navy's experience in the First World War was brief enough, but did not include a battle fleet engagement. After Japan entered the war on the side of the Allies (23 August 1914), the most formidable units of Admiral Count Maximilian von Spee's German East Asian squadron left their anchorage at Kiaochow Bay on the Shantung Peninsula and steamed eastward across the Pacific, where they defeated a British force at Coronel (1 November) before being crushed at the Falklands (8 December). Meanwhile, the Germans left behind surrendered their base at Tsingtao to a predominantly Japanese allied force (7 November) after scuttling the small or obsolete warships Spee had left behind. The Japanese navy secured Germany's island colonies, the Marshalls and the Carolines, while the army occupied the Shantung Peninsula. Afterward Japan practically sat out the rest of the war, aside from sending a light cruiser and fourteen destroyers to the Mediterranean to bolster Allied convoys. This small force, under Rear Admiral Kozo Sato, gained valuable experience in anti-submarine warfare operations (albeit without sinking a single u-boat).[45]

After the First World War the Navy General Staff focused its attention on preparing for a future war with the United States, just as us navy leaders focused primarily on the threat from Japan. In the inter-war Japanese navy, strategic, tactical and qualitative innovations all focused on what one work has called the quest to 'outrange' the enemy – whether it be in carrier operations, battleship gunfire or the range of torpedoes fired by smaller surface warships and submarines. Such efforts further extended the navy's operational range deep into the Pacific and, on a tactical level, held the promise of allowing Japanese units to strike from distances at which the enemy would be unable to strike back.[46] As early as 1927, officers at the Naval Staff College wargamed a carrier-based attack against the us navy's base at Pearl Harbor, Hawaii, 4,000 miles east of Japan, but throughout the inter-war period the mainstream of Japanese strategic thinking on war with the United States remained essentially defensive, centred around the notion of luring the us navy into a Tsushima-like battle fleet engagement in the western Pacific. For its part, the us navy calculated that the Japanese had the ability to launch a carrier-based attack on Pearl Harbor and simulated it in manoeuvres in 1932 and again in 1938. The Japanese took notice when the British navy used carrier-based aircraft to sink or damage units of the Italian fleet at Taranto in November 1940; meanwhile, Pearl Harbor became an even more tempting target once President Franklin Roosevelt ordered the main body of the us Pacific Fleet to be based there, rather than at San Diego. By January 1941 Admiral Isoroku Yamamoto (commander of the Combined Fleet since 1939) was planning for a surprise knockout blow at Pearl Harbor that would improve Japan's chances of winning a longer war against the United States. The attack would also cover a concurrent invasion of the East Indies staged from French Indochina, which Japanese troops from China (partially occupied since the onset of a full-scale Sino-Japanese war in 1937) seized in July 1941. In late November Yamamoto set in motion an elaborate plan to strike more or less simultaneously at American and British possessions on both sides of the international date line, on the morning of 7–8 December: Pearl Harbor, Wake Island and Guam, the Philippines, Malaya, Singapore and North Borneo.[47]

While Yamamoto directed the series of offensives from Tokyo, Vice Admiral Chuichi Nagumo commanded the First Air Fleet in the attack on Pearl Harbor. Appointed to the post eight months earlier, Nagumo was a curious choice; he had no prior experience in naval aviation and opposed the idea of attacking Pearl Harbor. His force consisted of the carriers

Akagi, Kaga, Hiryu, Soryu, Shokaku and *Zuikaku,* two battle-ships, one light and two heavy cruisers, eleven destroyers and three submarines. Five midget submarines were sent ahead to infiltrate the harbour prior to the air assault. Approaching Hawaii undetected on the morning of 7 December, Nagumo's carriers launched 350 aircraft in two waves that bombed Pearl Harbor and other targets on the island of Oahu for two hours, sinking four of the us Pacific Fleet's eight battleships and caus-ing at least some damage to every other ship present. They also destroyed or damaged nearly 350 planes on the ground. In the attack the Japanese lost just 29 planes, one submarine and all five midget submarines. Nagumo caused significant damage to American naval power in the Pacific but failed to deliver the knockout blow Yamamoto had hoped for: none of the Pacific Fleet's carriers was in Pearl Harbor at the time of the attack and, aside from the battleships *Arizona* and *Oklahoma,* all of the sunken or damaged warships were eventually repaired and returned to service. Nevertheless, the us navy's temporary paralysis enabled Yamamoto's ships to land troops at several places in the Philippines and secure both Wake Island and Guam before the end of the month. Meanwhile, Vice Admiral Nobutake Kondo led an amphibious assault on British Malaya and Borneo, spearheaded by a force of two battleships, one light and seven heavy cruisers, covered by naval aircraft operating out of Japanese bases in French Indochina. On 10 December the latter sank the only British capital ships in East Asian waters, the battleship *Prince of Wales* and the old battle cruiser *Repulse,* which had arrived off the coast of Malaya just days before the onset of hostilities. The Japanese soon blockaded and besieged the surviving British forces at Singapore, which capitulated on 15 February 1942. By then Borneo had fallen, the Philippines were almost completely occupied, and the Japanese were look-ing forward to their next conquests: the Dutch East Indies, New Guinea and Australia.[48]

In January 1942 the surviving British naval forces in the East Indies joined Dutch, American and Australian units in the joint 'ABDA' command, under the overall leadership of an American admiral. After the fall of Singapore the Japanese focused on Java, which depended on a lifeline from Darwin, Australia. On

19 February Nagumo practically destroyed the northern Australian port with the same force he had used earlier to attack Pearl Harbor, minus two carriers, the two battleships and four of the destroyers. The *Kaga*, *Akagi*, *Hiryu* and *Soryu* launched 188 aircraft that day, and all but two returned safely. After isolating Java, the Japanese secured the conquest of the Dutch East Indies by crushing the ABDA squadron in the Battle of the Java Sea (27 February–1 March 1942), an encounter of cruisers and destroyers in which the light carrier *Ryujo* came to the aid of the Japanese force.[49] As the Japanese completed their conquest of the East Indies, the British assembled a new Eastern Fleet at Ceylon, including three carriers, five old battleships and seven cruisers. Yamamoto promptly sent Nagumo with his entire Pearl Harbor force, supplemented by two additional battleships, for a raid into the Indian Ocean with the goal of crippling the new British fleet and destroying its bases on Ceylon. After engine trouble forced the *Kaga* to turn back, Nagumo proceeded with the *Akagi*, *Hiryu*, *Soryu*, *Shokaku* and *Zuikaku*, whose aircraft dominated a four-day battle (5–9 April 1942) off Ceylon, sinking the British carrier *Hermes*, two heavy cruisers and four smaller warships along with 93,000 tons of Allied shipping, while also bombing the British bases at Colombo and Trincomalee. Nagumo lost no warships of his own. Coinciding with the conquest of Burma (completed May 1942), a Japanese landing on Ceylon would have further endangered India. Fearing the worst, the British withdrew half of their Eastern Fleet to the Arabian Sea and the other half to the coast of East Africa, to guard the convoy route between the Cape of Good Hope and the Red Sea. But after giving the British a beating Nagumo withdrew from the Indian Ocean, and the Japanese navy never threatened India again.[50]

In the first months of the war, the Ceylon raid was the only carrier operation that rivalled Pearl Harbor in its audacity. The navy used submarines for its other bold strokes, deploying nine off the coasts of Oregon and California in the winter of 1941–2, where they caused more alarm than damage, especially after *I-17* used its deck gun to shell a pier and an oil derrick at Santa Barbara (28 February 1942). Before being recalled, they sank just five merchantmen totalling 30,370 tons. All nine boats returned home safely. A raid by three midget submarines on the harbour of Sydney, Australia (31 May 1942), fared far worse, as all three units were lost and no damage done.[51] Meanwhile, after the sortie into the Indian Ocean Nagumo's carrier force returned home for a refit before the Midway campaign. The *Shokaku* and *Zuikaku* (in better shape than the rest for having missed the Darwin raid earlier) were detached to a force under Vice Admiral Takeo Takagi and sent to the Coral Sea, between northeast Australia and the Solomon Islands, to cover a Japanese amphibious landing on the southern coast of New Guinea. Takagi's other ships included the light carrier *Shoho*, six heavy and three light cruisers. In the Battle of the Coral Sea (7–8 May 1942) they met an American force including the carriers *Lexington* and *Yorktown* and eight heavy cruisers. The engagement ended with no clear winner, but the amphibious force had to turn back. While the Japanese lost the *Shoho*, their first significant material casualty of the war, the Americans lost the much larger *Lexington*. The *Shokaku* and *Yorktown* both suffered serious damage, the latter so much that the Japanese came away thinking they had sunk it. While the *Yorktown*, repaired at Pearl Harbor, would fight at Midway a month later, the *Shokaku* would not. The *Zuikaku* emerged from the battle unscathed but lost enough aircraft and pilots to be held back from Midway as well.[52]

Yamamoto's strategy for the Midway campaign was to secure the island, at the western end of the Hawaiian chain 1,200 miles (1,930 kilometres) from Pearl Harbor, in order to draw out and overwhelm the degraded US Pacific Fleet in a decisive battle. On this occasion the entire Combined Fleet sortied, including Admiral Yamamoto in the flagship *Yamato* in overall personal command. Vice Admiral Nagumo led the way with a force including the carriers *Kaga*, *Akagi*, *Hiryu* and *Soryu*, two battleships, one light and two heavy cruisers; other units in the fleet included the light carriers *Hosho* and *Zuiho*, four battleships, three light and eight heavy cruisers. At the same time, Vice Admiral Boshiro Hosogawa led a diversionary assault on the Aleutian Islands with the Fifth Fleet, including the light carriers *Ryujo* and *Junyo*, four light and three heavy cruisers. Nagumo opened the battle at 04:30 on 5 June 1942 by launching 108 of his 234 aircraft against Midway. When this first wave made its bombing run two hours later, the island's anti-aircraft guns shot down or damaged all but 41 of the planes, seriously reducing the striking power of Nagumo's four carriers and giving Yamamoto second thoughts about the deployment of the four light carriers, none of which would participate in the ensuing battle. Steaming toward Midway from Pearl Harbor, an American force under Admiral Chester Nimitz, including the carriers *Yorktown*, *Hornet* and *Enterprise* (total 233 aircraft), escorted by one light and seven heavy cruisers, launched its first planes between 07:00 and 08:00. They made their first contact with the Japanese fleet after 09:00, just as Nagumo was hesitating over whether to arm his planes for a second attack on Midway or for battle with the approaching American force. Some of the *Hornet*'s torpedo planes spotted the *Kaga* after 09:00 but failed to damage it in their attack. Then, between 10:20 and 10:30, dive-bombers from the *Enterprise* scored hits on the *Akagi* and *Kaga*, while dive-bombers from the *Yorktown* set the *Soryu* ablaze. The intense fires rendered the three Japanese carriers useless for the rest of the battle; the *Kaga* and *Soryu* each remained afloat for another nine hours before sinking, while Yamamoto ordered destroyers to torpedo the burning hulk of the *Akagi* at 05:00 the following morning. Meanwhile, the *Hiryu*, which had taken a course to the north of the other Japanese carriers, remained unscathed and launched a strike against the *Yorktown* around 11:00, and a second strike at 13:20. The first wave took an hour to reach its target, the second around 90 minutes, but both scored hits, and the *Yorktown* had to be abandoned just before 15:00. By then, American planes had spotted the *Hiryu*, and at 15:50 the *Hornet* and *Enterprise* launched all of their remaining aircraft for a strike against it. They found their prey just after 17:05, catching the crew taking its evening meal in no great sense of urgency. Four bombs tore through the *Hiryu*'s flight deck, putting it out of action and igniting fires below. Amid an intense but futile effort to save the ship, the crew remained aboard for another ten hours; the *Hiryu* finally sank at 08:20 on 5 June. In the predawn hours of the 5th, shortly after Yamamoto ordered the remaining ships to withdraw, the heavy cruisers *Mikuma* and *Mogami* collided, leaving both damaged and capable only of a reduced speed. On 6 June aircraft from the *Hornet* and *Enterprise* attacked the two ships as they straggled behind the rest of the retreating Japanese fleet; the *Mikuma* sank after dark that evening, while the *Mogami* escaped with heavy casualties. The *Yorktown*, abandoned two and a half days earlier, remained afloat until the morning of 7 June, when a Japanese submarine torpedoed and sank it. Meanwhile, Hosogawa's Fifth Fleet landed troops that occupied the islands of Attu (5 June) and Kiska (7 June) in the Aleutians, but this costly diversion failed to draw significant American forces away from the main body of the fleet at Midway.[53]

The Battle of Midway, coming just six months after Pearl Harbor, was the turning point of the Pacific theatre of the Second World War. Even after losing four carriers, the Japanese still had the strongest fleet in the Pacific, but Yamamoto would not get the short war his country needed. His chief of staff, Vice Admiral Matome Ugaki, blamed the defeat on arrogance: 'we had become conceited because of past success'.[54] In any event, the need to fight on dispelled their depression. Shortly after Midway the focus of the fighting shifted back to New Guinea and the adjacent Solomon Islands, where the Japanese began to build an airfield on Guadalcanal. In August 1942 an American-Australian force counter-attacked in New Guinea, while us Marines landed on Guadalcanal, in the latter case touching off a bitter battle the Japanese vowed not to lose, ultimately giving it priority over New Guinea. As both sides poured troops into the island, the navies concentrated their forces in the Solomons chain, with Yamamoto directing the various components of the Combined Fleet from aboard the flagship *Yamato*. During the fifteen-month war of attrition in the Solomons (August 1942–November 1943) the us navy added far more warships than it lost, including a number of units laid down since Pearl Harbor, while Japan's industrial base could not compensate for the losses its navy suffered. Yamamoto achieved a last victory in the Battle of the Santa Cruz Islands (25–7 October 1942), fought 500 miles east of Guadalcanal, where a force including the carriers *Shokaku*, *Zuikaku*, *Junyo* and *Zuiho* defeated an American force including the carriers *Enterprise* and *Hornet*, sinking the latter, but three of the Japanese carriers suffered damage and the situation on Guadalcanal remained unchanged.

Even after the Japanese abandoned Guadalcanal in February 1943, the contest continued to the northwest in the Bismarck Archipelago, until American carrier strikes finally destroyed the Japanese stronghold of Rabaul in November. Meanwhile, in the northern Pacific sideshow to the main campaign, an American counter-attack drove the Japanese out of the Aleutian Islands by the end of July. Further casualties included Yamamoto (18 April 1943), whose plane was shot down in the Solomons. While the *Hornet* was the most significant US navy ship sunk during the campaign, Japanese losses included the carrier *Ryujo* along with the battleships *Hiei* and *Kirishima*. Ultimately Guadalcanal was lost because the United States could reinforce and resupply its forces on the island, while Japan could not. After the island was abandoned, devastating losses in shipping would cripple Japanese efforts to sustain garrisons on other islands they had occupied in their initial conquest of the western Pacific. In eight months alone (March–October 1943) the Japanese lost 1,052,740 tons of shipping, including 676,410 tons in military and naval transport vessels, two-thirds of it sunk by American submarines.[55]

Admiral Mineichi Koga succeeded Yamamoto as commander of the Combined Fleet but could do nothing to reverse the decline of the navy's fortunes. Avoidable losses in home waters weakened the fleet still more: a magazine explosion destroyed the battleship *Mutsu* at anchor at Hashijimira (June 1943), while an American submarine sank the carrier *Chuyo* off Yokosuka (December 1943). Meanwhile, the loss of the Solomons exposed the position of Japanese forces in the Marshall Islands, 1,000 miles to the northeast, where US Marines took Tarawa in November 1943. After the loss of the Marshalls, Koga moved the forward anchorage of the Combined Fleet from Truk in the Carolines to Palau, 1,200 miles to the west; a week later (17–18 February 1944) an American task force including eight carriers and six battleships destroyed what was left of the base at Truk, sinking the light cruisers and destroyers Koga had left behind. After Koga's plane disappeared en route to Palau (31 March), Admiral Soemu Toyoda took over as head of the Combined Fleet. Thereafter, the American offensive moved on from the Carolines northward into the Marianas. In mid-June US troops landed on Saipan, just 1,500 miles south of the Japanese home islands, where Admiral Nagumo (in disgrace since Midway) was in charge of the naval defences. Toyoda responded by sending Vice Admiral Jisaburo Ozawa with the recently organized First Mobile Fleet to counter-attack. In the ensuing Battle of the Philippine Sea (19–20 June), fought just to the west of the Marianas, the Japanese deployed nine carriers (*Shokaku*, *Zuikaku*, *Junyo*, *Ryuho*, *Zuiho*, *Hiyo*, *Taiho*, *Chitose* and *Chiyoda*), five battleships (among them the giant *Yamato* and *Musashi*), eight heavy and two light cruisers. This was by far their largest force of the war to date but it was still dwarfed by the opposing Admiral Raymond Spruance's US Fifth Fleet, which included fifteen carriers, seven battleships, eight heavy and thirteen light cruisers. In the first hours of action on the 19th, American submarines torpedoed the *Taiho* (at 09:10) and the *Shokaku* (at 12:20), both of which exploded and sank later that afternoon. The two fleets disengaged for a full day before the battle resumed during the last daylight hours of the 20th, at which time 216 planes from eleven American carriers attacked the Japanese fleet, sinking the *Hiyo* at 20:30 and seriously damaging three other carriers. Greatly outnumbered in any event, Ozawa's force suffered from the inexperience of his pilots, who failed to sink a single American warship. Saipan soon fell to the Americans, and Admiral Nagumo took his own life rather than surrender. American submarine attacks later in the summer of 1944 further degraded the Japanese carrier fleet, claiming the *Taiyo* (in August) and the *Unyo* (in September), both off the coast of China.[56]

The next great American amphibious operation targeted Leyte in the Philippines, where US troops began landing in mid-October 1944. Toyoda's strategy for the Battle of Leyte Gulf (24–25 October) called for Ozawa's badly weakened carrier force to lure the main striking power of the US Third and Seventh fleets, under the overall command of Admiral William Halsey, out into the Philippine Sea and away from the waves of American transports preparing to land troops on Leyte. The US fleets would then be fallen upon by a battleship force under Vice Admiral Takeo Kurita, advancing through the Philippine islands from the west, in two columns. Ozawa had at his disposal just the carriers *Zuikaku, Zuiho, Chitose* and *Chiyoda*, along with the half-carrier hybrids *Ise* and *Hyuga* (battleships fitted with flight decks aft following the loss of the carriers at Midway in 1942), supported by three light cruisers and destroyers, while Kurita's force included the *Yamato*, the *Musashi*, five other battleships, thirteen heavy and three light cruisers. The American armada they faced included thirteen carriers, eighteen escort carriers, eighteen battleships, and scores of cruisers and destroyers. The battle opened on the morning of 24 October, when land-based Japanese aircraft sank the American light carrier *Princeton*. That afternoon more than 250 aircraft from Halsey's carriers pounded Kurita's main column as it passed through the Sibuyan Sea, focusing on the *Musashi*, which sank at 18:35. Thereafter Halsey took the bait as the Japanese had hoped, and chased Ozawa's force to the northeast, out into the Philippine Sea. On the night of 24–25 October six old American battleships left behind by Halsey (five of which had been at Pearl Harbor on 7 December 1941) engaged another column of the Japanese battleship force in the Surigao Strait, the southern approach to Leyte Gulf. American battleships and destroyers used gunfire and torpedoes to sink the battleships *Fuso* and *Yamashiro*, along with one heavy and one light cruiser, while losing no units of their own. Meanwhile, Kurita's main column sank the escort carrier *Gambier Bay* off the island of Samar, north of Leyte Gulf, at 08:00 on the morning of 25 October, but strikes launched from other escort carriers and fire from the smaller American warships protecting them ultimately turned back his force, in the process damaging three of his heavy cruisers so badly that they had to be scuttled. Thus, the American landings on Leyte continued unmolested, while out in the Philippine Sea, Halsey finished the battle by sinking all four carriers in Ozawa's decoy force: the *Chitose* at 08:30, the *Zuikaku* at 13:15, the *Zuibo* at 14:25 and the *Chiyoda* around 15:45. Counting two heavy cruisers sunk the day before the battle and two light cruisers the day after, Japanese losses included four carriers, three battleships and nine cruisers, against two carriers (one light and one escort) for the Americans.[57]

For the Japanese navy, Leyte Gulf was an exercise in futility. Halsey had taken the bait and pursued Ozawa, leaving the landing force at Leyte vulnerable to attack, but the US navy enjoyed such superiority that his error in judgement had not mattered. The day after the defeat, the remaining units of the Combined Fleet were divided into two forces, one based at Singapore and the other in Japan's Inland Sea. American forces retook the Philippines with no further interference from the Japanese navy; indeed, over the last nine and a half months of the war its ships rarely ventured out. On 7 April 1945, six days after the onset of the Battle of Okinawa, the battleship *Yamato* went on a suicide sortie from the Inland Sea down to the embattled island, accompanied by a light cruiser and eight destroyers. After American carriers launched hundreds of aircraft to attack the small group, only four of the destroyers survived to return to their base. The 'battle' cost 3,665 Japanese lives. The crew of the giant *Yamato* alone accounted for 2,498 of the dead, more than the total number of Americans killed at Pearl Harbor on 7 December 1941 and, by far, the greatest number of fatalities ever suffered in a single warship sinking. Between the defeat at Leyte Gulf and the end of the war in August 1945, most of the other larger warships of the fleet were destroyed by bombs or torpedoes in or near Japanese home waters: the carriers *Amagi*, *Kaiyo*, *Shinano*, *Shinyo* and *Unryu*, the half-carrier hybrids *Hyuga* and *Ise*, the battleships *Kongo* and *Haruna*, six heavy and five light cruisers. The last significant units lost on the high seas were also the largest Japanese ships claimed by the British navy during the war: the heavy cruiser *Haguro*, sunk by destroyers on 15 May 1945, and its sister ship *Ashigara*, torpedoed by a submarine on 8 June, both while on missions to evacuate isolated island garrisons in the eastern Indian Ocean.[58] Aside from the *Yamato*'s final sortie, the navy played no role in either of the last major battles of the war, Iwo Jima and Okinawa, leaving it to army troops and, in the latter case, kamikaze pilots to make US forces pay dearly for their victories.

CONCLUSION

Unlike the Imperial German navy of the First World War, which surrendered almost its entire battle fleet intact, the

Imperial Japanese navy of the Second World War went down fighting, leaving few larger units to surrender to the Allies on 2 September 1945: the battleship *Nagato*, the carriers *Hosho*, *Junyo*, *Katsuragi* and *Ryuho*, two heavy cruisers and three light cruisers. Of 153 submarines known to have sortied during the war, just 22 survived to be handed over. Casualty figures reflected the decision to fight to the end, as naval deaths alone numbered 300,386, just a few thousand less than the total figure for all branches of the United States armed forces on all fronts. Another 114,493 civilian naval employees died, most of them in the aerial bombing of shipyards and bases.[59] In all of history, no other defeated navy has ever suffered destruction on such a scale, either in lives of personnel or tonnage of *matériel*.

For a half century before its demise in 1945, the Imperial Japanese navy was the standard bearer of Japanese imperialism. Without it, Japan obviously never could have created an empire beyond its home islands. The fleet grew to such a strength that in 1941–2 it posed the greatest security threat to the United States since the British invasion in the War of 1812. In order to defeat the Japanese, the United States, in turn, assembled the largest navy the world had ever known, the foundation of the force that would attempt to dominate the world's oceans during the ensuing era of the Cold War.

EIGHT

Red Star Rising:
The Soviet Navy, 1956–91

The Cold War provided the context for a dramatic revival of Russian sea power, begun in the late 1940s but accelerated after 1956 under the direction of Admiral Sergei G. Gorshkov. The build-up made the Soviet Union the world's second sea power after the United States. While intercontinental ballistic missiles ultimately became the focal point of the US-Soviet military rivalry, it was the operational reach of the Soviet navy – including surface vessels and submarines cruising wherever there were American warships – that carried the Cold War to every corner of the planet. By denying the US navy command of the world's oceans, Gorshkov's fleet played an important role in Soviet strategy without ever achieving, or seeking to achieve, command of the sea in its own right.[1]

GORSHKOV'S FLEET

In the decade between the end of the Second World War and Gorshkov's appointment to command the Soviet navy, the fleet grew considerably but to no coherent grand design. The Soviet navy of 1945 included 3 battleships, 9 cruisers, 53 destroyers and 176 submarines, over half of the latter in the Pacific Fleet. Because the Allies had all but destroyed the German navy, the Soviets received most of their naval reparations from the Italian fleet: the battleship *Giulio Cesare* (renamed *Novorossiysk*), cruiser *Duca d'Aosta* (renamed *Stalingrad*, later *Kerch*), ten destroyers and ten submarines. The German cruiser *Nürnberg* (renamed *Admiral Makarov*) also passed into Russian service. Once the prizes arrived, the Soviet navy returned the battleship

Arkhangelsk (ex-*Royal Sovereign*) and eight destroyers to Britain, and the cruiser *Murmansk* (ex-*Milwaukee*) to the United States.[2]

Joseph Stalin's vision for the postwar Soviet fleet included giant battleships supported by battle cruisers. Eight 75,000-ton battleships armed with nine 16-inch guns were to be backed by a class of 36,500-ton battle cruisers with nine 12-inch guns. While none of the battleships was ever laid down, in 1951 and 1952 work began on the battle cruisers *Stalingrad* and *Moskva*, for the Black Sea and Baltic fleets, respectively. Admiral Nikolai G. Kuznetsov, navy commissar from 1939 to 1947, clashed with Stalin over the postwar fleet plan and was banished to Vladivostok, where he commanded the Pacific Fleet until 1951. Thereafter he returned to Moscow, resumed overall command of the navy, and actively sought to cancel the projected battleship class as well as the battle cruisers just laid down. Kuznetsov favoured aircraft carriers over battleships and battle cruisers, and wanted a larger submarine force. Nikita Khrushchev characterized Kuznetsov as 'too outspoken and stubborn for Stalin's taste', yet the admiral had a rare ability to survive disagreements with the ageing dictator.[3] Ultimately Stalin and Kuznetsov agreed on a large programme of cruisers, which remained the focal point of the Soviet surface fleet through the 1960s. Five 11,500-ton *Chapayev* class cruisers laid down in 1939 were completed during the 1950s, and in 1952 the navy commissioned the 13,600-ton *Sverdlov* (illus. 25), the first of a projected class of 25 cruisers. The *Chapayev*s and *Sverdlov*s carried a primary armament of twelve 6-inch guns. Smaller surface warships included 70 destroyers of the *Skorij* class (completed 1949–53) and 31 of the *Spokoiniy* (NATO 'Kotlin' and 'Kildin')[4] class (completed 1955–8). Shortly before Stalin died in March 1953, the navy drafted plans to arm the *Skorij* and *Spokoiniy* class destroyers with missiles. Beginning in the late 1940s the Soviets developed a variety of guided (cruise) and ballistic missiles, building their own expertise on a foundation of captured German technology. In 1955 the Soviet Union deployed its first anti-ship missiles on aircraft, but at that stage no Russian warship had yet been armed with missiles.[5]

Immediately after Stalin died, Kuznetsov halted work on the battle cruisers *Stalingrad* and *Moskva*, and cancelled plans for

25 A Soviet *Sverdlov* class cruiser, photographed in 1957.

26 The Soviet battleship *Oktyabrskaya Revolutsia* (ex-*Gangut*) in 1936, after modernization.

the class of 75,000-ton battleships. The navy's three older battleships soon left service as well. The *Oktyabrskaya Revolutsia* (ex-*Gangut*; illus. 26) and the *Parizhkaya Kommuna* (ex-*Sevastopol*), both commissioned in the Imperial Russian navy in 1914, were retired in 1954 and 1957, respectively, while the former Italian prize *Novorossiysk* sank in 1955, victim of an old German mine in the Black Sea. As Stalin's successor,

Khrushchev, gradually consolidated his power, the navy's construction projects remained in doubt. The twenty-first *Sverdlov* was laid down in 1955, but later that year Khrushchev cancelled the programme. Fourteen of the cruisers entered service, the last in September 1955; the seven units begun after January 1953 were broken up on the stocks.[6] Khrushchev agreed with Kuznetsov on the need for a large submarine force but clashed with the admiral over the cruiser programme and the notion that the future Soviet navy should include aircraft carriers. In December 1955, just months after promoting Kuznetsov to the new rank of fleet admiral (the naval equivalent of marshal of the Soviet Union), Khrushchev tired of the admiral's 'obstinacy and arrogance' and sacked him. The minister of defence, Marshal G. K. Zhukov, joined other Soviet political and military leaders in endorsing Khrushchev's vision of a future naval service centred around submarines and land-based aircraft armed with anti-ship missiles.[7]

In January 1956 Khrushchev appointed Vice Admiral Sergei G. Gorshkov to succeed Kuznetsov as navy commander. Gorshkov, then just 45 years old, won the post over several more senior admirals, evidence of the degree to which Khrushchev trusted him to implement his vision. Early in his tenure Gorshkov took care to operate within the limits of Khrushchev's wishes, concealing his own general agreement with his predecessor on the navy's material needs. Khrushchev permitted new smaller surface warships as long as they were armed with missiles; in 1958 Gorshkov responded with the *Bedoviy*, a *Spokoiniy* (NATO 'Kildin') class destroyer that became the first Soviet surface ship in regular commission to be armed with missiles. It carried the first Soviet naval surface-to-surface missile (SSM), the Korabelnye Snaryad Shchuka or KSshch (NATO SS-N-1 'Scrubber'),[8] a shipboard version of Vladimir N. Chelomey's air-launched Shchuka missile, first deployed in 1955. Until such time as the Soviets developed a functional system of over-the-horizon (OTH) targeting, the effective range of the KSshch was limited to targets within sight of the firing ship. The next Soviet destroyers, eight Project 57B (NATO 'Krupny') class vessels (completed 1960–61), each carried twelve KSshch missiles. They entered service concurrently with the first Project 205 (NATO 'Osa') class fast attack craft, 300 of which were commissioned in the years 1959–70. Similar in concept to the Jeune Ecole's coastal torpedo boats, the 172-ton Osas were supposed to defend Soviet waters against larger enemy surface vessels. Each carried a formidable armament of four P-15 (NATO SS-N-2 'Styx') SSMs, the next Soviet ship-launched missile after the KSShch, which likewise had a range extending to the horizon. In 1967 a P-15 fired by one of ten Osas sold to Egypt became the first missile to sink a ship in combat, the Israeli destroyer *Eilat*.[9]

The four 4,400-ton Project 58 (NATO 'Kynda') class guided missile cruisers (completed 1962–5) featured the Soviet navy's first operational OTH missile, the P-35, a modified version of the P-5 (NATO SS-N-3 'Shaddock'). The naval Shaddock, designed by Chelomey, remained under the control of the firing ship after it passed beyond the ship's horizon thanks to radar video data from the fired missile relayed via an aircraft. The Kyndas carried 16 P-35s and, for air defence, 24 M-I (NATO SA-N-I) surface-to-air missiles, the Soviet navy's first operational SAMs. Gorshkov's next destroyers, specifically designed to defend other warships against air attack, likewise received M-I SAMs. The twenty units of the Project 61 (NATO 'Kashin') class, completed 1962–73, each carried 32 M-Is.[10]

The Kyndas were the largest Soviet surface warships to enter service between 1955 and 1967. Smaller than most destroyers commissioned in the early 1960s by the US and other Western navies, the 4,400-ton cruisers nevertheless represented an important break in Khrushchev's ban against surface vessels larger than destroyers. By the time the first of the Kyndas entered service, Gorshkov had won approval for two 14,590-ton helicopter carriers, the *Moskva* (built 1962–7) and *Leningrad* (1965–9), platforms for anti-submarine warfare marketed to Khrushchev as an antidote to the US navy's new Polaris missile submarines. The design accommodated up to twenty helicopters, launched from a flight deck aft of its centreline superstructure. Its shipboard arsenal included eighteen anti-submarine (NATO SUW-N-I 'Hormone') missiles and, for air defence, 44 M-II (NATO SA-N-3 'Goblet') SAMs. The *Leningrad* was laid down the day after the *Moskva* was launched, on the same slip at the Black Sea shipyard of Nikolaiev, which Gorshkov would later use to build much larger surface warships.[11]

While his subsequent projects would reveal a strong prejudice in favour of large surface vessels, during the Khrushchev years Gorshkov found it expedient to satisfy his master's desire for a formidable fleet of submarines. He inherited three attack submarine programmes: the 1,340-ton Project 613 (NATO 'Whiskey') class, including 215 units completed 1951–8; the 2,350-ton Project 611 (NATO 'Zulu') class, including 18 units completed 1952–5; and the 540-ton Project 615 (NATO 'Quebec') class, including 30 units completed 1954–7. Shortly after Gorshkov assumed command, the navy introduced three more attack submarine types: the 1,700-ton Project 633 (NATO 'Romeo') class, including 21 units completed 1957–62; the 2,485-ton Project 641 (NATO 'Foxtrot') class, including 62 units completed 1957–71; and the 5,300-ton Project 627 (NATO 'November') class, including 14 units completed 1959–63. The Novembers were the navy's first nuclear-powered submarines; Gorshkov inherited the first unit of the class, the *K 3*, later named *Leninskiy Komsomol*, laid down in the covered Arctic submarine yard at Severodvinsk in May 1954. It entered service in March 1959, four and a half years after the first US navy submarine of the same type, the *Nautilus*. Gorshkov also commissioned the navy's first guided missile submarines: the 5,500-ton nuclear-powered Project 659 (NATO 'Echo I') class, including five units completed 1961–2; the 6,000-ton nuclear-powered Project 675 (NATO 'Echo II') class, including 29 units completed 1962–7; and the 3,750-ton diesel-powered Project 651 (NATO 'Juliett') class, including 16 units completed 1963–8. While the first Echos carried a submarine version of the P-5 Shaddock SSM, the remaining Echos and the Julietts received a modified Shaddock, the P-6. Shaddocks were also fitted aboard several Whiskey class attack submarines, which the navy converted to guided missile submarines. To access the Soviet navy's aircraft-based OTH targeting system of the 1960s, the Echos, Julietts and converted Whiskeys had to stay on the surface while guiding their Shaddocks to their intended targets, a practice that left them vulnerable to attack. The navy took heart in the impressive speed of these classes, which theoretically would help them escape after firing their missiles. The 23- to 25-knot submerged speed of the Echos and the 30-knot submerged speed of the Novembers caused great concern in the US navy, whose fastest aircraft carrier, the nuclear-powered *Enterprise* (commissioned 1961), steamed at 32 knots. The narrowing speed gap of the early 1960s stood in sharp contrast to the gulf that had existed as recently as the 1950s, when the fastest Soviet submarines had been slower than the slowest American aircraft carriers. By the end of the decade the Soviets had produced history's fastest guided missile submarine, the single unit of the Project 661 (NATO 'Papa') class. A 5,200-ton nuclear-powered vessel armed with ten P-120 Ametist (NATO SS-N-9 'Siren') missiles, it achieved its record submerged speed of 44.7 knots during a patrol in 1970–71. Unfortunately for Gorshkov, the lone Papa took six years to build (1963–9) and cost too much to replicate.[12]

Alongside its attack submarines and guided missile submarines, the Soviet navy of the Khrushchev years added its first ballistic missile submarines. The initial milestone came in September 1955, in the last weeks of Kuznetsov's command, when a modified Zulu class attack submarine fired a Soviet army R-11 (NATO 'Scud') in history's first launch of a ballistic missile from a submarine. Starting in 1958, five Zulus refitted to carry R-11s functioned as the navy's first operational ballistic missile submarines. In 1961 they were rearmed with R-13 (NATO SS-N-4 'Sark') missiles, the Soviet Union's first genuine sea-launched ballistic missiles (SLBMs), which had a range of 350 miles (563 kilometres), a vast improvement over the R-11's 80 miles (129 kilometres). Following the initial Zulu conversions, Gorshkov laid down two classes of purpose-built ballistic missile submarines: the 2,900-ton diesel-powered Project 628 (NATO 'Golf') class, including 23 units completed 1959–62 (illus. 27), and the 6,000-ton nuclear-powered Project 658 (NATO 'Hotel') class, including eight units completed 1960–64. The first Hotel, *K 19*, entered service in November 1960, just eleven months after the first US navy ballistic missile submarine, the nuclear-powered *George Washington*, but the American vessel and its sister ships far surpassed the early Soviet ballistic missile submarines in both design and capability. While the *George*

27 A Soviet submarine of the 'Golf' class, photographed in 1965.

Washington carried sixteen Polaris SLBMS, which it could fire while submerged, the Zulus, Golfs and Hotels each carried three R-13 SLBMS, which had to be fired from the surface, in a launch process consuming some ten minutes per missile. At least in the 1950s and early 1960s, the Soviet navy hoped that sheer quantity would compensate for the lack of quality in most of its submarine types. By commissioning the first Soviet ballistic missile submarines, along with scores of attack and guided missile submarines, Gorshkov gave Khrushchev history's largest force of undersea boats. If measured in number of units alone, the fleet achieved its peak strength in 1958, when it had 475 submarines, of which well over half (258) had been commissioned since 1953. Thereafter the overall number of submarines fell, as obsolete units launched in the 1940s left service faster than they were replaced.[13]

The Soviet submarine fleet of the Khrushchev years may have been a hodgepodge of types generally inferior to their American counterparts, but aside from the smaller, older boats of 1940s vintage, the 540-ton Quebecs (intended for service in the Baltic and Black Sea) were the only units not capable of operating on the high seas. Thanks largely to the submarine build-up, in 1959 the Soviet Union passed Britain in overall warship tonnage to become the world's second naval power behind the United States; Britain retained second place in surface tonnage into the 1960s, until the completion of Gorshkov's first major surface warship projects. Gorshkov built new bases as well as new warships, in order to improve his navy's access to open water. In 1956 he took the provocative step of moving the main base of the Baltic Fleet from Kronstadt to the ice-free port of Baltiysk (formerly Pillau) near Kaliningrad (formerly Königsberg, East Prussia). He also built up the Northern Fleet (based at Severomorsk, a White Sea port near Murmansk, on the Kola Peninsula) from the smallest of the Soviet fleets to the largest, including most of the navy's submarines.[14]

The decline of Khrushchev's dictatorship began with his capitulation to the United States in the Cuban Missile Crisis of 1962, but within the Soviet leadership the setback played to Gorshkov's advantage. Because a US naval blockade had helped force the withdrawal of Soviet missiles from Cuba, afterward the admiral had an easier time gaining support for a fleet including significant surface warships. Just before Leonid Brezhnev replaced him in 1964, Khrushchev authorized four 6,000-ton Project 1134 (NATO 'Kresta I') class cruisers, completed between 1967 and 1969. Intended for anti-submarine warfare, they were armed with just four Shaddock SSMs but 42 M-1 SAMs, giving them a much stronger air-defence capability than the earlier Kynda class cruisers. Their ten 5,600-ton half-sisters of the Project 1134A (NATO 'Kresta II') class, completed 1969–77, shared the same characteristics but featured a more potent armament of eight RPK-3 (NATO SS-N-14) anti-submarine missiles and 48 M-11 SAMs. The next class of Soviet cruisers, the seven units of the 6,700-ton Project 1134B (NATO 'Kara') class, completed 1971–9, likewise carried eight RPK-3s but had an even more formidable air-defence capability, thanks to 72 M-11 and 40 RZ-13 (NATO SA-N-4 'Gecko') SAMs.[15]

The Soviet surface fleet of 1970 included two helicopter carriers and nineteen cruisers, but the latter included ten Sverdlovs (completed 1952–5), seven of which had not been modernized to fire missiles. That summer, Brezhnev allowed Gorshkov to begin his most ambitious surface warship project to date, the 36,000-ton Kiev, first of a class of four 'tactical aviation cruisers' that were aircraft carriers in all but name. The odd classification apparently was a device to circumvent the Montreux Convention, which restricted the right of passage through the Turkish straits of aircraft carriers and submarines, and might have prevented the completed ships from leaving the Black Sea shipyard at Nikolaiev for their intended stations (two with the Northern Fleet, two with the Pacific Fleet). The *Kiev*s also defied conventional classification because they resembled no other warships ever constructed. Instead of a carrier island, the design featured an extensive superstructure similar to a battleship of the Second World War; yet, like a carrier island, the superstructure was offset to starboard, to accommodate an angled flight deck extending from the stern of the ship to the port side of the superstructure. The design included a graceful battleship bow, since the flight deck did not extend forward. When completed, each of the *Kiev*s carried 31 Yak-38 (NATO 'Forger') vertical/short takeoff and landing (VSTOL) attack aircraft, which usually took off vertically since they lacked the assistance of the 'ski jump' ramp that was a standard feature of western European VSTOL carriers. The *Kiev* was completed in 1975, followed by the *Minsk* (built 1972–8), *Novorossiysk* (1975–82; illus. 28), and *Baku* (1978–87), each ship being laid down as soon as the launching of the one before vacated the slip at Nikolaiev. To supplement the striking power of their aircraft, the *Kiev*s carried 24 Bazalt (NATO SS-N-12 'Sandbox') SSMS. Their air-defence missiles included 72 M-11 and 40 RZ-13 SAMs.[16] When commissioned, the *Kiev* became the largest warship yet to serve in the Soviet navy, but the US navy's nuclear-powered carrier *Nimitz*, also completed in 1975, displaced over twice the tonnage and carried three times as many aircraft. Gorshkov failed to articulate a clear mission for the *Kiev*s, which were too small to be effective conventional aircraft carriers but far larger and less flexible than contemporary VSTOL carriers, such as Britain's *Invincible* class (completed 1980–85). If they were, indeed, large cruisers, they were woefully under-armed, packing less offensive firepower than the much smaller guided missile cruisers of the US navy.

The other major Soviet surface warships of the Brezhnev years were, indeed, large cruisers, the largest non-aircraft carrying ships built by any navy after the completion of the British battleship *Vanguard* (1946). The four 'missile cruisers' of the 24,000-ton *Kirov* class were the Soviet navy's first nuclear-powered surface warships. They carried an impressive arsenal of

28 The Soviet carrier *Novorossiysk* (1982).

20 P-500 Granit (NATO SS-N-19 'Shipwreck') missiles, 16 RPK-3 anti-submarine missiles and, for air defence, 96 S-300 (NATO SA-N-6 'Grumble') and 40 older RZ-13 SAMs. The *Kirov* (built 1974–80) was followed into service by its sister ships *Frunze* (1978–84) and *Kalinin* (1983–8), but the fourth unit, laid down in 1986, remained incomplete at the end of the Cold War. Built as fleet flagships, they replaced ageing *Sverdlov* class cruisers that had been modernized for such duties. To replace the rest of the *Sverdlov*s, Gorshkov ordered the four 10,000-ton cruisers of the *Slava* class, a more conventional design carrying sixteen Bazalt SSMs, with air defence provided by 64 S-300 and 40 RZ-13 SAMs. The first three *Slava*s entered service between 1982 and 1988 but, as with the *Kirov*s, the fourth unit of the class remained incomplete when the Cold War ended. Meanwhile, 6,200-ton destroyers of the *Sovremenniy* and *Udaloy* classes were intended to succeed the small missile cruisers that had entered service in the 1960s. The *Sovremenniy*s (twenty units laid down 1976–89) were land-attack destroyers with a primary armament of P-80 Moskit (SS-N-22 'Sunbeam') missiles, while the *Udaloy*s (four-teen units laid down 1979–90) were built for anti-submarine warfare and armed with RPK-3 missiles. The *Sovremenniy* class was the centrepiece of an amphibious warfare force including three assault ships of the 11,000-ton *Ivan Rogov* class (completed

1978, 1982 and 1989), which collectively could carry 1,650 troops, 30 tanks and 90 armoured personnel carriers.[17]

As the Soviet navy followed the lead of the US and Western navies in constructing cruiser-sized destroyers, it also replaced its older destroyers with destroyer-sized frigates. The 39 units of the 3,300-ton Project 1135 (NATO 'Krivak') class, completed 1970–90, were the first Soviet missile frigates. They were to be followed by the 3,500-ton *Neustrashimy* class, but just three units of the type were laid down (1986–90) and none completed before the end of the Cold War. Replacements for the Osa class missile boats and other obsolete missile-launching light craft included the Project 1234 (NATO 'Nanuchka') and Project 1241 (NATO 'Tarantul') class missile corvettes. The 'Nanuchkas', produced from 1967, and the 'Tarantuls', produced from 1970, pioneered the ducting radar system of fire control featured later aboard destroyers of the *Sovremenniy* class.[18]

A satellite-based OTH targeting system developed early in the Brezhnev era augmented the capabilities of all missile-launching Soviet warships. The first satellite test launch occurred in 1965, four years after the project began, and the system was fully deployed by 1973, one year after the Ocean Surveillance Information System (OSIS) gave the US navy its first satellite-based OTH targeting system. Because satellite-based missile fire control required the firing units to know their own precise location, these targeting systems had to be preceded into service by satellite navigation systems. On the Soviet side, the effort began in 1962 and was fully operational by 1971, although some Whiskey and Zulu class submarines navigated via satellite as early as 1969. The new space-based technologies benefited Soviet surface vessels but were more crucial for the submarines, which by the early 1970s were deployed worldwide. While Gorshkov focused an increasing share of Soviet naval resources on large surface warship projects, the navy of the Brezhnev era still had the world's largest undersea fleet. By the mid-1970s it included 409 submarines, down from the peak of 475 in the late 1950s, but most units were larger than their earlier counterparts and 95 were nuclear powered.[19]

The Soviet navy continued to build diesel-powered attack submarines through the end of the Cold War: the 3,900-ton Project 641 BUKI (NATO 'Tango') class, including 19 units completed

1972–81, and the 3,075-ton Project 877 (NATO 'Kilo') class, including 28 units completed 1982–93. All other classes of submarines built after the 1960s were nuclear powered. Among the attack submarines, the Project 671 (NATO 'Victor') class included 48 units completed 1968–91. Built in three sub-classes displacing between 5,100 and 6,000 tons, the Victors carried 82R (NATO SS-N-15 'Starfish') anti-submarine missiles in addition to torpedoes. Smaller classes of attack submarines included the 3,680-ton Project 705 (NATO 'Alfa') class, seven units completed 1972–83; the 8,500-ton Project 685 (NATO 'Mike') class, a single unit completed 1983; the 7,900-ton Project 945 (NATO 'Sierra') class, four units completed 1984–93; and the 9,100-ton Project 971 (NATO 'Akula') class, six units completed 1984–9. The Alfas, like the Victors, carried 82R anti-submarine missiles, while the Akulas were equipped with S-10 (NATO SS-N-21 'Sampson') strategic guided missiles; otherwise, all attack submarine classes were armed with torpedoes alone. Of the lot, the Alfas were the fastest, with a submerged speed of over 40 knots. The Alfa design also featured a titanium hull that allowed deeper dives than a conventional steel hull. The newest attack submarines were joined by another two classes of nuclear-powered guided missile submarines: the 4,900-ton Project 670A (NATO 'Charlie') class, including seventeen units completed 1968–80, and the 14,600-ton Project 949 (NATO 'Oscar') class, including ten units completed 1980–94. The Charlies were armed with 8 P-20 (NATO SS-N-7) missiles or older P-120s, the Oscars with 24 P-500 Granit SSMs.[20]

The ballistic missile submarines built during and after the Brezhnev era were a vast improvement over their predecessors. All were nuclear powered, and all had far greater firepower than the Golfs, Hotels and converted Zulus of the Khrushchev years, which had been limited to just three missiles apiece. The 9,600-ton Project 667A (NATO 'Yankee') class, including 34 units completed 1967–72, were armed with 16 R-27 (NATO SS-N-6 'Sawfly') SLBMs, which they could fire while submerged. The Yankees were roughly equal in capability to the American Polaris/Poseidon ballistic missile submarines, the first of which had entered service eight years before the first Yankee. When the United States subsequently decided to stop building new ballistic missile submarines for more than a decade (none was commissioned from 1967 to 1981), the Soviet Union made the most of the opportunity to catch up. The navy commissioned 43 submarines of the Project 667 (NATO 'Delta') class in the years 1972–92, but most were in service by the time of Brezhnev's death in 1982. The Deltas were built in four sub-classes ranging in size from the 11,750-ton 'Delta I' to the 13,500-ton 'Delta IV'. The first Deltas carried 12 R-29 (NATO SS-N-8 'Mod I Sawfly') SLBMs, missiles with a range of 4,000 miles (6,440 kilometres) that could strike any target in the United States from the security of the Sea of Okhotsk (for Pacific Fleet units) or Barents Sea (for Northern Fleet units). The firepower of the Deltas compelled the US navy to adopt new anti-submarine warfare strategies, since it could no longer depend upon its own warships intercepting Soviet submarines before they reached launching areas in the middle of the Pacific or Atlantic oceans. Later Deltas carried sixteen SLBMs of an improved R-29 type, either the R-29U (NATO SS-N-18 'Stingray') or the R-29RM (NATO SS-N-23 'Skiff'). While the Delta IVs were still under construction, the isolated Arctic shipyard at Severodvinsk began work on the six units of the 25,000-ton Project 941 (NATO 'Typhoon') class, designed by Sergey N. Kovolev. The largest submarines ever built, the Typhoons were armed with 20 R-39 (NATO SS-N-20 'Sturgeon') SLBMs, missiles with a range of almost 4,500 miles (7,240 kilometres). Commissioned in the years 1981–9, the Typhoons were all assigned to the Northern Fleet. In case of nuclear war with the United States, Soviet navigation satellites would have guided the Typhoons to breaks in the Arctic icecap, through which they would fire their missiles. In surfaced displacement (18,500 tons), length (562 feet; 171 metres) and speed (25 knots submerged), the Typhoons surpassed the battleship *Dreadnought* of 1906. They were among the most remarkable warships in naval history, and arguably the most impressive achievement of the Soviet military-industrial complex. The Typhoons were much larger than the American *Ohio*s (18,750 tons submerged) but arguably not as powerful, since each of the *Ohio*s carried 24 Trident SLBMs.[21] By the late Cold War years, both navies were basing a growing number of their ballistic missiles aboard submarines, but for the Soviet Union, the share of the overall arsenal entrusted to the navy was far smaller than that of the United States. While the Soviets stopped the Typhoon programme at six boats, the Americans had built twelve *Ohio*s by the time the Soviet Union collapsed in 1991, and another six thereafter.

During his last years in office Gorshkov finally secured permission to build a conventional aircraft carrier, with much of the construction accomplished during the brief reigns of Yuri Andropov (1982–4) and Konstantin Chernenko (1984–5). The 60,000-ton ship, laid down in 1983, was named *Leonid Brezhnev* in honour of the late dictator, whose support had enabled the admiral to construct a formidable fleet of surface warships. The carrier had an angled-deck and a 12-degree 'ski jump' bow ramp, to compensate for its lack of launching catapults. It could operate less than half the aircraft of a US navy supercarrier (a mixture of 30 jets and helicopters, within the ranges of 18–24 aircraft and 6–12 helicopters) but, unlike its American counterparts, supplemented the offensive power of its air group with a formidable missile-launching capability including sixteen P-500 Granit SSMs. In a further distinction from American carriers, the *Leonid Brezhnev* also provided for most of its own air defence with 144 SAMs (NATO SA-N-7 'Gauntlet'). In service, its aircraft included Su-27 (NATO 'Flanker'), MiG-29 (NATO 'Fulcrum') and Su-25 (NATO 'Frogfoot') jets. As late as 1989 the Soviet navy still referred to the ship as a 'heavy aircraft-carrying cruiser', maintaining the fiction (as it had with the *Kiev* class) that the ship was not an aircraft carrier and thus could pass from its Black Sea construction site at Nikolaiev through the Turkish Straits to its future duties with the Northern Fleet. Work on a sister ship, the *Riga*, began in 1985, shortly after the launching of the *Leonid Brezhnev*. Chernenko's successor, Mikhail Gorbachev, permitted work to begin on the ship prior to the promulgation of his domestic reform agenda at the 27th Party Congress (1986) and negotiations with the United States to end the Cold War. Work also continued on the long-delayed fourth missile cruiser of the *Kirov* class, which Gorbachev named *Yuri Andropov* to honour his political mentor.[22]

In dealing with the Soviet navy, Gorbachev proved to be every bit as revolutionary as he was in his domestic and foreign policies. In December 1985 he forced the 75-year-old Gorshkov to retire, one month short of his thirtieth anniversary in office. While Gorbachev sought to rescue his country from its financially ruinous arms races with the United States, between 1988 and 1991 signing the agreements that ended the Cold War, Gorshkov's successor, former submariner Admiral of the Fleet Vladimir N. Chernavin, co-operated fully with his master's policies. Chernavin first saved money by reducing the size of the active fleet and scrapping older warships, then by decommissioning newer warships, then by practically halting new construction. After Gorbachev's anti-corruption campaign brought to light the abuses of the Brezhnev era, the aircraft carrier named after the late dictator became the *Tblisi*. During 1990, after his policy of openness (*glasnost*) spawned separatist movements in the Soviet Union's non-Russian republics, the names of their capitals were removed from warships: the *Kiev*'s sister ship *Baku* became the *Admiral Gorshkov*; the carrier *Tblisi* was renamed again, as *Admiral Kuznetsov*; and its sister ship *Riga*, still under construction at Nikolaiev, became the *Varyag*. Even though he had already signed the first of the us-Soviet agreements intended to end the Cold War, late in 1988 Gorbachev let the navy lay down another aircraft carrier at Nikolaiev, the 65,000-ton *Ulyanovsk*, shortly after the launching of the *Varyag*. The *Admiral Kuznetsov* finally entered service early in 1991; when the Soviet Union collapsed at the end of that year, the *Varyag* was almost complete, the *Ulyanovsk* 40 per cent finished and nearing launch. Neither the *Varyag* nor the *Ulyanovsk* would ever be commissioned.[23]

PERSONNEL: PRIVILEGES AND PROBLEMS

By the last years of the Brezhnev era the naval officer corps reflected the malaise plaguing Soviet society as a whole. Most officers were the sons of officers or of Communist party officials, and when it came to promotions or assignments, personal connections often mattered more than talent. In the early 1980s roughly 50 per cent of all naval officers were alumni of a single prep school, the exclusive Nakhimov Naval Preparatory School in Leningrad, where boys aged fifteen to eighteen completed their last three years of secondary education before securing admission to one of eleven Higher Naval schools. Founded during the Second World War as one of three military prep schools for teenaged sons of men killed in action, Nakhimov lost its egalitarian character during the 1950s as its original clientele dwindled in number; it became, instead, the preserve of sons of the privileged elite. Instead of a single naval academy the Soviet system of naval education included eleven smaller, specialized Higher Naval schools: five for the preparation of surface warfare officers, two for ship-based engineers and one apiece for submariners, land-based engineers, electronics officers and political officers. Thus, the preparatory experience at Nakhimov provided an important common bond (at least for half of the officer corps) that otherwise would not have existed. While competitive examinations determined admission to the Higher Naval schools, graduates of Nakhimov were all but guaranteed places.[24]

By the 1980s the Soviet navy was commissioning between 1,500 and 2,000 new naval officers every year, 85 per cent of whom had completed a five-year course of study at one of the eleven Higher Naval schools. Even though only three of the eleven were designated as engineering schools, owing to their common curricular emphasis on mathematics, the sciences and engineering all awarded their graduates the equivalent of a baccalaureate degree in engineering. Among the remaining 15 per cent of new officers most were products of a ten-week Officer Candidate School curriculum, completed after graduation from a university or technical college. Direct commissioning from the enlisted ranks, common from the Bolshevik Revolution through the Second World War, remained possible but became increasingly rare. According to one Soviet source, volunteers from among naval conscripts completing their required term of service 'enjoy[ed] certain advantages for entry' into the Higher Naval schools, but apparently very few availed themselves of the opportunity.[25] The Marshal Grechko Naval Academy in Leningrad (officially designated the 'Order of Lenin and Ushakov Naval Academy named after Marshal of the Soviet Union A. A. Grechko', following the death of the former defence minister in 1976) served as a naval war college for the Soviet fleet, providing a two-year course to prepare senior officers destined for higher command or staff roles. Naval officers could also receive postgraduate training at the General Staff Academy in Moscow or at naval technical schools in Kronstadt and Leningrad.[26]

While personal connections mattered a great deal, at least formally the Soviet navy assigned its newly commissioned officers under a merit system, giving preference to the graduates of the Higher Naval schools with the highest class rank. After Gorshkov took command of the navy, the Northern Fleet and Pacific Fleet became the most popular, since units assigned to those commands spent the most time at sea, beyond Soviet waters; both postings also qualified as 'remote' locations warranting bonus pay. Once assigned, officers were rarely transferred between fleets. In contrast to their counterparts in other navies, Soviet officers frequently served for several years aboard ships of the same type or even the same ship, in the latter case for up to six years. Owing to infrequent transfers, ship commanders typically had the same junior officers for years at a time and thus wielded a great deal of power over their future career paths. In the late Brezhnev years 90 per cent of Soviet naval officers were serving the 25 years required for a pension (which, for most, included their five years of study at a Higher Naval School). Unlike the US navy, the Soviet navy had no 'up-or-out' promotion system; thus, being passed over for promotion did not end an officer's career. Officers not chosen for command positions continued to advance on the career tracks within their specialities, and could even eventually serve aboard ship as a specialist at a higher rank than the ship's commanding officer, an impossibility in most other navies at most times in history. More often than not, these senior specialists were in engineering or electronics, areas from which few ship commanders were chosen.[27]

As of the early 1980s, 95 per cent of naval officers belonged to the Communist party or the Komsomol (Young Communist League), compared to 80 per cent of all Soviet military officers. While all officers bore some degree of responsibility for the political education of the enlisted men under their command, such duties fell primarily to the political officer (*Zampolit*) assigned to each ship or unit. Whereas the military and naval political commissars of the inter-war years were drawn from among civilian Communist party loyalists and held ranks equal to the commanders of the units or ships in which they served, the post-1945 political officer usually was an army or navy officer by training who happened to be active in the party, and was subordinate to the unit or ship commander. By the end of the Cold War most of the navy's political officers were trained at the Naval Higher School offering that speciality. Aboard ship they typically served as the commander's chief personnel officer, co-ordinated health and recreation programmes, and functioned as a personal counsellor (in the latter case, much like a chaplain in Western military or naval service).[28] Ironically, a political officer led the only confirmed mutiny to occur aboard a Soviet navy ship during the era of the Cold War. On the night of 7–8 November 1975, while its base at Riga was distracted by the annual celebration of the Bolshevik Revolution holiday, the 'Krivak' class frigate *Storozhevoy* put to sea under the command of Captain Valery M. Sablin, bound for the Swedish island of Gotland, where the mutineers hoped to secure political asylum. Pursued by nine other Baltic Fleet units and eventually bombed by Soviet aircraft, the ship offered no resistance before surrendering just 30 miles (48 kilometres) short of Gotland, six hours after leaving Riga. Within days, Sablin and others involved in the mutiny were tried, convicted and executed.[29]

Only one officer joined Sablin in the *Storozhevoy* mutiny. The loyalty of the rest reflected the overall political reliability and professionalism of the naval officer corps. In a country in which life was often harsh and freedoms – most notably the right to travel – extremely limited, naval officers received good treatment and, depending upon their assignment, had the opportunity to visit other parts of the world. Officers were paid on a complex system reflecting rank, position, seniority, speciality and location (with service in the 'remote' Northern and Pacific fleets, as well as submarine service, adding bonus pay). In the 1980s, before Gorbachev's economic policies unleashed runaway inflation, newly commissioned naval officers received basic pay of 170 rubles per month, roughly the average monthly wage for all Soviet citizens, but a sum 24 times greater than the basic pay of first-year naval conscripts. (In comparison, in 2003, the basic monthly pay of a newly commissioned US navy officer was only slightly more than twice as high as that of an entering sailor). On land and aboard ship, officers enjoyed far better living conditions and better food than their men, and had free access to alcohol. As one historian has noted, in the Soviet fleet 'the gulf between standards' for officers and seamen was 'strangely reminiscent of the situation in the Tsarist navies'.[30]

Whereas American naval education emphasized the ideal of preparing the officer for a general leadership role, Soviet naval education placed a premium on technical proficiency in the officer's chosen speciality. The difference reflected the realities of command in a conscript navy, in which the common manpower could be expected to develop little depth of special or technical knowledge during their relatively brief term of active service. After the Second World War, the Soviet army and air force conscripted young men for three years of active duty; for the Soviet navy, the term was four years, except in the naval infantry and naval aviation, which served the same three-year term as their army and air force counterparts. The Soviet Union's Universal Military Service Law of 1967 fixed the age of induction at 18 and reduced all terms of service by one year, leaving the navy with a three-year term (two for the marines and aviators). Students pursuing post-secondary degrees at universities or technical colleges were eligible for educational deferments and, upon graduation, served two years (eighteen months in land-based services); in 1989 Gorbachev ordered the further reduction of this term to one year for both sea and land service, before releasing all university and technical college graduates from military service for the good of the economy. To compensate for the shorter training time, under the 1967 law all males were required to join a local unit of the Voluntary Society for Co-operation with the Army, Air Force and Navy (DOSAAF) at age 16, and receive 140 hours of pre-military training under DOSAAF supervision during their last two years of secondary school.[31]

By the 1980s the navy took 8 per cent of the annual pool of conscripts; along with the strategic rocket forces (a separate branch within the Soviet military), it received the best of the lot. Since most naval conscripts had pre-military training in a naval DOSAAF unit, most were ethnic Russians. The Slavic nationalities of the Soviet Union (Russians, Ukrainians and Belorussians) accounted for more than 90 per cent of the navy's common manpower and virtually all of its officers; most of the rest were Latvians or Estonians. Central Asian Muslims and men of the Caucasian nationalities, considered the least desirable conscripts, very rarely entered naval service. The near absence of non-Russian speakers made assimilation and training at least somewhat easier than in the Soviet army, but the sheer numbers of men cycling through the service on an annual basis posed a daunting challenge. In a naval establishment numbering roughly half a million men (including officers and NCOs), 65,000 conscripts entered every six months, while almost as many were discharged owing to the very low rate of voluntary re-enlistment. Indeed, among the common manpower, by the onset of the Gorbachev era conscripts serving their mandatory three years outnumbered warrant officers and other re-enlisted men by a ratio of 7:1. The dearth of technical knowledge among NCOs left officers responsible for many of the duties fulfilled by petty officers in other navies, including the repair and maintenance of shipboard equipment. Prior to a reform introduced in 1971, NCO status was open on a seniority basis to any conscript who volunteered to re-enlist. Very often the volunteers were the worst of the lot, who sought to remain in service because of poor prospects in civilian life. The new system of warrant officers was based on talent in one's specialization. Warrant officers re-enlisted for five-year terms and enjoyed the same pay scale as junior commissioned officers; whereas the basic pay for conscripts in the mid-1980s was 7 rubles per month, warrant officers started at the national average wage of 170 rubles per month and could earn as much as 250. Like junior officers, they had a minimum of 30 days of leave per year, three times as much as a second- or third-year conscript. But not enough men met the new, higher standards, leaving the navy short of NCOs and forcing it to resort to a mixed system including some serving on the new (1971) system and others on a revival of the old system, under which conscripts could volunteer to re-enlist for terms of two, four or six years.[32]

The half million men in Soviet naval service as of the mid-1980s included 200,000 aboard ships, 60,000 in naval aviation and 16,000 in naval infantry. The rest served in various other roles ashore, including a staggering 58,000 involved in some form of education or training. Conscripts could be sent aboard ship after as little as nine weeks of basic training, but roughly 75 per cent of them received additional training in a speciality before going to sea. After induction, sailors were allowed no leave during their first year of service and just ten days per year in the second and third years. Officially no conscript could serve within 1,000 kilometres (620 miles) of his home, a rule which, for example, meant that no Estonians, Latvians or Leningrad Russians were supposed to serve in the Baltic Fleet. Exceptions to this longstanding rule increased as time went on. By the end of the Brezhnev era parents with the right personal connections or enough money to place a bribe could secure for their sons a posting closer to home; through these means, even Latvian and Estonian conscripts made their way into the Baltic Fleet.

Aboard ship or ashore, living conditions were usually spartan and at times harsh. Naval housing on bases tended to be dilapidated and crowded, even for officers and their dependants, especially in Vladivostok, where some apartments were shared by three or four families. Surface warships built in the Stalin era lacked the most basic comforts for their crews, but those constructed under Gorshkov showed gradual improvement. Ships built in the 1970s and '80s were centrally air conditioned; by then, older vessels carried portable air conditioners during Mediterranean and other warm-weather deployments. Older, smaller Soviet surface warships had no mess; crewmen took food from the galley back to their berths to eat it. Right up to the food crisis of the late Gorbachev years, the navy typically received better food than the army and the civilian population, including a daily serving of meat and no shortage of coffee. As in the rest of the Soviet armed forces, bullying of first-year men by older conscripts was common, accepted and at times brutal. In one particularly demeaning ritual, newly inducted men were forced to exchange their new uniforms for the worn clothing of the older conscripts. As Gorshkov expanded the surface fleet, cruises abroad became more common and also grew longer. Shore leave was restricted, and even in other Communist countries the sailors went ashore only under strict supervision. Shore leave was seldom granted even for men aboard ships that spent long periods anchored in the same Soviet port. At least officially, alcohol was not allowed aboard Soviet naval vessels. According to regulations, officers and NCOs could drink while off duty, but the ordinary sailor was not to drink at all. Nevertheless, alcoholism was just as significant a problem for the navy as for the armed forces in general and Soviet society as a whole.

COLD WAR OPERATIONS

Until the Khrushchev era, the Soviet navy, like the Imperial Russian navy, maintained its largest force in the Baltic and its second largest force in the Black Sea. Under Lenin and Stalin, Soviet warships rarely left coastal waters; foreign port visits became more frequent after 1945, but only to the Communist satellite states bordering the Baltic and Black Sea.[33] During Kuznetsov's last years in command, the construction of the *Sverdlov* class and completion of the *Chapayev* class increased the visibility of the surface fleet. After Stalin's death, Khrushchev sent these cruisers, escorted by destroyers, on the navy's first visits to non-Communist countries. In June 1953 the *Sverdlov* became the first Soviet warship to visit a NATO country, steaming to Britain to represent the Soviet Union at an international naval review off Spithead coinciding with the coronation of Queen Elizabeth II. During 1954 two of its sister ships called at Helsinki and Stockholm; then, in 1955, two *Sverdlov*s and four destroyers visited Portsmouth. The following year the cruiser *Ordzhonikidze*, escorted by two destroyers, carried Khrushchev to Britain for a state visit. Other cruises during 1956 included a sortie through the Bosphorus and Dardanelles by the Black Sea Fleet commander, Admiral V. A. Kasatonov, with the cruiser *Mikhail Kutuzov* and two destroyers. Kasatonov visited Albania and Yugoslavia, Communist states whose harbours the Soviets coveted as potential submarine bases, to circumvent Montreux Convention limits on the passage of submarines through the Turkish straits. Soviet-Yugoslav relations, previously poisoned by the personal animosity between Stalin and Marshal Josip Broz Tito, improved in the Khrushchev years, but not enough for Tito to allow Soviet forces to be based in Yugoslavia. The navy ultimately had better luck in Albania, basing eight Whiskey class submarines in the Gulf of Valona in 1960. The following year, however, a breach in Soviet-Albanian relations cancelled the arrangement. In the late 1950s and early 1960s, the navy supported Khrushchev's diplomatic outreach to the Arab world by sending warships to various Arab Mediterranean ports; the cruiser *Zhdanov* called at Latakia, Syria, in 1957, on the first such visit. Elsewhere in the Muslim world, Khrushchev enlisted the navy in his courtship of Indonesia as a Soviet ally. In 1959 a cruiser and two destroyers from the Pacific Fleet visited Jakarta; over the next three years, the Soviet navy transferred fourteen Whiskey class submarines, the cruiser *Ordzhonikidze*, eight destroyers and dozens of smaller craft to the Indonesian navy. The naval aid initiative coincided with the breakdown of Sino-Soviet relations, and ended in failure after President Sukarno chose Beijing over Moscow, adopting a pro-Chinese outlook before he was ousted in 1965.[34]

Owing to its weakness in surface warships, the Soviet navy played no visible role in the Cuban Missile Crisis of 1962. Indeed, no Soviet warship had visited Cuba in the years since Fidel Castro's takeover in 1959, and none would call there for another seven years after the crisis. During the brief US naval blockade of Cuba in October 1962, the only Soviet naval units active in the West Indies or western Atlantic were non-nuclear submarines, all of which were tracked by the US navy.[35] The Brezhnev era ushered in a more assertive posture that went hand in hand with Gorshkov's steady build-up of the Soviet surface fleet. The navy maintained a continuous cruising presence in the Mediterranean from 1964 onward, and during the Arab-Israeli war of 1967 made its greatest effort thus far, dispatching 70 warships of various sizes to the Eastern Mediterranean. The next Arab-Israeli war, in 1973, brought 96 Soviet warships to the same waters (including 5 cruisers; 16 destroyers, frigates and corvettes; 8 amphibious ships; 38 intelligence and support ships; and 23 submarines), a force much larger than the 60 warships attached to the US Sixth Fleet during the crisis. Between the two wars, the Soviet navy conducted ten joint exercises with the armed forces of Egypt and Syria, at least six of which involved amphibious landings. Such demonstrations forced the US navy, heretofore most concerned about Soviet submarines, to take seriously the surface dimension of Soviet sea power. In 1967 Gorshkov initiated the practice of having Soviet destroyers join submarines in following US navy carrier battle groups wherever they went. In 1968, when the United States responded to North Korea's internment of the intelligence ship USS *Pueblo* by dispatching the carrier *Enterprise* to the Sea of Japan, a November class nuclear-powered attack submarine shadowed it across the Pacific. At the peak of the *Pueblo* crisis, sixteen Soviet warships, auxiliary ships and surveillance vessels challenged the *Enterprise* and its battle group as they cruised off the Korean coast. Soviet warships never attempted a similar display off the coast of Indochina during the US war in Vietnam (1965–73) but during those years made frequent calls at Singapore, which Brezhnev courted as an ally after Khrushchev's failure to lure Indonesia into the Soviet orbit. The Soviets initiated talks as soon as the city-state declared its independence in 1965, in the hope that their navy could gain access to its strategically located anchorage after the last British forces withdrew. In the early 1970s some Soviet warships were repaired in Singapore's shipyards, but negotiations for a base had produced no result by 1975, when North Vietnam's conquest of South Vietnam gave Gorshkov's navy access to Camranh Bay.[36]

This strategic windfall was followed by a far more significant setback in the Mediterranean, when Egypt's President Anwar Sadat, after saving face in his 1973 war against Israel, changed sides in the Cold War and, in 1976, rescinded the Soviet navy's docking rights in Egyptian ports. Thereafter, the large Soviet Mediterranean squadron had to use inferior facilities in Syrian ports and depend more than before on a train of auxiliary vessels. By 1987 the Soviet navy typically maintained 40 to 50 ships in the Mediterranean, of which between 10 and 20 were surface warships or submarines, the rest oilers, tenders and supply ships of various types, shuttling through the Dardanelles and Bosphorus from the Black Sea.[37]

Operations in the brief era of East–West détente included the first visit by Soviet warships to the United States, when two destroyers called at Boston in 1975; the us navy reciprocated by sending a destroyer and a frigate to Leningrad. But in naval operations, as in the overall superpower relationship, such gestures of friendship did not signal an end to aggressive Soviet behaviour. That same year, when Portuguese colonial rule in Africa finally collapsed, Gorshkov's surface ships deployed to the waters off southern Africa in a show of support for Marxist movements attempting to seize power in Angola and Mozambique. In February 1976 the 'Kresta ii' class cruiser *Admiral Makarov* even provided fire support for MPLA guerrillas operating near the coast in Angola. After the Communist victory in Vietnam the Soviet Union initially avoided antagonizing the United States in southeast Asia, but in November 1978 Moscow signed a new friendship treaty with Hanoi. The following spring, during the brief Sino-Vietnamese War, Soviet warships called at Camranh Bay and convoyed freighters rushing military equipment from Vladivostok to Haiphong. In November 1979, to celebrate the first anniversary of the friendship treaty, a Soviet cruiser and two destroyers visited Haiphong.[38] One month later, the Soviet invasion of Afghanistan marked the end of détente.

During the same years, Gorshkov orchestrated three of the largest manoeuvres ever attempted by any navy. In 1968 the exercise codenamed 'Sever' included ships from the Polish and East German navies as well as the Soviet fleet. The simulated high seas encounter with an enemy force ranged across the Baltic, Barents and Norwegian seas, as well as the North Atlantic. Two years later, the exercise 'Okean' involved roughly 200 ships and submarines in the Baltic, Barents and Norwegian seas, the Mediterranean, the Philippine Sea and the Sea of Japan, simulating anti-submarine, anti-carrier and amphibious warfare. Gorshkov used the manoeuvre as a near-full mobilization test, as other Soviet squadrons not involved in 'Okean' were deployed to Cuba and the Indian Ocean while the massive exercise was underway. In 1975 another multi-ocean 200-ship simulation, codenamed 'Vesna' (but called 'Okean 75' by the us navy), featured the first extensive test of the Soviet satellite-based missile fire control system, in targeting exercises in the Atlantic, Pacific and Indian Oceans and the Mediterranean Sea. 'Vesna' also emphasized amphibious operations, simulating landings and the escorting of convoys by the Pacific Fleet in the Sea of Japan and the Northern Fleet in the Barents Sea. The West's largest naval manoeuvres of the Cold War paled in comparison: 'Ocean Safari 85', held in 1985, involved 157 warships from the US navy and nine European NATO navies.[39]

In the late Brezhnev years, as the Cold War returned in earnest, Soviet naval activity reached unprecedented levels. Warships from the East German and Polish navies joined units of the Soviet Baltic Fleet in provocative North Sea exercises in 1980 and again in 1981. In the autumn of 1981, amid the crisis over the growing strength of Poland's Solidarity movement, the navy conducted its largest Baltic manoeuvre ever. Codenamed 'Zapad', the exercise included ships sent from the Northern Fleet and Black Sea Fleet as well as Baltic units. Helicopters from the *Leningrad* and VSTOL aircraft from the *Kiev* supported landings of troops on the Soviet Baltic coast near the Soviet-Polish border. The amphibious manoeuvre came just months after a joint Soviet-Syrian military exercise involving the landing of 1,000 troops on the coast of Syria by the Soviet Mediterranean squadron. The Soviet naval posture in the Indian Ocean likewise became more aggressive, with a squadron of 20 to 25 surface units and submarines from the Pacific Fleet regularly assigned to the region. Operations on such a scale would have been impossible if not for the success of Soviet diplomacy in establishing friendships with Ethiopia and Yemen, which offered naval bases at Dehalak Island in the Red Sea and Socotra Island east of the Gulf of Aden. Soviet warships were also welcome at ports in India, thanks to a relationship that Gorshkov had nurtured since 1968, when he personally commanded the navy's first visits to Bombay and Madras. Thereafter, the Soviet Union became the principal source of warships for India.[40]

In operations, as in the construction programme, the interregnum between the death of Brezhnev and the accession of Gorbachev featured plenty of action. Indeed, the years 1984 and 1985 were the busiest ever for Soviet naval operations beyond coastal waters. The manoeuvre of 1984 surpassed in size and scope all but the exercises of 1970 and 1975, involving more than 180 ships and submarines from the Northern, Baltic and Black Sea fleets. During the manoeuvre the 14,590-ton helicopter carrier *Leningrad*, flagship of a group detached to the Caribbean, became the largest Soviet warship ever to visit Cuba; later in 1984, the same ship visited Yemen, heading a group including a cruiser and a destroyer along with smaller warships. Their presence in the western Indian Ocean at least temporarily reinforced the squadron there, which remained busy throughout the Iran–Iraq war (1980–88) detaching warships to escort Soviet tankers and merchantmen operating in the Persian Gulf.[41] By 1989 Gorbachev's efforts to end the Cold War had led to a warming of US-Soviet relations sufficient to warrant a naval visit to the United States (by the *Slava* class cruiser *Marshal Ustinov* and smaller warships, to Norfolk, Virginia), the first since 1975. The same year, the Soviets admitted the loss of the lone Mike class nuclear attack submarine. Previous accidental losses of nuclear-powered submarines (a November class attack submarine in 1970, a Charlie class guided missile submarine in 1983, and a Yankee class ballistic missile submarine in 1986) had been shrouded in secrecy.[42]

CONCLUSION

As in so many other areas, in naval-industrial resources the Soviet Union ultimately lacked the means to compete with the United States.[43] When the USSR collapsed at the end of 1991, the Soviet navy led the US navy in numbers of nuclear-powered submarines (209 to 114) and non-nuclear submarines (100 to none). It also enjoyed a great superiority in smaller types of surface warships, with more frigates (206 to 121), corvettes (162 to 19), minesweepers (205 to 23), patrol torpedo boats and missile boats (115 to none), and a lesser advantage in amphibious ships (75 to 66) and minelayers (3 to none). Based on the numbers and capability of these warship types, experts rated the Soviet navy superior to the US navy in most aspects of submarine, mine and amphibious warfare, as well as anti-ship missile firepower. But the Soviets never could match the global intervention capability of American carrier battle groups and assault ships. In sheer numbers the US navy enjoyed an overwhelming superiority over the Soviet navy in carriers (13 to 5) and helicopter carriers or assault ships (13 to 2), along with a marginal advantage in guided missile cruisers (45 to 31) and destroyers (51 to 40). The extent of nuclear propulsion in its surface fleet gave the US navy a significant qualitative edge, since most of its carriers and many of its larger surface vessels were nuclear powered, while the Soviet navy had no nuclear-powered surface warships other than the *Kirov* class cruisers. Even the greatest Soviet naval-industrial achievement, the construction of the six Typhoon class ballistic missile submarines, ultimately paled in comparison to the eventual eighteen units of the US navy's *Ohio* class.[44]

During the Cold War, the Soviet navy played a role *vis-à-vis* the US navy similar to that of the French *vis-à-vis* the British during much of the nineteenth century, with one important difference: the rivalry between the Soviet Union and the United States took on the character of a near-permanent war scare, the likes of which nineteenth-century Europe certainly had not seen. In such an atmosphere of ongoing tension, the United States could not be complacent about the quality of its fleet and, unlike Britain in the decades after 1815, did not have the luxury of behaving like a true hegemon. More often than not, the United States rather than the Soviet Union introduced the new naval and military technologies of the Cold War, raising the stakes but at the same time hoping eventually to achieve a level of power its rival simply could not match. Ultimately the strategy worked. The Soviet Union, like Japan before and during the Second World War, had to spend a far greater share of its national income on defence than the United States just to remain competitive; given the chronic productivity problems of the Soviet economy under communism, the effort was doomed to fail.

NINE

Upholding the Pax Americana:
The United States Navy since 1991

Alfred Thayer Mahan is dead. We have no fleets to fight.' A dozen years after the collapse of the Soviet Union, a retired American naval officer summed up the post-Cold War dilemma of the US navy in these terms.[1] In the late 1800s Mahan's blue-water battle fleet navalism had helped spur the navy out of its post-Civil War slumber. In the twentieth century the American fleet rose to face down the challenge of two formidable rivals, first the Imperial Japanese navy, then the Soviet fleet. But within a decade of the collapse of the Soviet Union the ex-Soviet navy was a shadow of its former self, as post-Communist Russia's economic problems brought a dramatic reduction in the size and scope of operations of the fleet. The US navy thus enjoyed the mixed blessing of being left without a serious rival, free to dominate the world's oceans as no navy had since the British fleet of the first decades after 1815, but also lacking the clear sense of purpose that had guided it for much of the twentieth century.

Like the former Soviet navy, the post-Cold War US navy endured a considerable reduction in size, from the 600-ship fleet of the late 1980s to barely 300 ships by 2003. During those years the scope of operations of this smaller fleet expanded to include a variety of missions in support of the new Pax Americana. In the Persian Gulf War of 1990–91 and interventions in Bosnia (1995), Kosovo (1999), Afghanistan (2001–2) and Iraq (2003), the navy provided indispensable carrier-based aircraft and ship-based cruise missile fire. The range of cruise missiles enabled US warships to launch punitive attacks against terrorist facilities in Sudan and Afghanistan (1998), demonstrating that a high-tech version of the old 'gunboat diplomacy' could be used to strike targets far from the sea. The US navy also facilitated humanitarian interventions in Somalia (1992) and Haiti (1993), and the impossibility of bringing naval resources to bear was at least one factor in the United States' refusal to get involved in the crisis in Rwanda (1995).

TRANSFORMATION OR CONTRACTION?: FROM THE 600-SHIP NAVY TO THE 300-SHIP NAVY

In 1991 the US navy had 13 aircraft carriers, 4 battleships, 45 cruisers, 51 destroyers, 121 frigates and scores of smaller vessels. Thirteen helicopter carriers or assault ships and 66 smaller landing ships provided a formidable amphibious capability, while the undersea arm of the service included 114 submarines on active duty, all nuclear powered. The formidable fleet, arguably the most capable in world history, already was somewhat smaller than the '600-ship navy' of President Ronald Reagan, achieved (albeit only briefly) in the late 1980s, before the end of the Cold War ushered in a decade of steady reduction in the size of the force.[2]

Fifteen carrier battle groups formed the centrepiece of the Reagan-era fleet. By the onset of the presidency of George Bush (1989), the force included six nuclear-powered and nine non-nuclear units, with two of the latter out of service and under refit at any given time. The oldest carrier, the 62,600-ton (full load) *Midway* (commissioned 1945, last major refit 1986), was withdrawn from service just before the completion of the nuclear-powered *George Washington* (built 1986–92). The 78,500-ton *Forrestal* (1955; refit 1983–5) and its sister ships *Saratoga* (1956; refit 1980–83), *Ranger* (1957; refit 1984–5) and *Independence* (1959; refit 1985–8) were all slated to remain in service until replaced by nuclear powered units in the first decade of the twenty-first century. The 80,800-ton *Kitty Hawk* (1961; refit 1988–91) and its sister ships *Constellation* (1961; refit 1990–93), *America* (1965) and *John F. Kennedy* (1968; refit 1993–5) were to serve even longer, during the transition to an all nuclear-powered carrier fleet. Aside from the 89,600-ton *Enterprise* (1961; refit 1990–94), the nuclear-powered carriers

29 The carrier USS *Nimitz* (1975), with the guided missile cruisers *California* (1974), foreground, and *South Carolina* (1975).

were all units of the 97,000-ton *Nimitz* class, the largest warships ever constructed, of which five were in service by the end of the Cold War: the *Nimitz* (built 1968–75; illus. 29), *Dwight D. Eisenhower* (1970–77), *Carl Vinson* (1975–82), *Theodore Roosevelt* (1981–6) and *Abraham Lincoln* (1984–9). After the *George Washington* replaced the *Midway* in 1992, under the presidency of Bill Clinton the post-Cold War downsizing of the navy reduced the number of carriers from fifteen to twelve. In 1993–4 the *Forrestal*, *Saratoga* and *Ranger* left service without being replaced, and a scheduled refit for the *America* was cancelled. Thereafter the *John C. Stennis* (1990–95) replaced the *America*, the *Harry S. Truman* (1992–8) replaced the *Independence*, and the *Ronald Reagan* (1995–2003) replaced the *Constellation*. Thus, in the dozen years following the demise of its Soviet rival, the US navy's carrier force became smaller but much more modern and capable, emerging with twelve units (ten nuclear powered and two non-nuclear), of which one of the nuclear-powered ships was idled at any given time for a refuelling complex overhaul (RCOH), starting with the *Nimitz* (1998–2001) and followed by the *Dwight D. Eisenhower* and other units of the *Nimitz* class thereafter. In addition to replacing fuel rods and servicing the nuclear power plant, the RCOH process also updated all other systems on the carrier to make it the equal of the newest member of the class. CVN-77, named *George H. W. Bush* in 2002 after the former president's son, George W. Bush, succeeded Clinton, was initially projected for a new design but laid down as another unit of the *Nimitz* class, scheduled to replace the *Kitty Hawk* in 2008 or 2009. As of 2003 the *John F. Kennedy* was projected to remain in service a decade longer than the *Kitty Hawk*, as the last non-nuclear powered carrier in the US navy. At the turn of the century the typical air wing of an American carrier included three squadrons of FA-18 (Hornet) fighter/attack jets, one squadron of F-14 (Tomcat) fighters, one of EA-6B (Prowler) tactical electronic warfare jets, one of E-2C (Hawkeye) tactical warning and control planes, and one of SH-60 (Seahawk) helicopters, totalling 60 to 70 aircraft in all.

The most controversial warships in the Reagan-era naval build-up, the recommissioned battleships of the 57,540-ton *Iowa* class, did not survive long into the 1990s. Laid down in 1940–41 and completed in 1943–4, the four *Iowa*s had been inactive since the 1950s except for the *New Jersey* (recommissioned 1967–9, for service during the Vietnam War). The *New Jersey* was the first to return to service (1982), followed by the *Iowa* (1984), *Missouri* (1986) and *Wisconsin* (1988). Tomahawk cruise missile launchers supplemented the firepower of their original battery of nine 16-inch guns; they were also equipped with Harpoon anti-ship missiles and, for close range defence, Phalanx rapid-fire 20-millimetre guns. As before, the ships proved to be very expensive to operate, requiring a crew of almost 2,000 (enough to man four cruisers). A powder explosion destroyed one turret of the *Iowa* during a training exercise in 1989, killing 47 sailors and leading to the premature decommissioning of the ship in 1990. The remaining three units were still with the fleet at the time of the Persian Gulf War, but were decommissioned in 1991–2. After all four *Iowa*s were finally stricken in 1995, plans called for at least three to be preserved as museum ships.

The end of the Cold War also brought a dramatic reduction in the number of US navy cruisers. As of 1991 the oldest cruiser still in service was also the largest: the 16,600-ton nuclear-powered *Long Beach* (completed 1961). Other nuclear-powered cruisers included the 7,980-ton *Bainbridge* (1962), the 8,930-ton *Truxtun* (1967), two units of the 10,150-ton *California* class (1974–5) and four of the 11,000-ton *Virginia* class (1976–80). Conceived as escorts for nuclear-powered aircraft carriers, they were far more expensive to build and maintain than conventionally powered warships of a similar size. After the *Arkansas* (1980), the navy commissioned no new nuclear-powered vessels other than aircraft carriers and submarines, and all nine nuclear-powered cruisers left service between 1994 and 1999. Nine cruisers of the 7,590-ton *Leahy* class (completed 1962–4) and nine of the 7,890-ton *Belknap* class (1964–7) were also withdrawn from service in the years 1993–5. At the turn of the century the 27 active cruisers in the fleet all belonged to the 9,600-ton *Ticonderoga* class (1983–94). The first ships equipped with the Aegis air defence system, their armament initially included 68 SM-1 SAMS and 20 ASROC anti-submarine rockets (later replaced by 88 SM-2 SAMS in the five oldest units of the class, and 122 SM-2s or Tomahawk cruise missiles in the remaining ships). All of the *Ticonderoga*s also were equipped with eight Harpoon SSMs, two 5-inch guns, and torpedo tubes, and all were later fitted with Phalanx rapid-fire 20-millimetre guns. They could operate two SH-60 helicopters from a deck immediately aft of the superstructure.

Among its smaller surface warships, the US navy of 1991 still included several destroyers of the 5,650-ton *Farragut* class (completed 1959–61) and the 4,530-ton *Charles F. Adams* class (completed 1961–4), all of which were decommissioned by 1993. In the late Cold War years the 31 units of the 8,040-ton *Spruance* class (completed 1975–83) formed the core of the destroyer force, supplemented by the four units of the 9,200-ton *Kidd* class (completed 1981–2), modified *Spruance*s laid down for the Shah of Iran but taken over by the US navy after the Iranian revolution of 1979. While the *Spruance*s were designed primarily for anti-submarine warfare in carrier battle groups, the *Kidd* version of the same type emphasized air defence. The 46 frigates of the 4,070-ton *Knox* class (completed 1969–74) joined the *Spruance*s in giving the US navy the anti-submarine warfare capability essential to counter the formidable undersea fleet of the Soviet Union. By the turn of the century, the *Spruance*s and *Kidd*s had been superseded by the multi-role destroyers of the *Arleigh Burke* class, which featured the Aegis air defence system, and a size and striking power rivalling that of the *Ticonderoga* class cruisers. Initially designed to displace 8,315 tons (full load), later ships of the class reached 9,200 tons. Their armament included 90 SM-2 SAMS and Tomahawk cruise missiles (96 in later models), one 5-inch gun, torpedo tubes and Phalanx rapid-fire 20-millimetre guns. They could operate one SH-60 helicopter from a deck at the stern. The *Arleigh Burke* was completed in 1991; by 2003 another 40 units of the class had entered service, eight were under construction, and an additional thirteen had been ordered. Meanwhile, between 1991 and 1994 all 46 *Knox*s left service, and by 2003 all four *Kidd*s and all but fourteen of the *Spruance*s had been retired. In lieu of the *Knox*s and *Spruance*s, the burden of anti-submarine warfare fell to the 55 frigates of the 3,660-ton *Oliver Hazard Perry* class (completed 1979–89). The last 25 units of the class were completed with lengthened hulls (and five of the original 'short hull' units were lengthened retroactively) in order to accommodate two SH-60 helicopters operating from a stern deck. Their armament included 40 SM-1 or Harpoon missiles, one 3-inch gun, torpedo tubes, and Phalanx rapid-fire 20-millimetre guns. In 2003 the last pair of 'short hull' ships of the class were decommissioned, leaving only the 30 'long hull' units in service. The demise of the Soviet fleet affected the anti-submarine warfare branch more dramatically than any other element of the US navy. In 1991 the American fleet had included over 130 warships specifically designed to counter the undersea threat; by 2003 barely a third as many ships (the surviving *Spruance*s and *Perry*s) filled that role, and the United States had not commissioned a new anti-submarine warfare vessel since 1989.

In 1991 the US navy's amphibious warfare units included thirteen helicopter carriers or assault ships, the largest warships of the fleet aside from aircraft carriers. Seven surviving 18,000-ton *Iwo Jima* class helicopter carriers, dating from the 1960s, had been joined by five 39,400-ton *Tarawa* class assault ships (completed 1976–80) and the first of the 40,500-ton *Wasp* class assault ships (completed 1989). The *Iwo Jima*s were decommissioned as another six *Wasp*s entered service (1992–2001), leaving the navy with twelve assault ships. The *Iwo Jima*s, *Tarawa*s and *Wasp*s could each carry around 2,000 Marines, but beyond that their capabilities varied dramatically. While the *Iwo Jima*s had hangar space for a maximum of 19 CH-46 Sea Knight helicopters, the *Tarawa*s could carry 30 and the *Wasp*s between 30 and 32, along with six Harrier VSTOL jets. Between 1991 and 2003 the navy pared its amphibious support fleet from 66 vessels to 26, by decommissioning all tank landing ships (LSTS) along with the oldest dock landing ships (LSDS) and amphibious transport docks (LPDS). At the turn of the century the LSDS included three units of the 14,000-ton *Anchorage* class (completed 1969–72), eight of the 15,940-ton *Whidbey Island* class (1985–92) and four of the 16,700-ton *Harper's Ferry* class (1995–8), each capable of carrying 400 troops along with equipment and supplies. The eleven surviving LPDS, all belonging to the 17,000-ton *Austin* class (1965–71), could each carry more than 800 troops. New amphibious warships under construction as of 2003 included three LPDS of the 24,900-ton *San Antonio* class (to be completed 2005–6), while those ordered included two more *San Antonio*s and an eighth *Wasp* class assault ship. The *San Antonio*s, delayed considerably in their design phase, received top priority owing to the age of the *Austin*s, which were obsolete after nearly four decades in service, having never been significantly refitted.

In contrast to the Soviet submarine force, which to the end included a large number of diesel-electric units, the US navy commissioned its last non-nuclear submarine in 1959 and had an all-nuclear undersea force after 1990. The eighteen ballistic missile submarines of the 18,750-ton *Ohio* class (completed 1981–97; illus. 30), each armed with 24 Trident SLBMs, housed a significant element of the American nuclear deterrent. They replaced units of the 7,890-ton *Ethan Allen* class (decommissioned 1985–92) and 8,250-ton *Lafayette* class (decommissioned 1986–95), all of which carried sixteen SLBMs. The 62 attack submarines of the 6,900-ton *Los Angeles* class (completed 1976–96) were armed with torpedoes, supplemented by Tomahawk cruise missiles starting in 1983. While older units of the class carried as few as eight Tomahawks, which had to be launched via

30 USS *Ohio* (1981).

torpedo tubes, later units were fitted with vertical launch systems and carried as many as twenty cruise missiles. They replaced the 42 attack submarines of the 4,780-ton *Sturgeon* class (completed 1966–75), which were decommissioned starting in 1990. Reflecting the shift of emphasis from nuclear deterrence to land-attack and intervention capabilities as the Cold War gave way to the Pax Americana, in 2002 plans were set in motion to withdraw the oldest four *Ohio*s from service for reconstruction as guided missile submarines; instead of 24 Trident SLBMs, they would carry 154 Tomahawk cruise missiles, and also deploy navy SEAL teams for special operations. During the 1990s the navy began to build newer, larger attack submarines to replace the oldest units of the *Los Angeles* class, twelve of which would be out of service by 2003. The 9,150-ton attack submarines *Seawolf* and *Connecticut* (completed 1997–8) were armed with torpedoes, carried 50 Tomahawks and could also be used to sow mines. A third unit of the class, the *Jimmy Carter* (under construction as of 2003), had the same capabilities but was modified to accommodate SEAL teams and conduct undersea recovery operations. Four attack submarines of the

7,800-ton *Virginia* class (under construction as of 2003) likewise were designed to accommodate SEAL teams as well as fire torpedoes or Tomahawk cruise missiles.

By 2003 the US navy had been reduced to just over 300 ships, and not enough were being built on an annual basis to maintain even that level of force. No new frigates had been commissioned since 1989, no cruisers since 1994, and carriers were being completed at the rate of one every five or six years. In the Quadrennial Defense Review (QDR) of 2001, discussion included a possible further force reduction from twelve carriers and twelve amphibious assault ships to just six carriers and eight amphibious assault ships, with a corresponding reduction in the need for escort ships. The sheer cost of the navy's standard warship types – for example, roughly $4.5 billion for a *Nimitz* class carrier, $1.65 billion for a *Virginia* class submarine and $1 billion for a *Ticonderoga* class cruiser – caused considerable political difficulties at budget time.[3] The need to build and maintain a fleet strong enough to counter the Soviet navy had disappeared, and no other equally compelling justification had replaced it. Yet in the first years of the Pax Americana, the United States placed greater demands on its smaller navy, leading to a tempo of operations that only accelerated the ageing of individual ships. In April 2003 almost two-thirds of the navy's ships were away from their home ports and slightly more than half were on overseas deployment. Such activity stood in sharp contrast to the British navy in the early wooden-ship years of the Pax Britannica, when most of the fleet was laid up in peacetime.

Enjoying an absolute domination of the world's oceans at a time of rapid technological change, the US navy of the 1990s and early twenty-first century had much more in common with the British navy of the 1870s and '80s. In each case, the hegemon adopted an almost leisurely approach to warship construction, typically reacting to developments abroad rather than seeking to pioneer new designs. In the post-Cold War situation, US navy talk of a 'revolution in military affairs' and 'transformation' of warfare at least partially masked this relative lack of action, but could not hide the fact that in the 1990s the navies and shipyards of Europe, constructing smaller ships in smaller classes, were responsible for most of the technological breakthroughs. The US navy especially admired the smaller surface combatants produced in northern Europe. Sweden's 620-ton, 38-knot corvette *Visby* (launched 2000), a revolutionary vessel designed with no right angles and a low-weight, high-strength hull made of plastic and carbon fibre, was considered the first operational model of a 'stealth' surface warship. At the same time, Norway's 260-ton patrol boat *Skjold*, an air-cushion catamaran capable of 57 knots, armed with 8 SSMs and one SAM, fascinated the US navy so much that in 2002 it was leased for further trials in American waters.[4] American designers also admired variations of a fast transport type with a catamaran hull, produced in the 1990s in Australia. In 2001–3 a 750-ton Australian catamaran capable of 38 knots while carrying a 1,200-ton load (or 48 knots with a 400-ton load) served with the US navy under the name *Joint Venture*, after which two similar vessels were ordered from US shipyards. Plans called for further experiments with two other leased Australian catamarans during 2003, one as a fast tank transport for the US army, the other as a mine countermeasures ship.[5]

In the early years of the twenty-first century, confusion reigned over the future direction of US naval construction. Under the Clinton administration, planning for future warships had focused on three projects: DD-21, a stealthy land-attack destroyer of roughly 10,000 tons to follow the *Arleigh Burke* class; a far less well-developed plan for a cruiser (CG-21) to follow the *Ticonderoga*s; and a new generation of aircraft carrier to follow the *Nimitz* class. As an alternative to the DD-21, Vice Admiral Arthur K. Cebrowski promoted the concept of the 'Streetfighter', a smaller surface warship that would be heavily armed for operations in inshore waters. Cebrowski first advocated the design in the last years of the Clinton presidency, while serving as director of the Naval War College in Newport, Rhode Island, where 'Streetfighter' had performed well in computer simulations of a war against China circa 2015. Summoned to Washington in 2001 to serve as director of the Office of Force Transformation in Donald Rumsfeld's Defense Department, Cebrowski unleashed a debate at least vaguely reminiscent of the *furor* over the Jeune Ecole in the 1880s, with the alleged virtues of the smaller warship contrasted against the ostensible obsolescence of larger types. Like the torpedo boats and light cruisers of the Jeune Ecole, 'Streetfighter' gained popularity mostly because of its projected cost (much lower than that of the DD-21 programme), but its advocates ultimately erred in marketing the type as practically a 'disposable' warship, calling into question whether it would be politically possible to produce and man such vessels if, in time of war, they might be so readily sacrificed against formidable enemy targets at sea or ashore.[6] In the end the 'Streetfighter' advocates helped kill the DD-21 project – cancelled by the Bush administration in late October 2001 – without achieving a consensus about what to put in its place. The subsequent experimental destroyer or DD(X) concept embodied several features of the DD-21 but in a multi-role (rather than land-attack) destroyer. The future 'family' of American warships was still projected to include a cruiser, now labelled CG(X) and charged with a missile-defence role, as well as a small 'littoral combat ship' (LCS) to appease the 'Streetfighter' advocates. As of 2003 the LCS was projected to be larger than the original 'Streetfighter', perhaps displacing 2,500 tons, featuring design elements of the Norwegian *Skjold* and the high-speed Australian catamarans leased by the US navy for experimental purposes. In 2003 the navy ordered the construction of an experimental littoral support craft or LSC(X), a small aluminium catamaran flat-top capable of carrying two helicopters. Both the LCS and LSC were to accommodate navy SEAL teams. Design and material elements pioneered in the Swedish *Visby* appeared to be most relevant to the DD(X) and CG(X), albeit in larger hull sizes, but as of 2003 the only US navy warships actually under construction that included 'stealthy' design features were the LPD *San Antonio* and its two sister ships.[7] Meanwhile, opponents of continuing the *Nimitz* carrier programme hoped that CVN-76 (the *Ronald Reagan*), completed in 2003, would be the last of its class; speculation in the 1990s included designs that were not only smaller but also not nuclear powered. The decision to build CVN-77 (the *George H. W. Bush*) as a *Nimitz* class carrier, coinciding with the defeat of DD-21, disappointed advocates of a more rapid transformation. The CVNX project designation for the eventual replacements for the

Enterprise (around 2013) and *John F. Kennedy* (around 2018) confirmed that future carriers would continue to be nuclear powered. Plans called for CVN-77 to be a 'transition ship' to the future design.[8]

'ZERO DEFECTS': LIFE IN A SHRINKING FLEET

In 1990 the US navy had 74,400 officers and 530,100 enlisted men; by 2003 the force had been reduced to 54,400 officers and 323,100 enlisted men. In the post-Cold War US navy under the Pax Americana, as in the post-Napoleonic British navy under the Pax Britannica, the shrinking size of the fleet limited career opportunities for officers and created a 'zero defects' mentality, in which most officers lived in fear of making a career-ending mistake or failing to measure up to expectations. Critics within the officer corps alleged that most of their peers had become selfish 'careerists' who placed their own concerns over pay and promotion ahead of all else. In many cases an officer's first loyalty was to his sub-branch within the navy, since the carrier aviators, submariners and surface warfare officers tended to form distinct camps dedicated to self-preservation. The Defense Department and successive presidential administrations only reinforced these internal divisions by respecting them, at least informally, in rotating the post of Chief of Naval Operations among the three. Thus, Admiral Frank Kelso (CNO 1990–94), a submariner, was followed by Admiral Jeremy 'Mike' Boorda (CNO 1994–6), a surface warfare officer, who was succeeded by Admiral Jay Johnson (CNO 1996–2000), a naval aviator. In the prevailing climate, officers sympathetic to change rarely risked advocating it for fear of being ostracized or, worse yet, passed over for promotion. Admiral Vernon Clark (CNO 2000–04) was credited with improving the atmosphere within the corps, but as late as 2003 one admiral proposed that junior officers wishing to air their views in the US Naval Institute's monthly *Proceedings* be allowed to do so anonymously, 'to protect [the] writers from vengeful seniors'.[9]

Compared to the US army and air force, the navy seemed to have greater (or at least more publicized) difficulties adjusting to changing values and attitudes in American society as a whole. When a powder explosion aboard the battleship *Iowa* in 1989 killed 47 sailors, the navy's initial explanation blamed the accident on sabotage by one of the dead sailors, allegedly a homosexual attempting to kill another sailor who had spurned his advances. The evidence was flimsy and the navy's version of the story both outraged the public and ruined the life of the other sailor, who had survived the explosion. In 1991 a scandal involving incidents of sexual harassment at the annual Tailhook convention of naval aviators caused further public outcry over the treatment of women in the navy, where they had served alongside men since 1978. The Tailhook scandal dogged Admiral Kelso for most of his tenure as CNO and helped force him to retire a few months earlier than scheduled, in 1994. His successor, Admiral Boorda, weathered the subsequent storm over the Clinton administration's policies regarding homosexuals in the armed forces but ultimately fell victim to a scandal of his own, committing suicide in 1996 upon learning that *Newsweek* magazine was investigating whether he had really been awarded a combat decoration he had worn since the Vietnam War. Further tarnishing the navy's image, during this same turbulent decade the US Naval Academy at Annapolis was hit by some of the worst scandals since its opening in 1845. Following an investigation of cheating incidents dating from 1992, the Secretary of the Navy expelled 24 midshipmen in 1994. To make matters worse, in 1996 five current and former midshipmen were charged with running a car theft operation.[10]

In 2003 the Naval Academy had a student body of 4,200; every year an average of a thousand new officers graduated from the four-year programme. Because Annapolis enrolments remained stable despite the 25 per cent reduction in the size of the officer corps between 1990 and 2003, opportunities for young men seeking to enter the corps via a thirteen-week Officer Candidate School (OCS) after graduation from civilian colleges and universities became somewhat restricted. Nevertheless, once commissioned, officers experienced less of the traditional prejudice in favour of Annapolis graduates than had once been common. Admiral Boorda rose to CNO despite having entered the navy as an enlisted man after dropping out of high school; in 1962 he completed OCS (which at the time still admitted men without college degrees), received his commission, and went on to become the first former enlisted man to reach the navy's highest office. Admiral Clark likewise did not attend the Naval Academy, entering the service in 1968 from OCS after earning a degree at Evangel College in Missouri. In 2003 three of the six highest-ranking admirals were not Annapolis graduates.[11]

The all-volunteer enlisted personnel of the navy were traditionally less well educated than their army and air force counterparts, and far less so than the civilian population of the United States. Of those enlisting in the navy in 1997, just 3.7 per cent had attended a college or university for a semester or more, compared to 10 per cent of army enlistees, 19.8 per cent of air force enlistees and 45.5 per cent of all civilians aged 18 to 24. The rate improved to 7.7 per cent by 2002 but still lagged behind the other services, the increase coming when the onset of a recession at the turn of the century ended the American economic boom of the 1990s and drove more young people to seek employment in the armed forces. In 2003 the entering sailor earned a basic pay of $12,768 per year, a total supplemented by allowances for housing and clothing, duty at sea, duty in submarines or naval aviation, remote 'hardship' postings, hazardous duty and service in 'imminent danger' or under 'hostile fire.' In comparison, the lowest-paid officer, a newly commissioned ensign, earned a basic pay of $26,204 per year, supplemented by the same array of allowances, but junior officers earned less and received lower allowances than senior enlisted personnel. Thus the high percentage of naval personnel on overseas shipboard deployment (20 per cent in 2003) received compensation for the inconvenience, but the strain of such assignments on the personal or family life of those deployed tended to depress re-enlistment rates. Re-enlistments declined during the 1990s, as stormy times within the service coincided with an economic boom in the civilian sector, but by 2002 the re-enlistment rate rebounded to 70 per cent. Enlistments were for a period of four years, and all prospective sailors (at least since the late 1970s) had to be high school graduates. Newly commissioned officers also served at least four years, except for engineer officers, who served a minimum of five years, and pilots or flight officers, who served eight to ten years.[12]

At the turn of the century the US navy attracted fewer women and minorities than the army or air force. In 1999 women accounted for 14.3 per cent of the navy's officers and 13.6 per cent of enlisted personnel; four years later, just thirteen of 305 flag officers (rear admirals and above) were female. In some respects, however, the navy offered women greater opportunity than the other armed services. As of 1996 the air force had just ten female pilots with three more in training, while the navy had 246 female pilots with another 102 in training. Under the Clinton administration, the repeal of combat exclusion provisions increased the number of jobs open to women; in the navy, only the SEALS and submarine duty were still limited to men. Meanwhile, the African American share of the navy remained considerably lower than the figure of roughly 25 per cent for enlisted personnel in the armed forces as a whole, and 12 per cent of the overall population. In 2002 the navy's 305 flag officers included just ten African Americans (3.3 per cent). The dearth of minority senior officers contrasted sharply with the Marine Corps, where the 99 generals included seven African Americans (7.1 per cent).[13]

WAR AND INTERVENTION UNDER THE PAX AMERICANA

The first exercise of American naval and military power in the post-Cold War world came several months before the final collapse of the Soviet Union, in the Persian Gulf War of 1990–91. The conflict began in August 1990, when Iraq's President Saddam Hussein ordered troops into neighbouring Kuwait. Iraq quickly conquered the country and proclaimed its annexation, prompting the Kuwaiti government to appeal to the United States and the United Nations for help. The UN ultimately gave Iraq until 15 January 1991 to withdraw from Kuwait, by which time the United States had organized a coalition for a military campaign to be launched in case Saddam Hussein disregarded the deadline. When the United States and its allies initiated Operation Desert Storm on 17 January, the US navy had over 130 warships of all types stationed in the region, including the carriers *Theodore Roosevelt*, *John F. Kennedy*, *Midway*, *Saratoga*, *Ranger* and *America*, the battleships *Missouri* and *Wisconsin*, the amphibious assault ships *Tarawa* and *Nassau*, six *Iwo Jima* class helicopter carriers, 18 cruisers, 14 destroyers, 18 frigates and at least a dozen submarines. From their stations in the Persian Gulf and Red Sea, the carriers participated in a campaign of air strikes lasting 37 days, supplemented by Tomahawk cruise missile launches from the *Missouri*, the *Wisconsin*, smaller surface warships and submarines. Warships from more than a dozen allied countries supplemented the American effort. US and allied ground forces liberated Kuwait during a brief campaign (23–7 February), after which President George Bush resisted the temptation to press on to Baghdad and overthrow Saddam Hussein, since such an action would have overstepped the UN mandate supporting the campaign and likely split the allied coalition. Most of Iraq's small fleet of patrol boats, minesweepers and fast attack craft was destroyed piecemeal, British navy helicopters alone accounting for fifteen sinkings. Most Iraqi warships that survived the war saved themselves only by defecting to neutral Iran. The US and its allies lost no warships in the conflict, but three US navy units were damaged by Iraqi mines: the frigate *Samuel B. Roberts*, put out of action for 18 months, requiring repairs costing $96 million; the cruiser *Princeton*, out for two months, at a cost of $17 million; and the assault ship *Tripoli*, out for one month, at a cost of $4 million. Although the Iraqi armed forces were very badly overmatched, American respect for Saddam Hussein's minefields and arsenal of missiles (which included Russian Scud ballistic missiles, launched during the war at targets in Israel and Saudi Arabia, and Chinese Silkworm anti-ship missiles, fired at coalition warships) influenced the decision not to place the US navy's most valuable assets at risk. Of the five nuclear-powered carriers then in service, only the *Theodore Roosevelt* deployed to the war zone. Four of the other five carriers involved in the war would be out of service by 1995, along with the battleships *Missouri* and *Wisconsin*, the six *Iwo Jima* class helicopter carriers, and roughly half of the smaller surface combatants that saw action in the conflict.[14]

In the years after the Persian Gulf War the navy facilitated us-led international interventions in Somalia and Haiti. Each country had experienced an internal political breakdown accompanied by some degree of famine, both problems more extreme in the Somalian case. Larger warships involved in Operation Restore Hope in Somalia (1992–4) included the aircraft carrier *Abraham Lincoln*, the assault ship *Peleliu* and the helicopter carriers *Inchon*, *Guadalcanal* and *New Orleans*. Operation Support Democracy in Haiti (1993–5) initially included a mixture of six cruisers, destroyers and frigates, which joined three Canadian warships in enforcing un sanctions against the Haitian dictatorship. us Marines from the assault ship *Wasp* later maintained order in the wake of the collapse of the dictatorship, until un troops arrived to oversee the transition to a new government.[15] Neither operation was particularly successful; in 1994 us forces left Somalia in chaos, while in Haiti the new regime in the long run proved to be just as corrupt as the old.

The American intervention in Bosnia (1995) proved to be far more decisive. Up to that point the United States had not been directly involved in the break-up of Yugoslavia, which began in the summer of 1991 but took an especially violent turn after the secession of Bosnia in the spring of 1992. Over the persistent protests of Russia, which supported Serbian leader Slobodan Milošević's quest to hold together the Yugoslav union by force, the United States and nato gradually became more involved in pressuring the Serbs to negotiate a compromise peace. From 1992 to 1996 us navy destroyers and frigates participated in nato patrols of the Adriatic Sea to enforce a un arms embargo on the former Yugoslavia, and during the summer of 1995 us and nato aircraft attacked Serbian targets in Bosnia. The carrier air wing of the *Theodore Roosevelt* supplemented nato aircraft based at Aviano, Italy, in the brief air campaign over Bosnia. The air strikes, coinciding with Croatian and Bosnian counteroffensives against the Serbs, forced Milošević to accept a peace deal at the end of that year, after which us and nato ground forces occupied Bosnia to enforce the settlement.[16]

Naval actions during 1998 foreshadowed future conflicts after the turn of the century, targeting suspected strongholds of the terrorist group al Qaeda as well as alleged chemical and biological weapons manufacturing sites in Iraq. In early August 1998 al Qaeda terrorists bombed the US embassies in Kenya and Tanzania, prompting Clinton to order retaliatory cruise missile strikes against suspected al Qaeda facilities in Sudan and Afghanistan two weeks later. The Tomahawks were launched from two US navy warships in the Indian Ocean and covered the longest distance to date of any cruise missile strike, with accuracy made possible by satellite guidance technology developed in the Cold War competition with the Soviet Union and further improved during the 1990s. The operation demonstrated that a high-tech version of the old 'gunboat diplomacy' could be used to strike targets even in landlocked or near-landlocked countries far from blue water. The strikes did little to weaken al Qaeda and nothing to deter its followers; the US navy would learn this hard lesson two years later, in October 2000, when al Qaeda members detonated a bomb against the hull of the *Arleigh Burke* class destroyer *Cole* during a port call in Yemen, killing seventeen sailors and disabling the ship.[17] Meanwhile, later in 1998 American attentions returned to Iraq when the government of Saddam Hussein stopped co-operating with the regime of UN arms control inspections imposed after the Persian Gulf War. The United States responded with Operation Desert Fox (16–19 December 1998), a series of punitive strikes against suspected chemical and biological sites, as well as military targets in general within Iraq. The carrier air wings of the *Enterprise* and *Carl Vinson* joined US and British air force planes in bombing raids while the ships of their battle groups in the Persian Gulf fired more than 200 cruise missiles into Iraq.[18]

The following year the focus shifted back to the Balkans, where the relative calm that had followed the Bosnian peace settlement of 1995 was broken when Serbian leader Milošević began to drive ethnic Albanians out of Kosovo, a predominantly Albanian but historically Serbian region of Yugoslavia. During Operation Allied Force (March–June 1999) warships from the US and ten other NATO navies supplemented the efforts of aircraft based at Aviano, Italy. The *Theodore Roosevelt* joined British and French carriers in launching sorties against targets in

Kosovo and Serbia, while other US and British units fired Tomahawk cruise missiles. As in Bosnia in 1995, in Kosovo the Serbs ultimately agreed to a settlement enforced by US and NATO ground troops, under which Albanian refugees were allowed to return to their homes.[19]

During his campaign for the presidency in 2000, George W. Bush criticized the Clinton administration's commitment of US armed forces to 'nation-building' interventions in Somalia, Haiti, Bosnia and Kosovo, while Condoleeza Rice, his future national security advisor, drew loud cheers at that summer's Republican party convention when she declared that 'George W. Bush . . . recognizes that America's armed forces are not a global police force'.[20] But just as the Pax Britannica of the nineteenth century had transcended British partisan politics to be upheld, in the long run, regardless of which party happened to be in power, the interventionist and policing roles of the American armed forces established under Clinton continued and, indeed, took on a far more sweeping scope under Bush, following the attacks on the World Trade Center in New York and the Pentagon in Washington by the terrorist group al Qaeda on 11 September 2001. On that day, the carriers *George Washington*, *John F. Kennedy* and *John C. Stennis* were pressed into service to provide air cover over major coastal cities in the United States, while the Aegis air defence systems of seven *Ticonderoga* class cruisers and six *Arleigh Burke* class destroyers contributed to the North American Air Defense Command's efforts to monitor potential further threats to US terrritory. In October 2001, when the United States and a coalition of allies launched Operation Enduring Freedom against al Qaeda and its Taliban hosts in Afghanistan, the navy contributed the carriers *Enterprise*, *Carl Vinson* and *Kitty Hawk* to the effort. The *Kitty Hawk*, rushed to the Arabian Sea from its home port of Yokosuka, Japan, without most of its air wing, embarked helicopters and over 1,000 special operations troops (including navy SEALs), which used the ship as a staging area. Supplementing the air strikes, US and British naval units fired Tomahawk cruise missiles into Afghanistan. Until such time as the United States could negotiate land access to Afghanistan via Uzbekistan and other former Soviet Central Asian republics, much of the effort had to be sustained by naval forces, despite the more than 300 miles (480 kilometres) that separate the Arabian Sea from the southern border of Afghanistan. Shortly after the operation began, the *Theodore Roosevelt* arrived to give the force a fourth carrier, while the assault ships *Peleliu* and *Bataan* brought additional helicopters, Harrier VSTOL aircraft and US Marines. The *John C. Stennis* arrived two months later, in December 2001, to relieve the *Carl Vinson*. Refuelled with the help of tankers from US bases in the Gulf states, carrier-based aircraft struck targets as far as 900 miles (1,450 kilometres) inland. By December 2001 al Qaeda had been routed from Afghanistan and the Taliban regime replaced by a pro-Western provisional government.[21]

As Afghanistan became the first 'nation-building' project of the Bush administration, the Pax Americana promised to take on a far more aggressive character. In his State of the Union Address before the US Congress in January 2002, Bush labelled Iraq, Iran and North Korea 'the Axis of Evil', condemning all three as rogue states that sponsored terrorism and threatened others with weapons of mass destruction.[22] Over the year that followed, the United States gradually increased the pressure on the regime of Saddam Hussein. When the Iraqi dictator allowed UN weapons inspectors back into his country after an absence of four years, then failed to allow them free rein to conduct their investigations, the United States resolved to depose him by force if he did not agree to leave Iraq peacefully. In sharp contrast to the last war against Iraq a dozen years earlier, this time the coalition opposing Saddam Hussein included military and naval units from just the United States, Britain, Australia and Poland (in the case of the latter two, token forces). On 19 March 2003, shortly after the expiration of an American ultimatum, coalition forces invaded Iraq. Because US allies in crucial neighbouring states, Turkey and Saudi Arabia, refused to support the intervention, the war had to be run from Kuwait, the smaller Persian Gulf states including Bahrain (where the US Fifth Fleet had established a base in 1993) and air bases far removed from the theatre of operations. Under these conditions the US navy shouldered much more of the burden than it had in the Persian Gulf War of 1990–91, and the US

Marines accounted for a far greater share of a much smaller ground force (roughly half the size of the army deployed in 1990–91). At the start of the war, the carriers *Theodore Roosevelt* and *Harry S. Truman* were in the eastern Mediterranean with the assault ship *Iwo Jima*, three dock landing ships and an armada of supply ships, carrying the equipment for an infantry division that the United States hoped to send via Turkey into northern Iraq. When the Turks refused to allow the troops to pass through, the two carriers remained in the Mediterranean while the cruisers and destroyers of their battle groups relocated to the Red Sea, in order to fire cruise missiles through Saudi airspace into Iraq. Even though the Tomahawks were much more accurate than a dozen years earlier (hitting the desired targets over 98 per cent of the time, compared with a success rate of less than 85 per cent in the Persian Gulf War), the Saudis protested when a small number of the missiles fell on their territory. The navy responded by sending the ships on to the Persian Gulf. The supply ships joined them there, unloading the equipment for the additional infantry division in Kuwait, where the troops were finally readied to go into Iraq only after the collapse of Saddam Hussein's regime (9 April 2003). Meanwhile, the carriers *Kitty Hawk*, *Constellation* and *Abraham Lincoln* were in the Persian Gulf from the start of the war, launching air strikes against Baghdad and other targets while the ships of their battle groups fired cruise missiles. In the three weeks prior to the fall of the Iraqi capital, us navy ships fired 800 cruise missiles. The large contingent of us Marines sent into Iraq from the Gulf deployed from seven assault ships (the *Boxer*, *Bonhomme Richard*, *Saipan*, *Kearsarge*, *Bataan*, *Tarawa* and *Nassau*) and ten dock landing ships. us and coalition naval forces suffered no material losses or damage during the brief war. The Iraqis managed to launch just one Silkworm missile in the general direction of the Persian Gulf, which struck a pier in Kuwait City, detonated, and damaged an adjacent shopping mall. The handful of small Iraqi naval vessels played no role in the war other than laying a few mines off the port of Umm Qasr near Basra, where their presence did little to disrupt the coalition's war effort but much to delay the subsequent importation of humanitarian aid.[23]

During the Iraq war of 2003 US naval resources were stretched thinner by the concurrent sabre-rattling of North Korea, which took advantage of the United States' preoccupation with Saddam Hussein to resume a nuclear weapons programme it had agreed to suspend in the early 1990s. Because the *Kitty Hawk*, normally based at Yokosuka, Japan, had been moved to the Persian Gulf, in late March the navy deployed the carrier *Carl Vinson* and its battle group to the Sea of Japan. Meanwhile, the assault ship *Essex* and two dock landing ships cruised in East Asian waters, and a second carrier battle group led by the *John C. Stennis* put to sea from San Diego for a Pacific cruise. The crisis over North Korea may have played a role in the curious voyage of the carrier *Nimitz* and its battle group, which left San Diego on 3 March bound for the Persian Gulf, where it was supposed to relieve the *Abraham Lincoln* around the time the crisis in Iraq came to a head, leading to speculation that both carriers would be on station at least for the initial strikes against Saddam Hussein. Instead, the *Nimitz* lingered in the Pacific, putting in at Pearl Harbor in mid-month, before finally passing into the Indian Ocean in late March and arriving in the Persian Gulf on 7 April, two days before the fall of Baghdad. By then an additional carrier was no longer needed, and the *Abraham Lincoln* steamed for home. In late April, following the collapse of Saddam Hussein's regime, the *Kitty Hawk* and *Constellation* steamed for their home ports as well. At the same time, an easing of tensions in the North Korean crisis prompted the relocation of the *Carl Vinson* to the Philippine Sea and the return of the *John C. Stennis* to San Diego. The coincidence of the war in Iraq and the crisis over North Korea had required the simultaneous deployment of eight of the navy's eleven active carrier battle groups and nine of its twelve amphibious assault groups. So many American warships had not been at sea at any time since 1991, and then the overall fleet had been almost twice as large.[24]

CONCLUSION

Like the British navy during the era of the Pax Britannica, the US navy of the early twenty-first century policed the world's oceans and littoral regions, not just in defence of its own territory and interests, but in support of moral and legal positions it had taken and had persuaded others to take. The fall of Saddam Hussein marked the onset of another ambitious American exercise in 'nation-building', and raised the question of whether the intervention in Iraq would spark an increase in Arab terrorism against the United States, as many predicted, or have the positive effect of encouraging better behaviour by other rogue states fearful of meeting a similar fate. The latter had been the case at the dawn of the Pax Britannica, when punitive action taken against one of the North African pirate states typically had an impact on all of them.

The Bush administration's willingness to pursue the invasion of Iraq alone if necessary was reminiscent of Britain's post-Palmerston preference to act unilaterally rather than compromise its own goals or ideals for the sake of accommodating allies. Whereas Britain, between 1815 and 1865, more often than not had policed the world in league with other countries, from 1865 until the end of the Pax Britannica the British typically operated alone. Even though many rival powers may have privately applauded these unilateral actions, publicly they opposed British domination in the international arena. Ultimately, in the Anglo-Boer War (1899–1902), the British found themselves embroiled in a messy and costly conflict in which practically the entire world cheered for their opponents to win. The marked isolation of Britain and clear rejection of its international leadership confirmed that the Pax Britannica was dead. In 2003 the opposition to US action in Iraq voiced by significant former enemies (Russia and China) and ostensible friends (France and Germany) called into question whether the more aggressive posture of the post-11 September Bush presidency had not placed the United States in a similar position, just a dozen years into the era of the Pax Americana. It remained to be seen whether the Iraq war of 2003 would be the United States' version of the Anglo-Boer War, a conflict the Americans would win, but at such a high price in international goodwill that the damage to its reputation would be irreparable. In any event, as long as the United States remained the only superpower in the international arena, its navy would continue to serve as the strong arm of the world's policeman.

References

ONE · RULING THE WAVES: THE BRITISH NAVY, 1815–1902

1 Fred T. Jane, *The British Battle Fleet* (London, 1915; reprint, London, 1990), vol. I, p. 193; Lawrence Sondhaus, *Naval Warfare, 1815–1914* (London, 2001), p. 2.

2 Jane, *The British Battle Fleet*, vol. I, p. 211; Colin White, *Victoria's Navy: The End of the Sailing Navy* (Annapolis, MD, 1981), p. 10; Philip Pugh, *The Cost of Seapower: The Influence of Money on Naval Affairs from 1815 to the Present Day* (London, 1986), pp. 335–7; Robert Gardiner, *Frigates of the Napoleonic Wars* (Annapolis, MD, 2000), p. 61.

3 Andrew Lambert, 'Introduction of Steam', in *Steam, Steel and Shellfire: The Steam Warship, 1815–1905*, ed. Robert Gardiner (London, 1992), pp. 17–24; David K. Brown, *Paddle Warships: The Earliest Steam Powered Fighting Ships, 1815–1850* (London, 1993), p. 79.

4 Andrew Lambert, 'The Screw Propeller Warship', in *Steam, Steel and Shellfire*, pp. 33–46; Sondhaus, *Naval Warfare*, p. 67.

5 David K. Brown, 'The Era of Uncertainty', in *Steam, Steel and Shellfire*, pp. 76–8; *Conway's All the World's Fighting Ships, 1860–1905*, pp. 4–5, 12–18.

6 David K. Brown, *Warrior to Dreadnought: Warship Development, 1860–1905* (London, 1997), p. 14; John F. Beeler, *British Naval Policy in the Gladstone-Disraeli Era, 1866–1880* (Stanford, CA, 1997), pp. 19, 91.

7 Brown, *Warrior to Dreadnought*, p. 203; *idem*, 'The Era of Uncertainty', pp. 84–6; *Conway, 1860–1905*, pp. 26–7; Denis Griffiths, 'Warship Machinery', in *Steam, Steel and Shellfire*, p. 176.

8 Brown, 'The Era of Uncertainty', p. 92; Griffiths, 'Warship Machinery', p. 176; Sondhaus, *Naval Warfare*, pp. 140, 143–4.

9 Beresford to House of Commons, 13 December 1888, quoted in Charles William de la Poer Beresford, *The Memoirs of Admiral Lord Charles Beresford* (Boston, 1914), vol. II, p. 360. See also Aaron L. Friedberg, *The Weary Titan: Britain and the Experience of Relative Decline, 1895–1905* (Princeton, NJ, 1988), p. 146; Arthur J. Marder, *The Anatomy of British Sea Power: A History of British Naval Policy in the Pre-Dreadnought Era, 1880–1905* (New York, 1940), pp. 105–6.

10 Jon Tetsuro Sumida, *In Defence of Naval Supremacy: Finance, Technology and British Naval Policy, 1889–1914* (Boston, 1989), pp. 13–16; John Roberts, 'The Pre-Dreadnought Age, 1890–1905', in *Steam, Steel and*

Shellfire, p. 116; Brown, *Warrior to Dreadnought*, pp. 124–32; *Conway, 1860–1905*, pp. 32–3, 76–7, 66, 82.

11 Pugh, *The Cost of Seapower*, p. 16; W. Mark Hamilton, *The Nation and the Navy: Methods and Organization of British Navalist Propaganda, 1889–1914*, p. 9; Friedberg, *The Weary Titan*, p. 155; Brown, *Warrior to Dreadnought*, pp. 137–46; Roberts, 'The Pre-Dreadnought Age', p. 117; *Conway, 1860–1905*, pp. 34–7, 90–91.

12 Michael Lewis, *A Social History of the Navy, 1793–1815* (London, 1960), p. 198; *idem, The Navy in Transition, 1814–1864: A Social History* (London, 1965), pp. 56, 63–71, 123; Peter Kemp, *The British Sailor: A Social History of the Lower Deck* (London, 1970), p. 189.

13 Lewis, *The Navy in Transition*, pp. 53, 61, 80, 116.

14 *Ibid.*, pp. 57, 126; John Wells, *The Royal Navy: An Illustrated Social History, 1870–1982* (London, 1994), p. 33.

15 Lewis, *The Navy in Transition*, pp. 74, 114–16; *idem, A Social History of the Navy*, pp. 189–90.

16 Lewis, *The Navy in Transition*, p. 53.

17 *Ibid.*, pp. 79, 93.

18 *Ibid.*, p. 79; Sondhaus, *Naval Warfare*, p. 64.

19 Kemp, *The British Sailor*, p. 189, observes that this was especially the case in matters of discipline.

20 Lewis, *The Navy in Transition*, p. 82; Sondhaus, *Naval Warfare*, pp. 9–17, 20, 22, 28, 30.

21 Lewis, *The Navy in Transition*, p. 103; *idem, A Social History of the Navy*, pp. 143–5, 148. Lewis's data for the years 1793–1815 is based upon a sample including roughly 40 per cent of all officers serving in those years; his data for 1815–49 is based upon roughly 60 per cent serving in those years.

22 White, *Victoria's Navy: The End of the Sailing Navy*, p. 65; Lewis, *The Navy in Transition*, p. 107.

23 White, *Victoria's Navy: The End of the Sailing Navy*, p. 67; Wells, *The Royal Navy*, p. 6. Lewis, *The Navy in Transition*, p. 111, notes that the old ship of the line *Prince of Wales* replaced the *Britannia* in 1869, and was renamed *Britannia*. Subsequent replacements likewise retained the name *Britannia*.

24 White, *Victoria's Navy: The Heyday of Steam*, pp. 77–8.

25 Lewis, *A Social History of the Navy*, pp. 31, 36, 62–74, 177; *idem, The Navy in Transition*, pp. 20–26, 30, 36–41. On the limitations of Lewis's data see note 21 above.

26 Eugene L. Rasor, *Reform in the Royal Navy: A Social History of the Lower Deck, 1850 to 1880* (Hamden, CT, 1976), pp. 107–10.

27 Isaac Edward Land, 'Domesticating the Maritime: Culture, Masculinity, and Empire in Britain, 1770–1820', PhD diss., University of Michigan, 1999, pp. 209, 251; Kemp, *The British Sailor*, p. 188; White, *Victoria's Navy: The End of the Sailing Navy*, p. 67; Lewis, *A Social History of the Navy*, p. 139. On the Quota Act of 1795, by which localities usually used to empty their prisons, see Rasor, *Reform in the Royal Navy*, p. 22, and Lewis, *The Navy in Transition*, p. 174. The most dramatic short-term emigration of British seamen into foreign service came in 1822–5, during

Cochrane's tenure as commander of the Brazilian navy. See chapter 3 below. On the number of former British subjects in the American navy, Rasor, *Reform in the Royal Navy*, p. 27, notes that as late as 1878 some 30 per cent of American seamen were born in the British Isles.

28 Rasor, *Reform in the Royal Navy*, p. 29.

29 *Ibid.*, p. 100; White, *Victoria's Navy: The End of the Sailing Navy*, pp. 68, 78; Kemp, *The British Sailor*, pp. 200–202; Lewis, *The Navy in Transition*, p. 184.

30 White, *Victoria's Navy: The End of the Sailing Navy*, pp. 68–70; Land, 'Domesticating the Maritime', p. 251; Rasor, *Reform in the Royal Navy*, pp. 26, 33; Kemp, *The British Sailor*, p. 202. Graham to Napier, March 1854, quoted in Lewis, *The Navy in Transition*, p. 186.

31 White, *Victoria's Navy: The End of the Sailing Navy*, pp. 75, 77; Rasor, *Reform in the Royal Navy*, pp. 12, 43; Land, 'Domesticating the Maritime', p. 251.

32 Rasor, *Reform in the Royal Navy*, pp. 39, 42, 55, 59, 64–5, 67, 71, 116–17; Kemp, *The British Sailor*, p. 205; White, *Victoria's Navy: The End of the Sailing Navy*, p. 77.

33 Kemp, *The British Sailor*, pp. 192, 194, 198, 202.

34 Palmerston to Admiral Napier, in 1847, quoted in White, *Victoria's Navy: The End of the Sailing Navy*, p. 133.

35 Kenneth Bourne, *Palmerston: The Early Years, 1784–1841* (New York, 1982), pp. 59–61, 80, 82.

36 Basil Lubbock, *Cruisers, Corsairs & Slavers: An Account of the Suppression of the Picaroon, Pirate & Slaver by the Royal Navy during the 19th Century* (Glasgow, 1993), pp. 94–5, 327–31, 364, 374–5, 384, 617; Regis A. Courtemanche, *No Need of Glory: The British Navy in American Waters, 1860–1864* (Annapolis, MD, 1977), p. 88.

37 White, *Victoria's Navy: The End of the Sailing Navy*, p. 129; Lubbock, *Cruisers, Corsairs & Slavers*, pp. 354, 407; Raymond Howell, *The Royal Navy and the Slave Trade* (New York, 1987), p. 12; Courtemanche, *No Need of Glory*, pp. 89, 92.

38 Howell, *The Royal Navy and the Slave Trade*, pp. 21–5, 36, 67, 114, 184–5, 195–205, 208.

39 Jasper Ridley, *Lord Palmerston* (New York, 1971), pp. 359, 374–5, 380–89.

40 *Ibid.*, p. 366.

41 Andrew Lambert, *The Last Sailing Battlefleet: Maintaining Naval Mastery, 1815–1850* (London, 1991), pp. 8, 99.

42 C. I. Hamilton, *Anglo-French Naval Rivalry, 1840–1870* (Oxford, 1993), p. 3.

43 Sondhaus, *Naval Warfare*, p. 22.

44 John C. K. Daly, *Russian Seapower and 'the Eastern Question', 1827–41* (Annapolis, MD, 1991), pp. 1–13; Anthony J. Watts, *The Imperial Russian Navy* (London, 1990), pp. 11–12; Maurice Dupont and Etienne Taillemite, *Les guerres navales françaises du Moyen Age à la guerre du Golfe* (Paris, 1995), pp. 227–8; Fred T. Jane, *The Imperial Russian Navy*, 2nd edn (London, 1904; reprint edn London, 1983), pp. 128–30. According to Dupont and Taillemite, Ibrahim's fleet at Navarino included 3 ships

of the line, 12 frigates and 22 corvettes or smaller warships. English-language sources usually count one of the French frigates as a ship of the line.

45 Sondhaus, *Naval Warfare*, pp. 27–8.

46 Hamilton, *Anglo-French Naval Rivalry*, p. 11; Daly, *Russian Seapower and 'the Eastern Question'*, p. 143; François Ferdinand d'Orléans, Prince de Joinville, *Essais sur la marine française* (Paris, 1853), p. 10.

47 Hamilton, *Anglo-French Naval Rivalry*, p. 21; Lawrence Sondhaus, *The Habsburg Empire and the Sea: Austrian Naval Policy, 1797–1866* (West Lafayette, IN, 1989), pp. 102–3; Lambert, *The Last Sailing Battlefleet*, p. 38. Prussia had no naval forces at the time, and contributed to the effort by sending troops to the Rhine, while a rebellion in Georgia kept the Russian Black Sea Fleet from participating. See Daly, *Russian Seapower and 'the Eastern Question'*, pp. 159–63.

48 Sondhaus, *The Habsburg Empire and the Sea*, pp. 103–4; Lambert, 'Introduction of Steam', p. 23.

49 Daly, *Russian Seapower and 'the Eastern Question'*, pp. 171–3; Lambert, *The Last Sailing Battlefleet*, p. 87; Sondhaus, *The Habsburg Empire and the Sea*, pp. 127–36.

50 Jack Beeching, *The Chinese Opium Wars* (New York, 1975), pp. 84–104 *passim*.

51 *Ibid.*, pp. 111–12; Lambert, 'Introduction of Steam', p. 28.

52 W. H. Hall, *Narrative of the Voyages and Services of the* Nemesis, *from 1840 to 1843*, 2nd edn (London, 1845), p. 121 and *passim*.

53 *Ibid.*, pp. 478–9 and *passim*; Beeching, *The Chinese Opium Wars*, pp. 144–56; Lambert, 'Introduction of Steam', pp. 22, 29.

54 Unless otherwise noted, the sources for this section are Andrew Lambert, *The Crimean War: British Grand Strategy against Russia, 1853–56* (Manchester, 1991), pp. 3, 9–22, 60, 102–6, 135–40, 146, 218, 230–34, 246–8, 296–8; F. N. Gromov, Vladimir Gribovskii and Boris Rodionov, *Tri Veka Rossiiskogo Flota* (St Petersburg, 1996), vol. III, pp. 191–6; David Woodward, *The Russians at Sea: A History of the Russian Navy* (New York, 1966), pp. 99–104, 109; Watts, *The Imperial Russian Navy*, pp. 12–13.

55 D. Bonner-Smith and A. C. Dewar, eds, *Russian War, 1854: Baltic and Black Sea: Official Correspondence* (London, 1943), pp. 210–27; Andrew Lambert, *Battleships in Transition: The Creation of the Steam Battlefleet, 1815–1860* (Annapolis, MD, 1984), pp. 95–6; George Sydenham Clarke, *Russia's Sea-Power Past and Present; or, The Rise of the Russian Navy* (London, 1898), pp. 89–90.

56 Lambert, *Battleships in Transition*, p. 41; John Campbell, 'Naval Armaments and Armour', in *Steam, Steel and Shellfire*, p. 167; Clarke, *Russia's Sea-Power*, p. 93; Bonner-Smith and Dewar, eds, *Russian War, 1854*, pp. 3–5.

57 Dundas to Secretary of the Admiralty, 13 August 1855, in D. Bonner-Smith, ed., *Russian War, 1855, Baltic: Official Correspondence* (London, 1944), p. 184; see also *ibid.*, pp. 8–12; Hamilton, *Anglo-French Naval Rivalry*, p. 77; Clarke, *Russia's Sea-Power*, p. 94; Watts, *The Imperial Russian Navy*, p. 13; Lambert, *Battleships in Transition*, pp. 50–52, 113;

    idem, 'The Screw Propeller Warship', p. 44.

58 See report of Lyons to Secretary of the Admiralty Thomas Phinn, 10
    September 1855, in A. C. Dewar, ed., *Russian War, 1855, Black Sea:*
    Official Correspondence (London, 1945), p. 291.

59 Andrew Lambert, 'Iron Hulls and Armour Plate', in *Steam, Steel and*
    Shellfire, p. 52; James Phinney Baxter, *The Introduction of the Ironclad*
    Warship (Cambridge, MA, 1933), pp. 78–86.

60 Hamilton, *Anglo-French Naval Rivalry*, p. 77; Clarke, *Russia's Sea-Power*,
    p. 94; Watts, *The Imperial Russian Navy*, p. 13; Lambert, *Battleships in*
    Transition, pp. 50–52, 113; *idem*, 'The Screw Propeller Warship', p. 44.

61 J. Y. Wong, *Deadly Dreams: Opium, Imperialism and the 'Arrow' War*
    (1856–1860) in China (Cambridge, 1998), pp. 99, 280, 487–9 and *passim*;
    Beeching, *The Chinese Opium Wars*, pp. 246–325; Dupont and
    Taillemite, *Les guerres navales françaises*, pp. 244–5.

62 Brown, *Warrior to Dreadnought*, pp. 71–3. On Gladstone's earlier opposi-
    tion to Palmerston, see Ridley, *Lord Palmerston*, pp. 255, 387–8.

63 Pugh, *The Cost of Seapower*, p. 37.

64 Theodore Ropp, *The Development of a Modern Navy: French Naval Policy,*
    1871–1904, ed. Stephen S. Roberts (Annapolis, MD, 1987), p. 205. See
    text of British naval intelligence office memorandum of 28 October
    1896 in Marder, *The Anatomy of British Sea Power*, pp. 578–80.

65 Marder, *The Anatomy of British Sea Power*, p. 263.

66 Friedberg, *The Weary Titan*, p. 162.

67 *Ibid.*, p. 159; White, *Victoria's Navy: The Heyday of Steam*, pp. 138–9. The
    only naval guns brought to bear in the war were 7-inch breech-loaders
    dismounted from the protected cruisers *Terrible* and *Powerful*, and
    hauled inland for the defence of Ladysmith. Royal Marines and seamen
    also served ashore during the war, alongside army troops. See White,
    ibid., pp. 152–4, and Peter Padfield, *Rule Britannia: The Victorian and*
    Edwardian Navy (London, 1981), p. 207.

68 Goschen, quoted in M. C. Morgan, *Foreign Affairs, 1886–1914* (London,
    1973), p. 29.

69 Friedberg, *The Weary Titan*, pp. 181, 189, 206. For a detailed account of
    the negotiations and the treaty, see Ian H. Nish, *The Anglo-Japanese*
    Alliance: The Diplomacy of Two Island Empires, 1894–1907 (London,
    1966).

70 White, *Victoria's Navy: The Heyday of Steam*, pp. 155, 170.

71 *Ibid.*, p. 170; Friedberg, *The Weary Titan*, p. 207.

72 Graham and Gladstone quoted in Friedberg, *The Weary Titan*, p. 140.

TWO · THE CHALLENGER: THE FRENCH NAVY, 1840S–1890S

1 Stephen S. Roberts, 'The Introduction of Steam Technology in the
    French Navy, 1818-1852', PhD diss., University of Chicago, 1976, pp.
    25–6; Hans Busk, *The Navies of the World: Their Present State, and Future*
    Capabilities (London, 1859), p. 75; Lambert, *The Last Sailing Battlefleet*,
    pp. 10, 142–3; *idem, Battleships in Transition*, p. 97. Henri Legohérel,
    Histoire de la Marine française (Paris, 1999), pp. 75–6, gives figures of 103
    ships of the line and 54 frigates in 1815 (which must include warships

still on the stocks), declining to 71 ships of the line and 41 frigates in
1817. Richard Harding, *Seapower and Naval Warfare, 1650–1830*
(London, 1999), p. 294, gives figures of 33 ships of the line and 40
frigates in 1830.

2 Gardiner, *Frigates of the Napoleonic Wars*, pp. 29–30, 87–91; Lambert, *The
Last Sailing Battlefleet*, pp. 18, 54, 134; Jane, *The British Battle Fleet*, vol. I,
p. 211.

3 Roberts, 'The Introduction of Steam Technology', pp. 57–108, 228. See
also Lambert, 'Introduction of Steam', pp. 15–21; François Ferdinand
d'Orléans, Prince de Joinville, *De l'état des forces navales de la France*
(Frankfurt, 1844), p. 29.

4 Henri-Joseph Paixhans, *Nouvelle force maritime* (Paris, 1822), pp. 346–7
and *passim*.

5 Roberts, 'The Introduction of Steam Technology', pp. 91–2. Roberts,
pp. 60–61, contends that the Senegal steamer *Voyageur* had two shell
guns in 1820, which seems unlikely, given that Paixhans's first demonstrations for the French navy did not occur until 1824. These trials, held
at Brest during January and September 1824, involved a single shell gun
mounted on a pontoon firing at the *Pacificateur*. The January trials were
conducted at 640 yards, the September trials at greater distances, up to
1,280 yards. See Henri-Joseph Paixhans, *An Account of the Experiments
Made in the French Navy for the Trial of Bomb Cannon*, trans. John A.
Dalghren (Philadelphia, 1838), pp. 29, 43, and *passim*. The French original is *Expériences faites à Brest, en janvier 1824: du nouveau système de forces
navales* (Paris, 1837). This work was among the first Western military
titles translated into Japanese following Commodore Matthew C.
Perry's 'opening' of Japan in 1853, as *Bonbe Kanon* (1855).

6 Sondhaus, *Naval Warfare*, p. 23.

7 Roberts, 'The Introduction of Steam Technology', pp. 129–95 *passim*,
219–21. The government-run packet lines all failed, and in 1848 the
government turned over all of the steamers to the navy. See *ibid.*, p. 261.

8 Roberts, 'The Introduction of Steam Technology', pp. 234, 253, 263, 271.

9 Joinville, *De l'état des forces navales de la France*, pp. 14–15, 25–6, 35,
38–41. Joinville initially published this pamphlet as an article, which
appeared on 15 May 1844 in the *Revue des deux mondes*. See also Busk,
Navies of the World, p. 75.

10 Roberts, 'The Introduction of Steam Technology', pp. 359–63, 383–91.

11 Hamilton, *Anglo-French Naval Rivalry*, pp. 37, 43; Lambert, 'The Screw
Propeller Warship', pp. 36–9. Joinville, quoted in Joinville, *Essais sur la
marine française*, p. 157. According to traditional accounts, the *Napoléon* –
officially unnamed at the time of the Revolution – was to have been
named *Prince de Joinville*. The Second Republic's first navy minister
named the ship *24 Février*, in honour of the day the Revolution broke
out. It did not receive the name *Napoléon* until after its launch in May
1850. See Roberts, 'The Introduction of Steam Technology', p. 434.

12 Lambert, *Battleships in Transition*, pp. 99, 122–47; *idem*, 'The Screw-
Propeller Warship', pp. 37–41.

13 Lambert, 'The Screw-Propeller Warship', pp. 41, 46.

14 Napoleon III to Théodore Ducos (navy minister), Paris, 16 November

1854, text in Baxter, *Introduction of the Ironclad Warship*, pp. 342–4. Lambert contends that competent solid shot gunnery would have had the same effect at Sinope, where the Turks were overmatched in any event, and that the performance of the armoured batteries at Kinburn was 'much exaggerated'. Lambert, 'Iron Hulls and Armour Plate', pp. 52–3; *idem, Battleships in Transition*, p. 92.

15 Lambert, 'Iron Hulls and Armour Plate', p. 53. According to Joinville, *Memoirs of the Prince de Joinville*, trans. Lady Mary Loyd (New York, 1895), pp. 343–4, Dupuy produced a first draft of an armoured frigate as early as 1847, concurrently with his drawings of the future *Napoléon*, but did not pursue the project at the time owing to failures in experiments at Lorient in which the best French iron plates had not withstood heavy fire.

16 Sondhaus, *Naval Warfare*, pp. 73–6, 88–9, 109.

17 Richild Grivel, *De la guerre maritime avant et depuis les nouvelles inventions* (Paris, 1869), p. 282. Grivel criticized France's agreement to outlaw privateering in the Treaty of Paris (1856), pointing to the French tradition of successful commerce raiding, and to the fact that the United States, Spain and Mexico still had not acceded to the agreement.

18 Aube quoted in Théophile Aube, *A terre et à bord, notes d'un marin* (Paris, 1884), p. 158, and Ropp, *The Development of a Modern Navy*, p. 165.

19 Marder, *The Anatomy of British Sea Power*, pp. 86–7; Ropp, *The Development of a Modern Navy*, pp. 132, 155–6, 159–65.

20 John Roberts, 'Warships of Steel, in *Steam, Steel and Shellfire*, 1879–1889', pp. 96, 109; *Conway, 1860–1905*, pp. 211, 300, 303, 308–10, 320, 324, 327–8, 330–32.

21 *Conway, 1860–1905*, p. 327.

22 Campbell, 'Naval Armaments and Armour', p. 163; Griffiths, 'Warship Machinery', p. 177; Roberts, 'The Pre-Dreadnought Age', p. 113.

23 Michael Wilson, 'Early Submarines', in *Steam, Steel and Shellfire*, p. 154; *Conway's All the World's Fighting Ships, 1906–21* (London, 1985), p. 206; Ray Walser, *France's Search for a Battle Fleet: Naval Policy and Naval Power, 1898–1914* (New York, 1992), p. 136. See Paul Fontin and Mathieu Vignot, *Essai de stratégie navale* (Paris, 1893), p. 421. The two officers, writing under the pseudonyms 'Commandant Z' and 'H. Montéchant', for the most part echo the Jeune Ecole doctrines of the previous decade, advocating a campaign by cruisers and torpedo boats against the enemy [British] coasts and commerce.

24 James J. Tritten, 'Navy and Military Doctrine in France', in *A Doctrine Reader: The Navies of United States, Great Britain, France, Italy, and Spain*, ed. James J. Tritten and Luigi Donolo (Newport, RI, 1995), p. 55; Michael Wilson, 'Early Submarines', in *Steam, Steel and Shellfire*, p. 154; Nicholas A. Lambert, *Sir John Fisher's Naval Revolution* (Columbia, SC, 1999), p. 27.

25 *Conway, 1860–1905*, pp. 303–7.

26 Lambert, *Sir John Fisher's Naval Revolution*, pp. 73–86; Wilson, 'Early Submarines', pp. 155–7; *Conway, 1906–21*, pp. 86–9, 206.

27 Michèle Battesti, *La Marine au XIXe siècle: Interventions extérieures et colonies* (Paris, 1993), pp. 16–17; Legohérel, *Histoire de la Marine française*, pp. 80–81.

28 Roberts, 'The Introduction of Steam Technology', pp. 267–8, 279, 308–9.
29 *Ibid.*, pp. 124–5; Legohérel, *Histoire de la Marine française*, p. 82; Joinville, *Memoirs*, p. 50.
30 Jules de Crisenoy, *Our Naval School and Naval Officers: A Glance at the Condition of the French Navy prior to the late Franco-German War*, trans. Richard W. Meade (New York, 1873), pp. 10–15, 18, 32, 36–40; Ropp, *The Development of a Modern Navy*, pp. 8, 43–4; 'L'Ecole navale embarquée', http://www.defense.gouv.fr/marine/navires/ecoles/ecolenavale/enaval.htm (accessed 8 August 2002). See also René Monaque, *L'Ecole de guerre navale* (Vincennes, 1995).
31 Ropp, *The Development of a Modern Navy*, pp. 45–7; 'Amédée Courbet', http://www.netmarine.net/bat/flf/courbet/celebre.htm (accessed 8 August 2002).
32 Ropp, *The Development of a Modern Navy*, pp. 47–8.
33 *Ibid.*, p. 49; James J. Tritten, *Navy and Military Doctrine in France* (Norfolk, VA, 1994), p. 33.
34 Paixhans, *Nouvelle force maritime*, pp. 347–8.
35 Legohérel, *Histoire de la Marine française*, pp. 80–81; Lewis, *The Navy in Transition*, p. 184; Ropp, *The Development of a Modern Navy*, pp. 50–51.
36 Lewis, *The Navy in Transition*, p. 184; Ropp, *The Development of a Modern Navy*, pp. 51–2, 231.
37 Grivel, *De la guerre maritime avant et depuis les nouvelles inventions*, p. 281; Ropp, *The Development of a Modern Navy*, p. 231.
38 Hamilton, *Anglo-French Naval Rivalry*, p. 3; Dupont and Taillemite, *Les guerres navales françaises*, p. 227.
39 Roberts, 'The Introduction of Steam Technology', pp. 118–19; Dupont and Taillemite, *Les guerres navales françaises*, pp. 231–2. According to Joinville, most of Duperré's warships were also employed as troopships. 'With the exception of the admiral's ship of the line, it was a squadron of transport, not a squadron of war.' See Joinville, *Essais sur la marine française*, p. 6.
40 Dupont and Taillemite, *Les guerres navales françaises*, pp. 235–6; Roberts, 'The Introduction of Steam Technology', p. 181; Joinville, *Memoirs*, pp. 123–39.
41 Roberts, 'The Introduction of Steam Technology', p. 182; Sondhaus, *Naval Warfare*, p. 43.
42 Joinville, *Essais sur la marine française*, pp. 11, 22, 27; Roberts, 'The Introduction of Steam Technology', pp. 231–2, 339–40.
43 Legohérel, *Histoire de la Marine française*, p. 83.
44 Joinville, *Memoirs*, pp. 322–9; Joinville, quoted in *ibid.*, p. 322.
45 On the Tahiti crisis see Sondhaus, *Naval Warfare*, pp. 39–40.
46 Dupont and Taillemite, *Les guerres navales françaises*, pp. 237, 239.
47 Sondhaus, *The Habsburg Empire and the Sea*, pp. 157, 160; *idem*, *Naval Warfare*, p. 47; Hamilton, *Anglo-French Naval Rivalry*, p. 53.
48 Lyons, quoted in Lambert, *The Crimean War*, p. 260; Lambert considers the performance of the batteries to have been 'much exaggerated'. See also *idem*, 'Iron Hulls and Armour Plate', p. 52; Baxter, *Introduction of the Ironclad Warship*, pp. 78–86; Watts, *The Imperial Russian Navy*, p. 13;

Lyons to Secretary of the Admiralty Thomas Phinn, *Royal Albert*, 18
October 1855, in Dewar, ed., *Russian War, 1855, Black Sea*, pp. 346–7.
49 Dupont and Taillemite, *Les guerres navales françaises*, pp. 244–5;
Sondhaus, *Naval Warfare*, p. 66.
50 Sondhaus, *The Habsburg Empire and the Sea*, p. 192.
51 Dupont and Taillemite, *Les guerres navales françaises*, pp. 249–50;
Sondhaus, *Naval Warfare*, pp. 97–8.
52 Dupont and Taillemite, *Les guerres navales françaises*, pp. 251–4;
Lawrence Sondhaus, *Preparing for Weltpolitik: German Sea Power before
the Tirpitz Era* (Annapolis, MD, 1997), pp. 94–6.
53 Dupont and Taillemite, *Les guerres navales françaises*, pp. 246–8, 255–60;
David Lyon, 'Underwater Warfare and the Torpedo Boat', in *Steam,
Steel and Shellfire*, pp. 141–2; *Conway, 1860–1905*, p. 395.

THREE · SHAPING THE SOUTHERN COLOSSUS:
THE BRAZILIAN NAVY, 1822–31

1 Brian Vale, *Independence or Death! British Sailors and Brazilian
Independence, 1822–25* (London, 1996), pp. 1–8.
2 Luís Cláudio Pereira Leivas and Levy Scavarda, *História da Intendência da
Marinha* (Rio de Janeiro, 1972), p. 39. According to João de Prado Maia,
Através da Historia Naval Brazileira (São Paulo, 1936), p. 25, the arsenal
dated from 1764. The only Spanish naval arsenal in the New World was
at Havana; it ceased to build warships long before Cuba became independent in 1898.
3 Vale, *Independence or Death!*, p. 14; João de Prado Maia, *Quatro séculos de
lutas na Baía do Rio de Janeiro* (Rio de Janeiro, 1981), p. 27.
4 Vale, *Independence or Death!*, pp. 15–17, 20, 42, 44.
5 *Ibid.*, pp. 38, 40, 57, 76, 84, 93.
6 *Ibid.*, pp. 91, 109–10, 130–31, 147, 162, 166–7.
7 Brian Vale, *A War Betwixt Englishmen: Brazil against Argentina on the
River Plate, 1825–1830* (London, 2000), pp. 180, 239–40; *idem,
Independence or Death!*, pp. 168–9.
8 Vale, *A War Betwixt Englishmen*, pp. 256–7.
9 Vale, *Independence or Death!*, p. 173; Armando Amorim Ferreira Vidigal,
A evolução do pensamento estratégico naval brasileiro, 3rd edn (Rio de
Janeiro, 1985), p. 13.
10 Quoted in Vale, *A War Betwixt Englishmen*, p. 179.
11 Sondhaus, *Naval Warfare*, pp. 2–6; Donald L. Canney, *Sailing Warships of
the US Navy* (Annapolis, MD, 2001), pp. 199–200. The American totals
for 1830 include six ships of the line and seven frigates built, and four
ships of the line and nine frigates building. (Another four ships of the
line then on the stocks were never launched.) In 1830 only Britain,
France, Russia, the Netherlands, Sweden, Turkey and the United States
had larger navies than Brazil.
12 Vale, *Independence or Death!*, pp. 174–5.
13 *Ibid.*, pp. 16–17; Portugal, Escola Naval, 'História – Breve Resenha',
http://www.escolanaval.pt/ (accessed 25 February 2003).
14 Quote from Cochrane to Don Antonio Manuel Correa da Camara,

Valparaíso, 29 November 1822, in Thomas [Cochrane], Earl of
Dundonald, *Narrative of Services in the Liberation of Chili, Peru, and
Brazil, from Spanish and Portuguese Domination* (London, 1859), vol. II,
p. 8. See also Vale, *Independence or Death!*, pp. 18–20.

15 Vale, *A War Betwixt Englishmen*, p. 183; *idem, Independence or Death!*, pp.
20, 41–3, 45, 175, 188–98.

16 Manuel Moreira da Paixão e Dores, *Diário da Armada da Independência*,
ed. Max Justo Guedes, 2nd edn (Brasília, 1972), pp. 56–7, 59–60.

17 José Francisco de Lima, *Marquês de Tamadaré: Patrono da Marinha* (Rio
de Janeiro, 1983), pp. 67, 73–4.

18 Vale, *A War Betwixt Englishmen*, p. 16.

19 Cochrane to Don Antonio Manuel Correa da Camara, Valparaíso, 29
November 1822, in Dundonald, *Narrative of Services*, vol. II, p. 8. See
also Vale, *Independence or Death!*, pp. 98, 152–9; Sondhaus, *Naval
Warfare*, p. 16.

20 Vale, *Independence or Death!*, pp. 168, 170–71, 195.

21 Vale, *A War Betwixt Englishmen*, pp. 9, 18, 60–64.

22 Lima, *Marquês de Tamadaré*, p. 95.

23 Vale, *A War Betwixt Englishmen*, p. 38.

24 *Ibid.*, pp. ix, 123, 136, 183–4.

25 Vale, *Independence or Death!*, pp. 11, 29, 32, 43.

26 Vale, *A War Betwixt Englishmen*, pp. 17, 182–3.

27 Vale, *Independence or Death!*, p. 173; *idem, A War Betwixt Englishmen*,
pp. ix, 183.

28 Vale, *Independence or Death!*, pp. 22–3, 39.

29 Vale, *A War Betwixt Englishmen*, pp. 93, 182.

30 See Vale, *Independence or Death!*, pp. 1, 187.

31 *Ibid.*, pp. 1, 7, 10–13, 27.

32 Trajano Augusto de Carvalho, *Nossa Marinha: Seus Feitos e Glórias,
1822–1940* (Rio de Janeiro, 1986), pp. 12, 14, 16; Vale, *Independence or
Death!*, pp. 45–61. Quote from Cochrane to José Bonifacio d'Andrade y
Silva, 5 May 1823, in Dundonald, *Narrative of Services*, vol. II, p. 31.

33 Vale, *Independence or Death!*, pp. 63–9, 95–6.

34 Carvalho, *Nossa Marinha*, p. 20. The Portuguese garrison was finally
evacuated in March 1824.

35 Lima, *Marquês de Tamadaré*, pp. 74–5; Vale, *Independence or Death!*, pp.
137–9; Prado Maia, *Através*, p. 73.

36 Vale, *A War Betwixt Englishmen*, pp. 21–8.

37 *Ibid.*, pp. 29–49, 51–2, 54–8; Carvalho, *Nossa Marinha*, pp. 22, 24, 26.

38 Vale, *A War Betwixt Englishmen*, pp. 69–82; Carvalho, *Nossa Marinha*, p. 28.

39 Vale, *A War Betwixt Englishmen*, pp. 120–33; Zenithilde Magno de
Carvalho, *A marinha no Brasil colonial* (Rio de Janeiro, 1928), p. 789.

40 Vale, *A War Betwixt Englishmen*, pp. 66, 83–4, 95, 157–62, 171, 181.

41 *Ibid.*, pp. 92, 97–9, 105–15, 163, 196–7, 204; Horacio Rodríguez and
Pablo E. Arguindeguy, *El Corso Rioplatense* (Buenos Aires, 1996), pp. 383,
491–2; Lubbock, *Cruisers, Corsairs & Slavers*, p. 374. Numbers of corsairs
and prizes are from Vale. Rodríguez and Arguindeguy list 104
Argentinian privateers for 1825–8, and 10 naval vessels that functioned
as commerce raiders (see *ibid.*, pp. 565–6 and *passim*). As late as 1850

Brazil still imported 23,000 African slaves, but the trade had died out by 1855 (see Lubbock, p. 384). Brazil finally abolished slavery in 1888.

42 Lima, *Marquês de Tamadaré*, pp. 94–8; Vale, *A War Betwixt Englishmen*, pp. 139–45; Prado Maia, *Através*, pp. 99–100; Rodríguez and Arguindeguy, *El Corso Rioplatense*, pp. 446–50, 468–9.

43 Vale, *A War Betwixt Englishmen*, pp. 146, 150–56, 172–5; Carvalho, *Nossa Marinha*, p. 36.

44 Lima, *Marquês de Tamadaré*, pp. 99–101; Vale, *A War Betwixt Englishmen*, pp. 148–9.

45 Rodríguez and Arguindeguy, *El Corso Rioplatense*, pp. 377–9, 411–18; Vale, *A War Betwixt Englishmen*, pp. 190–95, 202–4.

46 Prado Maia, *Quatro séculos de lutas*, pp. 30–31; Vale, *A War Betwixt Englishmen*, pp. 212, 215, 219.

47 Rodríguez and Arguindeguy, *El Corso Rioplatense*, pp. 371, 430–32, 438–9; Carvalho, *Nossa Marinha*, p. 44.

48 Vale, *A War Betwixt Englishmen*, pp. 214–15, 223–4.

49 Lima, *Marquês de Tamadaré*, p. 129; Vale, *Independence or Death!*, pp. 174–5; *idem*, *A War Betwixt Englishmen*, p. 234.

50 Lima, *Marquês de Tamadaré*, pp. 102–4, 106–10, 113–16, 118–22; Prado Maia, *Quatro séculos de lutas*, pp. 32–5; Arthur Cezar Ferreira Reis, *A Historia Paraense e a Marinha de Guerra do Brasil* (Belém, 1941), p. 20; Washington Perry de Almeida, *Guerra dos Farrapos: A acção da Marinha Imperial na Guerra dos Farrapos* (Rio de Janeiro, 1935), *passim*.

51 Ferreira Vidigal, *A evolução do pensamento estratégico naval brasileiro*, p. 14.

FOUR · PRESERVING THE UNION: THE UNITED STATES NAVY, 1861–5

1 On Welles's Mexican War experience see John Niven, *Gideon Welles, Lincoln's Secretary of the Navy* (New York, 1973), pp. 212–32. Since civilians rarely served as bureau chiefs, Welles faced considerable opposition from naval officers during these years.

2 E.g. Robert M. Browning, Jr, 'Defunct Strategy and Divergent Goals: The Role of the United States Navy along the Eastern Seaboard during the Civil War', *Prologue: Quarterly of the National Archives and Records Administration*, XXXIII (2001), pp. 9–79.

3 George Brown, *The Union Army*, vol. VII: *The Navy* (Madison, WI, 1908), p. 29.

4 Raimondo Luraghi, 'Background', in *The Confederate Navy: The Ships, Men and Organization, 1861–65*, ed. William N. Still, Jr (Annapolis, MD, 1997), pp. 7–8; Donald L. Canney, *The Old Steam Navy* (Annapolis, MD, 1993), vols I and II, appendices; Brown, *The Navy*, pp. 30, 33, 43–4.

5 Donald L. Canney, *Lincoln's Navy: The Ships, Men and Organization, 1861–65* (Annapolis, MD, 1998), p. 17.

6 Canney, *The Old Steam Navy*, vol. I, pp. 91–125 *passim*, 168–78 *passim*.

7 Brown, *The Navy*, p. 50; Canney, *The Old Steam Navy*, vol. II, pp. 7, 14; Robert Holcombe, 'Types of Ships', in *The Confederate Navy*, pp. 51–3.

8 Canney, *The Old Steam Navy*, vol. II, pp. 8–10, 54.

9 William N. Still, Jr, 'The American Civil War', in *Steam, Steel and Shellfire*, p. 74; Holcombe, 'Types of Ships', p. 52; Canney, *The Old*

Steam Navy, vol. II, pp. 29–32. Most sources give no displacement figure for the *Virginia*, but Gromov *et al.*, *Tri Veka Rossiiskogo Flota*, vol. I, p. 226, lists the ship at 3,500 tons and the *Monitor* at 1,200 tons, most likely figures for full load. According to Brown, *The Navy*, p. 84, the *Monitor* displaced 1,245 tons and drew 11 feet 6 inches (3.5 metres) when fully loaded.

10 William H. Roberts, *Civil War Ironclads: The US Navy and Industrial Mobilization* (Baltimore, 2002), p. 22.

11 *Ibid.*, pp. 19, 23, 32, 42–4, 49, 57, 138.

12 Canney, *The Old Steam Navy*, vol. II, pp. 29–30, 33, 59–69, 75, 89–91, 138; *Conway, 1860–1905*, pp. 119–23.

13 Roberts, *Civil War Ironclads*, p. 162.

14 Canney, *The Old Steam Navy*, vol. II, pp. 21–5.

15 *Ibid.*, pp. 15–20; William H. Roberts, *USS New Ironsides in the Civil War* (Annapolis, MD, 1999), pp. 18–28.

16 Canney, *The Old Steam Navy*, vol. II, pp. 70–73, 79.

17 *Ibid.*, vol. II, pp. 38–55, 95–118, 138. The world's only other turreted stern-wheeler was HMS *Pioneer*, an unarmoured iron-hulled warship built at Sydney in 1863 for use against the Maori in New Zealand. See Brown, *Paddle Warships*, pp. 58–9.

18 Canney, *The Old Steam Navy*, vol. II, p. 78.

19 Holcombe, 'Types of Ships', pp. 52–6; Royce Gordon Shingleton, *John Taylor Wood: Sea Ghost of the Confederacy* (Athens, GA, 1979), p. 146.

20 See Kevin J. Foster, 'The Diplomats Who Sank a Fleet: The Confederacy's Undelivered European Fleet and the Union Consular Service', *Prologue: Quarterly of the National Archives and Records Administration*, XXXIII (2001), pp. 181–93.

21 Canney, *The Old Steam Navy*, vol. II, pp. 29–30; Warren F. Spencer, *The Confederate Navy in Europe* (Tuscaloosa, AL, 1983), p. 111.

22 Holcombe, 'Types of Ships', p. 57–8.

23 Lawrence Sondhaus, 'Die österreichische Kriegsmarine und der amerikanische Sezessionskrieg 1861–1865', *Marine – Gestern, Heute*, XIV (1987), pp. 81–2.

24 Holcombe, 'Types of Ships', pp. 58–61.

25 Spencer, *The Confederate Navy in Europe*, pp. 43, 55 and *passim*.

26 Sondhaus, 'Die österreichische Kriegsmarine und der amerikanische Sezessionskrieg', pp. 81–3.

27 *Conway, 1860–1905*, p. 136.

28 Still, 'The American Civil War', p. 61; Canney, *The Old Steam Navy*, vol. II, p. 131.

29 Chester G. Hearn, *Admiral David Glasgow Farragut: The Civil War Years* (Annapolis, MD, 1998), pp. xv–26; Donald Chisolm, *Waiting for Dead Men's Shoes: Origins and Development of the US Navy's Officer Personnel System, 1793–1941* (Stanford, CA, 2001), pp. 161, 191, 201, 263, 285. The Naval Academy was known as the Naval School from 1845 to 1850.

30 Chisolm, *Waiting for Dead Men's Shoes*, pp. 324–5.

31 Hearn, *Farragut*, pp. 26–37; Chisolm, *Waiting for Dead Men's Shoes*, p. 173.

32 Craig L. Symonds, *Confederate Admiral: The Life and Wars of Franklin Buchanan* (Annapolis, MD, 1999), pp. 115–9, 126; Brown, *The Navy*, pp.

23–4; Chisolm, *Waiting for Dead Men's Shoes*, p. 283. When Farragut's became the navy's first vice admiral in January 1865, Congress agreed to waive the age and service ceilings for officers reaching that rank. In July 1866 he became the first admiral. See Chisolm, *ibid.*, pp. 312, 324, 326.

33 Hearn, *Farragut*, pp. 32–3.

34 Symonds, *Confederate Admiral*, pp. 126, 134.

35 *Ibid.*, p. 143.

36 Brown gives the same figures as Symonds for the number of southerners resigning (126 of 253) at the rank of lieutenant and above. While the differences by age and rank were not dramatic, older, higher ranking officers were marginally less likely to leave the navy: 16 of 38 southern captains resigned (42.1 per cent); 34 of 64 southern commanders (53.1 per cent); 76 of 151 southern lieutenants (50.3 per cent). Brown, *The Navy*, pp. 21–2. Luraghi, 'Background', p. 8, contends that just 30 per cent of naval officers were southerners, a figure that is not likely even if those from Maryland and Delaware are counted as northerners. Roberts, *Civil War Ironclads*, p. 13, says 247 naval officers 'went south' in 1861, a figure that may be accurate if masters, passed midshipmen and midshipmen are counted as officers.

37 Symonds, *Confederate Admiral*, p. 144; Sondhaus, *Naval Warfare*, pp. 45, 97.

38 Hearn, *Farragut*, pp. 42–3, 53.

39 Symonds, *Confederate Admiral*, pp. 137, 143–5; Shingleton, *John Taylor Wood*, pp. 5, 15–17. Wood hesitated before embracing the Confederate cause, even though he was a nephew of Jefferson Davis. Buchanan's pro-slavery sentiments were well known, but as recently as the first week of April he had invited President Lincoln to his daughter's Washington wedding and obediently dispatched a ship to Charleston with supplies for the garrison of Fort Sumter.

40 Symonds, *Confederate Admiral*, pp. 140, 146–8, and *passim*.

41 Brown, *The Navy*, pp. 23–4; Clarence Edward Macartney, *Mr Lincoln's Admirals* (New York, 1956), p. 6.

42 Chisolm, *Waiting for Dead Men's Shoes*, pp. 326–7, 360.

43 Dennis J. Ringle, *Life in Mr Lincoln's Navy* (Annapolis, MD, 1998), pp. 2–8; Brown, *The Navy*, p. 24; Canney, *Lincoln's Navy*, p. 127.

44 Brown, *The Navy*, pp. 24, 32, 164; Joseph P. Reidy, 'Black Men in Navy Blue during the Civil War', *Prologue: Quarterly of the National Archives and Records Administration*, XXXIII (2001), p. 159; Browning, 'Defunct Strategy and Divergent Goals', pp. 176–7.

45 Ringle, *Life in Mr Lincoln's Navy*, pp. 16–18, 23.

46 Brown, *The Navy*, pp. 24, 43; Canney, *Lincoln's Navy*, p. 216; Ringle, *Life in Mr Lincoln's Navy*, p. 24.

47 Reidy, 'Black Men in Navy Blue', pp. 156, 158, 165n. According to Ringle, *Life in Mr Lincoln's Navy*, p. 148, the African American share of naval manpower slipped below 10 per cent during the 1890s and collapsed after recruitment ended in 1919, bottoming out in 1932 at less than 1 per cent. The figure of 90,000 Union navy seamen serving in the years 1861–5 reflects a downward revision of the traditional figure of 118,000, cited by Ringle, *ibid.*, p. 1, and Canney, *Lincoln's Navy*, p. 117,

which is now widely acknowledged as inflated by the double-counting of thousands of men who re-enlisted during the war.

48 The ten men who became the most prominent Union generals of the Civil War had an average age of 45 as of 1861 [Ambrose Burnside (37), Ulysses S. Grant (39), Henry Halleck (46), Joseph Hooker (47), George McClellan (35), Irvin McDowell (43), George Meade (46), John Pope (39), Winfield Scott (75), William Tecumseh Sherman (41)], while the ten who became the most prominent admirals had an average age of 56 [John Dahlgren (52), Samuel F. Du Pont (58), David Glasgow Farragut (60), Andrew Hull Foote (55), Louis M. Goldsborough (56), Samuel P. Lee (49), William McKean (61), Garrett Pendergrast (59), David Dixon Porter (48), Silas H. Stringham (63)].

49 Brown, *The Navy*, pp. 36–7, 40–41, 45, 47–8. For detailed studies of the North Atlantic and South Atlantic squadrons, see Robert M. Browning, Jr, *From Cape Charles to Cape Fear: The North Atlantic Blockading Squadron during the Civil War* (Washington, DC, 1993), and *idem*, *Success Is All That Was Expected: The South Atlantic Blockading Squadron during the Civil War* (Washington, DC, 2002).

50 Brown, *The Navy*, p. 55.

51 *Ibid.*, pp. 105–8.

52 *Ibid.*, pp. 109–13, 116–25, 127.

53 *Ibid.*, pp. 91–101; William N. Still, Jr, 'Operations', in *The Confederate Navy*, pp. 216–9, 224; Browning, 'Defunct Strategy and Divergent Goals', p. 173.

54 Hearn, *Farragut*, pp. 60–128, *passim*; Brown, *The Navy*, pp. 49, 181–98.

55 Hearn, *Farragut*, p. 76.

56 Brown, *The Navy*, pp. 56–9.

57 *Ibid.*, pp. 131–44; Roberts, *Civil War Ironclads*, pp. 91–4; Browning, 'Defunct Strategy and Divergent Goals', pp. 173–6.

58 According to Brown, *The Navy*, pp. 129–30, the *Montauk* sank the *Nashville* on 2 March 1863; Roberts, *Civil War Ironclads*, p. 89, places the action on 28 February. At Warsaw Sound (17 June 1863) the *Weehawken* struck the *Atlanta* five times in the fifteen-minute battle; the *Atlanta* fired seven shots but scored no hits. The *Atlanta* surrendered when a 15-inch Dahlgren shot went through its 4 inches of iron plating and 18 inches of wood backing. Afterward the Confederates increased the thickness of armour on some of their ironclads to 6 inches. Meanwhile, the US navy repaired the *Atlanta* and used it in Hampton Roads in 1864–5. Brown, *The Navy*, pp. 146–8, 268; Holcombe, 'Types of Ships', pp. 52–3; Canney, *The Old Steam Navy*, vol. II, p. 80.

59 Roberts, *Civil War Ironclads*, pp. 99–100, 103.

60 *Ibid.*, p. 104; *idem*, *USS New Ironsides*, pp. 80–83, 89–91; Lyon, 'Underwater Warfare and the Torpedo Boat', p. 135; Brown, *The Navy*, pp. 149–55; Browning, 'Defunct Strategy and Divergent Goals', pp. 176–7; Still, 'Operations', p. 222, alleges that the *David* 'badly crippled' the *New Ironsides*.

61 Brown, *The Navy*, pp. 251–67; Hearn, *Farragut*, pp. 257–91, 305; Canney, *The Old Steam Navy*, vol. I, p. 102; Still, 'Operations', pp. 231–2.

62 Still, 'Operations', p. 223; Lyon, 'Underwater Warfare and the Torpedo

Boat', p. 135; Roberts, *Civil War Ironclads*, p. 156.
63 Brown, *The Navy*, pp. 269–91; Roberts, *USS New Ironsides*, pp. 99–103.
64 Commander John Rogers led the Mississippi River squadron from its creation in May 1861 until Foote's arrival in September 1861. Clarence Edward Macartney, *Mr Lincoln's Admirals* (New York, 1956), pp. 88–110; Brown, *The Navy*, pp. 160–79. According to Macartney, the *Carondelet* was Foote's flagship at Fort Donelson.
65 Hearn, *Farragut*, pp. 98–113; Brown, *The Navy*, pp. 205–28; Still, 'Operations', pp. 226–8.
66 Brown, *The Navy*, pp. 235–49.
67 Reidy, 'Black Men in Navy Blue', p. 159, notes that in June 1864 on the Red River, the uss *Lafayette* towed a group of 600 runaway slaves to freedom aboard an empty coal barge.
68 Macartney, *Mr Lincoln's Admirals*, pp. 221–7, 254–5; Lambert, 'The Screw Propeller Warship', p. 42; Holcombe, 'Types of Ships', pp. 50–51. A court martial in April 1865 led to Collins's dismissal, but Secretary Welles later set aside the verdict, allowing Collins to serve again from 1866 until his death in 1875.
69 Shingleton, *John Taylor Wood*, pp. 143, 207–8. The most recent monograph on the *Shenandoah* is Stanley Fitzgerald Horn, *Gallant Rebel: The Fabulous Cruise of the CSS Shenandoah* (New Brunswick, NJ, 1947).
70 Brown, *Warrior to Dreadnought*, pp. 17–18.
71 Lambert, *Battleships in Transition*, pp. 84–5; Spencer, *The Confederate Navy in Europe*, p. 216; Courtemanche, *No Need of Glory*, pp. 39, 43, 48, 58, 62; Foster, 'The Diplomats Who Sank a Fleet', p. 191. During the *Trent* affair Palmerston decided not to send the armoured frigate *Warrior* (just completed in October 1861) to North American waters.
72 Shingleton, *John Taylor Wood*, p. 146.
73 The *Dunderberg* and *Onondaga* went to France, the *Catawba* and *Oneota* to Peru. See *Conway, 1860–1905*, p. 119; Canney, *The Old Steam Navy*, vol. II, pp. 64, 86, 126–9, 138. Of the three ironclads designed for high seas duty, only the large single-turret monitor *Dictator* was commissioned in the postwar era, on two separate occasions between 1865 and 1877. The triple-turret monitor *Roanoke* remained on hand in New York, to defend the harbour in case of war. Both the *Dictator* and *Roanoke* survived until 1883, when they were sold for scrap. The armoured frigate *New Ironsides* had a much shorter postwar life; laid up at Philadelphia after the war, it was destroyed by fire in December 1866. See Stanley Sandler, *The Emergence of the Modern Capital Ship* (Newark, DE, 1979), p. 69; Canney, *The Old Steam Navy*, vol. II, pp. 15–20, 62, 66–70; Roberts, *USS New Ironsides in the Civil War*, pp. 1–2.
74 Roberts, *Civil War Ironclads*, p. 172.
75 *Ibid.*, p. 170.

FIVE · BY REASON OR BY FORCE: THE CHILEAN NAVY, 1879–92

1 O'Higgins quoted in Francisco Ghisolfo Araya, 'Situacion estrategica naval', in *El Poder Naval Chileno* (Valparaíso, 1985), vol. I, p. 279.
2 For a brief overview of the performance of the Chilean navy in the War

for Independence, the War of 1836–9 and the War of 1864–6, see
Sondhaus, *Naval Warfare*, pp. 9–11, 42–3 and 98–9. For a detailed
overview of the same years, see Carlos López Urrutia, *Historia de la
Marina de Chile* (Santiago de Chile, 1969), pp. 13–225. See also
http://www.armada.cl/site/framesets/fset_altomando.html (accessed
5–17 March 2003).

3   Sergio Villabos R., *Chile y Perú: La historia que nos une y nos separa,
    1535–1883* (Santiago de Chile, 2002), pp. 117–20, 127; Enrique Merlet
    Sanhueza, *Juan José Latorre: Héroe de Angamos* (Santiago de Chile, 1997),
    pp. 71–2. J. Arturo Olid Araya, *Crónicas de Guerra: Relatos de un ex com-
    batiente de la Guerra del Pacífico y la Revolución de 1891* (Santiago de Chile,
    1999), p. 53; *Conway, 1860–1905*, pp. 410–11, 416, 418–19;
    http://www.armada.cl/site/framesets/fset_altomando.html (accessed
    5–17 March 2003). Some Chilean sources have the corvette *Magallanes*
    and the Peruvian frigate *Independencia* built in France rather than in
    Britain; *Conway, 1860–1905*, p. 413, and some other sources refer to the
    950-ton *Magallanes* as a screw gunboat. The *Valparaíso* was renamed in
    September 1876, after the death of Vice Admiral Manuel Blanco
    Encalada, a hero of Chile's War for Independence.

4   Gonzalo Bulnes, *Resumen de la Guerra del Pacífico* (Santiago de Chile,
    1979), pp. 20, 31, 34–5, 41; William F. Sater, *Chile and the War of the
    Pacific* (Lincoln, NE, 1986), pp. 6–7. By the mid-1870s an estimated 93 to
    95 per cent of the population of the Atacama Desert mining region was
    Chilean; the remainder were Bolivian officials and their dependants. In
    1878 the population of Antofagasta, the largest city on the coast of the
    Atacama, was 77 per cent Chilean, 14 per cent Bolivian and 9 per cent
    other nationalities. See Villalobos, *Chile y Perú*, p. 132; Bulnes, *ibid.*, p.
    20. Because many of the investors of the Compañía de Salitres de
    Antofagasta were British, at least one recent Marxist interpretation views
    the War of the Pacific as a conflict waged for the sake of British capital-
    ists. See Enrique Amayo, *La Politica Britanica en la Guerra del Pacífico*
    (Lima, 1988).

5   Villabos, *Chile y Perú*, p. 122.

6   Bulnes, *Resumen de la Guerra del Pacífico*, p. 43; Olid Araya, *Crónicas de
    Guerra*, p. 52.

7   Lawrence Sondhaus, *The Naval Policy of Austria-Hungary, 1867–1918:
    Navalism, Industrial Development, and the Politics of Dualism* (West
    Lafayette, IN, 1994), pp. 52–3; *Conway, 1860–1905*, pp. 414, 418–19;
    http://www.armada.cl/site/framesets/fset_altomando.html (accessed
    5–17 March 2003).

8   Congressman John Thomas (Ohio), speech of 1 March 1884, quoted in
    Charles D. Johnson, 'Chile as a Stepping Stone to United States Naval
    Greatness, 1879–1895', Master's thesis, California State University –
    Hayward, 1974, p. 20. Worden, interview published on 30 October
    1891, quoted in *ibid.*, p. 76. See also *ibid.*, pp. 5–22.

9   Eugenio Varela Munchmeyer, 'Manejo de crisis: Situacion Chile-
    Estados Unidos en 1891–1892', *Rivista de Marina*, CIX (1992), p. 56.

10 Merlet Sanhueza, *Juan José Latorre*, pp. 149, 151–2, 156; Pedro Espina
    Ritchie, *El Monitor Huáscar* (Santiago de Chile, 1969), pp. 107–9;

Conway, 1860–1905, pp. 233, 410–11.

11 Villabos, *Chile y Perú*, pp. 154–5; Merlet Sanhueza, *Juan José Latorre*,
    p. 156; *Conway, 1860–1905*, pp. 401–4, 406–7. Aside from the *Patagonia*,
    built by an Austrian shipyard in Trieste, all of these Argentinian warships
    were constructed in Britain.

12 Merlet Sanhueza, *Juan José Latorre*, pp. 161–4; *Conway, 1860–1905*,
    pp. 411, 414. Budget figures from Sater, *Chile and the War of the Pacific*,
    pp. 274, 276. The country's traditionally conservative elites did not mind
    the increase in spending, since the new taxes on nitrate exports allowed
    the abolition of all income and inheritance taxes.

13 Merlet Sanhueza, *Juan José Latorre*, p. 162.

14 Fernando Ruz Trujillo, *Rafael Sotomayor: El Organizador de la Victoria*
    (Santiago de Chile, 1980), pp. 122, 136; http://www.armada.cl/site/
    framesets/fset_altomando.html (accessed 5–17 March 2003).

15 Victor H. Larenas Q., *Patricio Lynch: Almirante, General, Gobernante y
    Diplomatico* (Santiago de Chile, 1981), pp. 16–19; Merlet Sanhueza, *Juan
    José Latorre*, p. 42. The *Chile*, a 48-gun frigate ordered in France during
    the war of 1836–9, reached Chile in 1840 and thereafter saw little active
    service. With the establishment of the Naval School in 1858, it became a
    training ship for the Nautical School (Escuela Náutica), a merchant
    marine academy opened in Valparaíso in 1834. See also
    http://www.armada.cl/site/framesets/fset_altomando.html (accessed
    5–17 March 2003); http://www.escuelanaval.cl/esna1.htm (accessed
    5–17 March 2003).

16 Merlet Sanhueza, *Juan José Latorre*, pp. 43-5. See also
    http://www.armada.cl/site/framesets/fset_altomando.html (accessed
    5–17 March 2003); http://www.escuelanaval.cl/esna1.htm (accessed
    5–17 March 2003).

17 Merlet Sanhueza, *Juan José Latorre*, p. 44; Luis Uribe Orrego, *Los
    Combates navales en la Guerra del Pacífico, 1879–1881* (Valparaíso, 1886),
    p. 9; Villabos, *Chile y Perú*, p. 115; http://www.armada.cl/site/framesets/
    fset_altomando.html (accessed 5–17 March 2003).

18 http://www.armada.cl/site/framesets/fset_altomando.html (accessed
    5–17 March 2003).

19 Carlos Maldonado Prieto, 'Estadio de Situación del Servicio Militar en
    Chile', *Security and Defense Studies Review*, 1 (2001), p. 84.

20 http://www.escueladegrumetes.cl/Esgrum.htm (accessed 13 March
    2003); http://www.esmeralda.cl/pags/buque/index.html (accessed 12–13
    March 2003). Uribe Orrego, *Los Combates navales*, p. 9, incorrectly states
    that the Apprentice Seamen's School was closed in 1876; that year, in
    addition to having its enrolment reduced, it lost its original name
    (Escuela de Aprendices de Marineros) in favour of Escuela de Grumetes.

21 Merlet Sanhueza, *Juan José Latorre*, pp. 71, 164; http://www.armada.cl/
    site/framesets/fset_altomando.html (accessed 5–17 March 2003);
    http://www.revistamarina.cl/revistas/1993/1/esarm.pdf (accessed 13
    March 2003).

22 The precise figure for 1867 (the first full peacetime year following the
    war with Spain) was 643. See Merlet Sanhueza, *Juan José Latorre*, p. 64.

23 William F. Sater, *The Heroic Image in Chile: Arturo Prat, Secular Saint*

(Berkeley, CA, 1973), p. 38.

24 Crew rosters in Vicente Grez, *El Combate Homérico: 21 de May de 1879*, 4th edn (Santiago de Chile, 1968), pp. 157–68.

25 http://www.armada.cl/site/framesets/fset_altomando.html (accessed 5–17 March 2003). Of the 27 flag officers (1 admiral, 6 vice admirals and 20 rear admirals) of 2003, two had British surnames, five had British maternal surnames, and one had both. The names included Dunsmore, Gibbons, Gordon, Hodgson, Jordan, Leighton, Robinson, St Lawrence and Young.

26 Bulnes, *Resumen de la Guerra del Pacífico*, pp. 43, 45, 51; Ritchie, *El Monitor Huáscar*, pp. 64–7; Conway, *1860–1905*, p. 401.

27 Ritchie, *El Monitor Huáscar*, pp. 67–71; José Rodolfo del Campo, *Campaña Naval 1879*, 3rd edn (Lima, 1979), pp. 83–93; Olid Araya, *Crónicas de Guerra*, pp. 15–51; Grez, *El Combate Homérico*, *passim* (with rosters indicating fate of the Chilean crews, pp. 157–68). Del Campo, a Peruvian war correspondent aboard the *Independencia*, and Olid, a teenage sailor aboard the *Covadonga*, provide perspectives from both sides of the battle at Punta Gruesa.

28 Ritchie, *El Monitor Huáscar*, pp. 80–87; Merlet Sanhueza, *Juan José Latorre*, pp. 97–100; Ruz, *Rafael Sotomayor*, pp. 122, 136.

29 Ritchie, *El Monitor Huáscar*, pp. 76–84, 88–9, 94–100; Merlet Sanhueza, *Juan José Latorre*, pp. 103–13; Uribe, *Los Combates navales*, p. 83n.

30 Ritchie, *El Monitor Huáscar*, pp. 86, 103–5; Bulnes, *Resumen de la Guerra del Pacífico*, pp. 79, 91, 95, 99, 107, 121, 131–57.

31 Ritchie, *El Monitor Huáscar*, p. 106; Bulnes, *Resumen de la Guerra del Pacífico*, pp. 180–81; Conway, *1860–1905*, pp. 418–19.

32 Ritchie, *El Monitor Huáscar*, pp. 108–9; Larenas, *Patricio Lynch*, pp. 34–86 *passim*; Bulnes, *Resumen de la Guerra del Pacífico*, pp. 188, 193, 207, 229–64 *passim*.

33 Larenas, *Patricio Lynch*, pp. 90–94; Sater, *Chile and the War of the Pacific*, p. 57; idem, *The Heroic Image in Chile*, pp. 16–17, 66–8; http://www.armada.cl/site/framesets/fset_altomando.html (accessed 5–17 March 2003).

34 Uribe, *Los Combates navales*, pp. 10, 127; Ritchie, *El Monitor Huáscar*, p. 110.

35 The Chilean constitution of 1833, as amended in 1871, limited presidents to a single five-year term, but the outgoing president usually manipulated the election to secure victory for a handpicked successor. The congress could check the powerful presidency only by refusing to pass the budget, and traditionally had resorted to this tactic to force presidents to make changes in their cabinet or, near the end of their term, to choose a successor acceptable to the congress. In the last months of 1890 the congress wanted Balmaceda to make changes in his cabinet and also did not approve of the candidate he had chosen to succeed him after his term expired (in September 1891). But when the congress showed its displeasure by refusing to pass a budget for 1891, Balmaceda declared that he would govern without it, under the same terms as the budget of the previous year. The congress then deposed him on the grounds that he had violated the constitution. According to

López Urrutia, *Historia de la Marina de Chile*, p. 317, in December 1890 a
group of naval officers considered kidnapping Balmaceda during a visit
to Talcahuano and exiling him to the Juan Fernández Islands, 400 miles
west of the Chilean mainland.

36 Merlet Sanhueza, *Juan José Latorre*, pp. 168, 174; http://www.armada.cl/
site/framesets/fset_altomando.html (accessed 5–17 March 2003).

37 Merlet Sanhueza, *Juan José Latorre*, pp. 166, 169, 173, 180;
http://www.armada.cl/site/framesets/fset_altomando.html (accessed
5–17 March 2003).

38 Merlet Sanhueza, *Juan José Latorre*, pp. 173–5, 180; Julio Pizarro
Arancibia, 'José Manuel Balmaceda a fines de su gobierno', *Revista de
Marina*, CVIII (1991), pp. 76–9.

39 Merlet Sanhueza, *Juan José Latorre*, p. 173; Olid Araya, *Crónicas de
Guerra*, pp. 249–50.

40 Merlet Sanhueza, *Juan José Latorre*, pp. 176, 186, 201, 205.

41 *Ibid.*, p. 174; Varela Munchmeyer, 'Manejo de crisis', pp. 56–66 *passim*;
Johnson, 'Chile as a Stepping Stone to United States Naval Greatness',
pp. 50–109 *passim*.

42 Merlet Sanhueza, *Juan José Latorre*, p. 180.

43 *Conway, 1860–1905*, pp. 402–4, 411–5.

44 Marc Lifsher, 'The Flip Side of Bolivia's Dilemma Over Sale of Its
Natural-Gas Riches', *Wall Street Journal*, 9 July 2002; 'Peru Woos
Bolivia Over Gas Pipeline', *Wall Street Journal*, 15 November 2002, A6.

45 'Fujimori Pediría que el Huáscar Sea Devuelto a Perú', *El Mercurio*
(Santiago de Chile), 13 August 1999, C2.

SIX · A PLACE IN THE SUN: THE GERMAN NAVY, 1898–1918

1 Bülow quoted in Terrell D. Gottschall, *By Order of the Kaiser: Otto von
Diederichs and the Rise of the Imperial German Navy, 1865–1902*
(Annapolis, MD, 2003), p. 226.

2 Bismarck quoted in Beresford, *Memoirs*, vol. II, p. 363. See also Tirpitz,
'Allgemeine Gesichtspunkte bei der Feststellung unserer Flotte nach
Schiffsklassen und Schiffstypen', July 1897, in Volker R. Berghahn and
Wilhelm Deist, *Rüstung im Zeichen der wilhelminischen Weltpolitik:
Grundlegende Dokumente, 1890–1914* (Düsseldorf, 1988), pp. 122–7.

3 Sondhaus, *Preparing for Weltpolitik*, pp. 101–218 *passim*; Rolf Hobson,
*Imperialism at Sea: Naval Strategic Thought, the Ideology of Sea Power and
the Tirpitz Plan, 1875–1914* (Boston, 2002), pp. 131–53.

4 Tirpitz, quoted in 'Relation über die Herbstmanöver der Marine im
Jahre 1893', Bundesarchiv-Marinearchiv, RM 4/62, fols 104–84; the
'Kritik' is in *ibid.*, fols 160–84. See also Sondhaus, *Preparing for
Weltpolitik*, pp. 141–2, 161–4, 171, 176, 189, 193; Gottschall, *By Order of
the Kaiser*, 114. Wilhelm II, like Tirpitz, read Mahan's first book within a
year of its appearance, after an American friend of the emperor,
Poultney Bigelow, sent him a copy of it. See Carl Boyd, 'The Wasted
Ten Years, 1888–1918: The Kaiser Finds an Admiral', *Journal of the Royal
United Service Institution*, CXI (1966), p. 293.

5 Hobson, *Imperialism at Sea*, pp. 178–246 *passim*; Ivo Lambi, *The Navy*

and German Power Politics, 1862–1914 (Boston, 1984), p. 66.

6 Tirpitz, quoted in Jonathan Steinberg, *Yesterday's Deterrent: Tirpitz and the Birth of the German Battle Fleet* (New York, 1965), p. 126.
  7 Tirpitz, quoted in Holger H. Herwig, *The German Naval Officer Corps: A Social and Political History, 1890–1918* (Oxford, 1973), p. 11.
  8 Sondhaus, *Preparing for Weltpolitik*, pp. 222–5; Erich Gröner, *Die deutschen Kriegsschiffe* (Koblenz, 1989), vol. I, pp. 26–41, 72–8, 118–29.
  9 Alfred von Tirpitz, *Erinnerungen* (Leipzig, 1919), p. 100n, notes that the coastal battleships of the *Siegfried* class formed a separate category under the First Navy Law but were 'rechristened, on paper, as battleships (*Linienschiffe*)' in the Second Navy Law of 1900. See also Sondhaus, *Preparing for Weltpolitik*, pp. 225–6.
 10 Gröner, *Die deutschen Kriegsschiffe*, vol. I, pp. 46–50.
 11 Unless otherwise noted, sources for this and the following paragraphs include Holger H. Herwig, *'Luxury' Fleet: The Imperial German Navy, 1888–1918*, rev. edn (Atlantic Highlands, NJ, 1987), pp. 54–76 *passim*; Sumida, *In Defence of Naval Supremacy*, pp. 50–100 *passim*; *idem*, 'Sir John Fisher and the *Dreadnought*: The Sources of Naval Mythology', *Journal of Military History*, LIX (1995), pp. 619–38 *passim*; Lambert, *Sir John Fisher's Naval Revolution*, pp. 93–157 *passim*.
 12 Sumida, *In Defence of Naval Supremacy*, p. 192; Herwig, *'Luxury' Fleet*, pp. 76–7, 80.
 13 Herwig, *The German Naval Officer Corps*, p. 69 and *passim*. Herwig's work exposes the flaws of earlier accounts, which draw a sharp contrast between the largely middle-class, supposedly liberal naval officer corps and an aristocratic, conservative Prussian army officer corps. E.g. Franz Carl Endres, 'Soziologische Struktur und ihr entsprechende Ideologien des deutschen Offizierkorps vor dem Weltkriege', *Archiv für Sozialwissenschaft und Sozialpolitik*, LXVIII (1932), pp. 282–319, and Wahrhold Drascher, 'Zur Soziologie des deutschen Seeoffizierkorps', *Wehrwissenschaftliche Rundschau*, XII (1962), pp. 555–67.
 14 Lawrence Sondhaus, '"The Spirit of the Army" at Sea: The Prussian-German Naval Officer Corps, 1847–1897', *International History Review*, XVII (1995), pp. 459–60. Adalbert received admiral's rank in 1854 and Stosch in 1875. Caprivi never received admiral's rank.
 15 Adalbert to Marineministerium, 8 February 1862, BA-MA, RM 1/143 (IX.4.1.4, F4203), fols 7-12, quoted in Sondhaus, '"The Spirit of the Army" at Sea', pp. 466–7.
 16 On the effects of 1870 on Tirpitz, see Volker R. Berghahn, *Der Tirpitz-Plan: Genesis und Verfall einer innenpolitischen Krisenstrategie unter Wilhelm II* (Düsseldorf, 1971), pp. 58–9.
 17 Sondhaus, '"The Spirit of the Army" at Sea', pp. 473–4. Characterization of Weickhmann by future admiral Ludwig von Schröder (who served under him in 1871–2), quoted in Hugo von Waldeyer-Hartz, *'Ein Mann': Das Leben des Admirals Ludwig von Schröder* (Braunschweig, 1934), p. 34.
 18 Sondhaus, '"The Spirit of the Army" at Sea', pp. 475–6. In 1877 the junior service even attracted a Hohenzollern, Prince Heinrich, younger brother of the future Emperor Wilhelm II. Heinrich's career followed

the same steps as any other sea officer, of course with more rapid promotions. He became a rear admiral in 1895, at 33.

19 *Ibid.*, pp. 480–82. Because the army officer corps historically had been predominantly noble, noblemen still accounted for a substantial share of it as late as 1914. According to Arden Bucholz, *Moltke, Schlieffen and Prussian War Planning* (New York, 1991), p. 3, in the 1890s roughly half of all Prussian army officers were nobles. Ulrich Trumpener, 'Junkers and Others: The Rise of Commoners in the Prussian Army, 1871–1914', *Canadian Journal of History*, IV (1979), p. 30, cites Karl Demeter's figures of 65 per cent as of the early 1860s and 30 per cent in 1913.

20 Sondhaus, '"The Spirit of the Army" at Sea', pp. 469, 474–5, 478, 482; Herwig, *The German Naval Officer Corps*, pp. 47, 63.

21 Sondhaus, '"The Spirit of the Army" at Sea', p. 471; Herwig, *The German Naval Officer Corps*, pp. 41–4.

22 Sondhaus, *Preparing for Weltpolitik*, pp. 87, 107; Herwig, *'Luxury' Fleet*, pp. 111, 127–36. For a more detailed analysis of the status of engineering officers and deck officers, see Herwig, *The German Naval Officer Corps*, pp. 102–73 *passim*.

23 Paul G. Halpern, *A Naval History of World War I* (Annapolis, MD, 1994), pp. 79, 81–2, 89, 93, 96–100; Gröner, *Die deutschen Kriegsschiffe*, vol. I, pp. 80, 131, 133, 137. See also John Irving, *Coronel and the Falklands* (London, 1927); Geoffrey Bennett, *Coronel and the Falklands* (London, 1962).

24 Halpern, *A Naval History of World War I*, pp. 44–7; Gröner, *Die deutschen Kriegsschiffe*, vol. I, p. 80.

25 The most recent of many English accounts of the battle is Keith Yates, *Flawed Victory: Jutland 1916* (London, 2000). See also V. E. Tarrant, *Jutland: The German Perspective* (Annapolis, MD, 1995). The best concise account is in Halpern, *A Naval History of World War I*, pp. 315–28. Other sources for this paragraph include Andrew Gordon, *The Rules of the Game: Jutland and British Naval Command* (Annapolis, MD, 1996), pp. 76–151, 433–99; Gröner, *Die deutschen Kriegsschiffe*, vol. I, pp. 46, 85, 129, 137, 139–40; *Conway, 1906–21*, pp. 13, 22, 25, 27–36, 146, 148, 152, 154. By the time of Jutland the British had in service 32 dreadnoughts and 10 battle cruisers, the Germans 17 dreadnoughts and 5 battle cruisers. Capital ships missing the battle (mostly owing to ongoing repairs or refitting) included four British dreadnoughts, one British battle cruiser and one German dreadnought.

26 Roger Chickering, *Imperial Germany and the Great War, 1914–1918* (Cambridge, 1998), pp. 91–2.

27 On the German Baltic campaign of 1917, see Gromov *et al.*, *Tri Veka Rossiiskogo Flota*, vol. II, pp. 113–7; Halpern, *A Naval History of World War I*, pp. 181, 193, 212–20.

28 Herwig, *'Luxury' Fleet*, pp. 197–8; *idem*, 'Innovation Ignored: The Submarine Problem – Germany, Britain, and the United States, 1919–1939', in *Military Innovation in the Interwar Period*, ed. Williamson Murray and Allan R. Millett (Cambridge, 1996), p. 229; Halpern, *A Naval History of World War I*, pp. 39, 293–9, 302–3, 332–43, 354, 357–60.

29 http://www.USMM.org/ww1navy.html (accessed 14 October 2001); Halpern, *A Naval History of World War I*, pp. 423, 432, 434–7.

30 Herwig, *'Luxury' Fleet*, pp. 247–51; Halpern, *A Naval History of World War I*, pp. 444–5.
31 Herwig, *'Luxury' Fleet*, pp. 254–7; Halpern, *A Naval History of World War I*, pp. 403, 448–9; *Conway, 1906–21*, pp. 139, 147–71 *passim*.
32 Herwig, 'Innovation Ignored', p. 231; *idem, 'Luxury' Fleet*, pp. 247, 291; *Conway, 1906–21*, p. 4. Some sources say 133 U-boats were sunk by anti-submarine operations. Only 320 U-boats actually sortied during the war.
33 Herwig, 'Innovation Ignored:', p. 231; Michael Gannon, *Operation Drumbeat* (New York, 1990), pp. xxi, 417; Axel Niestlé, *German U-Boat Losses during World War II: Details of Destruction* (Annapolis, MD, 1998), pp. 4, 303. Historians disagree over the number of German U-boats that sortied in the Second World War and the numbers sunk; Herwig has 784 of 940 lost; Niestlé, 757 of 859; and Gannon, 754 of 863.

SEVEN · EMPIRE BUILDER: THE JAPANESE NAVY, 1894–1945

1 All Japanese warship tonnage is given in normal displacement rather than standard displacement. Normal displacement, somewhat heavier than standard displacement but not as great as full load, was used for treaty quota calculations under the naval arms limits regime of 1922–36.
2 David C. Evans and Mark R. Peattie, *Kaigun: Strategy, Tactics and Technology in the Imperial Japanese Navy, 1887–1941* (Annapolis, MD, 1997), pp. 45, 47–8; Charles H. Fairbanks, Jr, 'The Origins of the *Dreadnought* Revolution: A Historiographical Essay', *International History Review*, XIII (1991), p. 261; Brown, *Warrior to Dreadnought*, p. 167; Hansgeorg Jentschura, Dieter Jung and Peter Mickel, *Warships of the Imperial Japanese Navy, 1869–1945*, trans. Antony Preston and J. D. Brown (Annapolis, MD, 1992), pp. 12–13, 71–2, 92–9; *Conway, 1860–1905*, pp. 217, 223.
3 Jentschura, Jung and Mickel, *Warships of the Imperial Japanese Navy*, pp. 16–19, 72–6, 99–102, 130–33, 160; *Conway, 1860–1905*, pp. 221–2, 224–6, 229–30.
4 Evans and Peattie, *Kaigun*, pp. 63–4, 67, 79–81.
5 Woodward, *The Russians at Sea*, pp. 138–42; *Conway, 1860–1905*, pp. 204, 220, 228–9.
6 *Conway, 1906–21*, p. 226.
7 *Ibid.*, pp. 228–9; Evans and Peattie, *Kaigun*, pp. 128, 159; Roberts, 'The Pre-Dreadnought Age, 1890–1905', p. 124; Jentschura, Jung and Mickel, *Warships of the Imperial Japanese Navy*, pp. 23–4.
8 Jentschura, Jung and Mickel, *Warships of the Imperial Japanese Navy*, pp. 22–8, 35–6, 77–8; *Conway, 1906–21*, pp. 229, 233–5.
9 Evans and Peattie, *Kaigun*, pp. 143, 186.
10 *Ibid.*, pp. 159–60; *Conway, 1906–21*, pp. 112–19, 229–35.
11 Jentschura, Jung and Mickel, *Warships of the Imperial Japanese Navy*, pp. 103–10, 133–43, 160–65.
12 Evans and Peattie, *Kaigun*, p. 186.
13 Jentschura, Jung and Mickel, *Warships of the Imperial Japanese Navy*, pp. 25, 77, 96, 101–2, 133.
14 Evans and Peattie, *Kaigun*, pp. 191–4; Erik Goldstein, 'The Evolution of

British Diplomatic Strategy for the Washington Conference', in *The Washington Conference, 1921–22: Naval Rivalry, East Asian Stability, and the Road to Pearl Harbor*, ed. Erik Goldstein and John Maurer (London, 1994), pp. 10–11, 14, 23; B. J. C. McKercher, 'The Politics of Naval Arms Limitation in Britain in the 1920s', in *ibid.*, pp. 38, 42; Thomas H. Buckley, 'The Icarus Factor: The American Pursuit of Myth in Naval Arms Control, 1921–36', in *ibid.*, p. 126.

15 William R. Braisted, 'The Evolution of the United States Navy's Strategic Assessments', in *The Washington Conference*, p. 104; Asada, 'From Washington to London', in *ibid.*, p. 149; Goldstein, 'The Evolution of British Diplomatic Strategy', pp. 7–27 *passim*; Buckley, 'The Icarus Factor', pp. 129, 131–2.

16 Evans and Peattie, *Kaigun*, pp. 194–6; Braisted, 'The Evolution of the United States Navy's Strategic Assessments', p. 106; Robert Jackson, *The Royal Navy in World War II* (Annapolis, MD, 1997), pp. 7–8.

17 Jentschura, Jung and Mickel, *Warships of the Imperial Japanese Navy*, p. 35; *Conway's All the World's Fighting Ships, 1922–46* (London, 1980), p. 173.

18 Sources disagree on the 'normal' or 'trial' displacement of these carriers; cf. Jentschura, Jung and Mickel, *Warships of the Imperial Japanese Navy*, pp. 25–8, 31–5, 40–44; *Conway, 1922–46*, pp. 179–80.

19 Evans and Peattie, *Kaigun*, pp. 223–32; Asada, 'From Washington to London', p. 175. Sources disagree on the 'normal' or 'trial' displacement of these cruisers; cf. Jentschura, Jung and Mickel, *Warships of the Imperial Japanese Navy*, pp. 79–84, 108–10; *Conway, 1922–46*, pp. 186–9.

20 Evans and Peattie, *Kaigun*, pp. 212–23; Asada, 'From Washington to London', p. 175; Jentschura, Jung and Mickel, *Warships of the Imperial Japanese Navy*, pp. 143–5, 169–71; *Conway, 1922–46*, pp. 192–3, 197–8; Herwig, 'Innovation Ignored', pp. 231–3.

21 Evans and Peattie, *Kaigun*, pp. 233–7; Asada, 'From Washington to London', pp. 176–8.

22 Stephen E. Pelz, *Race to Pearl Harbor: The Failure of the Second London Naval Conference and the Onset of World War II* (Cambridge, MA, 1974), pp. 59–64; Evans and Peattie, *Kaigun*, pp. 296–8; Buckley, 'The Icarus Factor', p. 142.

23 Evans and Peattie, *Kaigun*, pp. 370–90; Jentschura, Jung and Mickel, *Warships of the Imperial Japanese Navy*, pp. 38–53, 84–7, 111, 113, 145–51, 165–77; *Conway, 1922–46*, pp. 171–3, 178–85, 190–95, 198–204. The *Taiyo*, *Unyo* and *Chuyo* were classified as escort carriers, even though (at 20,000 tons) they were larger than many Japanese fleet carriers.

24 Evans and Peattie, *Kaigun*, pp. 362–5.

25 *Ibid.*, p. 366; Jentschura, Jung and Mickel, *Warships of the Imperial Japanese Navy*, pp. 55–60; *Conway, 1922–46*, pp. 183–6, 191–2.

26 Shizuo Fukui, comp., *Japanese Naval Vessels at the End of World War II* (Annapolis, MD, 1991), p. xi.

27 Evans and Peattie, *Kaigun*, pp. 9–10.

28 *Ibid.*, pp. 10–11; Arthur J. Marder, *Old Friends, New Enemies: The Royal Navy and the Imperial Japanese Navy* (Oxford, 1990), vol. I, p. 285; Edwin

P. Hoyt, *Yamamoto: The Man who Planned Pearl Harbor* (New York, 1990), pp. 21–4, 27.

29 Evans and Peattie, *Kaigun*, pp. 12–13, 23–4, 535–6, 550n; Hoyt, *Yamamoto*, pp. 41–5.

30 Evans and Peattie, *Kaigun*, pp. 402, 537, 545n.

31 *Ibid.*, pp. 403.

32 Asada, 'From Washington to London', pp. 151–4.

33 *Ibid.*, pp. 154–7, 172, 174, 180, 182; Evans and Peattie, *Kaigun*, pp. 526, 530. Hoyt, *Yamamoto*, pp. 48–9, 67–8, reflects the traditional postwar view that Yamamoto distinguished himself from most other junior and mid-career officers by sympathizing with the 'treaty faction', and at London 'sought compromise' with the British and Americans. Hiroyuki Agawa, *The Reluctant Admiral: Yamamoto and the Imperial Navy*, trans. John Bester (Tokyo, 1979), pp. 45–52 and *passim*, likewise characterizes Yamamoto as an opponent of the 'fleet faction' and advocate of compromise at London.

34 Evans and Peattie, *Kaigun*, pp. 457, 525–6; Asada, 'From Washington to London', p. 183.

35 Agawa, *The Reluctant Admiral*, p. 129.

36 On these and other problems plaguing the officer corps by the 1930s, see Evans and Peattie, *Kaigun*, p. 211; Marder, *Old Friends, New Enemies*, vol. 1, pp. 285–7.

37 Evans and Peattie, *Kaigun*, pp. 402–5, 593n.

38 *Ibid.*, pp. 11, 402, 405.

39 See *ibid.*, p. 405.

40 Quoted in Hoyt, *Yamamoto*, p. 129.

41 Evans and Peattie, *Kaigun*, pp. 41–7, 128; *Conway, 1860–1905*, pp. 217, 219–20, 229, 395–9.

42 Woodward, *The Russians at Sea*, pp. 122–5, 131–42; Evans and Peattie, *Kaigun*, pp. 75, 77, 100, 103, 105, 109. *Conway, 1860–1905*, pp. 204, 220, 228–9.

43 On the Battle of Tsushima and its aftermath, see Richard Hough, *The Fleet That Had To Die* (London, 1958), pp. 32–144, 156–86, 206–7; Woodward, *The Russians at Sea*, pp. 139–44, 151–3; Evans and Peattie, *Kaigun*, pp. 119–24.

44 Hoyt, *Yamamoto*, pp. 28–9.

45 Evans and Peattie, *Kaigun*, pp. 168–9.

46 *Ibid.*, pp. 238–98 *passim*.

47 Hoyt, *Yamamoto*, pp. 106–31; Evans and Peattie, *Kaigun*, pp. 471–82.

48 Paul S. Dull, *A Battle History of the Imperial Japanese Navy (1941–1945)* (Annapolis, MD, 1978), pp. 14–44. For exhaustive accounts of the attack on Pearl Harbor and the sinking of the British capital ships, see Gordon W. Prange, with Donald Goldstein and Katherine V. Dillon, *At Dawn We Slept: The Untold Story of Pearl Harbor* (New York, 1981), and Martin Middlebrook and Patrick Mahoney, *Battleship: The Sinking of the* Prince of Wales *and the* Repulse (New York, 1979).

49 Dull, *A Battle History*, pp. 49–93.

50 *Ibid.*, pp. 103–11; Edwyn Gray, *Operation Pacific: The Royal Navy's War against Japan, 1941–1945* (Annapolis, MD, 1990), pp. 111–23, 128.

51 Carl Boyd and Akihiko Yoshida, *The Japanese Submarine Force and World War II* (Annapolis, MD, 1995), pp. 65–8, 218.

52 Dull, *A Battle History*, pp. 115–31.

53 *Ibid.*, pp. 133–71; Hoyt, *Yamamoto*, pp. 157–68. See also Gordon W. Prange, with Donald M. Goldstein and Katherine V. Dillon, *Miracle at Midway* (New York, 1982), and Mark Healy, *Midway 1942: Turning Point in the Pacific* (Oxford, 1993).

54 Matome Ugaki, *Fading Victory: The Diary of Admiral Matome Ugaki, 1941–1945*, ed. Donald M. Goldstein and Katherine V. Dillon, trans. Masataka Chihaya (Pittsburgh, PA, 1991), p. 161.

55 Dull, *A Battle History*, pp. 175–296; Hoyt, *Yamamoto*, pp. 169–250; H. P. Willmott, *The War with Japan: The Period of Balance, May 1942–October 1943* (Wilmington, DE, 2002), pp. 168–9 and *passim*.

56 Dull, *A Battle History*, pp. 297–311, 343, 348; Evans and Peattie, *Kaigun*, p. 529.

57 Dull, *A Battle History*, pp. 313–31, 335–7.

58 *Ibid.*, pp. 332–5, 343–8; Gray, *Operation Pacific*, pp. 201–3, 238–9.

59 Mansanori Ito, *The End of the Imperial Japanese Navy*, trans. Andrew Y. Kuroda and Roger Pineau (New York, 1962), pp. 211, 216–21; Dull, *A Battle History*, pp. 343–8; Boyd and Yoshida, *The Japanese Submarine Force*, pp. 209–17. Ito classifies the ships sunk or foundered as a result of air raids on the Kure Navy Yard in July 1945 as 'not sunk', while Dull follows the more conventional approach of counting these sinkings as combat losses.

EIGHT · RED STAR RISING: THE SOVIET NAVY, 1956–91

1 George E. Hudson, 'Soviet Naval Doctrine and Soviet Politics, 1953–1975', *World Politics*, XXIX (1976), pp. 107–8.

2 Gromov *et al.*, *Tri Veka Rossiiskogo Flota*, vol. III, pp. 214–15.

3 Nikita S. Khrushchev, *Khrushchev Remembers: The Last Testament*, trans. and ed. Strobe Talbot (Boston, 1974), p. 20; Jürgen Rohwer and Mikhail S. Monakov, *Stalin's Ocean-Going Fleet: Soviet Naval Strategy and Shipbuilding Programmes, 1935–1953* (London, 2001), pp. 194–7; *Conway's All the World's Fighting Ships, 1947–1995* (London, 1995), pp. 341, 376–7. According to *Conway*, work began on a third postwar battle cruiser, the *Kronstadt* (laid down 1955), but Western intelligence agencies were confused over whether this hull, in a slip at Molotovsk (later Severodvinsk), was really the incomplete *Sovyetskiy Soyuz* class battleship *Sovyetskaya Byelorussiya* (laid down 1939). Norman Polmar does not mention this ship at all; he also has the *Stalingrad* being laid down in 1949 rather than 1951. There is also some confusion over whether the hull of the *Moskva* seen on the slip in Leningrad in 1952 was really the surviving hull of the pre-war battle cruiser *Kronstadt* (laid down 1939). See Norman Polmar, *The Naval Institute Guide to the Soviet Navy*, 5th edn (Annapolis, MD, 1991), pp. 78–9, 164.

4 In the mid-1950s the US and NATO started giving K-series code names to classes of Soviet warships, but from the late 1960s they were usually called by their Soviet names. Classes of Soviet submarines were labelled

alphabetically and randomly (starting with 'Whiskey') until the letters
A-Z had been used. In 1985 the US and NATO began a new series, starting
with 'Akula' ('shark' in Russian). See Polmar, *The Naval Institute Guide to
the Soviet Navy*, pp. 5, 94.

5 Rohwer and Monakov, *Stalin's Ocean-Going Fleet*, pp. 197–8, 201–2;
Norman Friedman, *Seapower and Space: From the Dawn of the Missile Age
to Net-Centric Warfare* (Annapolis, MD, 2000), pp. 135, 137; *Conway,
1947–95*, pp. 368, 379, 386–9.

6 *Conway, 1947–95*, pp. 367, 379. Five *Sverdlov*s were launched but never
completed, and two were never launched. Ten served into the 1980s.
According to Polmar, *The Naval Institute Guide to the Soviet Navy*, p. 164,
20 (not 21) *Sverdlov*s were laid down, of which three were launched but
never completed and three never launched. Polmar has 12 *Sverdlov*s
serving into the 1980s.

7 Rohwer and Monakov, *Stalin's Ocean-Going Fleet*, pp. 216–17; Hudson,
'Soviet Naval Doctrine', p. 98; Gromov *et al.*, *Tri Veka Rossiiskogo Flota*,
vol. III, pp. 224–6; Friedman, *Seapower and Space*, pp. 140–41; *Conway,
1947–95*, pp. 342–3. Khrushchev quoted in *Khrushchev Remembers*, p. 27.
Khrushchev used the sinking of the *Novorossiysk* (October 1955) as an
excuse to sack Kuznetsov. The admiral, 51 years old at the time, suffered
a heart attack in May 1955 and most likely would have had to retire in
any event.

8 As with warship types, the United States and NATO developed a series of
codenames for Soviet missile systems. They were numbered in
sequence, starting with an abbreviation indicating missile type (ss for
surface-to-surface, SA for surface-to-air, etc.) and also given a nickname.

9 Friedman, *Seapower and Space*, pp. 141–2; Khrushchev, *Khrushchev
Remembers*, pp. 28–34; *Conway, 1947–95*, pp. 351, 389, 417. During this
period the only new Soviet surface warships not armed with missiles
were four classes of small frigates (NATO 'Kola', 'Riga', 'Petya' and
'Mirka'), armed with conventional artillery, torpedoes and mines. The
'Grisha' class frigates of the 1960s were armed with SAMs but carried no
SSMs. See *Conway, 1947–95*, pp. 392–3, 395–6.

10 Friedman, *Seapower and Space*, pp. 141–2; *Conway, 1947–95*, pp. 349–50,
353, 380, 390.

11 Polmar, *The Naval Institute Guide to the Soviet Navy*, pp. 83, 144–5;
Conway, 1947–95, pp. 375–6.

12 Gromov *et al.*, *Tri Veka Rossiiskogo Flota*, vol. III, p. 254; *Conway,
1947–95*, pp. 396–402, 405; Friedman, *Seapower and Space*, pp. 99,
209–10, 219. The first US navy guided missile was the Regulus (1958).
To counter the threat from the faster Soviet submarines of the 1960s,
the US navy developed a submarine of its own fast enough to escort a
carrier battle group, armed with a SSM with greater OTH range than
the 'Shaddock.' The result was the *Los Angeles* class (from 1976), eventually armed with the satellite-guided Tomahawk cruise missile (after
1983).

13 Gromov *et al.*, *Tri Veka Rossiiskogo Flota*, vol. III, p. 254; Rohwer and
Monakov, *Stalin's Ocean-Going Fleet*, p. 209; *Conway, 1947–95*, pp. 356,
398–9, 401. In addition to the types mentioned in the paragraphs above, the

1958 total also included one 1,200-ton Project 617 (NATO 'Whale') class attack submarine (built 1951–2), decommissioned after a 1959 accident.

14 Polmar, *The Naval Institute Guide to the Soviet Navy*, pp. 15–17.

15 *Ibid.*, pp. 155–62; Hudson, 'Soviet Naval Doctrine', pp. 102–3; *Conway, 1947–95*, pp. 381–2.

16 Polmar, *The Naval Institute Guide to the Soviet Navy*, pp. 49, 137, 141–3; *Conway, 1947–95*, pp. 374–5.

17 Polmar, *The Naval Institute Guide to the Soviet Navy*, pp. 148–50, 152–3; *Conway, 1947–95*, pp. 382–4, 413. The *Kirov* was commissioned 21 years after the completion of the 15,750-ton icebreaker *Lenin*, the world's first nuclear-propelled surface ship, and 19 years after the guided missile cruiser USS *Long Beach*, the first nuclear-powered surface warship.

18 Friedman, *Seapower and Space*, p. 153; *Conway, 1947–95*, pp. 394–5, 414–15.

19 Friedman, *Seapower and Space*, pp. 155–9, 163, 166, 175; Paul M. Kennedy, *Rise and Fall of British Naval Mastery* (London, 1976), p. 333.

20 Polmar, *The Naval Institute Guide to the Soviet Navy*, p. 81; *Conway, 1947–95*, pp. 399, 405–10.

21 Polmar, *The Naval Institute Guide to the Soviet Navy*, pp. 83, 91, 96–100; Friedman, *Seapower and Space*, p. 206; *Conway, 1947–95*, pp. 403–4, 408.

22 Polmar, *The Naval Institute Guide to the Soviet Navy*, pp. 135–7; *Conway, 1947–95*, pp. 373–4, 382.

23 Polmar, *The Naval Institute Guide to the Soviet Navy*, pp. 2, 45, 135–7; *Conway, 1947–95*, pp. 372–4.

24 J. E. Moore, 'The Soviet Sailor', in *The Soviet Military: Political Education, Training and Morale*, ed. E. S. Williams (New York, 1986), pp. 167–8; Gregory D. Young, 'Mutiny on the *Storozhevoy*: A Case Study of Dissent in the Soviet Navy', Master's thesis, Naval Postgraduate School, 1982, pp. 64–5.

25 Moore, 'The Soviet Sailor', p. 68; Young, 'Mutiny', p. 65–6. Quote from V. Moradsov, *Life in the Soviet Navy* (Moscow, 1975), p. 22.

26 Moore, 'The Soviet Sailor', pp. 169–71.

27 Young, 'Mutiny', pp. 66, 68–9, 73.

28 *Ibid.*, pp. 13–15.

29 *Ibid.*, pp. 20–30. Estimates of the number of mutineers executed range from fewer than 15 to more than 80. The only officer involved aside from Sablin received fifteen years in a labour camp.

30 Moore, 'The Soviet Sailor', pp. 166, 170.

31 *Ibid.*, p. 162; Young, 'Mutiny', pp. 65, 67; Polmar, *The Naval Institute Guide to the Soviet Navy*, p. 64.

32 Sources for this paragraph and the rest of this section are Moore, 'The Soviet Sailor', pp. 161–7, 175; Young, 'Mutiny', pp. 44–5, 47–9, 54, 58, 61–4, 67, 75.

33 Polmar, *The Naval Institute Guide to the Soviet Navy*, p. 37.

34 *Ibid.*, pp. 37–9, 43, 446; Rohwer and Monakov, *Stalin's Ocean-Going Fleet*, p. 198; *Conway, 1947–95*, pp. 178, 379, 396. The former *Ordzhonikidze* served until 1972 as the Indonesian navy flagship *Irian*.

35 Bruce W. Watson, *Red Navy at Sea: Soviet Naval Operations on the High Seas, 1956–1980* (Boulder, CO, 1982), pp. 42–4; Donald W. Mitchell,

'Strategic Significance of Soviet Naval Power in Cuban Waters', in *Soviet Seapower in the Caribbean: Political and Strategic Implications*, ed. James D. Theberge (New York, 1972), p. 29.

36 Watson, *Red Navy at Sea*, pp. 8, 11–12, 85, 101–19, 136–8; Charles C. Peterson, 'Showing the Flag', in *Soviet Naval Diplomacy*, ed. Bradford Dismukes and James M. McConnell (New York, 1979), p. 106; Polmar, *The Naval Institute Guide to the Soviet Navy*, pp. 39–41, 43–4; *idem*, *Chronology of the Cold War at Sea, 1945–1991* (Annapolis, MD, 1998), pp. 136, 162; Friedman, *Seapower and Space*, pp. 173, 230.

37 Gordon H. McCormick, *The Soviet Presence in the Mediterranean* (Santa Monica, CA, 1987), pp. 13–16.

38 Watson, *Red Navy at Sea*, pp. 36, 62, 138–40; Polmar, *Chronology*, pp. 158, 160, 173; *Conway, 1947–95*, p. 381.

39 Watson, *Red Navy at Sea*, pp. 29–35; Polmar, *The Naval Institute Guide to the Soviet Navy*, pp. 26, 38, 40–41; Friedman, *Seapower and Space*, p. 159.

40 Watson, *Red Navy at Sea*, pp. 147–67; Polmar, *The Naval Institute Guide to the Soviet Navy*, pp. 17, 38–9. See also Geoffrey Jukes, *The Indian Ocean in Soviet Naval Policy* (London, 1972).

41 Polmar, *The Naval Institute Guide to the Soviet Navy*, pp. 41–2, 44–5, 461.

42 *Ibid.*, p. 93; *idem*, *Chronology*, pp. 136, 216. The Soviet navy may have also lost one or more diesel submarines to accidents in coastal waters. Coincidentally, the US navy lost four submarines during the Cold War: the *Cochino* (SS-345) in 1949, the *Stickleback* (SS-415) in 1958, the *Thresher* (SSN-593) in 1963 and the *Scorpion* (SSN-589) in 1968.

43 Polmar, *The Naval Institute Guide to the Soviet Navy*, pp. 445–54.

44 *Ibid.*, pp. 3–4; Gromov *et al.*, *Tri Veka Rossiiskogo Flota*, vol. III, p. 311. According to Gromov, the Soviet navy of 1991 had 62 ballistic missile submarines: 13 Yankees, 43 Deltas and 6 Typhoons. Polmar gives a figure of 63 but does not account for them by class.

NINE · UPHOLDING THE PAX AMERICANA:
THE UNITED STATES NAVY SINCE 1991

1 John Byron, 'A New Navy for a New World', *US Naval Institute Proceedings*, CXXIX/3 (2003), p. 86.

2 Unless otherwise noted, sources for this section are *Conway, 1922–46*, p. 99; *Conway, 1947–95*, pp. 559, 570–74, 578–85, 587–9, 591–2, 598–601, 606–9, 612–13, 616–23; http://www.chinfo.navy.mil (accessed 8–11 April 2003); http://www.hazegray.org/worldnav (accessed 8–11 April 2003).

3 Scott C. Truver, 'Tomorrow's US Fleet', *US Naval Institute Proceedings*, CXXVIII/4 (2002), p. 78.

4 See Lawrence Sondhaus, *Navies of Europe, 1815–2002* (London, 2002), p. 328.

5 Robert J. Natter, 'Meeting the Need For Speed', *US Naval Institute Proceedings*, CXXVIII/6 (2002), pp. 65–7; A. D. Baker III, 'Combat Fleets', *US Naval Institute Proceedings*, CXXVIII/12 (2002), p. 88.

6 Greg Jaffe, 'Plans for a Small Ship Pose Big Questions for the US Navy', *Wall Street Journal*, 11 July 2001, A1, A10; Richard Brawley, 'Streetfighter Cannot Do the Job', *US Naval Institute Proceedings*, CXXVIII/10 (2002),

pp. 66–9.

7 Anne Marie Squeo, 'Navy to Scrap Plans for New Destroyer, Build Smaller Ships', *Wall Street Journal*, 31 October 2001, A11; Brawley, 'Streetfighter Cannot Do the Job', p. 67; Anne Marie Squeo and Greg Jaffe, 'Northrop Wins Warship Contract', *Wall Street Journal*, 30 April 2002, A6; George R. Worthington, 'We Have the Craft for Littoral Warfare', *US Naval Institute Proceedings*, CXXVIII/10 (2002), p. 128; *idem*, 'Littoral Warfare Needs a Specific Ship', *US Naval Institute Proceedings*, CXXIX/1 (2003), pp. 90–91; Henry C. Mustin and Douglas J. Katz, 'All Ahead Flank for LCS', *US Naval Institute Proceedings*, CXXIX/2 (2003), pp. 30–33; Norman Friedman, 'World Naval Developments', *US Naval Institute Proceedings*, CXXIX/4 (2003), pp. 4–6.

8 http://www.hazegray.org/worldnav (accessed 8–11 April 2003).

9 Bill Hamblet, 'In Search of the Zero-Defects Monster', *US Naval Institute Proceedings*, CXXVII/10 (2001), pp. 48–9, disputes the pervasive nature of the 'zero-defects' mentality. See also Jan M. van Tol, 'Using Anonymity is Dysfunctional', *US Naval Institute Proceedings*, CXXIX/4 (2003), p. 48.

10 Charles C. Thompson, *A Glimpse of Hell: The Explosion on the USS* Iowa *and its Cover-Up* (New York, 1999); William H. McMichael, *The Mother of All Hooks: The Story of the US Navy's Tailhook Scandal* (New Brunswick, NJ, 1997); 'Navy's Top Officer Dies of Gunshot, Apparently Self-Inflicted', 16 May 1996, http://www.cnn.com/US/965/16/boorda.6p/index.html (accessed 10 April 2003); Jeffrey Gantar, Tom Patten and Michael O'Donnell, *A Question of Honor: The Cheating Scandal that Rocked Annapolis and a Midshipman Who Decided to Tell the Truth* (Grand Rapids, MI, 1996); 'Five with Ties to Naval Academy Charged with Car Theft', 13 April 1996, http://www.cnn.com/US/9604/12/newsbriefs/ (accessed 10 April 2003).

11 http://www.chinfo.navy.mil (accessed 8–11 April 2003); http://www.defenselink.mil (accessed 10–11 April 2003).

12 James M. Murphy, 'Expand Education for Sailors', *US Naval Institute Proceedings*, CXXIX/2 (2003), p. 58; http://www.chinfo.navy.mil (accessed 8–11 April 2003); http://www.navy.com (accessed 10 April 2003); http://www.dfas.mil/money/milpay/pay/2003paytable.pdf (accessed 10 April 2003).

13 'Flag and General Officers and Senior Enlisted Leaders of the Naval Services', *US Naval Institute Proceedings*, CXXIX/5 (2003), pp. 143–64; http://www.gendercenter.org/military.htm (accessed 10 April 2003); http://www.africanamericans.com (accessed 10 April 2003).

14 http://www.desert-storm.com/soldiers/navy.html (accessed 11 April 2003); Polmar, *Chronology*, p. 223; Conway, *1947–95*, pp. 188–9; http://www.britishwarships.cjb.net (accessed 13 January 2002); Worthington, 'We Have the Craft for Littoral Warfare', p. 128; Conway, *1947–95*, pp. 188–9, 559–618 *passim*.

15 http://www.chinfo.navy.mil (accessed 8–11 April 2003).

16 http://www.afsouth.nato.int/factsheets/STANAVFORMED.htm (accessed 18 January 2002); http://www.navyhistory.com/CVN70TR.html (accessed 20 January 2002).

17 'Us Missiles Pound Targets in Afghanistan, Sudan', 20 August 1998, http://www.cnn.com/us/9808/20/us.strikes.01/ (accessed 11 April 2003); Friedman, *Seapower and Space*, p. 7; Harold W. Gehman, 'Lost Patrol: The Attack on the *Cole*', *US Naval Institute Proceedings*, CXXVII/4 (2001), pp. 34–7.

18 http://www.defenselink.mil/specials/desert_fox/index.html (accessed 18 January 2002).

19 Richard Cobbold, 'Kosovo: What the Navies Did', *US Naval Institute Proceedings*, CXXV/10 (1999), p. 87; http://www.afsouth.nato.int/fact-sheets/STANAVFORMED.htm (accessed 18 January 2002); http://www.defenselink.mil/specials/kosovo/index.html (accessed 20 January 2002).

20 Speech by Condoleeza Rice, Gov. George W. Bush's International Affairs Adviser, to the Republican National Convention, 1 August 2000, http://www.cnn.com/ELECTION/2000/conventions/republican/transcripts/rice.html (11 April 2003).

21 John D. Gresham, 'Forces Fighting for Enduring Freedom', *US Naval Institute Proceedings*, CXXVII/11 (2001), p. 45; Scott C. Truver, 'The us Navy in Review', *US Naval Institute Proceedings*, CXXVIII/5 (2002), pp. 79–82; Phil Wisecup and Tom Williams, 'Enduring Freedom: Making Coalition Naval Warfare Work', *US Naval Institute Proceedings*, CXXVIII/9 (2002), pp. 52–5.

22 'President Delivers State of the Union Address', 29 January 2002, http://www.whitehouse.gov/news/releases/2002/01/200020129-11.html (accessed 11 April 2003).

23 'Status of the Navy', http://www.chinfo.navy.mil/navpalib/news/.www/status.htm (accessed 3 March–21 April 2003); http://www.cnn.com (accessed 19 March–11 April 2003); Vice Admiral Timothy Keating, briefing from Fifth Fleet headquarters, Bahrain, aired on c-span, 12 April 2003.

24 'Status of the Navy', http://www.chinfo.navy.mil/navpalib/news/.www/status.htm (accessed 3 March–21 April 2003); http://www.cnn.com (accessed 19 March–11 April 2003).

Bibliography

MEMOIRS, PUBLISHED DOCUMENTS AND CONTEMPORARY
PUBLICATIONS

Aube, Théophile, *A terre et à bord, notes díun marin* (Paris, 1884)
Beresford, Charles William de la Poer, *The Memoirs of Admiral Lord Charles
  Beresford*, 2 vols (Boston, 1914)
Bonner-Smith, D., ed., *Russian War, 1855, Baltic: Official Correspondence*
  (London, 1944)
Bonner-Smith, D., and A. C. Dewar, eds, *Russian War, 1854, Baltic and Black
  Sea: Official Correspondence* (London, 1943)
Busk, Hans, *The Navies of the World: Their Present State, and Future
  Capabilities* (London, 1859)
Clarke, George Sydenham, *Russia's Sea-Power Past and Present; or, The Rise of
  the Russian Navy* (London, 1898)
Crisenoy, Jules de, *Our Naval School and Naval Officers: A Glance at the
  Condition of the French Navy prior to the Late Franco-German War*, trans.
  Richard W. Meade (New York, 1873)
Da Paixão e Dores, Manuel Moreira, *Diário da Armada da Independéncia*, ed.
  Max Justo Guedes, 2nd edn (Brasília, 1972)
Dewar, A. C., ed., *Russian War, 1855, Black Sea: Official Correspondence*
  (London, 1945)
Dundonald, Thomas [Cochrane], Earl of, *Narrative of Services in the
  Liberation of Chili, Peru, and Brazil, from Spanish and Portuguese
  Domination*, 2 vols (London, 1859)
Fontin, Paul, and Mathieu Vignot, *Essai de stratégie navale* (Paris, 1893)
Grivel, Richild, *De la guerre maritime avant et depuis les nouvelles inventions*
  (Paris, 1869)
Hall, W. H., *Narrative of the Voyages and Services of the* Nemesis, *from 1840 to
  1843*, 2nd edn (London, 1845)
Jane, Fred T., *The Imperial Russian Navy*, 2nd edn (London, 1904; reprint,
  London, 1983)
—, *The British Battle Fleet*, 2 vols (London, 1915; reprint, London, 1990)
Joinville, François Ferdinand d'Orléans, Prince de, *De l'état des forces navales
  de la France* (Frankfurt, 1844)
—, *Essais sur la marine française* (Paris, 1853)
—, *Memoirs of the Prince de Joinville*, trans. Lady Mary Loyd (New York,
  1895)

Khrushchev, Nikita S., *Khrushchev Remembers: The Last Testament*, trans. and
  ed. Strobe Talbot (Boston, 1974)
Olid Araya, J. Arturo, *Crónicas de Guerra: Relatos de un ex-combatiente de la
  Guerra del Pacífico y la Revolución de 1891* (Santiago de Chile, 1999)
Paixhans, Henri-Joseph, *Nouvelle force maritime* (Paris, 1822)
—, *An Account of the Experiments made in the French Navy for the Trial of Bomb
  Cannon*, trans. John A. Dalghren (Philadelphia, 1838)
Tirpitz, Alfred von, *Erinnerungen* (Leipzig, 1919)
Ugaki, Matome, *Fading Victory: The Diary of Admiral Matome Ugaki,
  1941–1945*, ed. Donald M. Goldstein and Katherine V. Dillon, trans.
  Masataka Chihaya (Pittsburgh, 1991)
Uribe Orrego, Luis, *Los Combates navales en la Guerra del Pacífico, 1879–1881*
  (Valparaíso, 1886)

SECONDARY SOURCES

Agawa, Hiroyuki, *The Reluctant Admiral: Yamamoto and the Imperial Navy*,
  trans. John Bester (Tokyo, 1979)
Amayo, Enrique, *La Politica Britanica en la Guerra del Pacifico* (Lima, 1988)
Araya, Francisco Ghisolfo, 'Situacion estrategica naval', in *El Poder Naval
  Chileno* (Valparaíso, 1985), vol. I, pp. 271–312; vol. II, pp. 401–72,
  605–44
Asada, Sadao, 'From Washington to London: The Imperial Japanese Navy
  and the Politics of Naval Limitation, 1921–1930', in *The Washington
  Conference, 1921–22: Naval Rivalry, East Asian Stability and the Road to
  Pearl Harbor*, ed. Erik Goldstein and John Maurer (London, 1994), pp.
  147–91
Baker III, A. D., 'Combat Fleets', *US Naval Institute Proceedings*, CXXVIII/12
  (2002), p. 88
Battesti, Michèle, *La Marine au XIXe siècle: Interventions extérieures et colonies*
  (Paris, 1993)
Baxter, James Phinney, *The Introduction of the Ironclad Warship* (Cambridge,
  MA, 1933)
Beeching, Jack, *The Chinese Opium Wars* (New York, 1975)
Beeler, John F., *British Naval Policy in the Gladstone-Disraeli Era, 1866–1880*
  (Stanford, CA, 1997)
Bennett, Geoffrey, *Coronel and the Falklands* (London, 1962)
Berghahn, Volker R., *Der Tirpitz-Plan: Genesis und Verfall einer innenpolitis-
  chen Krisenstrategie unter Wilhelm II* (Düsseldorf, 1971)
Berghahn, Volker R., and Wilhelm Deist, *Rüstung im Zeichen der wilhelminis-
  chen Weltpolitik: Grundlegende Dokumente, 1890–1914* (Düsseldorf, 1988)
Bourne, Kenneth, *Palmerston: The Early Years, 1784–1841* (New York, 1982)
Boyd, Carl, 'The Wasted Ten Years, 1888–1918: The Kaiser Finds an
  Admiral', *Journal of the Royal United Service Institution*, CXI (1966),
  pp. 291–7
Boyd, Carl, and Akihiko Yoshida, *The Japanese Submarine Force and World
  War II* (Annapolis, MD, 1995)
Braisted, William R., 'The Evolution of the United States Navy's Strategic
  Assessments in the Pacific, 1919–31', in *The Washington Conference,*

1921–22: Naval Rivalry, East Asian Stability and the Road to Pearl Harbor,
ed. Erik Goldstein and John Maurer (London, 1994), pp. 102–23

Brawley, Richard, 'Streetfighter Cannot Do the Job', *US Naval Institute
Proceedings*, cxxviii/10 (2002), pp. 66–9

Brown, David K., 'The Era of Uncertainty, 1863–1878', in *Steam, Steel and
Shellfire: The Steam Warship, 1815–1905*, ed. Robert Gardiner (London,
1992), pp. 75–94

—, *Paddle Warships: The Earliest Steam Powered Fighting Ships, 1815–1850*
(London, 1993)

—, *Warrior to Dreadnought: Warship Development, 1860–1905* (London,
1997)

Brown, George, *The Union Army*, vol. vii: *The Navy* (Madison, wi, 1908)

Browning, Robert M., Jr, *From Cape Charles to Cape Fear: The North Atlantic
Blockading Squadron during the Civil War* (Washington, dc, 1993)

—, 'Defunct Strategy and Divergent Goals: The Role of the United States
Navy along the Eastern Seaboard during the Civil War', *Prologue:
Quarterly of the National Archives and Records Administration*, xxxiii
(2001), pp. 169–79

—, *Success is All That Was Expected: The South Atlantic Blockading Squadron
during the Civil War* (Washington, dc, 2002)

Bucholz, Arden, *Moltke, Schlieffen and Prussian War Planning* (New York,
1991)

Buckley, Thomas H., 'The Icarus Factor: The American Pursuit of Myth in
Naval Arms Control, 1921–36', in *The Washington Conference, 1921–22:
Naval Rivalry, East Asian Stability and the Road to Pearl Harbor*, ed. Erik
Goldstein and John Maurer (London, 1994), pp. 124–46

Bulnes, Gonzalo, *Resumen de la Guerra del Pacífico* (Santiago de Chile, 1979)

Byron, John, 'A New Navy for a New World', *US Naval Institute Proceedings*,
cxxix/3 (2003), pp. 86–8

Campbell, John, 'Naval Armaments and Armour', in *Steam, Steel and
Shellfire: The Steam Warship 1815–1905*, ed. Robert Gardiner (London,
1992), pp. 158–69

Canney, Donald L., *The Old Steam Navy*, 2 vols (Annapolis, md, 1993)

—, *Lincoln's Navy: The Ships, Men and Organization, 1861–65* (Annapolis, md,
1998)

—, *Sailing Warships of the US Navy* (Annapolis, md, 2001)

Carvalho, Trajano Augusto, *Nossa Marinha: Seus Feitos e Glórias, 1822–1940*
(Rio de Janeiro, 1986)

Carvalho, Zenithilde Magno de, *A marinha no Brasil colonial* (Rio de Janeiro,
1928)

Chickering, Roger, *Imperial Germany and the Great War, 1914–1918*
(Cambridge, 1998)

Chisolm, Donald, *Waiting for Dead Men's Shoes: Origins and Development of
the US Navy's Officer Personnel System, 1793–1941* (Stanford, ca, 2001)

Conway's All the World's Fighting Ships, 1860–1905 (London, 1979)

Conway's All the World's Fighting Ships, 1906–21 (London, 1985)

Conway's All the World's Fighting Ships, 1922–46 (London, 1980)

Conway's All the World's Fighting Ships, 1947–95 (London, 1995)

Courtemanche, Regis A., *No Need of Glory: The British Navy in American*

Waters, 1860–1864 (Annapolis, MD, 1977)

Daly, John C. K., *Russian Seapower and 'the Eastern Question', 1827–41* (Annapolis, MD, 1991)

Del Campo, José Rodolfo, *Campaña Naval 1879*, 3rd edn (Lima, 1979)

Drascher, Wahrhold, 'Zur Soziologie des deutschen Seeoffizierkorps', *Wehrwissenschaftliche Rundschau*, XII (1962), pp. 555–67

Dull, Paul S., *A Battle History of the Imperial Japanese Navy (1941–1945)* (Annapolis, MD, 1978)

Dupont, Maurice, and Etienne Taillemite, *Les guerres navales françaises: du Moyen Age à la guerre du Golfe* (Paris, 1995)

Endres, Franz Carl, 'Soziologische Struktur und ihr entsprechende Ideologien des deutschen Offizierkorps vor dem Weltkriege', *Archiv für Sozialwissenschaft und Sozialpolitik*, LXVIII (1932), pp. 282–319

Evans, David C., and Mark R. Peattie, *Kaigun: Strategy, Tactics and Technology in the Imperial Japanese Navy, 1887–1941* (Annapolis, MD, 1997)

Fairbanks, Charles H., Jr, 'The Origins of the *Dreadnought* Revolution: A Historiographical Essay', *International History Review*, XIII (1991), pp. 246–72

Ferreira Reis, Arthur Cezar, *A Historia Paraense e a Marinha de Guerra do Brasil* (Belém, 1941)

Ferreira Vidigal, Armando Amorim, *A evolução do pensamento estratégico naval brasileiro*, 3rd edn (Rio de Janeiro, 1985)

Foster, Kevin J., 'The Diplomats Who Sank a Fleet: The Confederacy's Undelivered European Fleet and the Union Consular Service', *Prologue: Quarterly of the National Archives and Records Administration*, XXXIII (2001), pp. 181–93

Friedberg, Aaron L., *The Weary Titan: Britain and the Experience of Relative Decline, 1895–1905* (Princeton, NJ, 1988)

Friedman, Norman, *Seapower and Space: From the Dawn of the Missile Age to Net-Centric Warfare* (Annapolis, MD, 2000)

—, 'World Naval Developments', *US Naval Institute Proceedings*, CXXIX/4 (2003), pp. 4–6

Fukui, Shizuo, comp., *Japanese Naval Vessels at the End of World War II* (Annapolis, MD, 1991)

Gannon, Michael, *Operation Drumbeat* (New York, 1990)

Gantar, Jeffrey, Tom Patten and Michael O'Donnell, *A Question of Honor: The Cheating Scandal that Rocked Annapolis and a Midshipman Who Decided to Tell the Truth* (Grand Rapids, MI, 1996)

Gardiner, Robert, *Frigates of the Napoleonic Wars* (Annapolis, MD, 2000)

Gehman, Harold W., 'Lost Patrol: The Attack on the *Cole*', *US Naval Institute Proceedings*, CXXVII/4 (2001), pp. 34–7

Goldstein, Erik, 'The Evolution of British Diplomatic Strategy for the Washington Conference', in *The Washington Conference, 1921–22: Naval Rivalry, East Asian Stability and the Road to Pearl Harbor*, ed. Erik Goldstein and John Maurer (London, 1994), pp. 4–34

Gordon, Andrew, *The Rules of the Game: Jutland and British Naval Command* (Annapolis, MD, 1996)

Gottschall, Terrell D., *By Order of the Kaiser: Otto von Diederichs and the Rise of the Imperial German Navy, 1865–1902* (Annapolis, MD, 2003)

Gray, Edwyn, *Operation Pacific: The Royal Navy's War against Japan,
1941–1945* (Annapolis, MD, 1990)

Gresham, John D., 'Forces Fighting for Enduring Freedom', *US Naval
Institute Proceedings*, CXXVII/11 (2001), pp. 45–7

Grez, Vicente, *El Combate Homérico: 21 de May de 1879*, 4th edn (Santiago de
Chile, 1968)

Griffiths, Denis, 'Warship Machinery', in *Steam, Steel and Shellfire: The
Steam Warship, 1815–1905*, ed. Robert Gardiner (London, 1992), pp.
170–78

Gromov, F. N., Vladimir Gribovskii and Boris Rodionov, *Tri Veka Rossiiskogo
Flota*, 3 vols (St Petersburg, 1996)

Gröner, Erich, *Die deutschen Kriegsschiffe, 1815–1945*, 8 vols (Koblenz, 1989)

Halpern, Paul G., *A Naval History of World War I* (Annapolis, MD, 1994)

Hamblet, Bill, 'In Search of the Zero-Defects Monster', *US Naval Institute
Proceedings*, CXXVII/10 (2001), pp. 48–9

Hamilton, C. I., *Anglo-French Naval Rivalry, 1840–1870* (Oxford, 1993)

Hamilton, W. Mark, *The Nation and the Navy: Methods and Organization of
British Navalist Propaganda, 1889–1914* (New York, 1986)

Harding, Richard, *Seapower and Naval Warfare, 1650–1830* (London, 1999)

Healy, Mark, *Midway 1942: Turning Point in the Pacific* (Oxford, 1993)

Hearn, Chester G., *Admiral David Glasgow Farragut: The Civil War Years*
(Annapolis, MD, 1998)

Herwig, Holger H., *The German Naval Officer Corps: A Social and Political
History* (Oxford, 1973)

—, *'Luxury' Fleet: The Imperial German Navy, 1888–1918*, rev. edn (Atlantic
Highlands, NJ, 1987)

—, 'Innovation Ignored: The Submarine Problem – Germany, Britain and
the United States, 1919-1939', in *Military Innovation in the Interwar
Period*, ed. Williamson Murray and Allan R. Millett (Cambridge, 1996),
pp. 227–64

Hobson, Rolf, *Imperialism at Sea: Naval Strategic Thought, the Ideology of Sea
Power and the Tirpitz Plan, 1875–1914* (Boston, 2002)

Holcombe, Robert, 'Types of Ships', in *The Confederate Navy: The Ships, Men
and Organization, 1861–65*, ed. William N. Still, Jr (Annapolis, MD,
1997), pp. 40–68

Horn, Stanley Fitzgerald, *Gallant Rebel: The Fabulous Cruise of the CSS
Shenandoah* (New Brunswick, NJ, 1947)

Hough, Richard, *The Fleet That Had To Die* (London, 1958)

Howell, Raymond, *The Royal Navy and the Slave Trade* (New York, 1987)

Hoyt, Edwin P., *Yamamoto: The Man Who Planned Pearl Harbor* (New York,
1990)

Hudson, George E., 'Soviet Naval Doctrine and Soviet Politics,
1953–1975', *World Politics*, XXIX (1976), pp. 90–113

Irving, John Irving, *Coronel and the Falklands* (London, 1927)

Ito, Mansanori, *The End of the Imperial Japanese Navy*, trans. Andrew Y.
Kuroda and Roger Pineau (New York, 1962)

Jackson, Robert, *The Royal Navy in World War II* (Annapolis, MD, 1997)

Jentschura, Hansgeorg, Dieter Jung and Peter Mickel, *Warships of the
Imperial Japanese Navy, 1869–1945*, trans. Antony Preston and J. D.

Brown (Annapolis, MD, 1992)

Johnson, Charles D., 'Chile as a Stepping Stone to United States Naval
    Greatness, 1879–1895', Master's thesis, California State University –
    Hayward, 1974

Jukes, Geoffrey, *The Indian Ocean in Soviet Naval Policy* (London, 1972)

Kemp, Peter, *The British Sailor: A Social History of the Lower Deck* (London,
    1970)

Kennedy, Paul M., *The Rise and Fall of British Naval Mastery* (London, 1976)

Lambert, Andrew, *Battleships in Transition: The Creation of the Steam
    Battlefleet, 1815–1860* (Annapolis, MD, 1984)

—, *The Crimean War: British Grand Strategy against Russia, 1853–56*
    (Manchester, 1991)

—, *The Last Sailing Battlefleet: Maintaining Naval Mastery, 1815–1850*
    (London, 1991)

—, 'Introduction of Steam', in *Steam, Steel, and Shellfire: The Steam Warship,
    1815–1905*, ed. Robert Gardiner (London, 1992), pp. 14–29

—, 'Iron Hulls and Armour Plate', in *Steam, Steel and Shellfire: The Steam
    Warship, 1815–1905*, ed. Robert Gardiner (London, 1992), pp. 47–60

—, 'The Screw Propeller Warship', in *Steam, Steel and Shellfire: The Steam
    Warship, 1815–1905*, ed. Robert Gardiner (London, 1992), pp. 30–46

Lambert, Nicholas A., *Sir John Fisher's Naval Revolution* (Columbia, SC,
    1999)

Lambi, Ivo Nikolai, *The Navy and German Power Politics, 1862–1914*
    (Boston, 1984)

Land, Isaac Edward, 'Domesticating the Maritime: Culture, Masculinity
    and Empire in Britain, 1770–1820', PhD diss., University of Michigan,
    1999

Larenas Q., Victor H., *Patricio Lynch: Almirante, General, Gobernante y
    Diplomatico* (Santiago de Chile, 1981)

Legohérel, Henri, *Histoire de la Marine française* (Paris, 1999)

Lewis, Michael, *A Social History of the Navy, 1793–1815* (London, 1960)

—, *The Navy in Transition, 1814–1864: A Social History* (London, 1965)

Lima, José Francisco de, *Marquês de Tamadaré: Patrono da Marinha* (Rio de
    Janeiro, 1983)

López Urrutia, Carlos, *Historia de la Marina de Chile* (Santiago de Chile,
    1969)

Lubbock, Basil, *Cruisers, Corsairs & Slavers: An Account of the Suppression of
    the Picaroon, Pirate & Slaver by the Royal Navy during the 19th Century*
    (Glasgow, 1993)

Luraghi, Raimondo, 'Background', in *The Confederate Navy: The Ships, Men
    and Organization, 1861–65*, ed. William N. Still, Jr (Annapolis, MD,
    1997), pp. 1–20

Lyon, David, 'Underwater Warfare and the Torpedo Boat', in *Steam, Steel,
    and Shellfire: The Steam Warship, 1815–1905*, ed. Robert Gardiner
    (London, 1992), pp. 134-46

Macartney, Clarence Edward, *Mr Lincoln's Admirals* (New York, 1956)

Maldonado Prieto, Carlos, 'Estadio de Situación del Servicio Militar en
    Chile', *Security and Defense Studies Review*, 1 (2001), pp. 84–92

Marder, Arthur J., *The Anatomy of British Sea Power: A History of British Naval*

Policy in the Pre-Dreadnought Era, 1880–1905 (New York, 1940)

—, Old Friends, New Enemies: The Royal Navy and the Imperial Japanese Navy, 2 vols (Oxford, 1990)

McCormick, Gordon H., The Soviet Presence in the Mediterranean (Santa Monica, CA, 1987)

McKercher, B. J. C., 'The Politics of Naval Arms Limitation in Britain in the 1920s', in The Washington Conference, 1921–22: Naval Rivalry, East Asian Stability, and the Road to Pearl Harbor, ed. Erik Goldstein and John Maurer (London, 1994), pp. 35–59

McMichael, William H., The Mother of All Hooks: the Story of the US Navy's Tailhook Scandal (New Brunswick, NJ, 1997)

Merlet Sanhueza, Enrique, Juan José Latorre: Héroe de Angamos (Santiago de Chile, 1997)

Middlebrook, Martin, and Patrick Mahoney, Battleship: The Sinking of the Prince of Wales and the Repulse (New York, 1979)

Mitchell, Donald W., 'Strategic Significance of Soviet Naval Power in Cuban Waters', in Soviet Seapower in the Caribbean: Political and Strategic Implications, ed. James D. Theberge (New York, 1972), pp. 27–37

Monaque, Rene, L'Ecole de guerre navale (Vincennes, 1995)

Moore, J. E., 'The Soviet Sailor', in The Soviet Military: Political Education, Training and Morale, ed. E. S. Williams (New York, 1986), pp. 161–75

Moradsov, V., Life in the Soviet Navy (Moscow, 1975)

Morgan, M. C., Foreign Affairs, 1886–1914 (London, 1973)

Murphy, James M., 'Expand Education for Sailors', US Naval Institute Proceedings, CXXIX/2 (2003), pp. 57–9

Mustin, Henry C., and Douglas J. Katz, 'All Ahead Flank for LCS', US Naval Institute Proceedings, CXXIX/2 (2003), pp. 30–33

Natter, Robert J., 'Meeting the Need For Speed', US Naval Institute Proceedings, CXXVIII/6 (2002), pp. 65–7

Niestlé, Axel, German U-Boat Losses during World War II: Details of Destruction (Annapolis, MD, 1998)

Nish, Ian H., The Anglo-Japanese Alliance: The Diplomacy of Two Island Empires, 1894–1907 (London, 1966)

Niven, John, Gideon Welles, Lincoln's Secretary of the Navy (New York, 1973)

Padfield, Peter, Rule Britannia: The Victorian and Edwardian Navy (London, 1981)

Pelz, Stephen E., Race to Pearl Harbor: The Failure of the Second London Naval Conference and the Onset of World War II (Cambridge, MA, 1974)

Pereira Leivas, Luís Cláudio and Levy Scavarda, História da Intendência da Marinha (Rio de Janeiro, 1972)

Perry de Almeida, Washington, Guerra dos Farrapos: A acção da Marinha Imperial na Guerra dos Farrapos (Rio de Janeiro, 1935)

Peterson, Charles C., 'Showing the Flag', in Soviet Naval Diplomacy, ed. Bradford Dismukes and James M. McConnell (New York, 1979), pp. 88–114

Pizarro Arancibia, Julio, 'José Manuel Balmaceda a fines de su gobierno', Revista de Marina, CVIII (1991), pp. 76–9

Polmar, Norman, The Naval Institute Guide to the Soviet Navy, 5th edn (Annapolis, MD, 1991)

—, *Chronology of the Cold War at Sea, 1945–1991* (Annapolis, MD, 1998)

Prado Maia, João de, *Através da Historia Naval Brazileira* (São Paulo, 1936)

—, *Quatro séculos de lutas na Baía do Rio de Janeiro* (Rio de Janeiro, 1981)

Prange, Gordon W., with Donald Goldstein and Katherine V. Dillon, *At Dawn We Slept: The Untold Story of Pearl Harbor* (New York, 1981)

—, *Miracle at Midway* (New York, 1982)

Pugh, Philip, *The Cost of Seapower: The Influence of Money on Naval Affairs from 1815 to the Present Day* (London, 1986)

Rasor, Eugene L., *Reform in the Royal Navy: A Social History of the Lower Deck, 1850 to 1880* (Hamden, CT, 1976)

Reidy, Joseph P., 'Black Men in Navy Blue during the Civil War', *Prologue: Quarterly of the National Archives and Records Administration*, XXXIII (2001), pp. 155–67

Ridley, Jasper, *Lord Palmerston* (New York, 1971)

Ringle, Dennis J., *Life in Mr Lincoln's Navy* (Annapolis, MD, 1998)

Ritchie, Pedro Espina, *El Monitor Huáscar* (Santiago de Chile, 1969)

Roberts, John, 'The Pre-Dreadnought Age, 1890–1905', in *Steam, Steel and Shellfire: The Steam Warship, 1815–1905*, ed. Robert Gardiner (London, 1992), pp. 112–33

—, 'Warships of Steel, 1879-1889', in *Steam, Steel and Shellfire: The Steam Warship, 1815–1905*, ed. Robert Gardiner (London, 1992), pp. 95–111

Roberts, Stephen S., 'The Introduction of Steam Technology in the French Navy, 1818–1852', PhD diss., University of Chicago, 1976

Roberts, William H., *USS New Ironsides in the Civil War* (Annapolis, MD, 1999)

—, *Civil War Ironclads: The US Navy and Industrial Mobilization* (Baltimore, 2002)

Rodríguez, Horacio, and Pablo E. Arguindeguy, *El Corso Rioplatense* (Buenos Aires, 1996)

Rohwer, Jürgen, and Mikhail S. Monakov, *Stalin's Ocean-Going Fleet: Soviet Naval Strategy and Shipbuilding Programmes, 1935–1953* (London, 2001)

Ropp, Theodore, *The Development of a Modern Navy: French Naval Policy, 1871–1904*, ed. Stephen S. Roberts (Annapolis, MD, 1987)

Ruz Trujillo, Fernando, *Rafael Sotomayor: El Organizador de la Victoria* (Santiago de Chile, 1980)

Sandler, Stanley, *The Emergence of the Modern Capital Ship* (Newark, DE, 1979)

Sater, William F., *The Heroic Image in Chile: Arturo Prat, Secular Saint* (Berkeley, CA, 1973)

—, *Chile and the War of the Pacific* (Lincoln, NE, 1986)

Shingleton, Royce Gordon, *John Taylor Wood: Sea Ghost of the Confederacy* (Athens, GA, 1979)

Sondhaus, Lawrence, 'Die österreichische Kriegsmarine und der amerikanische Sezessionskrieg 1861–1865', *Marine – Gestern, Heute*, XIV (1987), pp. 81–4

—, *The Habsburg Empire and the Sea: Austrian Naval Policy, 1797–1866* (West Lafayette, IN, 1989)

—, *The Naval Policy of Austria-Hungary: Navalism, Industrial Development, and the Politics of Dualism, 1867–1918* (West Lafayette, IN, 1994)

—, '"The Spirit of the Army" at Sea: The Prussian-German Naval Officer Corps, 1847–1897', *International History Review*, XVII (1995), pp. 459–84

—, *Preparing for Weltpolitik: German Sea Power before the Tirpitz Era* (Annapolis, MD, 1997)

—, *Naval Warfare, 1815–1914* (London, 2001)

—, *Navies of Europe, 1815–2002* (London, 2002)

Spencer, Warren F., *The Confederate Navy in Europe* (Tuscaloosa, AL, 1983)

Steinberg, Jonathan, *Yesterday's Deterrent: Tirpitz and the Birth of the German Battle Fleet* (New York, 1965)

Still, William N., Jr, 'The American Civil War', in *Steam, Steel and Shellfire: The Steam Warship, 1815–1905*, ed. Robert Gardiner (London, 1992), pp. 61–74

—, 'Operations', in *The Confederate Navy: The Ships, Men and Organization, 1861–65*, ed. William N. Still, Jr (Annapolis, MD, 1997), pp. 214–38

Sumida, Jon Tetsuro, *In Defence of Naval Supremacy: Finance, Technology and British Naval Policy, 1889–1914* (Boston, 1989)

—, 'Sir John Fisher and the *Dreadnought*: The Sources of Naval Mythology', *Journal of Military History*, LIX (1995), pp. 619–38

Symonds, Craig L., *Confederate Admiral: The Life and Wars of Franklin Buchanan* (Annapolis, MD, 1999)

Tarrant, V. E., *Jutland: The German Perspective* (Annapolis, MD, 1995)

Thompson, Charles C., *A Glimpse of Hell: The Explosion on the USS* Iowa *and its Cover-Up* (New York, 1999)

Tritten, James J., *Navy and Military Doctrine in France* (Norfolk, VA, 1994)

—, 'Navy and Military Doctrine in France', in *A Doctrine Reader: The Navies of United States, Great Britain, France, Italy and Spain*, ed. James J. Tritten and Luigi Donolo (Newport, RI, 1995), pp. 37–75

Trumpener, Ulrich, '*Junkers* and Others: The Rise of Commoners in the Prussian Army, 1871–1914', *Canadian Journal of History*, IV (1979), pp. 29–47

Truver, Scott C., 'Tomorrow's US Fleet', *US Naval Institute Proceedings*, CXXVIII/4 (2002), pp. 78–86

—, 'The US Navy in Review', *US Naval Institute Proceedings*, CXXVIII/5 (2002), pp. 74–82

Vale, Brian, *Independence or Death! British Sailors and Brazilian Independence, 1822–25* (London, 1996)

—, *A War Betwixt Englishmen: Brazil against Argentina on the River Plate, 1825–1830* (London, 2000)

van Tol, Jan M., 'Using Anonymity is Dysfunctional', *US Naval Institute Proceedings*, CXXIX/4 (2003), p. 48

Varela Munchmeyer, Eugenio, 'Manejo de crisis: Situacion Chile-Estados Unidos en 1891–1892', *Rivista de Marina*, CIX (1992), pp. 56–66

Villabos R., Sergio, *Chile y Perú: La historia que nos une y nos separa, 1535–1883* (Santiago de Chile, 2002)

Waldeyer-Hartz, Hugo von, '*Ein Mann': Das Leben des Admirals Ludwig von Schröder* (Braunschweig, 1934)

Walser, Ray, *France's Search for a Battle Fleet: Naval Policy and Naval Power, 1898–1914* (New York, 1992)

Watson, Bruce W., *Red Navy at Sea: Soviet Naval Operations on the High Seas,*

1956–1980 (Boulder, CO, 1982)

Watts, Anthony J., *The Imperial Russian Navy* (London, 1990)

Wells, John, *The Royal Navy: An Illustrated Social History, 1870–1982* (London, 1994)

White, Colin, *Victoria's Navy: The End of the Sailing Navy* (Annapolis, MD, 1981)

—, *Victoria's Navy: The Heyday of Steam* (Annapolis, MD, 1983)

Willmott, H. P., *The War with Japan: The Period of Balance, May 1942–October 1943* (Wilmington, DE, 2002)

Wilson, Michael, 'Early Submarines', in *Steam, Steel and Shellfire: The Steam Warship, 1815–1905*, ed. Robert Gardiner (London, 1992), pp. 147–57

Wisecup, Phil, and Tom Williams, 'Enduring Freedom: Making Coalition Naval Warfare Work', *US Naval Institute Proceedings*, CXXIX/9 (2002), pp. 52–5

Wong, J. Y., *Deadly Dreams: Opium, Imperialism and the 'Arrow' War (1856–1860) in China* (Cambridge, 1998)

Woodward, David, *The Russians at Sea: A History of the Russian Navy* (New York, 1966)

Worthington, George R., 'We Have the Craft for Littoral Warfare', *US Naval Institute Proceedings*, CXXVIII/10 (2002), p. 128

—, 'Littoral Warfare Needs a Specific Ship', *US Naval Institute Proceedings*, CXXIX/1 (2003), pp. 90–91.

Yates, Keith, *Flawed Victory: Jutland 1916* (London, 2000)

Young, Gregory D., 'Mutiny on the *Storozhevoy*: A Case Study of Dissent in the Soviet Navy', Master's thesis, Naval Postgraduate School, 1982

NEWSPAPERS AND NEWS SERVICES (PRINT AND INTERNET)

El Mercurio (Santiago de Chile)
Wall Street Journal (New York)
http://www.cnn.com (accessed 19 March–11 April 2003)

OTHER INTERNET SOURCES

Portugal, Escola Naval, 'História – Breve Resenha', http://www.escolanaval.pt/ (accessed 25 February 2003)

'Amédée Courbet', http://www.netmarine.net/bat/flf/courbet/celebre.htm (accessed 8 August 2002)

'L'Ecole navale embarquée', http://www.defense.gouv.fr/marine/navires/ ecoles/ecolenavale/enaval.htm (accessed 8 August 2002)

http://www.africanamericans.com (accessed 10 April 2003)

http://www.afsouth.nato.int/factsheets/STANAVFORMED.htm (accessed 18 January 2002)

http://www.armada.cl/site/framesets/fset_altomando.html (accessed 5–17 March 2003)

http://www.britishwarships.cjb.net (accessed 13 January 2002)

http://www.chinfo.navy.mil (accessed 3 March–21 April 2003)

http://www.defenselink.mil (accessed 18–20 January 2002; 10–11 April 2003)

http://www.desert-storm.com/soldiers/navy.html (accessed 11 April 2003)

http://www.dfas.mil/money/milpay/pay/2003paytable.pdf (accessed 10 April 2003)
http://www.escueladegrumetes.cl/Esgrum.htm (accessed 13 March 2003)
http://www.escuelanaval.cl/esna1.htm (accessed 5–17 March 2003)
http://www.esmeralda.cl/pags/buque/index.html (accessed 12–13 March 2003)
http://www.gendercenter.org/military.htm (accessed 10 April 2003)
http://www.hazegray.org/worldnav (accessed 8–11 April 2003)
http://www.navy.com (accessed 10 April 2003)
http://www.navyhistory.com/cvn70tr.html (accessed 20 January 2002)
http://www.usmm.org/ww1navy.html (accessed 14 October 2001)
http://www.whitehouse.gov/news/releases/2002/01/200020129-11.html (accessed 11 April 2003)

Index

Adalbert, prince of Prussia 183–5
Adams, Charles F., American diplomat 115
Adriatic Sea 72–4, 281
Aegis air defence system 269–70
Afghanistan 261, 265, 282–4
al Qaeda, terrorist group 282–4
Albania 258–9, 282–3
Aleutian Islands 207, 228, 230
Alexandria 45; bombardment of (1882) 34, 43–4
Algiers, bombardment of (1816) 21, 34–5, 44; French conquest of (1830) 69–70
Amazonas, Francisco Manoel Barrosa da Silva, Baron do, Brazilian admiral 104–5
American Civil War (1861–5) 13, 26, 32, 57, 107–40, 142
Andropov, Yuri, Soviet president 250
Anglo-Boer War (1899–1902) 45–6, 175, 287
Anglo-Japanese alliance (1902) 46, 48, 206–7, 215
Arab-Israeli wars 259
Arabian Sea 227, 283–4
Argentina, and Argentinian navy 23, 71, 82, 88–90, 92, 95–106, 141, 144, 148–9, 166, 168–9
Arman, French shipbuilder 115
armoured warships, introduction of 12–15, 56
Armstrong, British armaments manufacturer 15–17, 59, 147–8, 160, 169
artillery 51–2, 54, 59, 203
Atlantic Ocean 75, 99, 115–16, 126–7, 133, 135, 137, 189, 249, 259, 262
Aube, Théophile, French admiral 57–61
Australia 30, 180, 200, 226–8, 274, 284
Austria (Austria-Hungary), and Austrian (Austro-Hungarian) navy 37, 45, 59, 69–74, 115–16, 146, 193, 204

Balmaceda, José Manuel, Chilean president 148–51, 164–8
Baltic Sea 27, 41, 73–4, 185, 237, 243–4, 254, 257–8, 261–2
Bancroft, George, American navy secretary 117
Barents Sea 249, 261–2
battle cruisers, introduction of 177–8, 203
Baudin, Charles, French admiral 67, 70–71
Beatty, David, British admiral 190–91
Beaurepaire, Teodoro de, Brazilian officer 86
Belgium 36, 70
Beresford, Charles, British officer 16
Bethmann Hollweg, Theobald von, German chancellor 181
Bismarck, Otto von, German chancellor 17, 171
Black Sea 12, 21–2, 40–41, 43, 45, 73, 237–8, 241, 243, 245, 250, 258, 260, 262–3
Blanco Encalada, Manuel, Chilean admiral 151
blockade, rules of 98–9, 126
Bolivia 142, 144–5, 157, 162–3, 169–70
Bolshevik Revolution (1917) 193, 252
Boorda, Jeremy 'Mike', American admiral 276–8
Borah, William E., American senator 207
Borda, Jean-Charles de, French officer 64
Borneo 225–6
Bosnia 265, 281–3
Bosphorus 38, 258, 260
Bouchage, François-Joseph Gratet du, French navy minister 62
Bouët-Willaumez, Louis, French admiral 75
Boxer Rebellion (1900) 46, 175

Brazil, and Brazilian navy 23, 31–2, 78–107, 139, 141–2, 148, 168–9
Brezhnev, Leonid, Soviet president 244–5, 247–8, 250–51, 259–60, 262
Brin, Benedetto, Italian naval engineer 15
Britain, and British navy 9–62, 64–74, 76–7, 79, 98, 100, 102–3, 115–16, 119, 126, 138, 142–4, 146, 148–9, 153–4, 164, 171–83, 188–97, 199–211, 215–16, 224–7, 234–6, 243, 245, 260, 264–5, 273, 276, 280, 282–4, 286–7; officers and seamen of, in foreign service 23, 26, 79, 85–92, 96, 99–102, 104–5, 151, 156–7
Brooke, John, Confederate artillerist 110
Broom, George, Brazilian officer 103
Brown, British armour manufacturer 15
Brown, William George, Argentinian admiral 95–7, 100–01
Brown-Curtis, American turbine manufacturer 204
Bruat, A. J., French admiral 41, 73
Buchanan, Franklin, Confederate admiral 119–22, 128, 133–4
Bülow, Bernhard von, German chancellor 171
Bush, George, American president 266, 280
Bush, George W., American president 268, 275, 283–4, 287

Cammell, British armour manufacturer 15
Camranh Bay 260–61
Canada, and Canadian navy 31, 138, 281
Cantiere Navale Adriatico, Austrian shipbuilder 115
Caprivi, Leo von, chief of German Admiralty 183, 185
Caribbean Sea 103, 124, 263
Carmen de Patagones, Battle of (1827) 100–01
Caroline Islands 206, 224
Castlereagh, Robert Stewart, Viscount, British foreign secretary 17
Cebrowski, Arthur K., American admiral 274
Charles x, king of France 70
Charleston, blockade of (1861–5) 107, 111, 113–14, 126, 131–3, 139
Chaumareys, Hugues de, French officer 62
Chelomey, Vladimir N., Soviet missile designer 239–40

Chernavin, Vladimir N., Soviet admiral 251
Chernenko, Konstantin, Soviet president 250
Chico Bank, Battle of (1828) 103–4
Chile, and Chilean navy 15, 23, 80–81, 85–8, 90, 93–4, 99–100, 106, 141–70, 182, 189
Chilean Civil War (1891) 150, 154, 156
China, and Chinese navy 38–9, 41–3, 46–7, 65, 75–6, 175, 189, 199–203, 206, 212, 219, 221–2, 225, 232, 259, 274, 287
Chuenpi, Battle of (1839) 38; Battle of (1841) 39
Churchill, Winston, First Lord of the Admiralty 181–2
Cisplatine War (1825–8) 82–3, 88–92, 95–106
Clark, Vernon, American admiral 276, 278
Clausewitz, Karl von 172–4
Clinton, Bill, American president 267, 274, 277, 279, 283
Cochrane, Thomas, earl of Dundonald, admiral 21, 23, 26, 80–82, 85–8, 90, 93–5, 142, 151
Codrington, Edward, British admiral 21, 35–6
Cold War 235, 246–7, 249–51, 254, 258–64, 266–7, 269, 272, 282
Coles, Cowper, British officer 112
Collins, Napoleon, American officer 137–8
Colonia, Battle of (1826) 97
commerce raiding 50, 57–8, 96, 99–103, 114–16, 137–8
Condell, Carlos, Chilean admiral 153, 158–9, 164
Confederate States of America, and Confederate navy 32, 57, 99, 107–11, 113–17, 120–21, 124–40, 143, 145
Congress of Paris (1856) 99, 126
Continental Iron Works, American shipbuilder 109
Coontz, Robert E., American admiral 207
Coral Sea, Battle of the (1942) 228
Corales, Battle of (1826) 89, 96–7
Coronel, Battle of (1914) 189, 224
Courbet, Amédée, French admiral 66, 75–6
Crimean War (1853–6) 12, 21–2, 24, 26–7, 32, 34, 39–41, 43–4, 54, 126
Crosbie, Thomas Sackville, Brazilian

officer 88
cruisers, steel, introduction of 15–16,
    57–9, 148
Cuba 116, 261, 263; Cuban Missile Crisis
    (1962) 244, 259
Cuhna Mattos, Brazilian politician 83
Cuniberti, Vittorio, Italian navy engineer
    203
Cushing, William, American officer 135

Dahlgren, John, American admiral and
    artillerist, 133
Dardanelles 38, 43, 258, 260
Darwinism 58, 174
Davis, Charles H., American officer 136
DeKay, George, Argentinian privateer 102
Denmark, and Danish navy 30; officers
    and seamen of, in foreign service 88–9
Desmadryl, Anatole, French officer 153
Dogger Bank, Battle of (1915) 190–91
Dom João (John VI), king of Portugal 78,
    83, 88, 98
Dom Miguel, Portuguese prince 83–4,
    103
Dom Pedro I, emperor of Brazil 78–84,
    86–8, 90, 92–3, 95, 98–9, 103–4, 142
Dom Pedro II, emperor of Brazil 84, 92,
    104–5
dreadnought battleships, introduction of
    178, 203–4
Dundas, James Deans, British admiral
    21, 40
Dundas, Richard Saunders, British
    admiral 22, 41
Duperré, Guy, French admiral 69
Du Pont, Samuel F., American admiral
    120–22, 126–7, 131–3, 136
Dupuy de Lôme, Stanislas, French naval
    architect 53, 55, 60, 64

Eades, James, American engineer 114
East Germany, and East German navy
    261–2
East India Company, British 38
Egypt, and Egyptian navy 35, 37–9, 43,
    71, 240, 259–60
electricity 15, 60
Elliot, George, British admiral 38–9
Entente Cordiale (1904) 47–8, 60–61,
    77, 178
Ericsson, John, Swedish-American ship-
    builder 109, 111–13
Errázuriz, Federico, Chilean president
    167

Exmouth, Edward Pellew, Lord, British
    admiral 21, 34
Eyre, William, Brazilian officer 101–2

Falklands, Battle of the (1914) 189, 224
Farragut, David Glasgow, American
    admiral 117–21, 124, 126, 129–31,
    134, 136
Fashoda Crisis (1898) 45
Feillet, Jean, French officer 153
Ferdinand VII, king of Spain 69
First World War (1914–18) 26, 47, 106,
    183, 187–99, 205–7, 215, 221, 224,
    234
Fisher, John, British admiral 46, 60–61,
    177–8, 182, 189, 203
flogging 28–9
Fontin, Paul, French officer 60
Foote, Andrew Hull, American admiral
    136
Fort Sumter 107, 121, 132–3
Fourichon, Martin, French admiral 75
Fournier, François, French admiral 60
Fox, Gustavus, American assistant navy
    secretary, 111–12, 132–3
France, and French navy 9–10, 12–17,
    30–31, 33, 35–43, 45–77, 98, 100,
    102–3, 106, 115–16, 119, 140, 143,
    146, 165, 168, 171–3, 177–8, 188, 195,
    197, 201, 204, 216, 264, 282, 287; offi-
    cers and seamen of, in foreign service
    86, 88–9, 99, 103
Franco-Chinese War (1884–5) 66, 75–6
Franco-Mexican War (1838) 67, 70
Franco-Prussian War (1870–71) 14, 57,
    75, 184–5
Frébault, Charles-Victor, French
    artillerist 64
French Indochina 65, 75–6, 225–6
Fujimori, Alberto, Peruvian president 170

Gambier, James, British admiral 30
Geneva Naval Conference (1927) 210
Germany, and German navy 17–18, 32,
    59–62, 77, 167, 171–201, 204,
    209–10, 221, 224, 234, 236–8, 287
    see also East Germany
Gibraltar 33, 45
Gladstone, William, British prime
    minister 44–5, 47
Goldsborough, Louis M., American
    officer 126–9
Gorbachev, Mikhail, Soviet president
    250–51, 254–6, 262

Gorshkov, Sergei G., Soviet admiral 236, 239–47, 250–51, 253, 257, 259–62
Goschen, George, First Lord of the Admiralty 45–6
Graham, James, First Lord of the Admiralty 22, 27, 47
Grau, Miguel, Peruvian admiral 158–9, 161
Greece, and Greek navy 23, 33, 82, 87–8
Greek War for Independence 35–6, 87
Grivel, Richild, French admiral 57
Guadalcanal, Battle of (1942–3) 230–31

Haiti 266, 281
Haldane, Lord Richard, British secretary for war 181
Halsey, William, American admiral 232–3
Hamilton, George, First Lord of the Admiralty 17
Hampton Roads, 126; Battle of (1862) 13, 110–12, 128–9, 134
Harrison, Benjamin, American president 168
Helgoland-Zanzibar Treaty (1890) 32
Hipper, Franz, German admiral 190–91, 195
Hirohito, Japanese emperor 219
Hitler, Adolf, German chancellor 197
Hong Kong 39, 42
Hope, James, British admiral 42
Hosogawa, Boshiro, Japanese admiral 228, 230
Hughes, Charles Evans, American secretary of state 207
Hussein, Saddam, Iraqi president 279–80, 282, 284–7
Hyatt, Edward, Chilean navy engineer 156

Ibrahim, pasha of Egypt 35–6
India 42, 116, 200, 227, 262
Indian Ocean 32, 189, 227–8, 234, 261–3, 282, 286
Indonesia 259–60
Indret, French engine manufacturer 51–2
Ingenieurskantoor voor Scheepsbouw, Dutch shipbuilder 210
Ingenohl, Friedrich von, German admiral 190
Inhaúma, Joaquim José Ignacio, Viscount de, Brazilian admiral 89, 104
Iquique 157, 159, 161, 163–5, 168; Battle of (1879) 158

Iran 269, 280, 284
Iran–Iraq War (1980–88) 263
Iraq 265, 279–80, 282; US invasion of (2003) 284–7
Island No. 10, Battle of (1862) 136
Israel 240, 260, 280
Italy, and Italian navy 15, 59, 116, 169, 204, 225, 236, 238, 281–2; officers and seamen of, in foreign service 99
Ito, Yuko, Japanese admiral 200, 216

Jaguary, Battle of (1826) 97
Japan, and Japanese navy, 43, 46, 77, 118–19, 148, 169, 189, 199–235, 264–5
Jauréguiberry, Jean-Bernard, French admiral 67
Java Sea, Battle of the (1942) 227
Jellicoe, John, British admiral 191
Jeune Ecole 15–16, 57–62, 66–7, 76, 148, 156, 173, 183, 200, 216, 240, 274–5
Jewitt, David, Brazilian officer 86
Johnson, Jay, American admiral 276
Joinville, François Ferdinand d'Orléans, Prince de 37, 52–3, 63, 70–71, 77
Jones, Catesby, Confederate officer 128
Jones, John Paul, American officer 158
Juncal, Battle of (1827) 97, 101
Jutland (Skaggerak), Battle of (1916) 190–92, 196

Kasatonov, V. A., Soviet admiral 258
Kato, Kanji, Japanese admiral 217–19, 221
Kato, Tomosaburo, Japanese admiral 217–18
Kawasaki, Japanese armaments manufacturer 204–5, 209, 214
Kelso, Frank, American admiral 276–7
Khrushchev, Nikita, Soviet premier 237–44, 248, 258–60
Kiaochow Bay 206, 224
Kiel, and Kiel Canal 184, 186–7, 192
Kinburn, bombardment of (1855) 41, 55, 73–4
Koga, Mineichi, Japanese admiral 231
Kondo, Nobutake, Japanese admiral 226
Korea 199, 222, 224. See also North Korea
Kosovo 265, 282–3
Kovolev, Sergey N., Soviet naval architect 249
Krupp, German armaments manufacturer 60, 149, 172, 204

Kurita, Takeo, Japanese admiral 232–3
Kuwait 279–80, 284–5
Kuznetsov, Nikolai G., Soviet admiral 237, 258

Laird, British shipbuilder 115–16
Lalande, Julien-Pierre, French admiral 71
Lamare, Rodrigo de, Brazilian officer 90–91, 93
Lara-Quilmes, Battle of (1826) 97
Latorre, Juan José, Chilean admiral 153, 159–63, 165–7
Lee, Samuel P., American officer 126
Lenin, V. I., Soviet premier 193, 258
Leyte Gulf, Battle of (1944) 232–4
Liaotung Peninsula 222, 224
Lincoln, Abraham, American president 107, 109, 125, 133
Lobo, Rodrigo José Ferreira, Brazilian admiral 85, 88–9, 95–8
London, Treaty of (1827) 35
London, Treaty of (1840) 37, 71
London Naval Conference, and Treaty (1930) 210–12, 219
London Naval Conference, Second (1935–6) 211
Los Pozos, Battle of (1826) 97
Louis XVIII, king of France 62
Louis Philippe, king of France 36, 52, 63, 70–71
Lynch, Luis, Chilean officer 146, 153
Lynch, Patricio, Chilean admiral 152–3, 159, 161–3
Lyons, Edmund, British admiral 41, 73–4

Mahan, Alfred Thayer, American officer and naval writer 172–4, 216, 224, 265
Malaya 225–6
Maria, queen of Portugal 83, 98, 103–4
Marshall Islands 206, 224, 231
Maximilian, emperor of Mexico 117
Mayo, Isaac, American officer 121
McKean, William, American officer 126
Mediterranean Sea 14, 28, 33–4, 43, 45–6, 53, 61, 67, 70–71, 108, 182, 224, 259–62, 285
Mehemet Ali, pasha of Egypt 35–8, 43, 71
Melville, Lord, First Lord of the Admiralty 22
Mervine, William, American officer 126
Mexican-American War (1846–8) 107, 118, 120
Mexico 23, 43, 74–5, 117, 143
Midway, Battle of (1942) 228–30, 232–3

Mill, John Stuart 28
Miller, British shipbuilder 116
Milne, David, British admiral 21
Milošević, Slobodan, Serbian president 281–2
Min River, Battle of the (1884) 76
missiles, introduction of 237, 239–40, 242–3
Mississippi River 107, 114, 122, 125–6, 128, 136–7
Mitchell, John K., Confederate officer 129–30
Mitsubishi, Japanese armaments manufacturer 205, 214
Mobile Bay, Battle of (1864) 117, 119, 133–4
Montreux Convention 244, 258
Montt, Jorge, Chilean admiral and president 150–51, 153, 160, 164–8
Moon Sound, Battle of (1917) 193
Moore, Guillermo, Peruvian officer 158–9
Morocco 71–2; Moroccan crisis (1905) 178

Nagumo, Chuichi, Japanese admiral 225–9, 232
Nanking, Treaty of (1842) 39
Napier, Charles, British admiral 21–3, 27, 40–41
Naples, and Neapolitan navy 72
Napoleon I, French emperor 9–10, 37, 50, 63
Napoleon III, French emperor 39, 53–5, 57, 64, 66, 69, 73–4, 117
Napoleonic wars 9–10, 19–20, 23, 25, 27–8, 36–7, 50, 62, 78
Navarino, Battle of (1827) 21, 34–6, 44
Near Eastern crisis (1832–3) 36
Near Eastern crisis (1839–40) 21, 26, 34, 36–8, 52, 68, 71
Nelson, Horatio 11, 21–2
Netherlands, and Dutch navy 34, 36, 52, 70; officers and seamen of, in foreign service 184
New Guinea 226, 228, 230
New Orleans 108, 114, 120, 128; Battle of (1862) 117, 129–31
Nimitz, Chester, American admiral 229
Normand, French shipbuilder 53
North Atlantic Treaty Organization 258, 262, 281–3
North German Confederation 75, 172, 188
North Korea 260, 284, 286
North Sea 178, 185, 188, 190, 192

Norton, James, Brazilian officer 89, 97,
    101–2
Norway, and Norwegian navy, 27, 274
nuclear propulsion, introduction of
    241–2
Nunes, Pedro, Brazilian officer 95

officers, policies regarding
    in Brazil 84–90, 104–5
    in Britain 19–25, 118
    in Chile 150–54
    in France 62–7
    in Germany 183–7
    in Japan 215–21
    in the Soviet Union 251–5
    in the United States 22, 117–22, 276–9
O'Higgins, Bernardo, Chilean president
    141–2, 152
Okinawa, Battle of (1945) 234
Ommaney, John, British admiral 21
Opium War, First (1839–42) 26, 34,
    38–9, 44, 152
Opium War, Second (1856–60) 34, 41–3,
    74, 119
Osumi, Mineo, Japanese admiral 219
Ottoman Empire, and Ottoman navy
    35–9, 43, 54, 182 see also Turkey
Ozawa, Jisaburo, Japanese admiral 232–3

Pacific Ocean 22, 114, 138, 188–9, 207,
    224–31, 236–7, 245, 249, 253–4, 260,
    262, 286 see also War of the Pacific
Pacifico, David, and 'Don Pacifico
    Affair' (1850) 33, 38, 44
Paixhans, Henri-Joseph, French
    artillerist 51–2, 54, 67, 69, 77
Palmerston, Henry John Temple, Lord
    30, 32–4, 36, 38–9, 42–4, 72–3
Panama, and Panama Canal 46, 147, 160
Paris, Treaty of (1856) 41; Peace
    Conference (1919) 195
Parker, William, British admiral 33, 39
Pax Americana 265, 272–3, 276, 279–87
Pax Britannica 9–10, 17–19, 22, 30, 33–4,
    38, 44, 46–8, 69, 273, 276, 283, 286–7
Pearl Harbor 218, 225–30, 233–4, 286
Pendergrast, Garrett, American officer
    126
Perry, Matthew Calbraith, American
    officer 118–19, 199
Persian Gulf 34, 263, 280, 282, 284–6;
    and Persian Gulf War (1990–91) 265,
    268, 279–82, 285
Peru, and Peruvian navy 23, 85, 140–46,

    156–64, 167–8, 170
Pescadores 199, 222
Philippines 147, 200, 225–6, 234, 261
Philippine Sea 286; Battle of the (1944)
    232
Pinto Guedes, Rodrigo, Brazilian admi-
    ral 88–9, 97–101
piracy 9–10, 30, 34–5, 42, 44, 47, 70
Plate, River 71, 80, 82, 85, 88–90, 92,
    95–104
Pohl, Hugo von, German admiral 190
Poland, and Polish navy 261–2, 284
Port Arthur 199, 203, 222–4
Port Hudson, Battle of (1863) 136
Port Royal, Battle of (1861) 127, 131
Portal, Pierre-Barthélemy, French navy
    minister 49, 53
Portales, Diego, Chilean minister 151
Porter, David, American officer 117
Porter, David Dixon, American admiral
    122, 125, 129–30, 135–7
Portsmouth (USA), Treaty of (1905) 224
Portugal, and Portuguese navy 23, 30,
    33, 36, 69–70, 78–88, 90–91, 93–5,
    97–8, 103–4, 106
Prat, Arturo, Chilean officer 147, 153,
    158–9, 163–4
Price, David, British admiral 22
Prussia, and Prussian navy 37, 69, 71,
    115, 172
P'ung Island, Battle of (1894) 222
Punta Angamos, Battle of (1879) 160,
    167

Raeder, Erich, German admiral 187
Ratsey, Edward, British admiral, 20
Reagan, Ronald, American president
    266, 268
Red Sea 32, 227, 262, 280, 285
Reed, Edward, British naval architect 13,
    144
religion, and naval personnel 25, 66–7, 187
Renshaw, W. B., American officer
    130–31
Reuter, Ludwig von, German admiral 196
Revolutions of 1848 72–3, 184
Rice, Condoleeza, American national
    security advisor 283
Rigault de Genouilly, French admiral 74
Riquelme, Ernesto, Chilean officer 153,
    158
Riveros, José Galvarino, Chilean admiral
    152, 159–63, 166
Roanoke Island, Battle of (1862) 127–8

Roosevelt, Franklin, American president
    225
Rosebery, Lord, British prime minister 45
Roussin, Albin-Reine, French admiral 102
Rozhestvensky, Zinovy, Russian admiral
    223–4
Rumsfeld, Donald, American defence
    secretary 274
Russia, and Russian navy 16–17, 22, 33,
    35–41, 43–6, 48, 54–5, 69, 71, 73–4,
    77, 169, 171, 177–8, 192–3, 197, 199,
    201, 203–5, 215, 221–4, 287; under
    the Soviet Union 236–65, 267,
    270–71, 279, 282
Russo-Japanese War (1904–5) 169, 199,
    201–3, 205, 222–4
Russo-Turkish War (1877–8) 144, 162,
    178

Sablin, Valery M., Soviet officer 254
Sadat, Anwar, Egyptian president 260
Santa Cruz Islands, Battle of the (1942)
    230
Santiago Bank, Battle of (1827) 101
Sardinia-Piedmont, and Sardinian navy
    72–4
satellites, for naval missile targeting 247,
    282
Sato, Kozo, Japanese admiral 224
Sato, Tetsutaro, Japanese officer 205
Saudi Arabia 280, 284–5
Scheer, Reinhard, German admiral
    190–92, 195
Schmidt, Erhard, German admiral 192–3
Sea of Japan 260–62, 286; Battle of the
    (1904) 223
seamen, policies regarding
    in Brazil 90–92
    in Britain 25–9
    in Chile 154–7
    in France 67–9
    in Germany 187–8
    in Japan 220–21
    in the Soviet Union 254–8
    in the United States 123–5, 278–9
Second World War (1939–45) 197, 200,
    212, 216, 220–21, 224–36, 252, 255,
    264
Selbourne, Lord, First Lord of the
    Admiralty 46
Semmes, Raphael, Confederate officer
    57, 121, 131, 137
Senna Pereira, Jacinto, Brazilian officer
    89–90, 97, 101

Serbia 281–3
Serrano, Ignacio, Chilean officer 158
Sevastopol, bombardment of (1854) 40, 55
Seymour, Beauchamp, British admiral 44
Seymour, Michael, British admiral 42
Shantung Peninsula 206, 222, 224
Shei-Poo, Battle of (1885) 76
Shepherd, James, Brazilian officer 88, 100
Shiloh, Battle of (1862) 136
Shubrick, William, American officer 120
Simpson, Juan, Chilean officer 161
Simpson, Robert, Chilean officer 151, 157
Singapore 225–6, 234, 260
Sino-Japanese War (1894–5) 199–201,
    216, 222
Sino-Japanese War (1937–45) 225
Sinope, Battle of (1853) 39, 54
slave trade 9–10, 30–32, 35, 44, 47, 70, 99
Solomon Islands 228, 230–31
Somalia 266, 281, 283
Sotomayor, Rafael, Chilean minister
    151, 159–60, 163
Soulin, Jean, Argentinian privateer 103
Spain, and Spanish navy 30–31, 69, 85–6,
    94–6, 142–3, 147, 152–4, 163
Spanish-American War (1898) 140
Spee, Maximilian von, German admiral
    189, 224
Spencer, John Poyntz, First Lord of the
    Admiralty 18, 26
Spruance, Raymond, American admiral
    232
Stalin, Joseph, Soviet premier 237–8,
    257–9
steam propulsion, advent of 11–12,
    50–52, 62, 67
Stimers, Alban Crocker, American naval
    engineer, 111–12, 132
Stopford, Robert, British admiral 21, 37,
    71
Stosch, Albrecht von, chief of German
    Admiralty 183–5, 187
Stringham, Silas H., American officer
    126–7
Sturdee, Doveton, British admiral 189
submarine, introduction of 60, 62, 133;
    warfare, unrestricted 193–4, 196–7
Sudan 265, 282
Suez Canal 43–4
Sukarno, Indonesian president 259
Sveaborg, bombardment of (1855) 41–2,
    74
Sweden, and Swedish navy 196–7, 274;
    officers and seamen of, in foreign

service 184
Syria 259–60, 262

Takagi, Takeo, Japanese admiral 228
Taiwan 76, 199, 222
Tamandaré, Joaquim Marques Lisboa, Marquis de, Brazilian admiral 87, 89, 100–01, 103–4
Tatnall, Josiah, Confederate officer 129
Taylor, John, Brazilian officer 87, 94, 105
Tewfik, khedive of Egypt 43–4
Thiers, Adolphe, French premier 37
Thornycroft, British shipbuilder 15
Tientsin, Treaty of (1858) 42
Tirpitz, Alfred von, German admiral 54, 171, 173–89, 193, 179
Tito, Josip Broz, Yugoslav president 259
Togo, Heihachiro, Japanese admiral 216, 222–4
Toro, Policarpo, Chilean officer 147
torpedo boats, introduction of 15, 57–9
Toyoda, Soemu, Japanese admiral 219, 231–2
Trafalgar, Battle of (1805) 11, 21, 50, 191
Triple Entente 171, 189, 206
Tsuboi, Kozo, Japanese admiral 216, 222
Tsushima, Battle of (1905) 202–3, 223–5
Turkey 284–5. *See also* Ottoman Empire
Tyler, John, American president 119

Ugaki, Matome, Japanese admiral 230
United Nations 169, 279, 281, 284
United States, and US navy 18, 24, 26, 30–31, 34, 39, 45–6, 71, 77, 82–3, 98–100, 102, 107–41, 143–4, 146–7, 160, 167–8, 182, 194–6, 199–201, 205–13, 217–18, 221–2, 224–37, 242–5, 247–51, 253, 255, 259–61, 263–87; officers and seamen of, in foreign service 86, 88–9, 96, 99, 102, 156
Uribe, Luis, Chilean admiral 153, 158, 161, 164, 166–7
Uruguay 71, 79, 82, 88, 95–8, 103, 105
Uruguay, River 89–90, 97–8

Venice, and Venetian navy 72–3
Versailles, Treaty of (1919) 196–7, 210
Vickers, British armaments manufacturer 202, 205
Vicksburg, Battle of (1863) 115, 136
Vietnam, US war in (1965–73) 260–61, 277
Vignot, Mathieu, French officer 60

Waddell, James, Confederate officer 138
War of 1812 117, 122, 235
War of the Pacific (1879–84) 141, 145–6, 148, 150–64, 167–9
Washington Naval Conference, and Treaty (1921–2) 199–200, 207–8, 210, 217–18
Weickhmann, Johannes, German officer 185
Welles, Gideon, American navy secretary 107, 111–12, 121
Wilhelm II, German emperor 171–4, 183, 186, 190, 192–3
Williams, John (Juan Guillermos), Chilean officer 157
Williams Rebolledo, Juan, Chilean admiral 157–8, 160, 163, 165–6
Winslow, John, American officer 137
Wood, John Taylor, Confederate officer 121, 138
Worden, John, American admiral 128–9, 132, 146
World War I *see* First World War
World War II *see* Second World War

Yalu, Battle of the (1894) 200–01, 222
Yamamoto, Gombei, Japanese admiral 216
Yamamoto, Isoroku, Japanese admiral 216, 219, 224–31
Yellow Sea 222; Battle of the (1904) 223
Yemen 262–3, 282
Yugoslavia 258–9, 281–2

Zédé, Gustave, French officer, 60
Zhukov, G. K., Soviet marshal 239